GEORGE HIGINBOTHAM AND EUREKA

The Struggle for Democracy in Colonial Victoria

George Higinbotham
Photo kindly supplied by Professor Stuart Macintyre

GEORGE HIGINBOTHAM AND EUREKA

The Struggle for Democracy in Colonial Victoria

GERALDINE MOORE

Australian Scholarly

Additional maps, information and images of persons who
figure in this book can be found on the author's website:
GeorgeHiginbothamAndEureka.net

First published 2018 by
Australian Scholarly Publishing Pty Ltd
7 Lt Lothian St Nth, North Melbourne, Vic 3051

Tel: 03 9329 6963 / Fax: 03 9329 5452
enquiry@scholarly.info / www.scholarly.info

ISBN 978-1-925801-49-1

Front Cover: The portrait of George Higinbotham, Trades Hall Council
Chamber. Courtesy of the Lovell Chen collection. Captured on 23 June 2017.

Back Cover: The General Elections: Interior of a Polling Booth, *Illustrated
Australian News*, 31 July 1880, p. 133. Trove

Cover design: Wayne Saunders

CONTENTS

FOREWORD

George Higinbotham cast a spell over his contemporaries. For nearly forty years he participated in the public life of colonial Victoria, pursuing a goal of complete self-government and civic virtue regardless of the political consequences. His devotion to principle allowed no compromise, so he held ministerial office for little more than five years. Insisting on an absolute freedom to speak and vote as he saw fit, he looked with distaste on the party spirit that seemed to him to 'deprive sane men of reason' and make 'men of honour utterly regardless for the obligation of truth'. But as Attorney-General from 1863 to 1869, he led the Government on a course of action that tested the limits of the Constitution and left a lasting political divide. The Governor he advised during this stormy period was just one of the casualties, for parliamentary colleagues reached a point when the conscience of 'King George' became too demanding. As one of them, William Shiels, put it, he was the 'most powerful and dreaded of leaders'.

Higinbotham set standards that few could meet. He was a man of honour, fastidious in his rectitude, unswerving in attachment to duty. With a dignified public presence went courtesy and respect for people of all stations – he hated all forms of privilege and disdained social distinctions. Nothing outraged him more than hypocrisy. He expected all citizens to do their civic duty and in 1873, as his parliamentary career drew to a close, he admonished them: 'you have no business to be indifferent to these public questions; you must not, as you do at present, appear to be utterly apathetic on all public affairs – utterly buried in your own personal and class occupations and interests, and indifferent to public and general interests'.

Higinbotham withdrew from Parliament in the belief that it had failed to uphold the principles of self-government. The Victorian

Constitution, which came into effect in 1855, had created a bicameral legislature, the one chamber popularly elected and the other restricted to a high property franchise. The Government was formed from the lower chamber, the Legislative Assembly, but reforming legislation was blocked by the upper one, the Legislative Council. To overcome this obstacle, Higinbotham hit in 1865 upon the device of the Assembly attaching a measure to impose tariffs to the Appropriation Bill that authorised public expenditure; and when the Council refused to pass it, bringing administration to a standstill, he arranged for the Government to borrow funds from a bank, which in turn recovered them through undefended legal action.

The constitutional crisis was eventually settled when the tariff was separated from the money bill and the Legislative Council acceded to both. But by then a further crisis arose from the Imperial Government's dismissal of the Governor for allowing his Ministers' irregular actions. Higinbotham denounced such interference as illegal, insisting that Victoria had full sovereignty in its domestic affairs. Furthermore, in 1867 he again attached a vote of monetary compensation to the Governor's family to an Appropriation Bill that was again rejected by the Council. The second crisis ended when the British Government offered a pension to the former Governor, but by then Higinbotham had lost patience with his less resolute colleagues. As a private Member, he moved and secured passage by the Assembly of resolutions to put 'an early and final step to the unlawful interference of the Imperial government in the domestic affairs of this colony'.

Its failure to do so lay behind his return to legal practice. Perhaps to make sure he did not return to Parliament, Higinbotham was appointed to the Supreme Court in 1880 and made Chief Justice in 1886. Even then, he refused to serve as Acting Governor since that would involve complicity in the 'sinister and clandestine policy' of the Colonial Office. And in a final act of principle, during the great industrial confrontation of 1890 he condemned the employers for refusing to negotiate with the unions, and contributed to their strike fund.

A younger generation of liberals revered Higinbotham. H.B. Higgins sought his nomination for admission to the Bar, Alfred Deakin arranged Higinbotham's appointment as Chief Justice, and both followed his example by refusing a knighthood. He was the greatest of Australian liberals, Deakin wrote, 'the noblest nature and the most refined', and in moments of confrontation a holiness of purpose crowned 'his singularly beautiful head and face', as if with a martyr's aureole – though it was Deakin who led the Victorian Government in breaking the Maritime Strike of 1890. We catch this difference in Deakin's tribute: 'His standards were too high, his temper too unbending, his scrupulousness to undiscriminating to render him a colleague whom it was easy to cooperate with or to understand'.

Many others have added their tributes: Higgins' niece Nettie Palmer, her husband Vance Palmer in his *National Portraits*, and a number of lawyers with similar sympathies – Maurice Blackburn, John Vincent Barry and, most recently, Michael Kirby. Higinbotham's family arranged for his son-in-law Edward Morris to compose a family memoir, but it was too filial. As Deakin observed, his 'influence was more magnetic, his thoughts – political, religious and social – more radical, and his will more dominating than Morris' *Memoir* describes'. Gwyn Dow explored those religious thoughts with acute insight in her account of his plan for public education, and I placed him at the forefront of my investigation of Victoria's liberal tradition.

When I wrote my own book in 1991, Gwyn Dow gave me a large body of material she collected to write *George Higinbotham: Church and State* (1964) and a substantial entry in the *Australian Dictionary of Biography* (1972). We were both intrigued by the gaps in the record. Before he died, Higinbotham issued strict instructions that all his papers were to be burned, and they were. He was an intensely private man who discouraged personal enquiries, and we wondered about his early life, his marriage, the sensitivity to slights and the dogmatism that brooked no contradiction. In the absence of information, it seemed there was no way of knowing more.

Now Geraldine Moore has proved us wrong. Through painstaking research and skilful use of the information made available through digitisation of historical sources, she has reconstructed crucial passages in the life of George Higinbotham. We knew that he arrived from London at the beginning of 1854, but not of his active involvement in the birth of Victorian democracy. He visited the Ballarat goldfields just a few weeks before the Eureka stockade and was convinced that the diggers had legitimate grievances. He objected from the outset to the provisions in the Constitution that withheld a full measure of responsible government and the undemocratic design of the Parliament. The principles that he expounded so insistently in the constitutional crises of 1865 and 1867 turn out to derive from the painful lessons he learned in 1855.

This book sheds new light on many other episodes. Perhaps most illuminating of all is Geraldine Moore's careful reconstruction of his tangled ancestry. We knew his father was part of Ireland's Protestant Ascendancy and that his mother had American ancestry and liberal views. We did not know that business failure resulted in their separation and George's upbringing in two separate circles, the one guided by Unitarian benevolence and the other by the unbending vigilance of the Orange Order. Readers will follow the consequences of this legacy throughout Higinbotham's family life and public career, and they will learn much else that casts new light on the apparent paradoxes that perplexed previous writers.

This is the first full biographical treatment of Higinbotham and the first to connect him properly to the political battles of colonial Victoria. He emerges undiminished, indeed enhanced by a deeper knowledge of this singular man.

Stuart Macintyre
August 2018

PREFACE

George Higinbotham was a Victorian colonial politician whose character and legacy have long been fiercely debated. Some historians admire him for his determination to achieve a just political system for Victoria based on his vision for a democratic and sovereign nation within the British Empire. Others regard him as a flawed character whose legacy was turmoil. He has been best known for his role in the constitutional crises of 1865 and 1867, and for his tireless work for the establishment of Victoria's public education system, but his influence on Victoria's politics began with his arrival in 1854 and continued until his death in 1892. His contemporary, Judge Redmond Barry, remarked that his contribution to the early history of Victoria was such that it would take six volumes to do justice to it.[1] This book highlights his role in the struggle for responsible government, but there are other facets to his life that are also interesting.

Higinbotham was an intensely private man who left instructions that, after his death, all of his personal papers were to be destroyed. His family dutifully carried out his wish. In doing so they destroyed a precious part of the early constitutional history of Victoria, and left a void in the story of Higinbotham's life that for the past century and a quarter has left us with many unanswered questions about the man, and obscured our understanding of what motivated his later political career. Without the tools that usually are considered essential to biography – such as letters, diaries, photos and personal memorabilia – a work that provides insights into the personal life of the subject is difficult to write. Inevitably, the reader will notice more than the usual occurrence of words such as 'perhaps' and 'may have' at various points in this book.

Higinbotham arrived in Melbourne in 1854, and for the next two years – during which momentous changes occurred in Victoria – he was one of four journalists who wrote anonymous editorials for the *Melbourne Morning Herald*. Until recently, Higinbotham's writings have not been identified.[2] The fragility of the original newspapers has made it necessary for researchers to use microfilm. The faded pages of the *Herald* made poor microfilm copies, and this has hampered a thorough examination of this important resource. However, the State Library of Victoria recently acquired computer-assisted microfilm readers that greatly improve the legibility of the copies. Before long, the Library will digitise many of the editions of this newspaper and make them available on the Internet.

Much of the new material about the early life of George Higinbotham in this book comes from his journalistic contributions to the *Melbourne Morning Herald* between March 1854 and July 1856. Because the articles were submitted anonymously, the task of identifying them has been lengthy and complex. Comparison with Higinbotham's written and spoken expression elsewhere has led to an identification of the characteristics of his style. His known views and favoured themes are another clue, and there are occasional references to biographical incidents that provide a further check. Elimination of the other known contributors by similar means also confirms the identification. The Appendix expands this discussion, and it is more fully expounded in the Appendix to my PhD thesis.[3]

A survey of the Melbourne *Herald* from 1854 to 1856 reveals a treasure trove of new material about Victoria in those years. It sheds new light on the perennial question of the motivations behind the conflict at Eureka (on both sides), and on its lasting significance. It also reveals a previously little-known constitutional crisis that occurred a year later, which adds to our understanding of colonial Victoria's turbulent birth.

From the *Herald* we also learn that certain significant personal events occurred during Higinbotham's first two years in Victoria. These left a lasting imprint upon him and shaped his view of colonial politics. It is now clear that, over a decade before his pivotal role in the great constitutional struggles of 1865 and 1867, Higinbotham was already influencing the course of events in Victoria through his anonymous journalism. This happened with respect to the battle at Eureka, and again in November 1855 following a memorandum from Governor Hotham to his ministry (known as Hotham's 'Minute') in which he claimed unconstitutional powers.

Some accounts advanced by historians of early colonial Victoria seek to diminish the political aspirations that motivated the battle at Eureka, and deny the existence of popular dissatisfaction with the 1855 Constitution. Such accounts have created a vacuum of historical context that has clouded our understanding of Higinbotham's political agenda and its popularity in his own time. But it was these events – Eureka and the Governor's Minute – rather than the constitutional struggles of the 1860s that launched Higinbotham's seventeen-year-long campaign to enshrine the principle of responsible government in the conduct of Victorian politics.

In 1893, just after Higinbotham's death, Price Warung (the pen-name of journalist William Astley) wrote:

> There has been no leader like him in Australian politics – none with the dash and daring, the courage and rectitude, the culture and resource. He broke the forces of Downing Street, and he took the heart out of the most arrogant and exclusive Chamber Australia has ever known. He won from privilege and class ground that they have never since been able to recover.[4]

This story of Higinbotham and his contemporaries who undertook the struggle for a democratic Constitution in Victoria brings a new dimension to our understanding of the history of Victoria.

INTRODUCTION

The Overlanders who followed Major Mitchell's exploratory journey in 1836 from Sydney south into the area that is now known as Victoria were astounded at the extent of the fertile and well-watered land that stretched before them. It promised to make them rich beyond imagining if they could secure the land for themselves. With similar ambitions, the whites who crossed Bass Strait to the Port Phillip region from Van Diemen's Land dreamt of making their fortunes. In 1835 John Batman negotiated a 'treaty' with the Aborigines, purporting to purchase a large area of land around the Yarra River for a white settlement. It may have been alarm at this initiative that pushed the Government to assert its claim to sovereignty of the land in order to forestall a rush of similar 'treaties'. But these entrepreneurial groups of white Europeans had first to contend with two enemies. The black custodians of the land for the past sixty millennia stoutly resisted their advance. The whites, however, knew that Aboriginal clubs and spears were no match for European firearms. Weakened by diseases that first appeared in Australia after the arrival of Europeans, the Aboriginal population, despite valiant resistance, faced successive setbacks, and its final defeat seemed inevitable. The whites were confident that before long, the land would be theirs.

The second enemy to these settlers arrived in the early 1850s and seemed to present a greater threat. It was the new Europeans who flocked to south-eastern Australia in their hundreds of thousands in search of gold. In following mining leads into pastoral runs, their interests often clashed with those of the pastoralists. They brought with them problems of law and order, interference with topsoil and watercourses, livestock and horses. The shepherds and agricultural labourers, upon whom the pastoral economy depended, left their employment to join in seeking their fortune on the goldfields. Upon the exhaustion of gold it was obvious that the gold seekers would clamour to settle upon the land, though with scant resources to pay a good price for it. The original settlers looked to the British Government to legitimise their conquests, and protect their investments. But, perhaps because it recognised that most of the newcomers too were British citizens, the Government gave contradictory signals. The early-comers saw that their best course was to persuade the British Government to cede self-government to the Colony, but on terms that would enable them to consolidate their claims to the land, and to entrench their power over the newcomers.

But times were changing. The newcomers came from a generation that was attuned to politics, for the widespread uprisings of 1848 across Europe had raised the popular aspiration for political rights. In Britain, the Chartist movement expressed the determination of working-class people to participate in the political life of the nation. The widespread movement in Ireland for Repeal of the *Act of Union* and the ill-fated 1848 Uprising demonstrated that there, too, the organised masses were determined to campaign vigorously for their rights. Among the newcomers there were many who recognised the importance of the new Victorian Constitution that the British Government had promised, for it would either concede or withhold the political rights that they considered their due.

The drafting of the new Constitution for Victoria began in 1853 and led eventually to its proclamation in November 1855. These three years were a time of heightened political tension. At the outset the Colonial Secretary, John Leslie Fitzgerald Foster, and the Attorney-General, William Foster Stawell, announced that the new Constitution would inaugurate a new era of 'responsible government', though what exactly this meant was never clearly articulated. A year later, the new Governor, Sir Charles Hotham, even went so far as to claim that the new Constitution was based upon the principle that 'all power proceeds from the people'.[1] But the new arrivals came to realise that such talk was a sham, for in reality they were firmly excluded from the process of drafting the Constitution. When the work of the drafters of the new Constitution was revealed and quickly adopted in the Victorian Legislative Council, the newcomers saw to their dismay that their views counted for nothing, and that under the proposed Constitution, they and their descendants would have to endure an undemocratic political system dominated by a landed oligarchy.

The drafters did not have everything their own way. A small minority in the Legislative Council valiantly sought to liberalise the provisions of the new Constitution, though on all but a few issues they were easily outvoted. In addition there was the *Melbourne Morning Herald,* which was widely read on the goldfields. One of Melbourne's leading barristers and a political liberal, Archibald Michie, had formed a syndicate that purchased the newspaper in 1853. Under Michie's editorship, the *Herald* repeatedly warned its readers about the anti-democratic nature of the recommendations for provisions of the new Constitution.

Resentment grew on the Victorian goldfields at the imposition of the gold licence fee, and particularly at the heavy-handed enforcement of it. The Government's failure to maintain law and order exacerbated the anti-Government feeling. Added to this was mounting frustration at the Government's implacable refusal to consult with the population of the goldfields over the provisions of the new Constitution. Resolutions at mass meetings and petitions were all ignored, and deputations were rebuffed. Matters came to a head in late November 1854 after a sequence of incidents – including murder, arson and looting – brought into focus the boiling anger of the Ballarat population. At a series of public meetings, the gold diggers articulated their demands, swore an oath of allegiance and appointed a deputation to negotiate with the Governor and the Goldfields Commissioner. Fearing attack, they built a wooden perimeter fence, known as a stockade, around the tents near the Eureka lead. They hoisted a flag that they called 'The Australian Flag', and commenced military drilling. Shortly before dawn on the morning of Sunday 3 December, soldiers surrounded the stockade and a battle began. According to the official report by Captain J.S. Thomas, at least thirty people were killed on the spot. Many others later died of their wounds. The 'rebellion' was at an end, but the repercussions for the Colony were to be long lasting.

Nine months before the conflict at Eureka, a twenty-eight-year-old Irish lawyer named George Higinbotham arrived in Victoria. He had worked for the *Morning Chronicle* in London as a reporter of debates in the House of Commons. In little more than a week after his arrival, he commenced work as a journalist with the *Melbourne Morning Herald*. In mid-October 1854, he travelled to Ballarat on *Herald* business and while there, he experienced the lawlessness and saw, with deep foreboding, the signs of the coming conflict. On his return to Melbourne, he wrote an article in the *Herald* urging immediate reform to avert a disaster. By early December when the conflict at Ballarat broke out, he was acting as the editor of the *Herald*. In this position he was suddenly faced with the necessity to make a weighty decision about the newspaper's stance in the conflict.

Higinbotham was horrified at the conflict at the Eureka goldfield, especially as the *Herald*'s correspondent at Ballarat was deliberately shot by a mounted trooper after the cessation of hostilities. He survived the attack but the gunshot wound caused lifelong pain, disability and an early death. Higinbotham reviewed his own political philosophy, and considered how such tragedies could be averted in the future. Eureka became for him the crucible of his campaign for political reform in Victoria.

Higinbotham was not by nature a radical. In fact his father's family were part of the Irish Protestant Ascendancy, a close-knit clan with a conservative ethos that stressed loyalty to the British Crown, allegiance to the established Church of Ireland and deep pride in British traditions, institutions and military achievements. Yet in some respects Higinbotham was atypical. This may have reflected his maternal heritage, for his maternal grandfather Joseph Wilson had fought with George Washington against the British, and according to family folklore, he had been one of Washington's aides-de-camp. No doubt he sensed the pride of his mother's family in the American victory, and of the ideals underlying the Declaration of Independence. His early exposure to the legends associated with the American Revolution inspired him and stayed with him throughout his life. Higinbotham's uncle, Thomas Wilson, was a founding benefactor of the Dublin Unitarian Church, whose congregation had traditionally provided a forum for political as well as religious reformers. From a young age, Higinbotham found himself torn between the contrasting political values of the maternal and paternal sides of his family. During his late adolescence and early adulthood, the Repeal movement, the Irish famine and the desperate and ill-fated political uprising of 1848, stimulated his search for a political philosophy that would heal a divided nation and prevent a recurrence of such tragedies.

After completing his university degree at Trinity College in Dublin, Higinbotham lived in London for five years, and during this time he became attracted to the ideas of an upper-class group of liberal thinkers who called themselves 'the Philosophical Radicals'. The leader of this group, Sir William Molesworth, took a keen interest in colonial affairs. He proposed his own model for a constitutional arrangement for colonial self-government. This arrangement provided for democratic decision-making within the domestic sphere by the local legislature, but prescribed loyal compliance by the colonial government with the directions of the British Government in matters concerning the Empire. Higinbotham became a firm advocate of this model, but in Victoria, the squatters and the Governor had no interest in promoting a broad-based colonial democracy and they contended for different constitutional arrangements.

In November 1855, the new Victorian Constitution was proclaimed. Far from ending the debate, the proclamation ignited a bitter contest in the Legislative Council regarding the correct interpretation of the Constitution. On the same day as the Governor, Sir Charles Hotham, proclaimed the new Constitution, he laid claims to certain powers that Higinbotham and others believed were both unconstitutional and incompatible with the promise that the Constitution would deliver responsible government. Ambiguities, discrepancies and arguments concerning the legality of the constitutional process kept alive the competing claims, and a long struggle ensued.

Between 1855 and 1878 there were four constitutional crises. These were episodes in which the constitutional mechanisms for the orderly conduct of government in Victoria appeared to fail, leading to bitter impasses that threw the Colony into upheaval. In three of these constitutional crises, 1855, 1865 and 1867, Higinbotham was a pivotal figure. The role that he played in the crises of 1865 and 1867 has long been known, and has drawn admiration from some historians and censure from others. The crisis of 1855 is one that historians have been scarcely aware of, and its significance has been under-appreciated. Higinbotham's role in it has until now been completely unsuspected. He led the opposition to Hotham's 'Minute' because he believed that the principle of responsible government was at stake. The aspiration for full responsible government had been clearly articulated in the agitation on the goldfields that preceded the battle at Eureka. Higinbotham supported the goldfields population in their view that colonial government should be based upon the will of the majority, for to him this was reasonable, necessary and entirely compatible with loyalty to the Crown. He continued the struggle to achieve this aspiration throughout the ensuing four decades of his life.

Despite the dark days of 1854 and 1855, the determination of the population of the goldfields to democratise the political system in Victoria continued apace. In the aftermath of Eureka, following a recommendation of the Royal Commission into the Goldfields, the Miner's Right replaced the hated gold licence fee. Those who purchased the Miner's Right (at a mere fraction of the cost of the previous licence fee) bought not only the right to dig for gold, but the rights to purchase land, to vote and to elect the members of the mining courts in their district. Courts of Mines were established on the goldfields, putting the administration of justice regarding mining matters into the hands of men who understood the complexities of gold mining, and who enjoyed the confidence of their peers. Hotham's unconstitutional claims fell into abeyance when he unexpectedly became ill and died a few weeks after announcing them. No successor ever attempted to revive them. After a short political struggle in 1856, the secret ballot was achieved. It was another milestone in democratising the political system of Victoria.

But still there was the undemocratic Constitution, and reform of that took a much longer struggle. By the end of Higinbotham's life in 1892, much had been achieved. He had awakened the Legislative Assembly to a clearer vision of its rightful place under a system of responsible government *vis-à-vis* the Legislative Council, the judiciary, the press and the Colonial Office in London. He had campaigned steadfastly against the British Government's practice of giving secret instructions to the Governors. He insisted that the practice amounted to interference in Victoria's domestic affairs and contravened the principle of responsible government. Shortly before his death the practice ceased. The restrictive property franchises for the Legislative Assembly and the Legislative Council, which disenfranchised many ordinary people, were progressively reformed, but it would take six decades before they would be entirely abolished.

The story of George Higinbotham's role in the epic struggle against oligarchy, corruption, and interference from London in the politics of colonial Victoria reveals a man with exceptional vision, leadership and determination. He was not alone. He had much popular support in Melbourne and on the goldfields. Others such as Archibald Michie, Henry Chapman, John O'Shanassy and Graham Berry played major roles in liberalising and reforming the Victorian political system. Shortly after Higinbotham's death, the principles that he fought for had even wider application when they were raised anew in the debates over the federation of the Australian colonies and the creation of an Australian Constitution. The historian Stuart Macintyre notes that eminent Australians such as Alfred Deakin (Australia's second Prime Minister), and Henry Higgins (Commonwealth Attorney-General and Justice of the High Court of Australia), acknowledged Higinbotham as their mentor and inspiration. Walter Murdoch, the author of Deakin's biography, wrote of Higinbotham that 'no man left a deeper or more lasting imprint upon the public life and parliamentary traditions of Victoria'.

If George Washington was the 'Indispensable Man' of United States history, George Higinbotham, for his principled leadership, was Victoria's 'Indispensable Man'. In so far as he inspired some members of the generation after him who achieved Federation, he may also have been Australia's Indispensable Man.

1

ARRIVAL IN VICTORIA

On 10 March 1854, the clipper *Briseis*, bearing both passengers and miscellaneous cargo, arrived in the new British colony of Victoria. It sailed through the heads into Port Phillip and cast anchor among a hundred or so other sailing ships that were riding at anchor in Hobson's Bay, Melbourne. After leaving Liverpool on 1 December 1853, the ship had encountered light winds for much of the passage, and the voyage had been protracted to one hundred days. Among the passengers who alighted from that ship was a young Irishman in his late twenties named George Higinbotham. He was of small to medium stature. His fashionable side-whiskers were neatly trimmed. He had a full head of brown hair, large soulful eyes and an erect bearing. In his trunk he had certain possessions that had been his daily companions on the voyage. They included the astronomy books that he had studied to familiarise himself with the constellations visible in the southern hemisphere, the diary of the voyage that he had been keeping, and the quadrant that he had been using (to the irritation of Captain Brown) to gauge the ship's longitude, and thereby to satisfy his own anxiety about the ship's progress. Also in the trunk were his wig and gown, for he had been called to the Bar at Lincoln's Inn in London and planned now to seek admission to practise at the Victorian Bar.

It was early autumn, a time when Victoria's short hot summer gives way to relatively settled and pleasant weather. To the Aboriginal people who had lived in the area for fifty thousand years, this was Eel Season – a season of plenty. The starchy roots of the water plants were now at their best for harvesting. The short-finned eels, having gorged themselves upon the small aquatic life of the river system of the south-eastern corner of Australia, were now in great abundance as they migrated back towards the open sea. From here, those that survived the traps of the Aboriginal people would start their 4,000-kilometre journey to the spawning grounds of the Coral Sea. Like nearly all of the Europeans who had so recently arrived, Higinbotham knew nothing of the ancient rhythms of this land, for he saw the country through European eyes.

In June 1851, the Port Phillip District of New South Wales had become the separate colony of Victoria, with its own legislature and a constitution based closely on that of the parent colony. Higinbotham was one of thousands of immigrants who were streaming into Victoria following the news of the gold discoveries at Forest Creek, Bendigo, Ballarat, Beechworth and the Ovens district. Over the two years 1852–54, the white population of Victoria increased by about 144,000 people to a total of about 312,000. The newfound wealth had suddenly transformed a remote colonial outpost relying on the pastoral industry into a rapidly expanding settlement with Melbourne as its commercial and industrial capital.

But it was not gold that attracted George Higinbotham to Victoria. To him this new British colony was of particular interest for another reason. He was a lover of British and American history, and to him Victoria was the arena for a historic experiment in creating a new model British colony. This colony had a unique opportunity to embrace the benefits of a constitution based upon the soundest and most advanced political principles, and to achieve this without the bloodshed that had attended the birth of the democratic polity in America. This was an opportunity to redeem the self-respect of the British Empire by showing that it had forever dispensed with the foolish and tragic policies that had first alienated and subsequently lost the American colonies to Britain eighty years previously.

In 1852, while Higinbotham had been working as a parliamentary reporter for the liberal London newspaper the *Morning Chronicle*, the staff had received the exciting news that the Fifth Duke of Newcastle, one of the proprietors of the newspaper, had been appointed Secretary of State for

War and the Colonies. In line with his liberal principles, in August 1853 the Duke had invited the Governor-General of the Australian colonies, Sir Charles Augustus FitzRoy, to establish new constitutions that would prepare the Australian colonies for responsible government. This was a bold initiative, for many in the British press debated the wisdom of allowing responsible government in colonies, especially those with a large population of convicts. As Victoria had never been a significant repository for transported convicts, Higinbotham hoped to find that its respectable citizenry would seize this golden opportunity to create a modern political system based upon respect for the traditional British institutions – the monarchy, the law and the church – yet enlightened with the liberal and democratic ideals that London's *Morning Chronicle* and other progressive voices advocated.

Like many before him, Higinbotham made do at first with a tent in Canvas Town on the south bank of the Yarra River, but soon moved to a boarding house in Fitzroy, on the eastern fringe of Melbourne.

Another immigrant to Melbourne at about this time described it is as follows;

> It was then a thriving village, in the by-streets of which, primeval trees or their stumps might still be seen, and where huge chasms sometimes interrupted communications between adjoining streets. The public buildings were ultra-provincial. The government offices were a two-storey villa, the law offices occupied a vacant corn store, the Public Works department was housed in a wooden shanty ... The Legislative Council met in a small brick building known as St Patrick's Hall ... the ill-lighted streets were also ill-paved, and the flag-ways made in patches or left unmade at the option of the owners of adjoining property. On windy nights one stumbled through some of the chief streets of Melbourne from fragments of solid flagging into unexpected pools of slush and mud.[1]

It is likely that Higinbotham had brought with him from London a letter of introduction to Archibald Michie, a senior barrister and part-owner of the *Melbourne Morning Herald*. While working in London, Higinbotham had formed an association with a mutual friend, Sir William Molesworth, Baronet, the Member for Southwark in the House of Commons. Molesworth was thirteen years older than Higinbotham, and supported the philosophy of Utilitarianism. He and his circle believed that it was the duty of the state to advance the welfare of the people. They agreed with many of the reforms advocated by the Chartists, but they rejected the confrontational strategies that the Chartists used to promote their cause. They envisaged that change would come through leadership of institutions such as Parliament and the press by men of education. Molesworth took a particular interest in the matter of self-government for the colonies. He did not accept that the devolution of responsible government would threaten loyalty to the British Empire, but rather argued that it would strengthen ties. The issue was highly topical as legislation regarding the Australian colonies was currently before the House of Commons.

Higinbotham's arrival in Melbourne was well timed, for the *Melbourne Morning Herald* had recently advertised for a parliamentary reporter. His four years of experience in reporting debates in the House of Commons for the *Morning Chronicle* stood him in good stead, and within eight days of his arrival he was writing for the *Herald*. Also writing for the *Herald* was Butler Cole Aspinall, an Englishman four years younger than Higinbotham and a former colleague from the *Morning Chronicle* who had arrived in Melbourne in late 1853. Like Higinbotham, Aspinall was a junior barrister who found journalism a convenient way of supplementing his income while he awaited legal briefs. He shared many of Higinbotham's liberal views and wrote in a style characterised by a harsh kind of humour and satirical overstatement.

In addition to Higinbotham and Aspinall, the *Herald*'s business manager Frederick Sinnett wrote occasional articles. Sinnett was a humourist who left the *Herald* in late 1854 to become the first editor of the Victorian edition of the satirical magazine, *Punch*. The *Herald* followed the widespread custom in the British Empire at that time for newspaper journalists to write anonymously. This was a useful strategy to circumvent the sedition and libel laws that served as a stern warning to journalists and newspaper proprietors about the consequences of expressing anti-government opinion. Aspinall, Sinnett, Michie and Higinbotham had moved in similar circles in London and shared similar views about constitutional principles, but despite this, their different writing styles and interests reveal four discernably distinct 'voices' in the editorials and leading articles of the *Herald* of the time.

The editorial team of the *Herald were* fearful that the historic and all-important constitutional process was being perverted by the naked self-interest of the great landowners and squatters, the government officials and the intriguers of the Colonial Office. They believed that, unless this tendency was redressed, it would lead to strife, and possibly to revolution. Alarmed that 'fearful mistakes' were being made, and that inadequate time had been allowed for public consultation, they worked tirelessly to rouse the population to address the dangers that they perceived.

Before Higinbotham's arrival, Archibald Michie, as the most senior and long-serving member of the editorial team, had written the majority of editorials and leading articles. Though he wrote anonymously, the body of his writing before Higinbotham's arrival allows us to identify his style, and to become familiar with his secular worldview and his favoured themes. We can then detect a contrast when Higinbotham writes editorials in a style that shows other characteristics and that reflect a distinctly Christian worldview. Michie's style was plain and unadorned, yet typically cogent, analytical and often highly polemical in tone, especially when he wrote about the issue of the drafting of the new Constitution. He felt so strongly about this matter that in August 1853 – one month before the Drafting Committee for the new Constitution was chosen – he resigned his seat in the Legislative Council and invested his life's savings in purchasing the majority shareholding in the *Melbourne Morning Herald*. He had moved the office to new premises, installed more modern printing machinery, and advertised for 'first class' staff. His intention was to provide editorial comment to the readership about what he saw as the single most important issue of the day: the drafting of the new Victorian Constitution. He declared that his aim was 'to imbue the minds of our readers with a sense of the importance of this question'. To the criticism that concentration on political philosophy would discourage people from buying the newspaper, he countered, 'If others neglect the all-important question of the new Constitution, we will not'.[2]

Michie was critical of the drafting process. He campaigned against the Drafting Committee's recommendations that candidates for membership of the Upper House of the new legislature must own property to the value of £10,000 and that the voters of the Upper House would also have to own property worth £100. He foresaw that this would create a privileged elite who would obstruct the will of the people as expressed by their representatives in the Lower House. The rival newspaper, the *Argus*, agreed that the property qualification for a seat in the Upper House was 'absurdly high'.[3] Michie objected, moreover, to the sweeping financial powers that were reserved to the Governor. These gave the Governor responsibility for a Civil List to cover his own salary and expenses, as well as those of his household, his Executive Council, the Legislative Council, the judges, the Auditor of Public Accounts, and all the responsible officers of the Government. The Governor would also be responsible for all pensions and compensation payments for loss of office that might be granted to any of these individuals.[4] Michie argued that this arrangement contravened the British tradition whereby 'the grand check afforded by the constitutional power over the purse-strings, and supposed to rest upon the Legislature is completely lost'. He pointed out that this would make the Governor more powerful than the sovereign in England, for he and the responsible officers whose salaries and pensions he controlled would become 'quite independent of the legislature'. What concerned him most of all was the recommendation that the new Constitution could only be amended in the future by the vote of a two-thirds majority of both Houses of the legislature.

Higinbotham expected to find that the citizens of Melbourne would be engaged in a vibrant debate about the merits of these constitutional principles. From boyhood he had heard from the Wilson side of his family the stirring stories of his maternal grandfather, Joseph Wilson (reputedly an aide-de-camp to George Washington), who had fought for the principle of self-government. Higinbotham's study of modern history at Trinity College expanded his appreciation of those weighty debates about constitutional principles that had accompanied the drafting of the American Constitution, yet to date in the Colony there had been little debate about broad constitutional principles in the process of drafting the new Victorian Constitution.

When Higinbotham commenced work as a parliamentary reporter at the *Melbourne Morning Herald*, he was just in time to hear the debates on the last phase of the passage of the draft Constitution Bill through the Victorian Legislature before its consideration by the British Parliament in London. The desultoriness and apathy that had accompanied much of the drafting of the Constitution Bill in the Legislative Council of Victoria suddenly turned to spirited debate, for the recommendations of the Drafting Committee were to be considered by the whole legislature, and the most controversial matters had been left until last. At the outset, the Colonial Secretary, John Foster, had assured the Council Members that 'responsible government' was fundamental to the new Constitution, but the recommendations of the Drafting Committee failed to clarify the mechanism by which it could be seen to operate.[5] Hugh Childers, the former Auditor-General, who had recently become the Collector of Customs, sought to allay growing popular disquiet over the powers of the proposed Upper House by giving the following undertaking to the Council:

> The lower house would have control over the money bills, while the upper house would have hardly a voice in the matter. The House which was elected would have the control over the entire funds of the Colony.[6]

In the same week, debate on the key issue of responsible government had also been stifled by the declaration of the Attorney-General, William

Stawell, to the Council, that 'the main principles of the Bill were two, call it three, viz, two chambers, both elected; and responsible government'.[7] Now Stawell sought to forestall renewed dissent by admonishing the Members of the Legislative Council that it was 'unbecoming for any member of the house to be guided by popular opinion'.[8] He argued that the population of the goldfields had refused the offer of a seat in the Legislative Council because they were too busy 'money-a-making' to be interested.[9] He did not mention that they had repeatedly petitioned and lobbied for the right to participate but had been rebuffed. Governor La Trobe had offered them a representative nominated by Government, but they had rejected this, not because of apathy but because they regarded a non-elected representative as 'a mock species of representation'.[10] John Foster went further, claiming that the public approved the draft Constitution. The great constitutional struggles of 1865, 1867 and 1878 in Victoria between the Legislative Council and the Legislative Assembly might never have occurred if the assurances of Foster, Childers and Stawell regarding responsible government had reflected reality, for the key issues at stake in these bitter battles to come were those of responsible government and the relative powers of the two Houses with respect to money bills. The contradictions and lack of parliamentary decorum may have struck the young parliamentary reporter, fresh from four years of observing the proceedings in Westminster. But he was more troubled by the failure to consult and the flouting of sound constitutional philosophy that underlay the process of designing the new Constitution.

On 25 March 1854 (eleven days after Higinbotham's arrival), the Constitution Bill passed its third reading. Thanks to the perseverance of Michie and others in the press, and to John Pascoe Fawkner, the Member for Talbot, and John O'Shanassy, the Member for Melbourne, in the Legislative Council, there were some significant changes. The attempt to give the Governor exclusive right to choose the ministry was defeated.[11] Both the *Melbourne Morning Herald* and the *Argus* recorded that there was much debate about this recommendation. The Irish Protestants William Stawell, Robert Molesworth (Solicitor-General) and Andrew Clark

(Surveyor-General) argued strongly for the Governor alone to choose the ministry, while the Congregationalist John Pascoe Fawkner, and the Catholic John O'Shanassy, who, despite their differences, constituted the main opposition in the Legislative Council, joined forces to oppose this proposal. They insisted that the Governor should act with the advice of his Executive Council, comprising the Ministers in the elected Government. Both newspapers record that, when the House divided, the Government's proposal was defeated by one vote. Neither newspaper's account makes any mention of a subsequent proposal for a clause excepting 'officers due to retire on political grounds' who were to be appointed by the Governor alone, yet in the final form of the Constitution Bill that was reserved for approval in London a new clause appeared that restored the Governor's exclusive right regarding 'officers due to retire on political grounds'.[12] The following year, this additional clause was to be the cause of a political crisis.

Yet several other important changes that the Legislative Council passed were implemented in their entirety. The proposed clause stipulating that a two-thirds majority in both Houses of the legislature would be required to change the Constitution was narrowly defeated. The proposed £10,000 property threshold for membership of the Legislative Council was reduced to £5,000. (This was still fifty times the figure of £100 that the British Parliament had set for the elective Members of the existing Legislative Council.)[13] Michie commented that the Colony had undergone a 'narrow escape' from inevitable revolution.[14] There were many features of the draft Constitution that still concerned him, but if a 50 per cent majority could be achieved, he reasoned that reform was a future possibility.

Having spent some years in reporting parliamentary debates, Higinbotham was eager to move into editorial writing. Only eight days after his arrival, his first leading article was published.[15] It expounded the difference between education and instruction. This was a characteristic preoccupation of his, and one that he often dwelt upon during his later parliamentary speeches in support of public education (which he termed 'public instruction').[16] As a devout Christian, Higinbotham believed that the term 'education' properly implies the development of an individual's spiritual, intellectual, moral, physical and religious nature. By contrast, he argued that education without a religious infusion is merely 'instruction'. A week later, he wrote another leading article advocating the abolition of public viewing of the executions of criminals. Higinbotham's son-in-law Edward Morris, who wrote a biography of his father-in-law in 1895, reported that as a young journalist he had strongly urged the abolition of the death penalty. The article employed revolting descriptions of an actual hanging along with forceful arguments denying the supposed salutary effect that witnessing such an execution was believed to have on members of the public. The article's combination of cogent argument with emotional language and powerful imagery were typical features of Higinbotham's literary style and of his parliamentary speeches a decade later.

The *Melbourne Morning Herald*

The *Herald* was the first newspaper in the Colony to use a steam printing press.[17] In its eagerness to be the first with the news from home, the *Herald* operated its own boat with five hands employed. It met the ships as they arrived without having to wait until they reached the wharf.[18] The *Herald*'s office was new, and conveniently located near the departure point for the goldfields coaches in Bourke Street. An article reporting the change to the new location announced that 'the advertising and publishing office of the journal will be at No. 9, Great Bourke Street, east of the Post Office and Messrs Symons and Perry's tea-rooms'.[19] Like its close rival, the *Argus,* the *Herald* had established agencies at all the diggings, and in other centres of population. The papers were delivered to these agencies and further distributed to smaller localities by private runners.[20] Miners in a locality often shared their newspapers, and the subjects of the articles were often discussed after work and on Sunday afternoons.[21] Between 1853 and 1855, the *Melbourne Morning Herald* also produced a weekly edition that featured all the main articles of the week. As late as August 1855 when the paper was in financial trouble, Michie claimed that the *Weekly Herald* still had 'the largest distribution of any newspaper on the goldfields'.

Each week the *Herald* published reports from the paper's unnamed 'own correspondents' who were stationed on the major goldfields. From these reports Higinbotham and the editorial team learned that tension was mounting on the goldfields over the issues of the gold licence fee and the harassment of the diggers to ensure compliance. There was widespread anger at the lawlessness that went unchecked on the goldfields, and a marked failure of confidence in the administration of justice. Increasingly there was frustration at the steadfast refusal of the Government to consult with the population of the goldfields over the issue of constitutional recognition of their right to vote. The *Herald*'s correspondents on the goldfields made no pretence of maintaining distance from the political agitation that they reported. They and the Melbourne editorial team saw themselves as participants in the struggle for political rights that was simmering on the Victorian goldfields.

Three months before Higinbotham's ship arrived in Melbourne, the diggers at both Bendigo and Ballarat had held public meetings to discuss several grievances, including the Constitution. At Bendigo they resolved to hold a Diggers' Congress and, after consultation with the populations of other major goldfields, to choose seven delegates who would negotiate with the Government in the interests of the mining population. The election of the seven members of the Diggers' Congress was scheduled for 24 January 1854, in order that the other diggings could be communicated with, and 'an entire and complete system of constitutional agitation established'.[22] Michie provided advice to the diggers that they should take care that the elections were properly conducted and to avoid inflammatory language. He reviewed their manifestos and congratulated them for rational argument and 'conclusions carefully arrived at'.[23]

Edmond Harrison, the *Herald*'s Bendigo correspondent, interspersed a report of the outcome of the Bendigo public meeting of 13 December 1853 with his own advice and views. He reported that meetings had taken place in most of the gullies expressing a determination to resist the new licence fee, and that subscriptions had been raised to support the continuation of the campaign. He cautioned the diggers to rely on 'peaceful, legitimate and constitutional agitation' to achieve their objectives, and congratulated them for exercising restraint. But he urged them to maintain their campaign, reminding them that 'taxation without representation is the very essence of tyranny'.[24] In June 1854, Harrison cautioned the diggers against supporting calls from extremists to implement 'Lynch Law' and to drive the Chinese from the diggings. He unleashed a diatribe against William Denovan who led the anti-Chinese agitation, commenting, 'this man's brains must certainly be in a queer state when he proposes an act of unreasonable tyranny to be perpetrated on the day commemorative of American independence', and he called for Denovan to be 'summarily stopped'.[25]

Soon after Higinbotham joined the *Herald*'s team, he too provided his own advice to the population of the goldfields. In July 1854 Smith O'Brien, the leader of the failed 1848 Uprising in Ireland, had been granted a pardon and released from imprisonment on Maria Island, Van Diemen's Land (Tasmania). O'Brien, a Protestant Member of the House of Commons, had joined Daniel O'Connell's Repeal Party, but finding himself unable to effect any change in British policy towards Ireland, he had later broken away and formed the Irish Confederation. *En route* to Europe he visited Melbourne, Geelong and Bendigo. At a public meeting before his arrival, the Bendigo diggers resolved to welcome him at a public dinner and to purchase a nine-pound (four kilogram) nugget of gold to be made into a ceremonial cup and presented to him as a memorial of his visit. The gold cup, which is now displayed in the National Museum of Ireland in Dublin, was more than 19 inches high (49 cm), decorated in Irish symbols and cost more than £800.[26] At some length, Higinbotham rebuked the Bendigo diggers for this effusive support for O'Brien. He denounced O'Brien's leadership of the 1848 Uprising as 'a gross blunder', which did not deserve to be celebrated for it was 'a subject for shame and grief'. Revealing his identification as a loyal Irish Protestant, he declared that the Irish population had no desire to bring about that separation from 'our mother country' that O'Brien had sought in Ireland.[27]

The new Governor

In June 1854, the *Herald*'s team welcomed the arrival in Melbourne of Sir Charles Hotham, the Colony's new Lieutenant-Governor. His high reputation for successful exploits preceded him for he had carried out British policy against the African slave trade in the Atlantic, defeated pirates in the Mediterranean and opposed populist forces in South America to advance British trading interests. His naval career was notable for outstanding achievements involving personal daring, diplomacy, seamanship, engineering skill, tactical cleverness, foreign language proficiency and command of men.[28] Higinbotham and the editorial team of the *Herald* held high hopes that, having been appointed by the Duke of Newcastle, Hotham's arrival would mark an improvement in the fortunes of the Colony. They looked forward to a constructive relationship with him in the implementation of a reformed political culture and the introduction of Victoria's new Constitution. Beginning in late June, the *Melbourne Morning Herald* featured a series of articles entitled 'Hints for the New Dynasty'. Higinbotham wrote the second of these, lyrically celebrating the historic opportunity presented to Hotham to witness the infancy of a colony soon to be a 'mighty nation'.[29] Successive instalments of the series urged Hotham to break with the policies of his predecessor and to institute reforms, particularly upon the goldfields.

In August, Hotham made a surprise visit to the diggings at Bendigo. Though some were suspicious of his intentions, the majority of the diggers gave the Governor and his young wife a hearty welcome, and then seized the opportunity to present him with a memorial setting forth their case for the complete abolition of the gold licence fee. Hotham addressed the diggers and promised that he would give their memorial serious consideration.[30] In the same month, he gave an address at a public meeting in Geelong in which he praised the new 'most liberal' Constitution.[31] It was a speech that he would never be allowed to forget. Three and a half months later, following the conflict at Eureka, Michie would bitterly remind him of this speech. Apparently echoing the sentiments of the liberal-minded Duke of

Newcastle who had appointed him to govern Victoria, Hotham announced to enthusiastic applause: 'when you adopted that Constitution, you adopted with it the principle that all power proceeds from the people … It is on this principle that the New Constitution is based.'[32]

To the *Herald*'s editorial committee, this pronouncement was astonishing since the people had not been consulted. The Constitutional Drafting Committee had been chosen by ballot from the Members of the Legislative Council of Victoria, but mysteriously, those chosen by this method were the same individuals as the Colonial Secretary Foster had previously identified as suitable for selection. The Council itself consisted of one-third unelected nominees while the remainder were elected by a restrictive franchise. An article in the *Argus* attacked the Legislative Council for its 'unconstitutional composition' and commented that since the days of separation from New South Wales, 'public opinion has never been properly represented there'.[33] The Bendigo goldfields population, which had lobbied and petitioned to be consulted in the drafting process, had been soundly rebuffed. At a meeting with the Colonial Secretary John Foster at Bendigo, a representative of the goldfields population, Dr John Downes Owens, lobbied Foster to allow consultation in the drafting of the new Constitution. Foster replied that the correct method was to send a petition to the Legislative Council. When the Bendigo diggers' delegates subsequently presented this petition in February, it was 'quashed for want of form'. When John Pascoe Fawkner moved a motion in sympathy with the aims of the petition, this also was defeated.[34]

It was inconceivable that the Governor was unaware of this. In the minds of the *Herald*'s editorial committee, the seeds of doubt were sown as to the bona fides of the new Governor.

2

MARRIAGE AND CAREER
IN TROUBLED TIMES

Higinbotham's career at the Bar in Victoria started slowly with few and sporadic briefs. By 27 March he had taken a room in Barristers' Chambers in Chancery Lane.[1] Higinbotham's son-in-law Edward Morris records that his finances were so low that he was close to despair while he awaited briefs. By luck a *cause célèbre* known as the Mackay–Harrison case indirectly provided him with a welcome spur to his career. In April 1854, the editor of the *Geelong Advertiser*, James Harrison, alleged that Dr George Mackay, a barrister who acted as prosecutor, had appeared in the Geelong Court in a drunken state. It was said that his wig had fallen off, and the courtroom had been in uproar. This may have been the same event that Morris briefly alluded to in the following account of a sudden change of fortune for Higinbotham in his early career at the Bar:

> One court day, a barrister in a large practice was drunk and incapable of work. Five of his briefs were brought in a hurry to Higinbotham, who acquitted himself well with them, and never afterwards lacked work.[2]

It is likely that the barrister in Morris's brief account was Dr George Mackay MLC, a senior Melbourne barrister who served on circuit as Crown Prosecutor in the Geelong Court. The fact that Higinbotham received five briefs for what was presumably only a day's work suggests that these were undefended prosecution briefs. If so, he would have received these from Robert Molesworth, the Acting Solicitor-General, on the authority of William Stawell, the Attorney-General.

Harrison called for Dr Mackay's dismissal. The *Melbourne Morning Herald* next reported that the Government directed Dr Mackay to bring an action for libel against the *Geelong Advertiser*. Mackay did so, and engaged three leading barristers to represent him, including Archibald Michie and Butler Cole Aspinall. Harrison subsequently alleged that the Bar had colluded to deny him representation, and that he had been forced to conduct his own case. An eminent but newly arrived senior barrister named Henry Samuel Chapman joined the fray, publicly rebutting Harrison's allegation. Harrison responded with a bitter, personal attack on Chapman.[3] As counsel for Mackay, Michie contended that his client had not been drunk but merely 'suffering a recovery', and that he had taken only two tablespoons of brandy in water on the morning of the court.[4] Mackay won the case with £800 in damages awarded against Harrison.

In Geelong, the court's judgment was seen as outrageous. Two public meetings were called, the first in Geelong, the second in Melbourne. Bitter accusations were exchanged between the adversaries. The size of the public meeting in Geelong underscored Mackay's unpopularity with the locals, and this may have worked in Higinbotham's favour. The five briefs to appear in court, as mentioned in Morris's account, may have been the first of many more in the aftermath of the public meeting. Despite winning the libel case, Dr Mackay found his credibility in court challenged, and his presence unwelcome in Geelong where further rowdy public meetings were held to protest the unpopular verdict. For some time afterwards, Stawell may have thought it prudent to allocate Mackay's prosecution briefs to another barrister. As Higinbotham was qualified and available, and an Irish Protestant like Stawell, Molesworth and Mackay, he was a natural choice.

His work as prosecutor at Geelong provided Higinbotham with valuable court experience and contacts. Although he welcomed the steady income, the work was not to his liking. He found the criminal justice system harsh and inequitable, and he saw that it particularly disadvantaged the poor.[5] This was a theme that he returned to in an article published in 1856, when his career was more established. A report of a Geelong legal case concerning a fourteen-year-old girl who was sentenced to death for her part in assisting a man to rape her much younger sister for financial gain, was the occasion for some writing of great pathos. Higinbotham noted that both girls were grossly neglected, and described the trial as a 'farce'. He described the moment after the judge passed the sentence of death by hanging on the older girl:

> She burst into a passionate and hysterical flood of tears … to her it may be that there were few other thoughts than of the green fields, and of such things as gave her natural clinging to the young life which she conceived was about to be violently torn from her. Perhaps may have flitted through her mind some thought of a mother, or sister, who may once have cared for her before her sorrowful fate carried her, a lone girl to the goldfield of Ballarat. If she could think at all, might she not reasonably wonder why, or to what purpose she had been born – why society had never attended to her assistance until it sent a judge and solicitor-general to Geelong to try her … There is neither Christianity nor economy in not caring for the ignorant and the poor.[6]

While Higinbotham's career at the Melbourne Bar had begun slowly, it soon improved. On 16 September he appeared in the County Court on behalf of George Black, the proprietor of the *Diggers' Advocate*, who was shortly to become a spokesman for the Ballarat diggers in the events immediately preceding the Eureka conflict. Further County Court appearances followed, and by the end of October he received his first brief in the Supreme Court.[7] In March, the month that marked the first anniversary of his arrival in the Colony, Higinbotham had three Supreme Court appearances.[8] His legal practice provided him with the income he needed to continue writing for the *Herald*, which was largely a labour of love.

As a journalist, Higinbotham would have spent time in the Legislative Council, which met in St Patrick's Hall, Bourke Street – a short walk from the *Herald* office. Here he would have listened to the debates, made notes and read parliamentary reports. It may have been here that he met Captain George Ward Cole, a Legislative Councillor who would become a long-term friend. Cole was a ship-owner, wharf-owner and general merchant, with banking, squatting and insurance interests.[9] In 1853, Cole represented Gippsland in the Legislative Council of Victoria. Perhaps Cole invited the young newcomer to a social event at his beachside house at Brighton. If so, it might have been here that Higinbotham met Margaret Foreman, an eighteen-year-old English immigrant who later became his wife. Theirs was to be a life-long union.

Margaret Foreman

The exact circumstances in which George Higinbotham met his future wife, Margaret Foreman, are unknown. Morris's biography describes her as 'a spinster, native of Kent',[10] but no photo of her survives, nor is there any description of her appearance, personality or her origins or background. The only anecdote we have is the recollection of the minister of St Luke's Church in South Melbourne that she was 'one of our district visitors', and 'a most sympathetic helper of the poor in all their troubles'.[11]

The historian Susan Priestley has researched Margaret Foreman and revealed that Margaret, her brother John and their widowed father arrived as government-assisted emigrants via the *Northumbria* in 1852. John found employment with Captain Cole, tending his horses. Cole owned a large house in William Street, Melbourne, and several valuable properties. One of these was St Ninians, a house of many rooms, set amid gardens, orchards and lawns on twenty-four acres of beachfront land at Brighton, a seaside town south of Melbourne. Margaret found employment with a Mrs Devlin, who Priestley suggests was the wife of Cole's business partner, Captain

Arthur Devlin.[12] Cole and Devlin jointly owned the Williamstown–Melbourne Ferry.[13]

Devlin was a larger-than-life adventurer and entrepreneur, who had built, owned and sailed a succession of merchant vessels, trading and speculating in various forms of merchandise. In 1851, he had sailed his ship from California to Australia, bringing back with him Edward Hargreaves, who later claimed to be the first discoverer of gold in New South Wales. Drawing on his experience of the Californian goldfields, Hargreaves demonstrated to his fellow Australians how to build and use a cradle to extract gold. From 1853 to 1856, Devlin was working in Queen Street, Melbourne, as a gold-buyer, and was living in the Melbourne suburb of Richmond.[14]

Though Cole and Devlin shared the same entrepreneurial spirit, they came from different social strata. Cole was born at Lumley Castle in Durham, and had served in the British Navy, in the West Indies, and at the British attack on Washington, before retiring on half-pay, and embarking on his business enterprises.[15] Devlin's father, Arthur, was a Catholic from Wicklow, Ireland, who had been involved in the 1798 Uprising. He had been given the option of exile, as an alternative to a trial, where, upon conviction, he would have faced execution by hanging. In Sydney Cove, he married a convict, Priscilla Squire, in 1806. Their son, Arthur, grew up to be adventurous, resourceful, financially shrewd, and a great mariner. But in Melbourne society of the 1850s, no amount of wealth, property or talent could expunge the indelible convict stain, and people of Devlin's ilk were often excluded from polite society. Devlin, like Higinbotham, insisted that his papers be destroyed after his death. In his case the motivation may have been to protect his descendants from the stigma he bore.

Stanley Leighton, an English barrister, landowner and (later) Conservative politician, who visited Melbourne in 1868, wrote in his journal:

> Higinbotham had married a woman beneath him in rank,
> who was not received in society … He was not to be seen at

the [Melbourne] Club, nor in general society for he declined
to go where his wife was not admitted.[16]

Leighton's remarks were in the context of a general attack on Higinbotham whose political views he deplored. He accused him of being 'greedy of power', 'a Deist in religion', and one whose political conduct was said to be the result of 'mental aberration'. In contrast to Leighton's harsh remarks about George and Margaret, Priestley's research shows that Margaret's family, although not wealthy, was literate and respectable. She was born in Deal, Kent. Her father, John Foreman, grew produce and may have worked on a local estate. She was the youngest child in the family, with a sister and one, or possibly two, brothers. Her signature on the marriage register was 'clear and regular', suggesting that she could write proficiently.[17] However, Leighton's disparaging remark about Margaret may have reflected the fact that two issues relegated her to a lower social status than her husband. She had been a servant before her marriage, and she had worked for Mrs Devlin, whose husband, Arthur Devlin, was the son of an Irish rebel and a woman convict.

Captain Cole's seaside home in Brighton in the 1850s was the location for the fashionable parties that he and his second wife, Thomas Anne (née McCrae), frequently gave, particularly in the warmer months. St Ninians was, at first, a double-storey brick building. Over time, ten guest-rooms, built of weatherboard, were added, along a veranda of one hundred feet (30.5 metres) in length. The shuttered windows of the guest-rooms overlooked Port Phillip Bay and their doorways opened on to a croquet lawn and gardens. Guests frequently stayed overnight after the journey on bad roads from Melbourne. While taking refreshments on the veranda, they could listen to musical performances and watch the ships passing and the sun setting over the bay. In the morning, they could stroll though colourful gardens and extensive orchards, view the coastal panorama and the abundant wildflowers and bird-life.[18] Might Higinbotham have met Margaret during a social occasion like this at St Ninians?

Top

Sir Archibald Michie
(1813–1899)

Photo courtesy of the
Parliamentary Library
of Victoria

Bottom

Lieutenant-Governor
Sir Charles Hotham
(1806–1855)

Batchelders, photographers

Photo courtesy of the
State Library of Victoria

Butler Cole Aspinall (1830–1875)

Photo courtesy of the Parliamentary Library of Victoria

Below

Captain George Ward Cole (1793–1879) and others in the garden of St Ninian's, Brighton

Photo courtesy of the Brighton Historical Society

As the Devlins lived in Richmond, and Higinbotham could not afford to be absent for long from his legal practice at Barristers' Chambers in Melbourne, it is likely that Higinbotham met Margaret Foreman in the environs of Melbourne. The story told by some descendants that the couple first met on the goldfields is therefore improbable. It may have been invented out of sensitivity about Margaret's connection with the Devlin family.

Perhaps it was Michie who introduced Higinbotham to Captain Cole. Like Michie, Cole was a man of strong political views. He opposed the transportation of convicts to the Australian colonies and he favoured the movement for separation of Victoria from New South Wales. He had supported the colonists' provocative gesture of electing Imperial legislators to the Legislative Council of New South Wales, to draw attention to the failure of the representation of the Port Phillip District in that Assembly.[19] However Cole and Higinbotham met, they found that their political views, while not identical, had much in common. Despite the difference of thirty-four years in their ages, they developed a close friendship that lasted until Cole's death twenty-five years later. At Cole's funeral, Captain Devlin and Higinbotham's brother Thomas were pallbearers, while George delivered a eulogy at the preliminary service.[20]

If indeed Higinbotham received such an invitation to St Ninians in 1854, he might have met Cole's business partner, Captain Devlin and his Irish wife, Esther (née McLelland). Devlin was forty-eight, and Esther was his second wife. The three little children of this marriage may have accompanied their parents. It may have been in such relaxed circumstances that twenty-eight-year-old George Higinbotham first met Mrs Devlin's eighteen-year-old servant, Margaret Foreman. She may have accompanied her employer on the outing, possibly to assist with the children, or in order to visit her brother John, at his place of employment.[21]

One of the few certain historical facts known about George and Margaret Higinbotham is that on 30 September 1854, they married in a brick school-room that doubled as the venue for services at All Saints Parish in St Kilda. They started married life in a newly built timber cottage of four rooms, with separate kitchen and stable, on a quarter-acre block on the east side of Montague Street, near the Bank Street corner in the suburb of Emerald Hill.[22]

A visit to the goldfields

In August, the *Herald*'s Ballarat correspondent sent an alarming report. Two armed intruders had overpowered the sleeping inmates of the *Herald* office at the Gravel Pit Hill, while a third removed a safe containing over £1,000 in valuables. Later that same day, a second theft had occurred.[23] As the *Herald*'s finances were in a precarious position, the news of this large loss came as a blow. On 20 September (ten days before Higinbotham's wedding), the *Herald* advertised vacancies for two parliamentary reporters. It may have been intended that Aspinall would accompany Higinbotham on a trip to the goldfields if both positions at the *Herald* could be filled, but it is unknown whether or not he did so.[24] Within days of his marriage, Higinbotham travelled to the Victorian goldfields. His wife, Margaret, may have accompanied him, and this may account for the belief of some descendants that the couple first met on the goldfields. It is likely that the purpose of the trip was to investigate the thefts, and to review security at the *Herald*'s offices on the other major goldfields. This excursion was to have a great influence on Higinbotham's life thereafter, for it brought him face-to-face with conditions on the goldfields, and set in motion a train of events that influenced the course of his later political outlook.

The *Herald*'s 'own correspondent' at Ballarat was George Collins Levey, a miner who used the latest quartz-crushing machinery and was also a gold-buyer.[25] It is likely that Higinbotham interviewed Levey. After returning from the goldfields, Higinbotham wrote an editorial about the unrest on the goldfields. He related it to the lawlessness that was prevalent on the goldfields. By way of an example, he wrote 'our own correspondent's losses by burglary are fresh in our recollection'.[26] The reference to 'our own correspondent' indicates that the writer was someone other than the newspaper's 'own correspondent'. In the course of his investigations he may also have interviewed Frank Hasleham, another freelance correspondent who wrote for the *Geelong Advertiser* as well as the *Melbourne Morning Herald*. Hasleham was a theatre critic, and had a reputation for his knowledge of the works of Shakespeare. Though he also wrote anonymously, his identity was revealed a few weeks later, because of a terrible ordeal that he suffered during and following the conflict at Eureka.[27]

During his visit to Ballarat, Higinbotham (and perhaps his wife Margaret) may have witnessed some of the ugly disturbances that formed the prelude to the battle at Eureka seven weeks later. On 16 October, around the time that Higinbotham is likely to have been at Ballarat, the local bank was robbed of £15,000. The next day a meeting of about 10,000 miners converged near the Eureka Hotel demanding justice for a murdered young miner named James Scobie, who had died from a blow to the head. The proprietor of the Eureka Hotel, James Bentley, his wife, Catherine Bentley, and two companions were charged in connection with Scobie's murder. Despite strong prima facie evidence implicating Bentley, the magistrate, John Dewes, dismissed the charges.[28]

There were gross irregularities in the conduct of the trial. Peter Lalor, who later came to prominence as the leader at the Eureka Stockade, observed the accused, Bentley, whispering to a juryman. During an adjournment, Bentley was also seen to enter the magistrate's room, and to remain there for about ten minutes.[29] The diggers were incensed by what many of them saw as collusion between the magistrate and the publican, and a blatant denial of justice. A public meeting was called with the purpose of composing a petition to the Governor. Indignation at the reports of the dismissal of charges against Bentley grew, and before long thousands had gathered. The meeting started peacefully but it soon degenerated into a wild and violent riot in which the discharged murder suspect, Bentley, became the target of an angry mob, who looted and burned his hotel and forced him to flee for his life.

Political agitation on the goldfields

Even before the crisis generated by the mishandling of the investigation into Scobie's murder, the population of the Victorian goldfields had grown increasingly indignant at the draft provisions of the new Constitution and the rebuff to their representations to Government. They were well informed about the development of the draft Constitution, for an efficient two-way communication had been established between the goldfields and the Melbourne office of the *Herald*. The correspondents on the major goldfields sent weekly updates of events in their localities for publication. The *Herald* in turn reported on the development of the new Constitution. Its cogently argued critiques of the recommendations of the drafting select committee provided the goldfields population with timely information and insightful commentary. The voice of the diggers was clearly heard in Melbourne, for the *Herald* fearlessly published the motions of public meetings on the goldfields, despite the risk of prosecution should the words it published be considered seditious.

From as early as 17 December 1853, concern had been expressed at a public meeting in Ballarat about the provisions recommended by the drafters of the new Constitution. Edward Kemp read aloud and denounced the provisions regarding the proposed property qualifications for both electors and members of the new legislature. He called for universal suffrage and vote by ballot, arguing that it was a fundamental principle of the British Constitution that there should be 'no taxation without representation'.[30] An example of even more robust dissent appeared in the *Herald* in January 1854 when it reported that, at a public meeting at View Point, Bendigo, on 31 December, about 1,500 people had unanimously passed a resolution containing the following declaration:

A free people can only assume a Constitutional Government through chosen representatives, informed of the interests, circumstances and desires of their correspondents, deliberately adopted in open and independent communication in national

> convention – we hereby, in full public assembly, make
> solemn declaration that the Legislative Council has usurped
> the people's authority, and does not represent, express or
> recognize the public opinion …

The *Herald* did not shrink from reporting the meeting's threat of civil disobedience to the proposed Constitution:

> Any such measure emanating from the Council would be
> regarded by the people as a violation of their inherent and
> inalienable rights, and without the force, the dignity and the
> obligation of constitutional law.[31]

The new Constitution threatened the goldfields population with a range of disadvantages. The worst of these was the property qualification of £2,000 to be eligible to stand for election to the proposed Legislative Assembly.[32] This effectively meant that few if any diggers could afford to stand, so that any digger who might meet the conditions for eligibility to vote would find his choice of candidate restricted to men of a privileged class. There was also the proposed unequal weighting of representation in the allocation of electorates that would see the goldfields population considerably under-represented. The historian Geoffrey Serle has calculated that under the provisions of the new Constitution, each Member of a squatting electorate would represent about 250 voters, but each Member of a goldfields electorate would represent about 1,850 voters. Thus the representation of the goldfields was close to one-eighth of that of the average squatting electorate.[33]

There was other inequitable legislation, such as the requirement that only those diggers who paid for an annual gold licence would be eligible to vote. As Michie had pointed out in an editorial, this amounted to 'selling the vote', for there was no other incentive for a digger to buy an annual licence, which would restrict his freedom to move to another goldfield at will.[34] Moreover, the goldfields population were subjected to a number of discriminatory taxes, such as the £50 annual storekeeper's licence (which the Colonial Secretary misleadingly characterised as a 'rent'), and the proposed £200 annual tax on wine and spirit merchants that threatened the livelihoods of many of the smaller operators.[35]

Higinbotham and the editorial team of the *Herald* were aware that the political agitation on the goldfields arose not only in response to the inadequacy of law and order and the imposition of unfair taxation, but also to dissatisfaction with the drafting of the new Victorian Constitution. As they saw it, both the injustices meted out to the goldfields population and the disdain for popular aspirations and liberal principles that was reflected in the new Constitution demonstrated the determination of an oligarchical clique to monopolise power and govern in its own narrow interests.

Following the trip, an article detailing Higinbotham's eyewitness accounts of the scandalous state of the administration of the law on the goldfields appeared in the *Melbourne Morning Herald*.[36] It differed from the typical reports of goldfields correspondents in that it covered events on three separate goldfields: Ballarat, Bendigo and Castlemaine. Higinbotham wrote in a grave and portentous tone, for he had witnessed some disturbing events. Speaking as a lawyer, he pronounced that certain proceedings that he had witnessed in the goldfields' courts were illegal. He reported that, at Castlemaine, the law against 'sly-grog' selling was usually only enforced if the seller 'offended a commissioner, or failed sufficiently to propitiate a policeman'. He continued on to Bendigo where he spent time watching and reporting upon the 'unjust, anomalous and injudicious proceedings' that took place in the Bendigo Courthouse.

He concluded:

> We have hitherto been proud to think that amidst all the turmoil and excitement of the discoveries here – in spite of the injudicious laws yet more injudiciously administered, the natural temperance and good sense of the people have freed us from the reproach of this wild and savage system of retribution. It is sad evidence of national folly and sin –

not confined to the ten thousand participants in the crime on which we are immediately commenting – that ... the goldfields should still be in a state rendering us liable to the perpetration of such an outrage ...[37]

With melancholy prescience he saw that a tragedy was unfolding. What he had seen of the maladministration of the goldfields during his visit had been so troubling to him that he had characterised it as 'sin'. Before any blood had been spilled, he had laid the blame for the state of affairs that led to the subsequent armed conflict on 'injudicious laws yet more injudiciously administered'. He called for an inquiry into the administration of the goldfields. In later years, George and Margaret Higinbotham may have preferred to avoid discussion of this trip, for to acknowledge it would have awakened painful memories. Though Higinbotham's warnings proved to be correct, they might have seemed to him in later years to be capable of being misinterpreted as excusing the illegality associated with the burning of the Eureka Hotel, and by extension with the conduct of the diggers seven weeks later in the last days before the battle at the Eureka goldfield.

An inquiry into the administration of the goldfields

The *Melbourne Morning Herald*'s call for an inquiry alarmed the Government and precipitated a chain of events. On 31 October William Mollison, who represented Kyneton in the Legislative Council, proposed an independent commission of inquiry into the administration of the goldfields. He explained that there were 'prejudicial reports abroad' and that he would like them inquired into. He particularly referred to a report of 'bribery of the most direct and bare-faced description ... particularly among the higher officials, in matters connected with the publicans' licences', and he also referred to 'a holy compact' between the magistrates and the publicans of the goldfields.[38] His quote referred to the previous day's *Melbourne Morning Herald*.

The Colonial Secretary, John Foster, dismissed the reports and the call for an inquiry, saying:

> You are not to put one hundred men on their trial because some 'anonymous scribbler,' some 'own correspondent' brings general charges; and then to show that the 'own correspondents' are totally unworthy of belief …

Following that, to the surprise of the Members of the Legislative Council, he announced that the Government had already set up its own Inquiry. William Wright, the Chief Commissioner of the Goldfields, perhaps perceiving that the real intent of the Government's Inquiry was to discover who had written the attack on the administration of justice on the goldfields, commented that there was 'no finding out the obscure persons who write for newspapers', yet he voiced support for the Inquiry, 'if only to prove that they are liars'.[39]

The *Argus* reported the Colonial Secretary's extraordinary revelation that the Commission of Inquiry had already been appointed and that the complaints from Ballarat, Bendigo and McIvor were all to be inquired into. The writer sarcastically observed that, despite Foster's assertion that the complaints of the press lacked credibility, he had detailed 'various steps about to be taken by the Government to remove the evils about which they protest', and that following these assurances, William Mollison's motion for an independent inquiry was withdrawn.[40] The *Argus* condemned Foster's remarks about the lack of integrity of the journalists as 'characteristic of the gentleman whose shifty policy has contributed more than anything else to the dissatisfaction that is prevalent'.[41] It expressed a lack of confidence in those appointed to conduct the Government's Inquiry, and scepticism about its likely outcome. The editorial staff of the *Melbourne Morning Herald* heartily agreed, remarking that anyone on the government-appointed commission who should report adversely would do so 'at their peril!'[42] Both newspapers defiantly asserted their confidence in their own sources, and declared that they would not reveal them, despite the penalties that they would incur if they were found guilty of libel.

It was clear that the Government and the leading newspapers were on a collision course, and that neither side would back away.[43] At this stage, one month before the conflict at the Eureka goldfield, both major metropolitan newspapers appeared to be siding with the diggers in their frustration at the failure of the Government to enforce law and order on the goldfields and to allow them their political rights. This united approach would soon prove to be transient.

3

REPORTING THE BATTLE AT EUREKA

The military conflict on the Eureka goldfield on 3 December 1854 was a seminal event in Australian history and an event of great emotional resonance for Higinbotham. His avoidance of any reference to it in his later years and the fact that Morris makes no reference to Eureka in his biography indicate that the subject was a painful one. As a journalist who was acting as editor of the *Herald* during the final days before the outbreak of hostilities, Higinbotham was forced to make weighty editorial decisions, some of which he may have regretted deeply. Eureka involved him in a conflict of loyalty between his kinship group and his colleagues on the editorial team of the *Herald*. Most importantly, the lessons he derived from Eureka caused him to consider aspects of his political philosophy in more depth, to attune it to the reality of colonial politics, and to develop an agenda for reform that would guide his future political career.

The discontent that had been building for months on the goldfields came to a head following the arrest of three men in connection with the burning of the Eureka Hotel. A 'Diggers' Rights Society' was formed at a public meeting on 23 October.[1] A month later this developed into the Ballarat Reform League, and its principles and objects, showing the influence of the British Chartist movement, were adopted at a public meeting. The document's opening sentence asserted 'the inalienable right of every citizen to have a voice in making the laws he is called upon to obey'. It declared that the League's object was 'to place the power in the hands of responsible representatives of the people to frame wholesome laws and carry on an honest government'. It objected to the proposed property qualifications for members and electors, and called for 'full and fair representation'.[2]

In late November 1854, following the report of a Board of Inquiry into the Scobie murder, a lengthy leading article in the *Melbourne Morning Herald* reviewed the sequence of events that had culminated in the crime five weeks earlier. The article carried the hallmarks of Higinbotham's style: the use of rhythm in building the argument, the vein of irony, the religious context, the grave tone and the liberal use of parentheses. He argued that injustice on the goldfields had been the motivation for the burning of the Eureka Hotel and that 'the "mob" ... could never have been hurried into outrage if it had not been first taught, by long experience to despair of obtaining justice by any other means'. He warned the Governor that worse would follow if the diggers' grievances were not addressed.[3] In the two weeks preceding the battle at Eureka, the *Herald*'s editorial team solidly supported the diggers in their grievances but begged them to refrain from lawlessness. A leading article in the *Melbourne Morning Herald,* probably written by Michie, called on the newly appointed Goldfields Commission of Inquiry to recommend the 'annihilation' of the government of the goldfields and an end to discriminatory laws against the diggers.[4]

All the grievances to date – the licence fee, its capricious enforcement, the failure to properly investigate Scobie's murder, the arbitrary arrest of three individuals in connection with the burning of the Eureka Hotel, the inequitable liquor laws, and the exclusion of the diggers from the drafting of the new Constitution – had now coalesced into a single issue: 'the social and political rights of the diggers'. The *Herald*'s correspondents at Ballarat, Bendigo, Creswick and the Ovens were all reporting the development of a unified political consciousness among the diggers and a steely determination to achieve their share of political power.

On 28 November, only four days before the conflict erupted at Eureka, two delegates of the Ballarat diggers, George Black and Thomas Kennedy, accompanied by the secretary of the Ballarat Reform League, John Basson

Humffray, met with Hotham, Stawell and Foster in Melbourne in a final effort to avoid conflict. It was a lengthy meeting and the Governor's record of it, transcribed from shorthand, extended to forty pages in length. The diggers' first 'demand' was for the release of McIntyre, Fletcher and Westerby – the three who had been convicted of offences in connection with the burning of the Eureka Hotel. Twenty-one pages of the transcript related to this issue and one page concerned the issue of the diggers' lack of access to land. The remaining eighteen pages concerned the complaint of the delegates that a number of the provisions of the new Constitution were so drafted as to deny the diggers appropriate political representation.[5]

Hotham largely left the issue of the Constitution to his Ministers, Stawell and Foster, and responded to the issue of the three men arrested for arson. He objected to the use of the word 'demand'. Black refused to soften the term, without authority from the diggers. He then stated that the second grievance was that no digger could be a member of the proposed Legislative Assembly 'unless he is worth one or two thousand pounds of freehold property'. Black pointed out that, instead of inserting into the Constitution Bill the requirement for diggers to take out a twelve-month licence in order to vote, the Legislative Council could have given the diggers the franchise without that qualification. Foster replied that the diggers were 'no more entitled to universal suffrage than any other class of the community'.[6] Stawell, however, disingenuously claimed that the diggers had failed to express their objections at the appropriate time:

> It is singular, Your Excellency, that those views were not more distinctly put forward when the Bill was under discussion but are now brought forward when the power does not exist, either in Your Excellency or in the Legislative Council to alter it.[7]

At a meeting on 9 January in Bendigo, Foster had assured a deputation of diggers' representatives who had raised this issue with him, that the Government was 'most desirous' to have members in the Legislative

Council who would truly represent the diggers. However, he claimed that 'the Colonial Government had not the power to enfranchise them until the New Constitution Bill had been approved of by the Home authorities'.[8] Now the Government Ministers blamed the diggers' representatives for not raising their objections earlier during the drafting phase. In deflecting responsibility for the near disenfranchisement of the diggers on to the Home authorities, Foster was doubly duplicitous. In the previous week he had twice used his casting vote as Chairman of the Drafting Committee to defeat initiatives to reduce the £2,000 property qualification for a member of the proposed new Legislative Assembly.[9] This meant that any diggers who might meet the criteria for eligibility to vote would find their choice of candidate restricted to men of a privileged class. Within a month of giving this assurance of his eagerness to enfranchise the diggers, Foster introduced the electoral scheme that proposed to reinforce their disadvantage by allowing far fewer representatives to the goldfields than other less populous areas.[10]

The Government had dismissed the clear and repeated expressions of public opinion at mass meetings on the goldfields. It had ignored two major petitions from the goldfields population. It had rebuffed their deputation's plea to the Legislative Council to be consulted about the Constitution.[11] The truth was that, even now, there was room to manoeuvre had the Governor wished to negotiate. The draft Constitution allowed for the possibility of change in the future, and even considering the position that would prevail at the time of its inauguration, the Governor, the Attorney-General and the Colonial Secretary could have given an undertaking to allow a motion to amend the new Constitution in this respect following its proclamation. But despite the earnest entreaties of Black, Kennedy and Humffray, their efforts met with united intransigence from the Governor, the Attorney-General and the Colonial Secretary. The one small concession that Hotham offered was to appoint one person, whom the diggers could elect, as a nominee member of the Legislative Council.[12]

Stawell's adamant assertion that it was too late to change the Constitution set in train fateful consequences. It ended any chance of a meaningful concession from Hotham to the representatives of the Ballarat diggers on both the major grounds of their complaint. From this point on, the confrontation at Eureka was inevitable.[13]

On the same day (28 November), a leading article, probably written by Aspinall, appeared in the *Melbourne Morning Herald* urging the readers to consider seriously the plight of the diggers at Ballarat. But it concluded on a note of caution to the diggers:

> The sword should never be drawn until an honest man's convictions tell him that it is the last sad remedy left, and that further submission to tyranny would be a crime. What mad man can yet say that it is the case here?[14]

On 29 November, the day after the deputation had met Hotham, the diggers heard of the Governor's intransigence at a 'monster meeting' on Bakery Hill. Some of them responded to a call to burn their gold licences. The *Melbourne Morning Herald* of that day featured an editorial written by Higinbotham. In it he praised the diggers as 'the salt of the earth' and declared that it was their constitutional right to hold a 'monster meeting'. However, he pleaded with them to refrain from illegality, invoking a memory that would have touched a nerve with many of the paper's Irish readers:

> Why did Daniel O'Connell, one of the greatest wielders of the popular will that ever lived 'in the tide of time' – why did he always abjure his excited and enthusiastic audiences in Dublin to shed no blood – to refrain from any, the slightest breach of the law? ... Because ... he felt that ... the masses ... were fathers, mothers, sons and daughters, husbands and wives; and that in these tender relations, they could have no interest in anarchy and bloodshed ... He besought ... the use of moral force alone, because he knew ... that any more violent means of influencing the British Government would end only in dividing the strength of his adherents ...[15]

O'Connell had famously cancelled the 'monster meeting' for Repeal of the *Act of Union* that was planned for Clontarf on 15 August 1843, because the British had surrounded the area with infantry and naval ships in the nearby Dublin harbour, and O'Connell feared a military attack on the crowd. The reference to 'the tide of times' comes from Shakespeare's *Julius Caesar*, Act III, Scene 1, where Caesar's corpse is referred to as 'the ruins of the noblest man that ever lived in the tide of times'. Although Higinbotham was opposed to Repeal, this reference suggests that it was his view that O'Connell, in putting the safety of his followers above his political objective, shared the noble and tragic attributes of Caesar.

Higinbotham was the only member of the *Herald*'s editorial team who had been in Ireland at the time of O'Connell's public meetings for Repeal. He prefaced his reference to O'Connell's endorsement of non-violence with the words, 'It is an assertion which, founded upon past observation, has with us, all the weight and moral force of a demonstration'. In this editorial, Higinbotham revealed his respect for Daniel O'Connell's concern for the Irish population and his own grave fear for the safety of the Ballarat population.

Two days before the battle at Eureka, Higinbotham wrote another editorial that explored the moral and religious dimension of the crisis. It urged the possibility that good could yet come from evil, declaring that the challenge of bringing this about constituted 'the highest exercise of natural faith'. It warned of the imminent danger that the goldfields were likely to become 'the arena of a conquest of brute force and tyranny over reason and humanity'. It pleaded for the immediate discontinuation of the licence fee before 'many a poor fellow has been unnecessarily sacrificed'. Gloomily it concluded with the observation that 'our apprehensions, unhappily, are at this moment, greater than our hopes'.[16]

An escalation of the conflict ensued, with the Goldields Commissioner, Robert Rede, ordering a new licence hunt. The diggers reacted with further militancy. The Eureka flag, bearing the Southern Cross, was hoisted, the diggers swore an oath of allegiance, vowed to defend themselves from harassment by the authorities, and commenced military drilling. Some time between three and five a.m. on Sunday 3 December, soldiers surrounded a defensive wooden stockade that the miners had built at the Eureka mine site, and a battle began. An eyewitness reported:

> Redcoats stormed through the front of the stockade cutting down diggers, while cavalry broke through the rear. To the cheers of troopers and traps, trooper John King … scaled the flagpole and tore down the insolent Southern Cross flag, which was thrown from man to man, and then trampled. The mounted police, perhaps too well primed with rum, skewered the dead and wounded. One pikeman's corpse had fifteen wounds.[17]

The battle was over in less than thirty minutes. According to the official report by Captain J.S. Thomas, 'not less than thirty were killed on the spot, and I know that many have since died of their wounds'.[18] The rebellion was at an end, but the repercussions were to last for decades.

Following the battle at Eureka, the close association between the *Herald*'s editorial team and the leaders of the diggers' movement continued. At the end of December, the *Government Gazette* announced the dismissal of many lower-ranking public servants, justifying it as an economy measure. The retrenchment was felt across Victoria including the goldfields population. Michie condemned the impact on the hundreds of 'unhappy postmen and poor clerks', declaring that no man deserved to be deprived of his income 'at an hour's notice'.[19] In the same week, the Goldfields Reform League of Sandhurst (Bendigo) complained that they had been forbidden by a proclamation to hold public meetings, and sought 'advice from counsel' as to whether they were obliged to comply with the proclamation. It was Higinbotham who provided the legal advice. He answered the enquiry as follows:

> What a question! Answer it ye long line of liberty's champions whose great names stir our hearts 'like the sound

of a trumpet': whose freely expressed souls have contributed so materially to make Englishmen what they are. Answer it shades of Cromwell, Hampden, Chatham, Fox! May Englishmen meet? ... To this proclamation we not only say it is not law, but that it is against the law.[20]

William Denovan, an activist among the diggers at Bendigo, paid tribute to the role of the *Melbourne Morning Herald*. Addressing a public meeting in late December in Bendigo, he praised the *Herald*'s 'noble stand against the Government' and recommended that the whole of the colonial press should imitate it.[21]

A critical time for the *Herald*

The apprehension of an imminent rebellion against authority on the goldfields was a time of great anxiety for the editors of Victoria's newspapers. In the case of the *Melbourne Morning Herald*, the clash at Eureka coincided with a time when the newspaper teetered on the brink of financial collapse. This crisis led to the resignation of Sinnett, the business manager, and forced Michie to undertake major legal and financial re-arrangements. The responsibility for editorial writing therefore devolved upon Higinbotham and Aspinall.

It was discovered that the *Herald* owed about £29,000. Michie later described himself as 'ruined ... and obliged to begin the world again', while claiming that Sinnett had 'millions in the bank'.[22] On 27 November, the firm of F. Sinnett and Co. was dissolved, and Sinnett's unpaid shares were transferred to Archibald Michie & Co. A second difficulty was that a bitter dispute between management and the Typographers Association was underway.[23] Both of Melbourne's leading daily newspapers, the *Argus* and the *Melbourne Morning Herald*, were facing tight financial constraints, and both had responded by cutting the wages of their typographers. A third complication was that, about the same time, the *Melbourne Morning*

Herald found itself the defendant in an action for libel, involving a claim for damages of £200.[24]

The indications of approaching conflict on the goldfields spelled danger for newspaper editors. Throughout the British Empire harsh penalties were prescribed for any who were convicted of criminal libel or sedition. Even reporting words uttered at a public meeting could result in prosecution if the words were deemed seditious.[25] All the editors of newspapers that had encouraged the diggers' cause had reason to be fearful. On the day of the military attack at Eureka, Henry Seekamp, editor of the *Ballarat Times*, was arrested in his office and subsequently convicted of sedition and sentenced to six months' imprisonment.[26] His newspaper had shown partisanship in the diggers' cause and indulged in inflammatory language. Seekamp had welcomed the formation of the Ballarat Reform League, declaring:

> This League is nothing more or less than the germ of Australian independence ... No power on earth can now restrain the united might and headlong strides for freedom of the people of this country, and we are lost in amazement while contemplating the dazzling panorama of the Australian future ... The League has undertaken a mighty task fit only for a great people – that of changing the destiny of a country.[27]

Higinbotham and Aspinall faced a huge dilemma in deciding how to report the turn of events at Ballarat. Aspinall's subsequent political activism and legal advocacy in the cause of the imprisoned diggers reveal that he was fiercely critical of the military intervention at Eureka. The stance that the *Herald* eventually adopted suggests therefore that it was the view of Higinbotham that prevailed. It contrasted markedly with the stances taken by the *Ballarat Times*, the *Argus* and the *Geelong Advertiser* in that it sought to allay fears by denying the evidence of preparations for a battle on the Eureka goldfield.

As the military conflict had approached, the *Argus*, which had supported the diggers as recently as 28 November, abruptly switched sides.

It asserted that there were many in the community who believed that 'an example must be made' of the diggers. Using italics for emphasis it continued:

> Now it must be evident to intelligent men that *there is a point at which Government must make a stand*, but everyone must know that unless a point be established somewhere *and maintained*, Executive authority becomes a laughing stock, and the community sinks into anarchy and confusion.[28]

The *Argus* urged the Government to take a stand against 'destroyers of law and order' and 'promoters of anarchy'.[29]

About six months later, the explanation for this reversal of stance came to light. In a series of two letters that were addressed to Edward Wilson, the editor of the *Argus*, and published in the *Age*, the Reverend David Blair accused Wilson of editorial inconsistency. Blair revealed that from 1852, he had written the earlier articles in the *Argus* sympathetic to the diggers, but that the change in the stance of the *Argus* (which Blair denounced as 'treachery') was because Wilson had written the later articles. Blair charged that 'dread of the physical force exhibited by the diggers brought you over at once to the side of what you call "law and order", but by which you really mean bayonets and slavery'.[30] Evidence of Wilson's views that supports Blair's claim can be found in private correspondence between Wilson and Hotham's Private Secretary, Captain Kay, dated 29 November 1854. Wilson wrote to Kay, assuring him of his support, and asked to be provided with 'authentic intelligence' from Ballarat so that he might influence 'the better class of diggers', and thereby 'prevent outrages'. He advised Kay that 'If the "respectable" men withdraw from the agitation it will at once assume an aspect of seediness under which it will crumble away rapidly'.[31]

By contrast, the *Geelong Advertiser* took a more courageous stand consistent with its support for the diggers. It published in full three reports from the freelance Ballarat correspondent, Frank Hasleham, in the one edition of 30 November. Using language connoting noble and heroic deeds, Hasleham reported that the diggers were undertaking military drilling and making bullets in preparation for war.

Hasleham wrote:

> A few men, whom accident, not merit, placed in high places, entrenched behind prerogative, the constitution, and similar shadows, tyrannize over men, many of whom are as much their superiors in intelligence, as they are their inferiors in deceit, impunity, recklessness, unstatesmanlike policy and unconstitutional government …

Most provocative was his appeal to the memory of the Rum Rebellion:

> This country was once before saved from ruin, and must be so again by the same means. This Augean stable must be cleansed, and then the young Hercules, the Digger, shall have doubly earned renown, having accomplished his second labour. Heaven help him. His is no easy task.[32]

The reference to the need to save the country again 'by the same means' was, on the face of it, a call to take up arms against the authorities.

The editor of the *Geelong Advertiser* implied solidarity with the diggers in their frustration with the Government but avoided openly committing himself regarding the looming confrontation. He wrote:

> We can well conceive with what painful feelings, each one of our readers must peruse our Ballarat correspondent's letter. A collision between the troops and the diggers has taken place, and several on both sides wounded, but none killed … Let us, instead of moralising, ACT. How? By insisting unanimously on the instant dismissal from office of those imbeciles who have been the direct cause of these sad occurrences.[33]

Three days previously, the *Argus* had reported the rumour that the Ballarat diggers had seized Commissioner Rede and Inspector Evans as hostages, but the rumour was later found to be false. Perhaps Higinbotham and Aspinall suspected, or hoped, that Hasleham had mistaken the situation, for not only did they take the step of censoring the inflammatory language in which his report had been couched, but they took the highly unusual step of publishing the report but prefacing it with the following disavowal of its veracity:

> We subjoin a version of the latest news, said to have been from Ballaarat, as taken from the Geelong paper. But at the same time, we are happy to say that we are in a position, on the highest authority in Melbourne, to give the Geelong statement the most unqualified contradiction.

Quoting from an unnamed 'authority', the *Melbourne Morning Herald*'s editorial reported that the public meeting of 29 November:

> did take place on Wednesday last and was attended by about two thousand persons, one thousand of whom were mere spectators, and took no part whatever in the proceedings … very little inflammatory speaking was heard, and no riot or disturbance took place. The motion to burn the licences was a signal failure, and the people had the good sense to render a perfect obedience to the laws of the land. We cannot but congratulate the diggers on their conduct on this occasion, and we trust that the same moderation will continue to mark all their proceedings.[34]

Perhaps having received an assurance from this unnamed 'authority' that the people on the Ballarat goldfield had shown 'perfect obedience to the laws of the land', the editor or editors may have decided to set the new facts in the Ballarat report in a context that emphasised the general tranquillity of the goldfield. Hasleham's report could be conveyed to the readers not as a balanced appraisal but an exaggeration based on a few isolated criminal acts. To this end the decision was made to publish a truncated version of the latest Ballarat report, and to omit the earlier reports, with their inflammatory language. To make certain of the point, they disavowed the report's veracity. It was an exceptional decision in response to a dilemma fraught with danger.

In stating that the diggers at the meeting on Bakery Hill behaved with 'good sense', 'moderation' and 'perfect obedience to the laws of the land', the editorial staff of the *Melbourne Morning Herald* misrepresented the situation, and misled their readership. The *Ballarat Times* had estimated the number of people assembled as ten thousand. Raffaello Carboni, a digger who was arrested and charged with 'high treason', later estimated the crowd at the meeting of 29 November at fifteen thousand.[35] Yet the *Melbourne Morning Herald* reported the total as only two thousand, of whom half it said were mere 'spectators'.

The description of the tone of the meeting as one of 'moderation' and exhibiting 'very little inflammatory speaking' was also misleading. Four resolutions had been passed. The first called for the 'instant dismissal' of Sergeant-Major Milne, and was passed unanimously. The second condemned:

> the insolent language used by the Colonial Secretary, the Surveyor-General, the Chief Commissioner of Goldfields and the Chairman of Committees, and their unwarrantable assertions respecting the veracity of the diggers and the respectability of the representatives of the Press on the Goldfields …

The third resolution of the meeting pledged the assembly to adopt the draft prospectus of the Ballarat Reform League, and to support the committee in attaining 'the full political rights of the people'.[36] The League's objectives comprised full and fair representation, manhood suffrage, abolition of the property qualification of members for the Legislative Council, payment of members and the short duration of Parliament. The assembly's final resolution expressed its 'utter want of confidence in the political honesty of the Government officials in the Legislative Council', and pledged to use 'every constitutional means to have them removed from the offices they disgrace ...'[37]

Was this attempt to downplay the volatility of the situation on the Ballarat goldfield motivated by fear of the sedition laws, misplaced trust in 'the highest authority', or mere wishful thinking? The decision to publish, but disavow the facts in the Ballarat correspondent's report of the diggers' preparation for armed conflict, sent a confusing message. Within seventy-two hours, it was clear that the editorial writer's report of the mood of the Ballarat goldfields' population was utterly mistaken.

Many readers of the *Melbourne Morning Herald*, after reading the 'unqualified contradiction' of the Ballarat correspondent's report of preparations for conflict on the goldfields, might have had their fears allayed. However, as they opened their newspaper that morning, a large party of military reinforcements, including soldiers and marines, with six cannon, were leaving Melbourne for Ballarat, and within twenty-four hours, Major-General Robert Nickle with another force of 800 men and four artillery pieces also left for Ballarat.

The following day (2 December), the *Melbourne Morning Herald* had to report that, despite its reassurance of tranquillity the day before, the Lieutenant-Governor had ordered that 'all the available military force in town will proceed forthwith to Ballarat'. It added, 'Martial Law has, we understand, been proclaimed at Ballarat'.[38] Notwithstanding his partisan language, the Ballarat correspondent had accurately reported the facts and the Governor was responding. If Higinbotham had indeed received reassurance of the peaceful state of affairs at the Ballarat goldfields from 'the highest authority in Melbourne', he had been deceived. He must have been greatly mortified when news of the military conflict broke.

In seeking to verify the report from Ballarat, had Higinbotham unwittingly become a pawn in the Governor's game? The military authorities at Ballarat had already received intelligence, through their spies and informers in the stockade, of the activities of the miners in preparing weapons and ammunition. It was later revealed that Sir Charles Hotham, in Melbourne, had been communicating directly with Commissioner Rede at Ballarat through encoded letters, and so would have been well informed of the situation.[39] The Colonial Secretary, John Foster, told the Goldfields Commission of Inquiry:

> It came accidentally to my knowledge that his Excellency also sent orders in cipher to the gold-fields ... Some were addressed to Colonel Rede. I know Colonel Rede had one because one of his answers came, in mistake, to my office; and I enquired into it then, and the cipher being a very plain one, I decoded it.[40]

It may have suited the Governor's purposes for an understated report of the treasonable activities of some individuals to be circulated to the population of Victoria through the *Melbourne Morning Herald*, thereby explaining to Melbourne readers the dispatch of troops to Ballarat, and preparing them for the subsequent charges of high treason against some of the leaders of the diggers' movement. It may also have suited the Governor's purposes for a false report to be circulated to the goldfields, through the efficient distribution arrangements of the *Melbourne Morning Herald*, that the view in Melbourne was that there was no cause for alarm and that nothing more than a precautionary increase in the military force at Ballarat was intended. That way, the element of surprise in the imminent dawn attack on the Eureka stockade was preserved.

The *Geelong Advertiser* attacked the *Melbourne Morning Herald*'s interpretation of events and denounced:

> the little specimen of 'toadyism' enunciated respecting the Ballarat intelligence. 'We are happy to say that we are in a position on the highest authority in Melbourne' to pooh-pooh the reports of any disturbance on the goldfields ...[41]

The person referred to as the 'toady' who had consulted 'the highest authority in Melbourne' before authorising the publication of the correspondent's truncated report was most likely to have been George Higinbotham. Tormented by an agonising and momentous decision under pressure of deadlines, the young journalist had attempted to seek clarification of the situation at Ballarat from 'the highest authority' only to be falsely advised. His good faith had been betrayed and now he faced the accusation that his motivation had been to curry favour with the Government. Was the 'highest authority in Melbourne' who had deceived him the Colonial Secretary? Was it the Attorney-General? Was it the Governor himself? Did the Governor assure the young journalist of the peaceable state of the goldfields while concurrently authorising the dispatch of a large force to deal with the agitators at Ballarat by means of a surprise attack on the stockade at dawn?

So many events crowded one on top of another, yet a decision of overriding importance had to be made. If the paper were seen to support the diggers' preparation for armed conflict, it might be shut down for sedition, especially if its reports caused diggers on other goldfields to join their comrades at Ballarat. If the *Herald* were to abandon the diggers after so many months of supporting their struggle, it would have invited the charge that, like the *Argus*, it had betrayed them at the critical time. The justice of the diggers' cause and the progress of their political aims were important considerations, but Higinbotham subscribed to O'Connell's view that it was not justifiable to risk the lives of the troops, the diggers and their families for a cause. Regrets and indelible memories, too painful to bear and to reveal, may explain the absence of any mention of Higinbotham's activities during the Eureka period in Morris's biography.

The shooting of Frank Hasleham

The news of the bloodshed at Eureka must have cast a pall over the editorial office of the *Melbourne Morning Herald*. But there was further horrifying news. Frank Hasleham, the freelance correspondent at Ballarat, became a victim of what the *Argus* condemned as the 'gross brutality' perpetrated by the Government forces after the end of all resistance from the diggers. According to Hasleham's own account, some hours after the affray he had been in the process of taking notes for the *Melbourne Morning Herald* when he was fired upon.[42] A group of mounted troopers had ridden towards him. One had signalled to him in a friendly way to approach, and unsuspectingly he had done so. At a distance of four paces, the trooper shot him in the chest with a pistol.[43] Hasleham managed to escape from the troopers but his ordeal did not end there. He reported that he had passed two weeks in hiding in a tent on the goldfields, under the summer sun, in great pain and 'with poverty as my nurse'. He received medical attention, but the doctor advised against removing the bullet, which had lodged in his shoulder. Months later, he applied for compensation, and was promised £400 compensation by a Board of Inquiry set up under John O'Shanassy, the Member for Kilmore, and at a later date, after further representations, he was promised an additional £200 which he did not receive.

He produced medical certificates attesting to the continuing pain and incapacity from his wound. He applied for a government position as Clerk of Courts at Ballarat, and submitted a character reference. However, in a note on his file, the Acting Resident Gold Warden, James Daly, opposed Hasleham's application because, 'during a period of disturbance, he was connected with the Press, and is still a correspondent of the *Melbourne Herald*'. He added that Hasleham ought not to be employed on the Ballarat goldfield because 'his private sympathies might seriously interfere with his efficiency as a Government servant'.[44]

Government antipathy for Hasleham stemmed from his writing immediately before the Eureka conflict, but despite his injury, Hasleham continued to write articles for the *Melbourne Morning Herald* attacking the Government.[45] Over the next few years, his misfortunes continued.[46] In 1856 Hasleham wrote to the Chief Secretary, William Haines, describing himself as being in great poverty as a result of his injury, and having to survive on loans from his friends.[47] Six years after the battle at Eureka, suffering from the constant pain in his shoulder and incapacity in his right arm, his character besmirched by ongoing accusations from Government authorities, and his finances in a desperate state, Hasleham managed to return to his family in Ramsgate, England, where he died a few weeks after arrival.

The editorial staff of the *Melbourne Morning Herald* must have been acutely conscious of Hasleham's plight. His own account of his wounding suggested a summary execution that had gone wrong. Acting Resident Gold Warden Daly's objection to a government appointment at Ballarat on the grounds that Hasleham was writing for the *Melbourne Morning Herald*, supports the view of the editorial committee of the *Herald* that Hasleham's ongoing ordeal at the hands of government authorities was in retaliation for the newspaper's anti-government stance.

Higinbotham would have been shocked and dismayed by the attack on a fellow journalist and colleague. It is likely that he would have met Hasleham on his visit to Ballarat seven weeks earlier, in the course of his enquiries about the burglaries at the *Herald* office. In performing the duties of editor at the *Herald*, he would have regularly handled reports from Hasleham. At a personal level, this incident confronted Higinbotham with the savagery of the conflict at Eureka. Perhaps he had been one of the 'friends' who lent money to Hasleham. His son-in-law, Morris, spoke of Higinbotham's generosity to those in need, writing, 'he let kindness of heart bear sway over his reason'.[48]

The memory of Hasleham's ordeal may have been a source of deep regret to Higinbotham, for in retrospect, his disavowal of the veracity of Hasleham's report of the diggers' preparations for conflict constituted an unwarranted attack on the correspondent's professional integrity. It played into the hands of officialdom, who justified the denial of Hasleham's plea for employment by casting aspersions on his character. The painful questions that it raised about the wisdom of the editorial decisions taken by the *Herald* immediately before the clash at Eureka, and the motivation for the attack on Hasleham, may partially explain Higinbotham's reluctance to reminisce about the battle at Eureka. Morris's bare acknowledgement of his father-in-law's twenty-seven months of work at the *Herald* and his studied avoidance of the impact of Eureka upon his subject may be sourced to the same sensitivity.

The *Herald's* editorial team in the aftermath

Michie and Aspinall refused to be intimidated by the attack on Hasleham. Indeed, it may have further enraged them. In the weeks following the conflict at Eureka, Aspinall defended without charge the African American John Joseph, and Michie defended without charge Jan Vennik, both of whom were charged with high treason.[49] Michie also defended the *Ballarat Times* journalist and sub-editor, John Manning, who, according to a police spy, had been undertaking military drill in the stockade on each of the two nights before the attack. The newspaper editorials and leading articles of the *Melbourne Morning Herald* undertook a passionate campaign on behalf of all the Eureka prisoners, and repeatedly called for an amnesty.[50] In an editorial, Michie contended that the prisoners had 'yielded their heads to their hearts' after suffering 'gross injustice and vindictiveness', and he denounced the actions of the Lieutenant-Governor, the Colonial Secretary and the Attorney-General as 'harsh', 'barbarous' and 'unconstitutional'. He reminded the readers that the awful penalty prescribed for high treason was 'the barbarous savagery of being *hanged, drawn and quartered*'.[51]

Several days after the notice appeared in the *Melbourne Morning Herald* confirming its change of management, the *Geelong Advertiser* reported that the *Herald's* new editor was 'Mr Aspinall, a young London barrister', and speculated that a changed political bias was already emerging.[52] This may have been an attempt to discover the new arrangements at the *Herald*. In answer to the speculations, the *Melbourne Morning Herald* published an editorial four weeks later, entitled 'Our Politics'. It may have been an attempt at a common platform by Higinbotham, Michie and Aspinall. It concluded as follows:

> Wherever, then, abuse is to be checked, wherever Downing
> Street trammels may be removed, wherever 'high-sighted'

local tyranny may call for opposition, wherever Victoria's young energies may be encouraged, we trust we shall be as reforming as the greatest radical may desire, but in a spirit of peace and reason such as the mildest and most conscientious Christian may approve.[53]

The barrister-journalists of the *Melbourne Morning Herald* expressed outrage that the Government had resorted to such heavy-handed means to deal with the situation on the goldfields. For months, the newspapers had revealed evidence of growing dissatisfaction at the administration of the goldfields, and of the criminal propensities of the ex-convicts, of whom Bentley was, arguably, an example.[54] Now, it seemed, the recent events had borne out all their warnings. If Higinbotham, Michie and Aspinall saw the treatment of Hasleham as a warning to the press from the Government circle that they should cease their criticism, their statement of editorial policy affirmed their determination not to comply. But despite the commitment to moderation in the common platform, the recent bloodshed had stirred powerful emotions, and cracks were appearing in the common approach and 'the spirit of peace and reason'.

Aspinall wrote satirical attacks particularly targeting the Governor and key Government Members.[55] Parodying the language of Hotham's proclamation in the *Gazette Extraordinary* of 4 December 1854, Aspinall proffered a list of cynical suggestions for the likely recommendations of the Commission of Inquiry into the Goldfields, beginning and ending with a bitter allusion to the fate of Frank Hasleham:

> Reporters, unless for papers decidedly anti-Government, are not to be shot at by private troopers, without express orders from headquarters ... women are also to be exempted because there is a scarcity of them in the colony, and children, because there is always an outcry against their being ill-used, and they make better marks for bad shooters when grown up than when they are infants ... We are given to understand

that the Government are determined on all these points,
and that the report of the Gold Commission will be such
as to warrant the proposed improvements. It is believed that
Sir George Grey will not complain of the alterations if their
necessity be properly represented at home. But no pseudo-
philanthropy for the ruffians – no pity for Mr Hasleham –
found armed with a pen and convicted of having used it too
often to tell the truth.[56]

This satirical reference to grossly immoral outcomes of the Inquiry into the
Goldfields being represented as reasonable to the new Secretary of State for
the Colonies, Sir George Grey, by unnamed persons in London, implies
that the same process might be operating regarding reports of the conflict
at Eureka.

Aspinall may also have been the unnamed 'own correspondent'
who reported favourably on the decision of the Bendigo Goldfields
Reform League to adopt a 'vigorous course regarding the conduct of the
Government during the late disturbances at Ballarat', and endorsed its
decision to petition the 'Home authorities' for the Governor's 'immediate
recall'. The distinctive style of writing with its bitter humour suggests
Aspinall rather than Edmond Harrison, who was the *Herald*'s Bendigo
correspondent. His style is apparent in the final lines in which he attacks
the Governor:

There is something so supremely ridiculous in the almighty
style of this Knight Commander of the Bath, visions of a
rampageous little schoolboy, with an unlimited quantity of
recumbent collar, and tiny breeches, buttoned to an equally
tiny waistcoat, stamping his foot in puny passion to all
around him, come up before one. Why, Sir Charles, you will
have a frightful reputation. Nurses will terrify naughty little
children by the mere mention of your name!

If so, he had travelled to Bendigo to address the Bendigo diggers and his role was not simply that of a reporter, but of an advocate, and possibly a political agitator.[57] On 13 January 1855, Aspinall addressed a public meeting attended by 4,000 people in Melbourne. Its purpose was to petition Sir Charles Hotham for a general amnesty for all the Eureka prisoners.[58]

The shock of Eureka reverberated throughout the Colony for months afterwards. Throughout the main centres of population in the Colony, public meetings took place, petitions were drafted, rumours circulated, recriminations were publicly aired, government buildings were sand-bagged, and feelings ran high about the fate of the prisoners taken from the battle. At the same time there were votes of thanks to the troops, demonstrations of loyalty to the Governor and prayers of thanks in churches for the restoration of peace. The political consensus that had existed between the editorial writers at the *Herald* showed signs of strain. For Higinbotham, this must have been a time of immense personal turmoil as he saw his colleagues Michie and Aspinall passionately embarking upon their role as leaders of the anti-Government agitation. But as a young man at the outset of his career, with a wife to provide for as well as himself, Higinbotham did not join in. He owed his improving career in part to the goodwill of the Attorney-General and he could not afford to jeopardise that.

4

A PHILOSOPHICAL WATERSHED

By a strange twist of fate, news of an appalling occurrence in Ireland added a further layer of complexity to Higinbotham's attitude to rebellion, whether in Victoria or at home. News from home of a rebel attack on a train near Enniskillen in Ireland was reported in the *Melbourne Morning Herald* five days after the battle at Eureka. The details at first were sketchy, but no doubt they were quickly supplemented by letters from home, for George Higinbotham's brother, Robert, was one of the organisers of a religious festival that had attracted about 800 people to embark on a fateful train trip in September. Morris provided a rare insight into Higinbotham's personal feelings when he wrote of his close relationship with his brother Robert. Though Morris had assisted in the burning of Higinbotham's personal papers, he described a range of memorabilia about Robert that had been amongst them. This included newspaper obituaries, a photograph, a book of sermons that Robert had published, some reminiscences by contemporaries, a letter from a relative, and the text of one of several poems written about him by William Alexander, Bishop of Derry and Raphoe. The closeness between the brothers would have meant that the news of the sabotage of the train would have been extremely disturbing.[1]

The train had been returning from Derry to Enniskillen when it left the tracks at a locality named Trillick.[2] Several large rocks weighing 'between one and a half, and eight hundred-weight' (seventy-six kilos and four hundred kilos) had been placed on a curving section of the line where it climbed an embankment leading to a bridge over a road. The rocks caused the derailment of the two engines at the front of the train. However, the carriages did not follow the engines down the embankment, because the connection to the carriages behind broke upon impact.[3] In the derailed engine, which had been flung on to its side, two firemen died and one of the two drivers was seriously injured. The passengers were Protestants from the Enniskillen area, who were returning at night after a day of religious festivities in Derry. The guest of honour, Lord Enniskillen, Grand Master of the Orange Order in Ireland, who was riding in the front carriage of the train, survived the ordeal. As the train was travelling very slowly, most of the passengers were either unhurt or sustained only minor injuries.

Earlier in the day, the Enniskillen excursionists had arrived in Derry. The city was festooned with banners commemorating historic Protestant victories. The visitors from Enniskillen were greeted at the station by a salute of artillery from the Apprentice Boys, and officially welcomed by a committee of dignitaries. Speeches were made. Standing with the official party was the Reverend Robert Higinbotham.[4]

The derailment at Trillick sent shock-waves through Ireland, for, had the plot gone according to plan, the carriages would have tumbled down the embankment after the engines, causing the loss of hundreds of Protestant lives. Had this act of sabotage succeeded, it would have aroused a massive retaliatory response against Catholics. The reports of the repercussions continued for many months with the arrest of seven suspects, who were eventually released, inquests, a government investigation, and a grand jury's assessment of the prima facie evidence. There were rumours about other collaborators who reportedly fled from Ireland, and complaints about the mistreatment of the imprisoned suspects. Somewhere amongst the papers that were burned after the death of George Higinbotham, there must have been newspaper cuttings and family correspondence relating to the derailment. Because of Robert Higinbotham's role in organising the event that involved the train excursion, the family must have been deeply shocked at the news of the attack and avidly interested in the process of bringing the perpetrators to justice.

Around the time of the newspaper report, Higinbotham would have learned of his brother's involvement via letters from home. The news of this second tragedy, coming in the same week as the bloodshed at Eureka, must have meant that George Higinbotham's first Christmas in Australia was an intensely miserable one. In the editorial for New Year's Day 1855, Higinbotham described himself as wrestling with his own anger towards Sir Charles Hotham and his duty as a Christian to think charitably.[5]

In the month following the incident, Lord Enniskillen received a deputation from the Apprentice Boys congratulating him on his 'late, providential escape from death'. The Reverend Robert Higinbotham presented a similar address on behalf of the Derry Working Committee.[6] The Apprentice Boys addressed their presentation to 'the Earl of Enniskillen and the Protestant Brethren', and in it they articulated a widely held Irish Protestant view of rebellion:

> We desire not wrongfully to lay to the charge of any men or body of men this fearful act; but we cannot shut our eyes to the fact that it has its origins and performance in that secret wicked system which concocted the Gunpowder Plot, carried into execution the massacre of 1641, induced the infamous Conrad de Rosen, on 12th July 1689, to drive under our walls, there to perish unprotected Protestants, from the hoary head to the infant on the mother's breast, and which has at various periods since imbrued the hands of our countrymen in blood. They are links in the same chain, and until that evil confederacy is destroyed at its foundations, we cannot expect safety, peace or comfort.[7]

At the first of the trials of the prisoners from Eureka, Attorney-General William Stawell drew upon this view that political acts (such as the diggers had undertaken) are, in reality, manifestations of a wider 'evil confederacy' that must be vigorously suppressed. In his opening address at the prosecution of John Joseph, Stawell implied that it was necessary to stop this particular 'conspiracy' in order to prevent other conspiracies. He told the jury:

> If men were allowed to organise such a conspiracy as this there is no saying how many wrong-headed men … may be unwittingly and unintentionally led into the most dreadful crimes and outrages.[8]

George Higinbotham's natural sympathies in the Irish incident would have been enlisted on the side of his brother and the Protestant population. But given his insights into the situation in Victoria, could he accept that the political movement that culminated in the battle at Eureka was simply another 'link' in the chain of evil confederacies that must be destroyed at its foundation? In many Irish households in Melbourne, the shock of the sabotage at Trillick is certain to have resonated for months in the aftermath. George and Margaret Higinbotham no doubt anxiously awaited letters from family members in Ireland bringing news of the capture of the perpetrators. George would have been deeply concerned that this criminal act in which innocent railwaymen died, and several hundred passengers narrowly escaped death, had so nearly touched his brother Robert.

Another brother, Thomas Higinbotham, was a civil engineer with renowned expertise in railway technology. In 1840 he had been assistant engineer of the South-Eastern Railway, and was the resident engineer of the Great Northern Railway Company, and in these capacities was responsible for the construction of several British lines. Thomas arrived in Melbourne in 1857 and came to live with George and Margaret. From May 1860 to January 1878, he was responsible for all railway construction in Victoria.[9] He must have had his own opinions regarding certain claims of technical problems with the second engine, and the ensuing debate about the construction of the track at Trillick (the contours of which were subsequently altered).

The derailment at Trillick showed that railway technology provided rebels with the opportunity for acts of sabotage on a grand scale. But the exceptionally broad gauge used in Ireland meant that the two engines, even after leaving the track on an uphill slope, remained upright. The broad base of the carriages ensured a low centre of gravity that prevented the heavily laden carriages from tipping when the derailment occurred. It may have been the breadth of the gauge that saved the lives of hundreds of passengers.

Six years after the derailment, Thomas Higinbotham was appointed Engineer-in-Chief of the Victorian Railways. In this capacity in the 1860s and 1870s, he insisted that the Victorian lines be constructed using a five feet, three inch gauge, which was known as 'the Irish gauge'. It was wider than that used in the neighbouring colonies and in most other countries of the world. The decision was much criticised, as it meant that passengers had to change trains when crossing colonial borders. His adamant insistence on the adoption of the wide gauge in Victoria may have been motivated by the lesson of Trillick in 1854. His obituary in the *Argus* stated:

> In 1871 when Mr Longmore was Minister for Railways, a strenuous effort was made to break the gauge of our railways. Mr Higinbotham almost single-handed opposed this, and contended that all our railways should be made on the same gauge.[10]

His brother George supported his stance.[11] In Ireland, the fear that rebels would use the railway tracks for sabotage was well founded. A warning of sabotage came in 1847, when John Mitchel of Young Ireland had advised Repeal wardens to study the tactical possibilities of railway cuts:

> Imagine a few hundred men lying in wait in such a spot with masses of rocks and trunks of trees ready to roll down – and a train or two advancing with infantry and the engine panting nearer and nearer until the polished studs of brass are distinguishable and its name may be nearly read; – 'Now, in the name of the Father and of the Son and of the Holy Ghost! – now'.[12]

In an editorial in the *Herald* written eleven months after news of the Trillick derailment, Higinbotham described the writer of these words as 'the unhanged and demoniacal John Mitchel ... the representative of an ignorant, brutal and unprincipled mob'.[13]

The combination of the news from Ireland and the battle at Eureka must have deepened the dilemma for Higinbotham. The Trillick incident would have re-awakened in him the age-old fear of the Irish Protestants that they might yet be driven from Ireland by an uprising directed against them. This now combined with the fear that he shared with many others in Victoria that further anarchy and bloodshed, perhaps compounded by religious, national and racial differences, could break out at any moment, ushering into this new society the deadly cycle of reprisals and counter-reprisals that had become endemic in Ireland.[14]

In his nine months in Victoria, Higinbotham had seen at close quarters how oppressive administration had escalated tensions on the goldfields to such a pitch as to cause deadly confrontation. Like Michie and Aspinall, he believed that the Government had provoked the bloodshed in Victoria by 'injudicious laws, yet more injudiciously administered'.[15] He might have been glad of the policy of anonymity at the *Melbourne Morning Herald*, for how, at a time like this, could he have explained to his family in Ireland that he had expressed any sympathy for the miners in Victoria during the recent confrontation? As loyal Protestants, might they not have viewed all these acts of rebellion as 'links in the same chain?' The visceral hatred of rebels felt by many of the Protestant Irish would have intensified after the recent sabotage. Higinbotham may have been uncomfortably aware that, even in faraway Australia, any editorial or article, written by him, that smacked of condoning preparedness to take up arms against the Government, might have seemed unpardonable to his immediate family, and to many of the kith and kin of the intended victims of the derailment at Trillick.

A theory of revolution

Eight months after the conflict at Eureka, in a leading article in the *Melbourne Morning Herald*, Higinbotham pondered the problem of rebellion in a religious and political context. The argument began in the context of the Genesis story of the fall of man. God imposes upon mankind the necessity to work, but with the promise of the bounties of Providence as a reward for honest labour. It argued that this concord between man and God could be disrupted by 'the hand of man interposing' with 'gratuitous malignity' to enact 'unequal and perverse legislation'. Higinbotham saw this as the cause of driving a population into 'some terrible reaction that cannot be misunderstood'. He further argued:

> This is the true theory of revolutions, which instead of being only crimes or misfortunes are more frequently the salutary crisis of some disease in the body politic that would otherwise concentrate itself upon the vitals.[16]

His experience of the conflict at Eureka had caused him to question the conservative Loyal Orange view of rebellion as an unpardonable and unnatural crime, and to arrive at a new view of rebellion as a symptom of a seriously defective political system. But the two perspectives on the recent Irish and Australian experiences of conflict could not easily be reconciled. Rather than retreat into a partisan view of these conflicts, an approach based upon a deeper analysis was called for. That approach, as Higinbotham's future conduct was to illustrate, meant withholding uncritical loyalty to either side, but holding fast to the fundamental principles of law, morality and good government. It involved reviving and fostering popular respect for the law and striving for a form of government that is founded and conducted upon honourable and equitable principles.

The Rev. Robert Higinbotham (1824–1857)

Image courtesy of St Columb's Cathedral, Londonderry, Northern Ireland

Below

Plaque in St Columb's Cathedral, Londonderry, Northern Ireland

Poem written by Bishop William Alexander

Image courtesy of St Columb's Cathedral, Londonderry, Northern Ireland

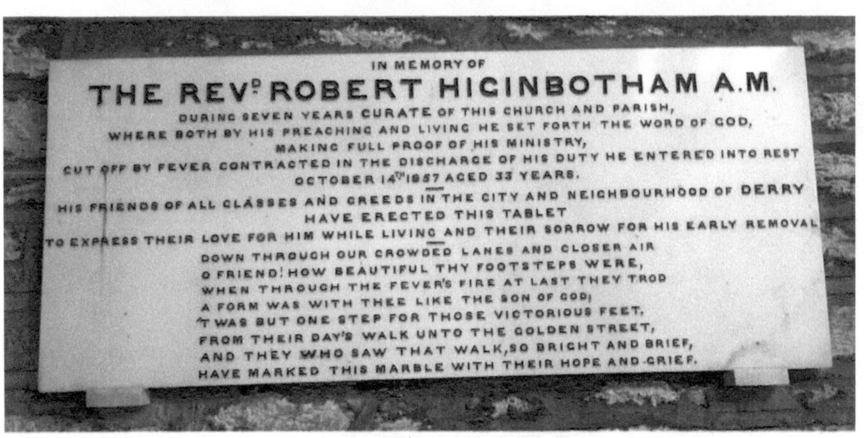

Top

Thomas Higinbotham
(1819–1880)

Image courtesy of the
State Library of Victoria

Bottom

George Higinbotham

Image courtesy of the
State Library of Victoria

Higinbotham's writing in response to Eureka

In September 1855, an editorial in the *Herald* (renamed as such in that month), committed the policy of the newspaper to advocacy of a political 'middle course'. While it endorsed democracy as a desirable system, it warned of the danger of slavishly following the popular will:

> Where two lines diverge, we shall usually be found pursuing that which takes the popular direction, but we should deem it false and base indeed, to pay that homage to the people universally, or to pander indiscriminately to the ignorance, the delusions and the passions of the multitude. This is the curse of liberalism when it bends public men into such vile and vicious obsequiousness to the popular will. At the same time, though the people may be often wrong in their judgement, they are generally right in their moral sentiments, and it is infinitely better for society to go with them, even in their errors, than to be the prostituted slave of a tyrant or an oligarchy ...[17]

Higinbotham was influenced by the views of the historian Lord Macaulay, who saw the British Crown, laws, religion and culture as the pinnacles of human progress. A rebellion might put at risk these boons that had been progressively won over previous centuries. Despite their shortcomings, Higinbotham believed that these social institutions offered the best hope for the advancement of society and the common good. Therefore they must be defended in their hour of need. But the current governing elite had betrayed the trust of the people by 'injudicious laws' and by authorising and endorsing wrongful actions. Were the rebels to be victorious, he feared that the upheaval might lead to unforeseen results such as a sudden and acrimonious separation from the Mother Country, to republicanism, to the triumph of Roman Catholicism, or to a descent into 'Lynch Law' as had recently happened in Ballarat in the case of James Bentley.[18]

Horrified by the bloodshed at Eureka and unwilling to join wholeheartedly in either supporting the illegality of the rebels, or in defending what he viewed as the illegality of the Government, Higinbotham decided to devote his life to promoting respect for the law and the development of a properly constituted, democratic government. For him, the lesson of Eureka was that, if British sovereignty was to continue, respect for the pillars of British society – the law, the Government, and the judiciary – which had fallen so low, must be restored in the hearts and minds of the people. Reform of the system was essential. The people must receive fair play from the Government, and they must be educated to prepare them for their role as responsible citizens in a democracy. Government must be made responsible to the people. Power must be exercised in an exemplary manner for the public good. The reputation of the law for impartiality must be rebuilt. Higinbotham saw a pressing need for a political system based upon the most advanced constitutional principles.

On 19 March 1855, not quite a week after the report of the public meeting at which Aspinall had roundly attacked the Governor and the Attorney-General, Higinbotham wrote an article in the *Melbourne Morning Herald* concerning the trials of the rebels. The tone was solemn, and it reflected upon the coming trials of the prisoners from Eureka from a legal perspective that seemed to be at the same time both a religious and a moral framework. He implied that convictions and executions were only to be expected. He took no pleasure in the prospect, and saved his condemnation for those who lacked feeling for their fellow-citizens who were facing judgment and probable execution. Without condoning the actions of the accused, he called on readers to feel compassion for them, castigating those who did not, as 'the most odious of all traitors'.

> We may say of the prisoners in the language of the law –
> 'God send them a good deliverance', and whoso will not join
> in that prayer, when he sees his fellow-countrymen in peril,
> and in his mind's eye follows them upon the dreadful track
> of justice to the place of execution must indeed be callous

and insensible to mercy. We brand and stigmatise him as
the basest and most odious of all traitors – because he rebels
and levies war against humanity itself – and therefore as to
prisoners when they come to be tried, without prejudicing
their case, whether guilty or innocent, we may be permitted
to say in the language of the Court itself 'May God send
them a good deliverance'.[19]

These sombre words may have reflected how profoundly Higinbotham
was affected by the gravity of the charges, and with what foreboding he
anticipated the trial outcomes and the public reaction to them. But the
article may have been more important for what it suggested, than for
what it said. He did not deny that there was a case for executions if the
prisoners were found guilty, but neither did he accept that anyone should
express satisfaction at the fate of the convicted. Those who would do so, he
castigated as worse human beings than the rebels themselves. He echoed
the words of the court that he anticipated would be spoken after the
sentence of death, but in pleading with the readers to have a merciful sense
towards their 'fellow-countrymen', he made a veiled appeal for mercy from
the authorities as well.

As defence attorneys for three of the prisoners, all of whom were
charged with high treason and were on trial for their lives, neither Aspinall
nor Michie could have written this editorial. Sinnett had severed his
connection with the paper after an acrimonious dispute with Michie about
his responsibility as manager for the paper's mounting debts.[20] The tone
of the editorial of 19 March showed that Higinbotham's involvement as
a journalist (and perhaps as an eyewitness) in the political upheavals in
the Colony had brought him face-to-face with the human tragedy behind
rebellion, and also its legal, moral and religious complexities.

Four days after the conflict at Eureka, Sir Charles Hotham addressed
the Legislative Council and delivered an explanation justifying his actions.
Higinbotham wrote a critique of his explanation entitled 'The Governor
and the Governed'. The article began with a series of mild, almost

dispassionate evaluations of the arguments put by Hotham to justify the action taken against the miners at Eureka, but each was lightly barbed with irony. Hotham's recent actions were recalled and, with consummate under-statement, contrasted with his public statements. As argument succeeded argument, the imagery became more graphic, the accusations graver. The portrait of Hotham that emerged was of a man whose words could not be trusted and whose motivations were unworthy. Higinbotham then broadened his attack to include the Legislative Councillors who had acquiesced in Hotham's justification for his decision to send the troops to attack the miners at Eureka. While being careful not to declare directly that they had colluded with Hotham in illegality, he nevertheless insinuated that they had done so. He implied that Hotham had authorised the shooting of Frank Hasleham, and he warned that loyalty to the Government was conditional upon the Government being able to demonstrate that it had acted lawfully. With bitter irony he wrote:

> A governor who dispenses with the laws and authorises the shooting of his fellow-citizens, even for a day, has reason to feel 'satisfaction' when he finds the Legislative Council admitting his right, and congratulating him on his intention 'to strike decisive blows' at men whose evil passions, if they were evil, had been aroused by difficulties which, as His Excellency admits, his utmost endeavours had been insufficient to stave off. He thanks the Honourable Members for being resolved to maintain the law. Perhaps he means the Martial.

> It is a very serious question in the first place as to whether the law has been maintained or infringed by His Excellency's adoption of those 'vigorous steps' upon which he now looks back with so much 'pride and satisfaction' …

> We are not clear as to the line beyond which his supposed right to dispense with trial by jury, and to shoot men like dogs ought to begin …

… Let him be one degree more frank, and announce his policy for the future; discontent will then have nothing to cling to, and juries will convict real rioters almost as speedily as troopers can shoot innocent reporters …

Our 'rallying round the authorities' lasts till they are on their trial, meanwhile all will support the law, knowing that according to strict law only can our several rights be maintained.

He concluded with an ironic flourish:

A popular representation would have had somewhat more to say against this brilliant novelty – Government by martial law.[21]

In writing that he was unsure about the line beyond which Hotham's supposed right to dispense with trial by jury, and to shoot men like dogs ought to begin, Higinbotham used ironic denial – a literary device characteristic of his style. This statement implies the opposite of its literal meaning. In fact his meaning is that Hotham *has* crossed the line into illegality. In referring to 'rallying round the authorities', clearly he was speaking for himself rather than the others on the editorial committee for, given their agitation and public denunciations of key government figures, Michie and Aspinall could not have described themselves as 'rallying round the authorities'. His appeal to both the readers' reason and emotions was expertly crafted. Like Mark Anthony's speech on the death of Caesar in Shakespeare's play *Julius Caesar*, his initial innocuous observations were something that readers would all have been inclined to agree with. But as the argument progressed, they would have found themselves entertaining doubts about the honourable intentions of the Governor, and gradually but inexorably become drawn to contemplate the shocking charge that his recent explanation to the Legislative Council revealed that he had made the decision to abandon recourse to law, and instead had sent the troops to attack the miners. The charges against Hotham climaxed with the hideous image of men being shot 'like dogs'. The style of the writing was consistent with Higinbotham's style as described by Morris:

> It is almost as if the words of Hamlet to the players were borne well in mind, 'in the very torrent, tempest, and (I may say) the whirlwind of passion, you must acquire and beget a temperance that may give it smoothness'.[22]

In Higinbotham's view, the Governor's actions had 'infringed' the law and the juries had failed in their duty to convict 'real rioters'. He did not join Aspinall and Michie in calling for an amnesty for the prisoners. Nevertheless, his reference to the attack on the reporter and to shooting men 'like dogs' indicated his firm conviction that those in authority were equally guilty of crimes. To Higinbotham, Eureka represented a tragic failure to uphold the law on both sides. An editorial that he wrote four years later, as editor of the *Argus*, expounded on his respect for the law:

> We should deeply grieve to see any wavering in that faith which a British population has almost invariably reposed in the supremacy, the might and the inflexible integrity of the law.[23]

The grave tone of Higinbotham's newspaper contributions during the Eureka period and its aftermath reveal how deeply the conflict had troubled him. They are readily distinguishable from Aspinall's contributions, for these became more inflammatory, and his political attacks more florid and savage. Despite the *Geelong Advertiser*'s report that Michie had transferred the editorship of the *Herald* to Aspinall, Michie continued to write editorials even whilst he was engaged in defending three of the Eureka prisoners.[24] Five months later, the recently established *Age* newspaper, which promoted itself as 'the People's Paper', also made veiled references to Michie as the proprietor and editor of the *Herald*.[25]

As the age of sailing ships gradually gave way to the age of steamships, the departure of a steamship for England was seen as an opportunity for speedy conveyance of news back to Britain. The major dailies compiled comprehensive summaries of recent economic and political developments and timed each to catch the bi-monthly steamer as it departed for home. Three months after Eureka, a major article in the *Melbourne Morning Herald* entitled 'Summary for the *James Baines*', further revealed Higinbotham's feelings about the recent conflict.[26] This article abstained from personal attacks, but spoke in generalities that nevertheless painted a damning picture of incompetent and corrupt government in the colony. Readers would have been in no doubt that Sir Charles Hotham was the object of the attack, though his name was never mentioned. The article must have been particularly galling to Hotham as it was addressed to British readers.

In examining the two 'not guilty' verdicts at the recent trials of the Eureka prisoners, Higinbotham dissented from both of the widespread opposing views about the significance of the verdicts and proposed his own:

> There are two extremes of opinion on this subject, with neither of which we can perfectly coincide. The Government people – the official party – are disappointed and enraged beyond all bounds. They say – without reflection on the self-condemnation they pronounce – that it is the result of general disaffection and widespread disloyalty among the people, and that both juries have undoubtedly perjured themselves.

> On the other hand, there are here, as there are everywhere, a few rabid stump orators and tap-room politicians who seem to think that all government is a curse and all authority a usurpation …

> We have found ourselves bound conscientiously to take a middle course … The summary is this – that while we

> think the prisoners very blameable, and guilty perhaps of grave misdemeanours, the executive flew too high in their prosecution, and compromised their success by resorting to the odious and terrific charge of high treason.[27]

Higinbotham's response to the conflict at Eureka was to abstain from partisanship and to embark upon what he called 'the middle course'. The concept reflected his reading of political philosophy and his religious belief.

Eureka had been a watershed for Higinbotham. Torn by competing loyalties between his professional colleagues and his kinship group, Higinbotham clung ever more steadfastly to the foundation of his political philosophy. He saw the illegal actions of the miners and Hotham's despotic style of governing partly as moral failings. But he saw Hotham's failings as the more reprehensible because of his willingness to use military force in preference to the processes of the law, his failure to keep to his word and his preparedness to sacrifice the lives of others. Higinbotham believed that Hotham's authorisation of the attack at Eureka emanated from a desire to please the Colonial Office and that the subsequent trials were an attempt to justify his action by imputing treasonable intentions to the miners.

Higinbotham drew several lessons from the conflict at Eureka. The first was that the law had been abused, and that it needed to be restored to its rightful place in the estimation of the public. The Governor's determination to secure convictions for high treason, to justify his actions, undermined public respect for the law and showed a fundamental flaw in the colonial political system. Like Michie, Higinbotham saw the 'bureaucratic origins' of the Governor's office as the fundamental cause of the problem. Sir Charles Hotham, he believed, regarded himself as answerable not to the people of the colony, but to Downing Street, and for this reason had been prepared to sacrifice the peace and welfare of the Colony when the actions of the miners challenged his authority. He believed that the relationship between Governors of the Colony, the Home Government and the Victorian legislature needed to be re-established on a sound constitutional footing that would be conducive to good government.

The willingness of the Legislative Councillors to approve the Governor's course of conduct indicated weakness and lack of principle. These perceptions spurred Higinbotham's long campaign against the Colonial Office during his parliamentary career and energised his campaigns for responsible government and democratic reform.

Higinbotham's abhorrence of demagoguery may have had its roots in the lead-up to the 1848 Uprising in Ireland and may have been further influenced by the writing of Carlyle. However, the burning of Bentley's hotel and the subsequent battle at Eureka demonstrated to him that such outbreaks of violence were the natural result when misrule of a population left no legitimate way to achieve redress.

In Higinbotham's writing in the days and weeks following the events at Ballarat, the influences of the French political theorist Alexis de Tocqueville, and the Scottish philosopher and writer Thomas Carlyle, can be traced. Both writers saw a close connection between religion and politics and it was this connection that particularly interested Higinbotham.[28] By 1857, Higinbotham's views had diverged from those of Carlyle on the issue of democracy. Morris notes that the following is an example of Higinbotham's editorial views:

> What Carlyle calls 'the mere counting of heads' is no doubt at all times a most fallible method of arriving at the truth, but in some form it is an essential of all electoral systems, nay, it is the electoral system itself, and defective as it is, human intelligence has as yet devised no better mode of picking out mankind's proper governors ...[29]

The bloodshed of Eureka heightened Higinbotham's abhorrence of demagoguery and mob rule, but it reinforced his sense of the urgent need for constitutional reform. Eureka strengthened his conviction that a popularly elected legislature, a responsible ministry and an independent judiciary were the essential bulwarks against such abuses of power as had led to the breakdown of civil society in Victoria.

5

AWAITING THE NEW CONSTITUTION

In July 1854, Higinbotham was still hopeful that the new Constitution would produce great blessings, 'because we hope that something like true government may yet be possible here'.[1] But in the third week of August the editorial team received alarming news. The Fifth Duke of Newcastle had assumed the new post of Minister of War. Sir George Grey, nephew of Henry George Grey, a former incumbent of the office, had become the new Secretary of State for the Colonies.

The *Herald* boldly declared its displeasure at the appointment and lamented the loss of Newcastle and his liberal predecessor, Sir John Pakington.[2] Henry George Grey, who had held office from 1846 to 1852, was a reformer in certain respects, but he was also a passionate Imperialist. He saw an ongoing role for the Australian colonies as repositories for Britain's convicts, and had no patience with colonists who opposed transportation; after all, he argued, they had made the choice to emigrate.[3] Although his name was associated with the introduction of responsible government into Canada, he expressed the view that it was not appropriate for the Australian colonies because of their convict origins and powerful cliques.[4] He believed that Britain should maintain control over some of the policies of its colonies, particularly their commercial and land policies, and therefore did not accept that the devolution of power from Britain to its Australian colonies ought to involve the principle of making the executive arm of colonial government answerable to an elected colonial legislature. Grey disliked party government and believed that it was the prerogative of the colonial Governor to select the ministry from amongst the members of the legislature 'in order to keep its composition in harmony with majority opinion in the assembly'.[5] His nephew, though nominally a Whig, appeared to have less interest in questions of the best model for devolution of power to the Australian colonies. His particular concern was to see that the position of the clergy of the Anglican Church in the colonies *vis-à-vis* those at home regarding appointments, remuneration and promotion should be regularised.

After the battle at Eureka, public attention shifted to the fate of the prisoners and the *Report* of the Royal Commission into the Goldfields. While waiting for the new Constitution to be voted upon at Westminster, and desperately hoping for removal of some of its undemocratic features, Higinbotham, Michie and Aspinall strove to keep the constitutional issue before the public mind.

Higinbotham and Chapman plan constitutional reform

In early 1855, a by-election occurred for the metropolitan seat of South Bourke. Michie and Higinbotham supported the candidacy of Henry Chapman, a fellow barrister. Three years earlier, Chapman had held office as Colonial Secretary in Van Diemen's Land (recently renamed Tasmania). A conflict had arisen between the majority of Legislative Councillors and the Governor over the issue of the Colony's continuing acceptance of transported convicts. Chapman had refused to support the Governor, Sir William Denison, and the Governor had suspended him from office.[6] Chapman had then sailed to London, intending to appeal to the Colonial Office. *En route* he had written a treatise explaining how the principles of responsible government and the separation of powers could be provided for in the Australian constitutions.[7] In this work, he criticised the existing arrangements for the drafting of the constitutions, and pointed out that the legislators were not representative of the colonial populations and were unfamiliar with constitutional principles.[8]

Like Molesworth, Higinbotham and the other colonial reformers, Chapman argued that the responsibilities of the Imperial Government should be distinguished from those of the colonial government. He concluded that 'the interference of the Imperial Government should be confined to subjects and questions which concern the Empire at large'. He urged that ministries should be responsible to elected legislatures and that the Governor in any of the Australian colonies was 'precisely in the position of the Crown at home'. Colonial government ought therefore to proceed, as in England, by means of a parliamentary majority.[9] Chapman did not have the opportunity to put his case to the Colonial Office in his capacity as Colonial Secretary, for in November 1852 he was notified that he had been dismissed. In October 1854 he began to practise at the Bar in Victoria, and four months later, after campaigning on the issue of responsible government, he was elected as a member of the Legislative Council.[10]

The events of December 1854 had made Higinbotham, Michie, Aspinall and Chapman suspicious of Hotham's real views about constitutional principles, and they foresaw an imminent contest over the interpretation of the new Constitution. It was clear that constitutional reform would not be achieved without a dire struggle. Chapman's success at the election secured for the *Herald*'s editorial team a powerful advocate to advance their cause in the Legislative Council.

A year after the Constitution Bill had left Victoria for consideration in London, there was still no news of its passage through the British Parliament. The *Age* and the *Herald* were both calling for a revised Constitution.[11] In June 1855, on the last day of the session of the Legislative Council, Chapman gave notice of a bold motion that he proposed to move on the first day of the next session in the event that the new Constitution was not proclaimed on or before that day. The motion would be addressed to the Governor-General (Sir William Denison) and would complain of the 'great and needless delay' by the Secretary of State for the Colonies in securing the Royal Assent to the Constitution. It would ask the Governor-General to request that the Queen should directly empower him as her representative to give the Royal Assent to the Constitution.[12]

Chapman's notice of motion was provocative for he planned to request that the Queen should bypass her Minister (the Secretary of State for the Colonies), the British Parliament and her Victorian Governor. He planned to ask her to allow her Royal Assent to be given to the original, unamended Victorian Bill, not by Sir Charles Hotham but by Sir William Denison as Governor-General. This may have been too radical for John O'Shanassy. The following day, the last of the session, O'Shanassy also gave notice of a motion for constitutional reform at the commencement of the next session. His proposed motion was milder as it did not call for the intervention of either the Queen or the Governor-General, nor for the bypassing of the British Parliament. His motion would be addressed to Sir Charles Hotham. It was to condemn the last four years of 'irresponsible government' and would call upon him 'to establish a system in consonance with the views and opinions of a free people – the enlightened system of Responsible Government'.[13] Thus the Legislative Council was on notice that, at the commencement of the next session, it would be presented with two options for pursuing the principle of responsible government.

Hotham was alarmed. He sent a dispatch to Lord John Russell, who had been appointed Secretary of State for the Colonies three months earlier, requesting urgent action on the Constitution and seeking advice as to how he should proceed in the event that O'Shanassy's motion should succeed. There was no confusion in his mind as to what the term 'responsible government' meant. He warned that 'a universal demand for Responsible Government will arise and they will refuse to proceed to an election unless the Government is to be chosen from the majority of the new Council'.[14] The stage was set for a great struggle.

In a leading article sent home to British readers via the bi-monthly steamer, Higinbotham complained of the following:

> We are grievously misgoverned … our finances are in a state of
> disorder, our legislature despised as a mockery, our executive
> hated as an imposition … we are tired and disgusted with
> delay in waiting for the New Constitution which we sent
> home so long ago that you seem to have forgotten it.[15]

He argued that the Victorian legislature was a 'sham'. He accused Sir
Charles Hotham of undermining loyalty to Britain, warned of the growth of
republican sentiment in Victoria and drew clear parallels with the situation
in the American colonies in 1776. He attacked the 'ghostly conclave in
Downing Street' and likened it to the papacy promulgating a dogma,
which in this case was 'irresponsible power'. On the same day the *Age*
also produced a fierce attack. The editor called for a revised Constitution,
warning: 'It will not be long before the entire population of Victoria will
unanimously declare that the real remedy for their grievances and their
wrongs embraces both the dismissal of Sir Charles Hotham and a revised
constitution: and this they will have – or the alternative'.[16]

Higinbotham envisages a new nation

By early August 1855, news arrived from Britain of yet another change to
the office of Secretary of State for the Colonies. Sir William Molesworth
was the new incumbent. Delighted that his former friend, the leader of the
Philosophical Radicals, was now in a position to implement his liberal ideals,
Higinbotham rejoiced in the belief that constitutional reform was imminent.
He redoubled his efforts over the next few weeks to rouse the public to demand
constitutional reform. His editorials expressed a new sense of purpose and
a passionate urgency. He condemned the lack of 'real political life' in the
Colony. He contrasted the community's apathy about constitutional matters
with the idealism of Algernon Sydney, the seventeenth-century English
political theorist. Sydney was beheaded in London in 1683 for his advocacy
of a system of government based upon the consent of the governed, and his
published opposition to the divine right of kings:

Who thinks himself capable of following a Sydney to the scaffold or a Washington to the field, or of dying for anything even 'on the floor of the House' or elsewhere, except for nuggets or a monopoly of tallow and fleeces! There is a new constitution coming out. Who cares about its qualities?[17]

He reminded the readers of the English 'Glorious Revolution' of 1688 – a landmark in the development of the supremacy of the British Parliament over the Crown. He urged them to assert their right to be governed by their own legislature, independently of that of England:

> This is the old-fashioned doctrine of the Pyms and Hampdens, the men that hurled defiance at the Stuarts, as we should – if we were like them and had not basely degenerated – at the insolence of Downing street and the usurpations of Parliament; and this is the sacred principle that America never lost sight of.[18]

Higinbotham gave free reign to his visions of the future of Victoria. He foresaw a 'majestic empire', and saw it as the duty of the founders of the country to consider their successors. He warned that succeeding generations might condemn those founders of the nation who would 'shrink from identifying themselves with the future freedom and glory of their descendants'.[19] He advocated public sale of land at 'a fair market price', and called for a land policy similar to that operating in South Australia that would 'gratify the popular demand and open the country to those with a genuine desire to settle upon it for their livelihood'.[20] He urged the Government to refrain from debasing itself by exploiting the purchasers through inflated prices. He called for self-sufficiency in supplying the Colony's food. With the Crimean War continuing, he warned that Victoria might yet be attacked by hostile powers, and called for the population to undertake military drill to secure the Colony's defence. 'Where is there such cavalry in the world as could be made of our stockmen ... As for infantrymen, who could match the digging population?'[21]

His chief concern was 'not for ourselves only or for our immediate descendants … but for the unborn generations that will come after us'.[22] The new nation would be a 'nursery to receive the contributions of the world'. He advocated extending citizenship to:

> the Frenchman and the American – the German and the Italian – the Hungarian and the Pole … or whatever race of men are capable of a natural and equal amalgamation with us – which all nations are not – in their pagan and idolatrous condition …[23]

Among the races that Higinbotham regarded as inferior were the Chinese. He warned of an inundation of Chinese bringing paganism and vice to the colony. He doubted that the Government's proposed poll tax would prevent the influx, and he urged that the will of the people for stronger measures should prevail over the Government's reliance on an ineffective poll tax.[24] Regrettably, this attitude towards the Chinese was common at the time amongst many Europeans in Victoria. Partly it was fuelled by the competition for gold, but there were also conflicts from time to time over other issues such as access to water. The fact that very few of the Chinese brought their wives to Australia created suspicion about their intentions regarding European women. The unfamiliar dress of the Chinese, their language and writing, as well as their religious and cultural traditions challenged European notions of propriety. In Higinbotham's vision for Victoria, Christianity, like democracy, was an essential element. Judged by the standards of his Irish Protestant community and his times, Higinbotham's respect for the religious impulses of other Christian believers was markedly tolerant, but this tolerance did not extend to the non-Christian Chinese. The members of the *Herald*'s editorial team varied in their views about this issue, but like Higinbotham, they agreed that the rule of law must prevail, and they condemned any descent into 'lynch law' or vigilantism.[25]

Governor Hotham's dispatch

In the same month there was disturbing news. Despite Governor Hotham's purported enthusiasm for the new Constitution as expressed in his speech at Geelong a year earlier, his true beliefs about the Constitution Bill came to light via a leaked dispatch from the register of official correspondence of the Colonial Office in London. The *Herald* reprinted an article from the London-based *Australian and New Zealand Gazette*. The article suggested that the dispatch had been made public inadvertently by the inexperience of the new Under-Secretary of the Colonial Office, James Ball. It revealed and commented upon the contents of a dispatch issued by Governor Hotham on 25 October 1854 to the Secretary of State for the Colonies. The date of issue was approximately two months after the accession of Sir George Grey to the office of Colonial Minister and at about the time that Victorians would have learned of his appointment. In the dispatch Hotham's views appeared to have changed markedly since he had hailed the new draft Constitution at Geelong as 'the most liberal constitution that was consistent with monarchy'. Now he argued that the proposed new Constitution would make Victoria 'a republic in reality'.[26] He warned of ill-effects if the draft Constitution were to receive Royal Assent. He urged that the power to appoint and dismiss the ministry should belong not to the Parliament but to the Governor, and that his choices should not be restricted to elected members of the Parliament.[27]

In choosing to reprint the article in the *Herald* in full, the editorial team sent a warning to their readers of the Governor's real intentions. Quoting from the dispatch, the author of the article reported that Hotham had charged that the members of the legislature were either stupid or venal for the recommendations that they had made. Hotham had couched his line of attack on the Constitution in terms that matched the known views of Sir George Grey's uncle and predecessor, Henry George Grey. He had particularly objected to the principle of allowing the legislature to control the executive arm of government, for he accused the Legislative Council of having adopted this recommendation 'with an eye to selling places'. For him, responsible government meant 'putting the appointment of all public officers in the hands of the Governor'.[28]

An anonymous letter to the *Herald* (which may have been the work of Henry Chapman) attacked Hotham's dispatch and questioned:

> whether the Executive Council of this colony, responsible for its actions to the country through Parliament is to appoint the officials necessary to carry out its schemes of government, or whether such schemes are to be appointed by the Governor, irresponsible, who cannot be called to account in the colony, and who is not answerable for the incapacity or dishonesty of these persons.[29]

The heady optimism with which Higinbotham, Michie, Sinnett and Aspinall had welcomed Hotham turned to deep dismay as the dispatch proved that Hotham was the implacable enemy of the constitutional principles that they advocated.

Higinbotham reacts to the new Constitution

On 16 July 1855, the Constitution Bill for Victoria received Royal Assent, and by late September Higinbotham read with deep despair the news that the Victorian Constitution Bill had passed through the British Parliament without the alterations that the *Herald*'s editorial team had advocated. According to an English newspaper report reprinted in the *Herald*, the Bill had been debated in a lack-lustre, late-night session that lasted about twenty minutes in the House of Commons with only twenty members present, many apparently 'half asleep'.[30] Neither Molesworth nor Grey had been present. The last hope of the *Herald*'s editorial team that the British Parliament might intervene to remove the 'fearful mistakes' that they had identified in the draft Victorian Constitution was finally dashed.

As the blow fell, Higinbotham characterised the political condition of the Colony as one of 'absolute quietude'. Employing a string of dissonant consonants to emphasise the oppressive tone of the sentence, he wrote with palpable emotion of:

> the stillness of a sullen acquiescence in acknowledged evils – the silence of an inexpressible disgust, and the stifled resolution that feels itself under the grasp of a loathsome incubus ...[31]

He declared in a leading article that the new Constitution had 'not one attribute of a legal constitution'. He added:

> The so-called Constitutional Act is no Act at all as binding upon the colony, but a mere document appended in a schedule to a statute, and referred to as a thing that may take effect and come into operation, under certain conditions and contingencies ...

Using an extended metaphor of putrescence, Higinbotham condemned the *Constitution Act* as grossly offensive to the colonial population. He argued that it lacked the force of an Act of the Imperial Parliament and should have been treated only as a draft sent back with amendments for reconsideration by the local Legislative Council. He insisted that the Legislative Council, at this stage, still had the option to amend it, by striking out 'all those clauses which are so hostile to the public interest and so hateful to the public sentiment'. He declared that if the Council should fail to do this, it would 'stink in the nostrils of the country'.[32]

Higinbotham particularly condemned the high property qualification for members of the legislature. He pointed out that it would debar many good candidates. He denounced the framers of the new Constitution as 'the slaves and lick-spittles of aristocracy' whose motive had been 'to confine the selection [of candidates] within the narrow and bigoted precincts of their own order'.[33] In another bitter leading article, Higinbotham absolved from blame those 'who thought they were really giving effect to our wishes', and directed it at:

those cunning and plausible politicians who concocted
this scheme of Government and sent it home under false
pretences and artful misrepresentations as the act and deed
of the people, when in reality, the object of the Bill is to
disqualify the people and to place all power in the hands of
a local aristocracy infinitely more odious and contemptible
than the gentlemen who used to be sent out from England to
govern us by the Colonial Office.[34]

This conviction persisted. In 1873, nineteen years after the conflict
at Eureka, he declared to the Legislative Assembly that the current
Government, as well as all previous Governments:

have sat down, contented with the invasion of the rights of
the people of this country to self-government. I do not wish
to give pain by referring to former events, and I will not do
so. But I will say this, without going further back ...[35]

At this point he went on to discuss events in the recent past. It is most likely
that the painful 'former events' that he referred to were the bloodshed
and deaths at Eureka. Though he pointedly never mentioned Eureka, it
is clear that he saw that conflict as a consequence of a chain of malign
influences leading back to the Colonial Office's failure to promote genuine
self-government in Victoria.[36] The religious references, arresting imagery,
rich language and forceful arguments of these editorials reveal the depth
of Higinbotham's disappointment with the form of the new Constitution
that had received Royal Assent. Like Michie, he feared that the framework
of Victoria's new political system betrayed the best interests of the Colony
and spelled disaster for its future.

The goldfields representatives enter the Council

In December 1855, two days after the first anniversary of the dawn battle at the Eureka goldfield, and ten days after Hotham had delivered his Minute, the Victorian Legislative Council assembled in St Patrick's Hall in Melbourne. The election of the new legislature with its Upper and Lower Houses as provided by the newly proclaimed Constitution of 1855 was still many months away. The Legislative Council was at this stage still a single House. The awareness of the bloody conflict a year earlier was heightened by the presence in the House that day of a man who had lost his right arm in the battle. It was Peter Lalor, brother of the Irish revolutionary James Fintan Lalor. As the conflict loomed at Ballarat in late November 1854, Peter Lalor had led the diggers to swear by the Southern Cross 'to stand truly by each other' to defend their 'rights and liberties'. For most of the past year, Lalor had been a fugitive in hiding with a price of £200 upon his head. If captured, he would have been charged with high treason, and possibly sentenced to hang. Now he took his place in the House as the Member for Ballarat.

Also in the House that day were seven other new representatives of the goldfields, some of whom had been prominent in the recent unrest. Henry Chapman and James Macpherson Grant, two of the lawyers who had volunteered their services in the successful defence of the prisoners from Eureka, took their places, as did Dr Thomas Embling, who had chaired a public meeting in Melbourne that had condemned the military action at Ballarat and called for redress of the miners' grievances and the dismissal of the Colonial Secretary, John Foster.[37] Flanked by the other new representatives, Lalor faced the Legislative Councillors who had retrospectively approved the dawn attack at Eureka.

John O'Shanassy, a long-standing critic of the Government, whose role in the recent Royal Commission into the Goldfields had done much to broker the peace, had been eagerly awaiting this day. On the last day of the previous session of the Council in June, he had given notice of a motion to call upon the Governor 'to establish a system in consonance with the views and opinions of a free people – the enlightened system of Responsible Government'. With the influx of new members it appeared that he might have the numbers to support his motion. He introduced the debate as the most important that had ever taken place within the walls of the House.

A dramatic shift in the political composition of the Legislative Council had set the scene for what was to become Victoria's first constitutional crisis. It followed events set in train twenty months earlier. The existing Legislative Council comprised 54 members, of whom the Crown nominated 18, and 36 were elected by means of a restricted franchise.[38] In March 1854 (three months before the arrival of Sir Charles Hotham), a Bill to extend the franchise, particularly in country districts, had been passed.[39] Governor La Trobe had reserved the Act for Royal Assent, and it had left Victoria, together with the reserved Constitution Act, for consideration in the British Parliament. La Trobe accompanied the Bill for the extension of the franchise with a letter describing it as a temporary measure that was designed to take effect only if there was a long delay in the Constitution Bill achieving Royal Assent.[40]

In April 1855, the eagerly awaited *Report* of the Royal Commission into the Goldfields was delivered. The most famous of its recommendations was the creation of a Miner's Right that could be purchased for merely five shillings. The previous gold licence fee had cost the miner £8 per year, or thirty-two times this amount. Importantly, the new Miner's Right granted its owner the rights to vote and to own land.[41] Another of the *Report*'s recommendations was for twelve members to be allotted to represent the goldfields as a temporary measure until the new Constitution should arrive. Eight of these members were to be elected and four were to be nominated by the Governor.[42]

In May, a dispatch arrived announcing that the *Franchise Extension Act* had received Royal Assent in February.[43] The date of Royal Assent was 8 February 1855, the very date on which Sidney Herbert briefly became the Secretary of State for the Colonies, and two weeks before Lord John Russell succeeded him in that office. However, the *Constitution Act* did not receive Royal Assent until five months later, in mid-July 1855. The delay in passing the Constitution had triggered the passage of the Franchise Extension Bill into law. The proclamation of the Act in Victoria stripped away the argument that Foster and Stawell had advanced previously that the Government had no power to enfranchise the diggers. At a meeting at Bendigo, Foster assured the diggers' representatives that the Government was 'most desirous' to have members in the Legislative Council who would truly represent the diggers, but that 'the Colonial Government had not the power to enfranchise them until the New Constitution Bill had been approved of by the Home authorities'.[44] The ensuing legislation therefore made provision for a further eight members to be elected and an additional four to be nominated by the Governor. Despite the fact that the Act allowed for four extra members to be nominated, only one member, Dr John Downes Owens, nominated under this Act, took his seat in the Council.[45]

The extension of representation to the country districts created consternation for the Government. When the Acting Colonial Secretary brought before the Council a Bill to define the districts that the Act would cover, the Speaker, Dr James Palmer, and the squatter, John Goodman, warned that the House would be 'swamped'.[46] Their fears were well founded. Compared with the £2,000 property qualification required for members of the Legislative Assembly under the new Constitution, the £100 required under the old Constitution was more affordable. The historian John Hirst argues that the property qualifications established in the New South Wales Constitution (on which the Victorian Constitution of 1851 was modelled) were derived in turn from the British property qualifications. He notes that in New South Wales, because of inflation associated with the gold rushes, the property qualifications excluded a smaller proportion of people than in Britain. This may also explain the relative ease with which a number of goldfields activists were elected to the old Legislative Council of Victoria in 1855.[47] This coupled with some enthusiastic fund-raising on the goldfields enabled a number of prominent leaders of the Eureka movement and their Melbourne supporters to be returned as elected representatives. Their period of office was brief because of the scheduled termination of the old Legislative Council, however their effect was remarkable. These members changed the political culture of the Legislative Council by demanding accountability, forcing debates on long-neglected issues of concern to the goldfields population and raising important constitutional principles. In their short time they challenged the legitimacy of the Government through a censure motion that came within one vote of succeeding. The movement for political reform that had developed upon the goldfields and erupted at Eureka had come of age as a new parliamentary force.

The historian Geoffrey Serle declares that, after the battle, 'the fillip given by Eureka died away fairly quickly', and that 'no organization of anything like a party emerged as a force for the democratic movement'.[48] Though the goldfields representatives did not constitute a formal political party, their legislative program showed a coherent platform of demand for reform of the goldfields. They also fearlessly demanded accountability from the Governor for the military intervention at Eureka, and compensation to the surviving victims of that conflict.

In the days preceding the proclamation of the new Constitution on 23 November 1855, five of the new members took their seats in the Legislative Council. Hotham's speech to the Legislative Council on the day referred to his wish that the representatives of the mining districts could have been present for the occasion, for he was unaware that in fact five of them were already present.[49] Over the next two weeks, three more took their seats. There were eight goldfields representatives. James Duncan Campbell Longden, editor of the *Ballarat Star*, who was also a mine manager and a sheep farmer, was elected for Avoca.[50] A digger named Daniel Cameron was elected for the Ovens district. For Castlemaine, two store-keepers, James Wheeler and Vincent Pyke, were elected.[51] Pyke opposed sectional taxation and argued that public rights to the land should take precedence over the rights of private property.[52] For Sandhurst (later named Bendigo), James Macpherson Grant and Robert Benson were elected. Grant was a solicitor who had acted without fee for eight of the thirteen prisoners arraigned for high treason following the battle at Eureka. He was known for his intense antipathy towards the squatters.[53] The *Herald*'s Bendigo correspondent reported that a 'well attended' meeting passed a motion 'that the electors of Bendigo, in public meeting assembled, cordially approve of the political principles of Mr J.M. Grant'.[54] Benson was chairman of the Bendigo Reform League and had been chosen at a public meeting to represent the diggers at the Goldfields Commission of Inquiry.[55]

The constituents of Ballarat elected Peter Lalor and John Basson Humffray, secretary of the Ballarat Reform League, which subsequently became the Victorian Reform League.[56] Humffray played a prominent role in the diggers' political campaign for improved law and order on the Ballarat goldfields. In the week before the battle at Eureka, he had accompanied the two delegates, George Black and Thomas Kennedy, who attempted unsuccessfully to negotiate with Hotham. During the trials of the prisoners, Humffray and Charles Nicholls (the vice-president of the Victorian Reform League), had unsuccessfully petitioned Sir Charles Hotham for an amnesty for the prisoners.[57]

Two urban radicals succeeded at by-elections. In September, Dr Thomas Embling was returned for the suburban electorate of North Bourke. Two days after the conflict at Eureka, Embling had chaired a public meeting at which two radical motions had been proposed and passed. The first called for the redress of the miners' grievances, and the second called for the immediate dismissal of the Colonial Secretary, John Foster.[58] At a second by-election in early November, the electorate of Melbourne returned Thomas Rae who opposed the squatters' claims to compensation. He supported the secret ballot and advocated making land available on long leases with easy terms.[59] In the colony's pastoral south-west, J.M. Knight was returned for the electorate of Villiers and Heytesbury. The Colonial Secretary, John Foster, had attempted to stand for election in this seat, and published a policy speech in which he announced his support for compensation payments to squatters whose land was resumed for sale.[60] But when the motion to endorse his candidacy failed, J.M. Knight, who had proposed the motion, stood in his stead and won by a narrow margin.[61] The ten new members took their seats in the single-chambered legislature. With this influx of new members, suddenly the long-standing preponderance of conservative members could no longer be relied upon.

Hotham and Stawell sensed the danger in the situation, for the reformers in the Council saw an opportunity to attempt to reform the Constitution by means of a simple majority while the legislature was still a single chamber. Applying Hotham's definition of responsible government, it was not necessary to wait for the implementation of the new bicameral legislature to declare that responsible government existed. It had done so from the time of the proclamation of the new Constitution. The unicameral legislature was therefore already competent to pass legislation, including constitutional reform, although it would still need Royal Assent in order to be valid legislation. But if a constitutional reform motion should succeed, it would mean a humiliating loss of face for Hotham. On the day that he proclaimed the new Constitution, Hotham embarked upon a desperate gambit to outwit the reformers. It would prove to be not only a trial of strength between determined adversaries, but the first parliamentary battle for the principle of responsible government in Victoria.

6

THE FIRST CONSTITUTIONAL CRISIS

On 3 December 1855, the first anniversary of the battle at Eureka, the Colony of Victoria received, with excitement and relief, the first reports via the steamer *Red Jacket* that the Russian port of Sebastopol had finally surrendered to the British, French and Ottoman Allied Forces. But amidst the ensuing jubilation at victory in the long-running Crimean War, an editorial in the *Herald*, written in the grave and portentous style of George Higinbotham, struck a jarring note:

> It is a great achievement for the Allies to have struck such a blow; and we may well enjoy our share of the exultation, but we must not forget our own little Czar, nor the preparations he is evidently making to establish a Lilliputian citadel against our rights and privileges.

From this opening shot, the article escalated into a full-blown assault on the Governor, Sir Charles Hotham, likening him to a Russian Czar for a memorandum that he had recently issued to his ministry prescribing the future conduct of the business of government in Victoria:

> We tell Sir Charles deliberately that this doctrine is disloyal and rebellious and more unconstitutional and treasonable

in a Governor than anything that was ever offered by the wildest demagogue at Ballaarat.[1]

In equally damning language Higinbotham denounced the 'meanness and treachery' of those Ministers who, in the context of accepting significant rises in their pensions, had offered no resistance to an ominous memorandum that Hotham had delivered. Higinbotham accused the Ministers of 'prostituting themselves', 'pimping for despotism' and 'betraying the liberties of the public'. He declared that the powers that Hotham claimed as Governor were unconstitutional and exceeded those enjoyed by the Queen *vis-à-vis* the British Parliament.

Hotham had delivered his memorandum – which became known as 'Hotham's Minute' – on 23 November 1855 when he had proclaimed the new Victorian Constitution. He placed in the hands of his new Chief Secretary, William Haines, a Minute to the Legislative Council concerning the future role of the Governor. Though he had already tendered his resignation, he claimed for himself and future Governors the following right:

> The Governor of this colony will always require that, previously to the introduction of any measure into Parliament, his sanction be obtained.

He also claimed that 'the Ministry should possess the confidence of the Governor', and warned that 'he would not be a party to the appointment of persons whose sole recommendation may be the advocacy of certain political principles'.[2] This was a reference to political parties.

It was some days before the press learned of the Governor's Minute, as the eagerly anticipated news of victory at Sebastopol overshadowed other news. But on the following Tuesday, when the Legislative Council assembled, five Ministers were conspicuously absent. These were William Stawell, the Attorney-General; William Haines, the Chief Secretary; Andrew Clark, the Surveyor-General; Hugh Childers, the Collector of

Customs; and Edward Grimes, the Auditor-General. Charles Pasley, the Colonial Engineer, announced to the House that the Ministers had resigned their offices, and he called for an adjournment of the House.[3]

The House did not adjourn. The veteran Opposition member, John Fawkner, queried Pasley's report that the Ministers had resigned. He informed the House that, on the previous day, 'a member of the Government' had reported that he had been dismissed from the Executive.[4] Fawkner objected to the Governor's assumption that he had the power to dismiss any member of the Executive without first receiving the Queen's assent. He condemned the Governor's action, for it did not follow from a vote of the House. Fawkner warned that the country was in great danger, for the Government was now 'more irresponsible than ever'. He suggested that the motive for the dismissal might have been to allow the re-appointment of the Ministers under the provisions of the new Constitution, and thereby to ensure their entitlement to enhanced pensions that they were otherwise not entitled to receive. He moved that the Governor be requested to lay before the House copies of all the correspondence on the subject and a statement of the reasons for his actions.[5]

Henry Chapman joined the attack, declaring that the Governor's Minute contravened British constitutional practice and the principle of responsible government. William Forlonge, one of the Colony's largest stockholders and occupiers of Crown lands, countered that it was Chapman's notice of motion from the previous session that had provoked the Governor's action.[6]

Both Higinbotham and Hotham had conducted their campaigns for their competing interpretations of the term 'responsible government' mindful of the views of the Secretary of State for the Colonies. But as the identity of the person occupying this office changed at intervals, it was not clear which view would ultimately prevail in the Colonial Office. Despite the lull during the Constitution Bill's sojourn in London, both knew that a contest was looming. Both were well aware of the growing political consciousness in the population, particularly on the goldfields. The success of both Henry Chapman and Thomas Rae at the recent metropolitan by-elections demonstrated that the city electors were in the mood for reform. The notices of motion in the Legislative Council indicated that the contest over responsible government was imminent. Higinbotham knew his adversary and was not caught off-guard when the Minute was handed down.

By identifying and articulating the issues at the outset, the *Herald* was able to launch a powerful press campaign that the *Age* wholeheartedly supported. The *Herald*'s reputation in constitutional matters gave credibility to its warning that Hotham's Minute was a claim for despotic powers for himself and his successors. In a situation where the Legislative Councillors were soon to face an election under the new Constitution, Higinbotham knew that they understood the necessity to defend their reputations. The *Herald*'s campaign of shaming the Ministers was designed to force them to acknowledge that they owed responsibility primarily to the electorate. In doing so, the campaign laid a foundation for the practice of responsible government for Victoria.

Higinbotham leads a press campaign against Hotham's Minute

In a stinging editorial in the *Herald,* Michie reiterated Chapman's and Fawkner's arguments linking the Governor's dismissal and immediate re-appointment of the Ministry with his Minute claiming extra-constitutional powers.[7] He accused the Governor of 'perceiving the hungry eagerness of his Executive to secure their pensions', and of seizing the opportunity to provide them with increased pensions under the new Constitution in return for their acceptance of 'conditions fatal to a constitutional system'. He accused the Ministers of selling out the public 'and the entire principle of responsibility'. Henry Miller subsequently estimated the additional cost to the Colony of the Ministers' pensions at the new rate would amount to £5,200 per annum.[8]

Higinbotham rejected Hotham's claim that the ministry should enjoy the Governor's confidence, arguing, 'they may be forced upon him in defiance of his dislike … he must stomach it as best he can'.[9] He then attacked another key element of the new Constitution that he believed undermined the principle of responsible government, namely that the Governor, rather than the legislature, controlled much of the Colony's finances. Clearly it was incompatible with the principle of self-government that the Governor had command of so much of the Colony's finances without being accountable to the elected legislature.[10] He pointed out the danger of the large annual Civil List that the new Constitution placed in the hands of such an 'errant governor':

> £62,000 independent of your votes, and in contempt of you for himself and his ministers. Enough to maintain the garrison, in spite of you, as long as he may think proper to hold out. But the supplies! You will stop them; will you? What supplies? For the police – the gaols – for the administration of justice – for your own security and convenience, in all departments of public life? … the more obstinate and wrong-headed your Governor, the more likely is he to avail himself of the resource you have placed in his hands.

The white heat of his anger was directed at the Ministers who had failed to protest at the Governor's Minute, with its claims to extra-constitutional powers, and who had agreed to accept dismissal and immediate re-appointment by the Governor as 'responsible ministers' without any consultation with the legislature. Some of these were the same people who, two years earlier, in drafting the new Constitution, had failed to ensure the new legislature would have the right to control the Colony's finances. He declared that their names would go down in history as 'the first to undertake and the first to betray the cause entrusted to their keeping'. He concluded with a challenge to the legislature to oppose Hotham's Minute, for 'the public are waiting to see whether it will prove the avenger or the accomplice of the crime'.[11]

The next day, the *Age* followed the *Herald*'s lead, publishing a lengthy attack. It estimated the gains that eight Ministers had recently made. Taking Childers as an example, it noted:

> As a pensioner, he was only entitled to two-thirds of his salary, namely £866.13.4d, but as Collector of Customs he has £1200 and as Commissioner for Trade and Customs he has £2000 … the Surveyor-General, Auditor-General and Colonial Engineer reap a similar benefit. To the Colonial Treasurer, the change … raises his salary from £600 to £2000 … The Solicitor-General profits in a similar manner … The Colonial Secretary and the Attorney-General are also pecuniary gainers by the change.[12]

Echoing the *Herald*'s challenge to the legislature, the *Age*'s editorial called upon the members of the legislature to condemn the 'knot of schemers' lest by their silence or inaction the members should appear to condone this 'flagrant outrage upon constitutional government'.[13] The *Age* condemned two irregularities. The first was the resignation and immediate re-appointment of Haines, Grimes, Stawell and Clark to the same positions they had held previously, but with enhanced pension rights in recognition of their new status as 'responsible ministers'. The second was the sudden hike in the salaries of Childers, Sladen, Molesworth and Pasley, which also gave them enhanced pension entitlements, as these were pegged to salary.

While the *Herald* was particularly concerned about the first issue because of the implications for the understanding of the principle of responsible government in the Colony, to the *Age* both issues revealed the Government's complicity in the unprincipled misuse of public money. The *Argus* distanced itself from the outcry. The *Age* accused it of being the mouthpiece of the Government.[14]

The week of editorial attacks in the *Herald* and the *Age* climaxed with a lengthy attack on Hotham in an extended summary for British readers.[15] On 30 November, the Ministers formally replied to Hotham's

Minute, declaring that they could not agree to accept its terms as defining responsible government. They requested that Hotham withdraw the Minute and allow the relation between the Governor and his advisors to be based on 'the broad principles of the Constitution and the enactment recently proclaimed'.[16] Then on 3 December, the House received a reply. Perhaps taken aback by what Higinbotham called 'the perfect howl and tempest of execration' directed at himself, Hotham sent a brief letter to the Council explaining that the Minute was merely 'an exposition of his own views', and not 'a dictation of the terms on which he expected a ministry to accept office'.[17] Higinbotham's response to Hotham's letter was scathing:

> When it comes to your intentions backed by force, the case
> is altered; and having … not retracted your avowal, we ask
> what security we have that you will not fulfil your threats
> whenever the occasion tempts you.

Higinbotham declared that 'the popular side' had won a moral victory. He observed:

> It triumphed for it extorted from the 'ministers' a confession
> of their error and guilt on the most essential point – their
> transaction with the Governor. His Excellency was reprehended
> and his principles repudiated by both parties … he is no longer
> to be permitted to dictate a policy, to exercise patronage or to
> indulge in any of the freaks of arbitrary power.[18]

The Governor's response did not constitute a retraction of his Minute, but merely a reassurance to the ministry that it was not directed against them. Indeed it is likely that Hotham had framed the Minute with some of the new representative members of the Legislative Council in mind. He did not revoke either his prohibition against the introduction of any measure into the legislature without his prior consent, or his claimed right to exclude candidates for the ministry whom he regarded as unsuitable.

By identifying and articulating the issues at the outset, the *Herald* launched a powerful press campaign, and the *Age* immediately added its whole-hearted support. The *Herald*'s reputation in constitutional matters gave credibility to its warning that Hotham's Minute was a claim for despotic powers for himself and his successors. In a situation where the Legislative Councillors were soon to face an election under the new Constitution, Higinbotham knew that they needed to protect their reputations. The *Herald*'s campaign of shaming the Ministers was designed to force them to confront the fact that they now owed responsibility primarily to the electorate. In doing so, the campaign laid an essential foundation for the practice of responsible government in Victoria.

The press campaign succeeded, and after a week-long delay the Ministers declared that they supported the principle of responsible government. In contrast to the perfunctory debates about key constitutional principles in the Legislative Council a year earlier, the highly charged and lengthy debate about responsible government now fully engaged the House. The *Age* and the *Herald* spared no efforts to ensure that the reading public grasped the full significance of the issues.

The Legislative Council responds to Hotham's Minute

On 5 December, the day after the *Herald* editorial denounced Hotham's unconstitutional claims, Dr Augustus Frederick Greeves moved a lengthy motion in the Legislative Council. The motion, which was in six parts, rejected 'the principles laid down in His Excellency's Minute to the Colonial Secretary', and was seconded by Henry Chapman.[19] Following the reading of each of the principles, tremendous groans resounded in the Council chamber. The motion also roundly denounced those who had accepted office on terms that were 'opposed to sound views of responsible government, and subversive of the principles of the Constitution'.[20]

Greeves, supported by O'Shanassy, Fawkner, Grant, Cameron and Benson, called upon the members to disavow having consented to any part of the proceeding, and to protest against it. Lalor reported to the House that Haines, as Chief Secretary, 'came down to that House and stated that he did not intend to ask it to appropriate the public money this session, but merely to lay on the table his plan of expenditure'.[21] The previous day, Chapman had made a similar accusation. He warned the Ministers that by expending the public money without the sanction of that House, they would be expending it 'unconstitutionally, unfairly and improperly', and that for such an act nothing less than their solemn impeachment would satisfy him.[22]

Lalor accused the Chief Secretary, William Haines, of collaborating with the Governor by depriving the House of 'the only means by which it could control His Excellency … the control of the public purse'.[23] Pyke declared that it was only the expressed indignation of the House that had prevented the Executive from carrying out its 'avowed intention' to expend the money of the country without the sanction of the Council.[24] Greeves called for an address containing the Council's resolutions to be presented to the Governor.[25] Speaking to the motion, Chapman declared that the term 'responsible government' had a defined political meaning in the constitutional vocabulary of England. His statement was greeted with cheers. He argued that it was obvious that the meaning of 'responsible government' that underlay the *Constitution Act* assumed the existence of the new legislature because the sixteenth clause provided that four of the Ministers must come from either the Legislative Assembly or the Legislative Council. The squatter Charles Griffith countered that this was a misunderstanding of the meaning of the term 'responsible government'. For him, 'the very power which the Governor possessed of dismissing his ministers constituted responsible government'.[26]

The ministry was at pains to rebut Higinbotham's argument in the *Herald* that it was guilty of 'an audacious attempt to secure the pensions and the larger salaries provided for by the Constitution, and to do so before the proper time'.[27] The next day, in response to the press attacks, the Attorney-General, William Stawell, defended the Government's position by distinguishing between the issues of the Governor's Minute and the dismissal and re-appointment of the ministry. He also insisted that the matter of the estimates was 'perfectly distinct'. The legal historian Charles Parkinson notes that, in explaining his conduct to the House, Stawell 'never revealed his involvement in pressing the Governor to issue new commissions for the responsible ministers'.[28]

Stawell excused his initial failure to dissent from the Governor's Minute, claiming that it had been due to 'the pressure of other business'. He insisted that the Ministers were not motivated by any thought of enhanced pensions, and declared that they would have received these pensions in any event.[29] He explained that their willingness to accept dismissal and re-appointment under the new Constitution was a rejection of the old system whereby 'blame … never rested on the right shoulders, nor credit either'. He argued that 'the country, the officers of the Government and all classes panted for the new Constitution'. He declared that the old Legislative Council was now 'gone, except so far as power given it to enable it to pass an electoral act'.[30] But as there would be months of delay before the new Parliament would assemble, an interim Government was a practical necessity. Without it, 'they would encounter such overwhelming difficulties from the mass of business that would present itself that it would be impossible to be got through efficiently'.[31]

Stawell insisted that the Ministers had not breached the principle of responsible government because they were responsible to the future legislature and because their motivation had been 'the good of the country'.[32] When challenged as to why the new Constitution failed to articulate clearly the principle of responsible government, Stawell dissembled, arguing on the one hand that they had introduced it 'as nearly as possible', and on the other hand that it was 'utterly impossible to define it'. He pointed out that 'it never had been done in any act in the sister colony'. Avoiding the term 'responsible government' and substituting the term 'political responsibility', Stawell said that it could not be defined for it was 'a creature of custom'.[33]

The House debates 'responsible government'

At first Stawell's statement was greeted with hisses, then a marathon debate followed on the question of whether responsible government could be said meaningfully to exist before the election of the new Parliament. Greeves called the process 'introducing a responsible government by the most gross violation of the principles of responsible government'. Stawell distinguished between legal responsibility and political responsibility. The latter, he said, was impossible to define. Robert Molesworth, as Solicitor-General, distinguished between the responsibility that existed between Governor and Ministers, and that which existed between the Ministers and the legislature. He argued that the components of responsible government were being introduced, but it was not possible to introduce all at the one time.[34]

Despite Stawell's attempt to divorce the issue of responsible government from the question of the Ministers' enhanced pensions, the lawyers in the Opposition clearly perceived that the two issues were connected. The Ministers' entitlement to the pensions was an important test of the meaning to be ascribed to responsible government under the new Constitution. According to the view of responsible government held by Higinbotham, Chapman, Greeves and the goldfields representatives, the Governor was obliged to take the advice of the legislature regarding appointment and dismissal of the ministry. Applying this interpretation, the current Ministers were not eligible for the enhanced pensions for they held office at the will of the Governor, not the legislature. As members of the Legislative Council, most had been appointed or nominated rather than elected. However, if 'responsible government' simply meant that Victoria would be governed by a ministry chosen by its own governor, with no implication that the ministry should hold office at the will of the legislature, then arguably they were entitled to the enhanced pensions. In asserting their entitlement as 'responsible officers', the Ministers were implicitly endorsing the interpretation of responsible government in the more limited sense that Governor Hotham advocated.[35]

The goldfields' representatives – Lalor, Grant, Benson, Pyke and Wheeler – delivered cogent speeches in support of Greeves' motions. Grant concentrated his attack on the failure of the ministry to object to Hotham's Minute, and reminded them that it had not been withdrawn. He declared that a ministry that chose to neglect the public liberties was unfit for office. However, he insisted that 'the very idea of their being responsible to an irresponsible Council one-third composed of nominees was ridiculous'.[36]

Lalor argued that, by accepting office under Hotham's Minute, the ministry had 'virtually trampled' on the new Constitution.[37] He said that in his wildest moments of political excitement, he had 'never claimed more liberty than was guaranteed by the British Constitution fully, fairly and entirely carried out, but he would never consent to having less'.[38] O'Shanassy attacked the Government for an appalling record of financial unaccountability, claiming that over the past four years they had spent 'an enormous sum … upon themselves, their officers and the patronage they wielded'. He asked, 'to whom were they to give an account of their stewardship? Did they consider themselves responsible to the Council?' He paused for a reply, but receiving only silence, he continued: 'if they were responsible, to whom were they responsible? And if not the whole thing was a delusion and a sham.'[39]

The Opposition demanded answers of Government members and fundamentally challenged their legitimacy as a Government and their honour and integrity as individuals. Peter Lalor, with his supporters in the legislature, particularly O'Shanassy, a fellow Catholic, and Fawkner, a Congregationalist, audaciously lectured the Ministers who had accepted re-appointment – Anglicans to a man – about constitutional principles. To the Government members and their supporters, this was the nightmare of mob rule that the military response at Eureka and the conservative safeguards in the new Constitution had been designed to circumvent.

The Ministers mouth support for responsible government

The Opposition was now ready to test its numerical strength in the Council. The alacrity of the Ministers in accepting Hotham's offer of enhanced pensions involved more than their financial entitlements; it raised questions about their personal integrity. At stake were their reputations with the electors at the coming elections under the new Constitution. But, Grant, Chapman, Michie and Higinbotham hoped that the public outcry over the pensions issue would deliver them the numbers in the Council, not only to censure the Government, but to quash Hotham's claims to the rights of patronage and to clear the way for reform of the Constitution.

In the newly expanded Council, 28 out of the 36 representative members supported Greeves' six-part motion.[40] The Government officials and nominee members as well as eight representative members, some of whom were squatters, opposed the motion. Francis Murphy, the Chairman of Committees, had reportedly attended a meeting with the representatives the week before the debate and pledged his support for Greeves' motion.[41] The *Age* confidently predicted that a large majority would support the motion.[42]

Of the 62 members of the newly expanded Legislative Council, 56 recorded a vote. A surprise defection from the ranks of the goldfields representatives was James Duncan Campbell Longden, the Member for Avoca, whom the *Age* roundly denounced as a traitor.[43] But the Government found an even more unlikely ally. James Harrison, the editor of the *Geelong Advertiser*, whose paper had robustly encouraged the diggers immediately before the battle at Eureka, and who had been a trenchant critic of the Government only a few months earlier, on this occasion supported the Government. This inconsistency may have been motivated by his deep-seated dislike of Henry Chapman, who had seconded and spoken in support of Greeves' motion.

In 1854, Harrison, as editor of the *Geelong Advertiser*, had denounced Dr George Mackay, the prosecutor at Geelong, for appearing in court in a drunken state. Mackay had engaged Michie to sue Harrison for libel. The case had gone badly for Harrison, for his integrity had been impugned and a large damages award had been made against him. Following the verdict, an extremely bitter public dispute arose in which Michie and Chapman were both aligned against Harrison. The affair became a *cause célèbre* with large rowdy public meetings in both Melbourne and Geelong. As both Michie and Chapman were now committed to the success of Greeves' motion, Harrison may have been motivated to even the score with both of his former adversaries by voting with the Government.[44]

With the fate of the Government hanging in the balance, Murphy, despite his earlier speech supporting the central principles of Greeves' motion, used his casting vote as Speaker to support the Government.[45] By so doing, Murphy not only saved the Government, but he defended the reputations of his Irish Protestant brethren Stawell, Clark and Molesworth against the attack from the Opposition in the Council. He saved the enhanced pensions of Childers, Grimes, Sladen, Stawell and Clark. The *Age* alleged that he also safeguarded his own position as President of the Roads Board. The editor reported that the salary for this position was £1,450 per annum, which he said was only exceeded in England by the salaries of Ministers of State. He added that the salary was 'mere pocket money' compared with the perquisites that accompanied it.[46]

Had Murphy not done so, a new and more radical ministry might have claimed the right to take office. There might have been a unique opportunity to reform the Constitution, by passing amending motions through the Council, for only a simple majority was required and there was, as yet, no house of review. Even if Royal Assent were to be withheld, the effect of any such amendment of the newly proclaimed Constitution would have caused great embarrassment and difficulty for Hotham, his Government, and the Colonial Office.

The Ministers had stared into the abyss of ignominy for the impression of venality created by their silence in response to Hotham's Minute, and their acceptance of his offer to re-appoint them as 'responsible ministers' under the new Constitution with enhanced pension entitlements. Their refusal to answer O'Shanassy's question, 'Did they consider themselves responsible to the Council?', only added to the impression of disingenuousness. They had narrowly saved themselves from utter disgrace with the plea that it had been a laudable eagerness for the principle of responsible government – rather than a reprehensible concern for their own pensions – that motivated their acceptance of Hotham's offer. Haines and Stawell had argued as much, and Grant had signalled preparedness to countenance it. But in order to salvage their reputations, they were forced to mouth a commitment to the principle of responsible government.[47]

In line with Stawell's statement that 'responsible government' could not be defined since it was 'a creature of custom', Lalor quoted from the famous contemporary British politician and historian, Lord Macaulay:

> It is evidently our wisdom to keep all the constitutional checks on misgovernment in the highest state of efficiency, to watch with jealousy the first beginnings of encroachment, and never to suffer irregularities, even when harmless in themselves, to pass unchallenged lest they acquire the force of precedents.[48]

This quotation, enunciated by the undisputed hero of Eureka, became a guiding principle of the popular movement in the decades ahead.[49]

A changed political landscape

Following the debate, the Ministers formally replied to Hotham's Minute, declaring that they could not agree to accept its terms as defining responsible government. They requested that Hotham withdraw the Minute 'and allow the relation between the Governor and his advisors to be based on the broad principles of the Constitution and the enactment recently proclaimed'.[50] The ironies were overwhelming, for, as at Eureka, although the representative members had lost the battle, they had won a tactical victory. They had emboldened their fellow Councillors to reject Hotham's views of 'popular responsible government', encompassing greatly enhanced powers for the Governor at the expense of the elected Government. They had forced a debate upon a key constitutional principle that had been left undefined in the Constitution. Together with the lawyers Grant and Chapman, they had made common cause with the long-standing popular advocates, O'Shanassy, Fawkner and with Dr Greeves. The battle lines over the issue of responsible government were now drawn and the stage was set for several decades of conflict over the issue.

Higinbotham must have sensed the personal animosity towards the *Herald* in Harrison's defection. Still smarting from Harrison's attack on him for his editorial decisions when the battle at Eureka was imminent a year earlier, Higinbotham could not resist the opportunity to retaliate. In a veiled attack on Harrison, he denounced those who were guilty of 'fawning upon the possessors of power', which he observed 'may be more properly designated as toadyism'.[51] The vendetta illustrated the corrosive nature of the politics of personality in the small community of Victoria, and its propensity to undermine collaborative effort in pursuit of a common cause. Though the animosity generated by the Mackay–Harrison legal case of 1854 may have provided a spur to Higinbotham's legal career, it had snatched victory from his grasp in 1855.

The press campaign succeeded, and after a week-long delay the Ministers declared that they supported the principle of responsible government. In contrast to the lacklustre debates about key constitutional principles in the Select Committee a year earlier, the highly charged and lengthy debate about responsible government now fully engaged the House. The *Age* and the *Herald* spared no efforts to ensure that the reading public grasped the full significance of the issues.

Still unaware of Molesworth's death on 22 October, Higinbotham warned of a 'pretty scene' in the House of Commons when Sir William Molesworth would drag his 'blundering official' through the mire for his 'Machiavellian tricks'.[52]

Following the loss of Greeves' motion, the *Argus* exulted in the defeat of the Opposition, accusing its members of planning to overthrow the Government in order to gain for themselves 'the sweets of place and power'.[53] Higinbotham, however, claimed victory for the press, arguing that its investigation had revealed, 'like lightning into a robbers' cave', the arrangement between the Governor and the Ministers, which he condemned as 'lawless usurpation on the one side and venal hypocrisy on the other'.[54] The *Age* and the *Herald* had pricked the conscience of the Government and the legislature. In drawing attention to the constitutional principles at stake, and promoting a public meeting to discuss the situation, they had played a leading role in challenging Hotham's Minute and Haines' complicity in surrendering the legislature's right to authorise the appropriation of the public money.

Hotham's plan for 'popular responsible government'

Hotham's motivation for his Minute can be gauged from his dispatch to the Colonial Office of 25 October 1854. In it he had advocated his own view of 'popular responsible government', which entailed 'putting the appointment of all public officers in the hands of the Governor'. Hotham had further requested that every office in the Colony 'shall be vested in the Governor'. Claiming that it was British practice, he argued that his principal advisors – the Colonial Secretary, the Attorney-General and the Controller of Customs – should continue in office, in all circumstances.[55] He had objected particularly to Clause 44 of the *Constitution Act* as passed by the Victorian Legislative Council, which described the manner in which the Ministry would be appointed.[56] He argued that a transfer of power from the Governor to 'a party in the legislature' would produce 'a great deal of mischief'. He requested that this clause be amended such that the Governor alone would appoint the ministry; or alternatively, that the Governor would have power to increase the size of the Executive Council so as to 'swamp the Heads of Departments who are in it'.

The Colonial Secretary, Sir George Grey, commented on the file, 'Sir C. Hotham's objection ... applies perhaps to the establishment of responsible government, though he does not admit this'.[57] Grey's successor, Lord John Russell, commented on the file, 'I believe *party appointments* to be a concomitant of "responsible government" …' and he directed that a dispatch be sent to Hotham informing him that 'I dissent from several of the remarks that you have made in reference to the 44th Clause of the Bill'.[58]

Despite the strong message that the Secretary of State for the Colonies had ordered to be sent to him, Hotham took a different view of his task. This may have been because he supported the view of the Permanent Under-Secretary of the Colonial Office, who had objected to the new Constitution, arguing that its adoption would make Victoria 'a republic'.[59] Perhaps, perceiving a difference between the administrators of the Colonial Office and the British Government, Hotham may have gambled that the official policy could yet be reversed, or at least modified before it was considered in the British Parliament, if both he and the Colonial Office could convince the Secretary of State for the Colonies of the need to do so. He was a conservative man whose remarkable successes in his past naval career owed much to his habit of making his own assessments and following his own instincts as to how British interests could best be served.[60] He may have believed that he saw more clearly than his political superiors in London that he would need to keep a tight reign on power to prevent a spate of reforms of the new Constitution. Democratic amendments would not only undermine his power in Victoria but would encourage populist agitation at home, for which his superiors might blame him.

The delay in the return of the new Constitution from the Parliament in London allowed for months of speculation as to how the new system would operate. On 1 August, the *Herald* published a lengthy letter to the editor, signed 'A Colonist' (possibly written by Henry Chapman), that quoted from Hotham's dispatch of 25 October 1854 to the Secretary of State for the Colonies.[61] The letter revealed Hotham's proposed amendments to Clause 44, and declared:

> The great point in question, then, is whether the Executive Council of this colony, responsible for its actions to the Country

through Parliament, is to appoint the officials necessary to carry out its schemes of government, or whether such officials are to be appointed by the Governor, irresponsible, who cannot be called to account in the colony, and who is not answerable for the incapacity or dishonesty of these persons.[62]

As part of its campaign for responsible government, the *Herald* accused the Government of irresponsibility, firstly because of financial incompetence, and secondly because it acted without consulting the Legislative Council.[63] Other newspapers and journals echoed the demand for responsible government.[64]

The offer of enhanced pensions may have secured the co-operation of the ministry to Hotham's Minute, but it was difficult to find inducements to offer to the other Legislative Councillors. The outcry in the press and subsequently in the House may have alarmed the members, for with the coming election in mind, they could not afford to compromise their own reputations in the eyes of the voters by appearing complicit in the pensions affair.

The spectacular successes of Hotham's naval career to date had earned him the reputation of a man who could achieve results in near impossible circumstances. Awareness of the financial deficit and the growing dissent on the goldfields may have led the Duke of Newcastle, Secretary of State for the Colonies, to select Hotham for the position of Lieutenant-Governor of this difficult colony.[65] But he may not have realised that Hotham's own anti-democratic political views and personal ambition would exacerbate the situation.

The year 1855 brought repeated frustration and humiliation for Hotham. At the instigation of the press, the Legislative Council had rejected his Minute. This followed hard on the failure to secure convictions against those charged after the battle at Eureka, and the unrelenting campaigns against him in the press. These stresses may have eventually taken their toll on his health.[66] A short illness led to his death on New Year's Day 1856. The unconstitutional claims were never revived, and most historians have treated the affair of Hotham's Minute as little more than a historical footnote.[67] But to Victorians of the time, the Minute was alarming. Had Hotham attempted to implement his plan for his own version of 'popular responsible government', he would have done so in open defiance of the British Government's instructions and the rule of law. This could have plunged the Colony into further conflict and division.

Fawkner told the House he had all along opposed the proposal to allocate large pensions to retiring officers, for 'it might have the effect of displacing good men in order to make room for favourites who would have a pension to retire upon'.[68] Indeed this seems to be a likely explanation of Hotham's motivation for the Minute. He sought to include his personal friend of many years, the Colonial Engineer, Charles Pasley, who as aide-de-camp to Captain Thomas of the 40th Regiment had commanded the skirmishers at the battle at Eureka.[69] He also proposed to include another who had not been elected: William Henry Fancourt Mitchell. Mitchell was a squatter on the Campaspe River whom La Trobe had appointed Chief Commissioner of Police, and who had recently returned from a period of paid leave of absence in Europe.[70] Mitchell's biographer describes him as 'one of the staunchest conservatives' and adds that, by the 1870s, he had become 'one of the most active defenders of the (Legislative) Council'.[71]

The amendment to Clause 44 allowed Hotham to grant retirement allowances to the existing Ministers who were due to retire 'on political grounds' at his own discretion. It gave him the opportunity to use this power in three ways. Firstly, he could use it to induce key Ministers to comply with his own chosen appointees to the ministry. Secondly, he could use it to bribe the Ministers to accept the restrictions on the powers of the Parliament that he had proposed in his Minute. Thirdly, he could use it to bind the ministry to his interpretation of the meaning of 'responsible government'. Though Hotham was the architect of the Minute, Stawell's failure as the Chief Law Officer of the Colony to oppose the Minute as contrary to the Constitution, and his dissembling about responsible government in answer to questions in the Legislative Council, suggest that Hotham's Minute suited his purposes as well.

Higinbotham denounces the ministry and the Constitution

The *Herald* took the lead in denouncing Hotham's Minute and the Ministers' initial failure to protest against it. Higinbotham declaimed at the hollowness of the Ministers' arguments:

> How can they dare to deny that they were parties to the compact … to plead that they did not read it, or that it did not strike them at first as so objectionable, is to confess themselves to be … egregious blockheads.[72]

Higinbotham was equally merciless in his treatment of the Governor's explanation that the Minute was only an expression of his views. He pointed out that the Governor had directed that the Minute be handed down by one generation of Chief Secretaries to the next. He referred to the 'exalted and majestic strain' of the language in which the Minute was couched, and described it as 'anything but a mere draft or a memorandum open to discussion'.[73]

Hotham's explanation of his Minute did not constitute a withdrawal of it but only a reassurance to the Ministers that it was not directed against them. His failure to withdraw the Minute recast the entire debate about the Constitution, for despite its faults, the Constitution now provided the Colony's main defence against the rogue Governor, as it invoked the authority of the British Government.

Confident that he now had Molesworth's powerful support as Secretary of State for the Colonies, Higinbotham attacked the Constitution as 'a transparent fraud upon the desire for responsibility and self-government' and championed a movement for its reform.[74] But his plan miscarried, for though the news had not yet arrived in Victoria, Sir William Molesworth had died in London on 22 October 1855 after a bout of gastric fever.[75]

7

CHALLENGING THE NEW CONSTITUTION

One month after the death of Hotham, Higinbotham wrote a lengthy 'Summary for Europe' in the *Herald*, entitled 'Political Retrospect'. While professing loyalty to the Crown, he declared that it was the view of 'lawyers as well as politicians of the first class' that the new *Constitution Act* was not legally in force. He argued that, although Victoria's *Constitution Act* had been amended in London, these amendments should then have been adopted by the Legislative Council of Victoria before being incorporated into the *Constitution Act*. The failure to do this meant, in his view, that the *Constitution Act* had not been validly enacted. He contended that 'the preponderance of argument and opinion' was with the view that the assent of the Crown to an amended Bill is not sufficient without the adoption of those amendments by the local legislature.[1] In a passionate polemic that built to a crescendo, he demanded 'co-equal and co-ordinate' rights for the local Parliament. He boldly declared that the Australian people 'repudiate and protest the interference of the Parliament at Westminster as a usurpation and a tyranny'. The argument climaxed with a famous phrase taken from the concluding paragraph of the American Declaration of Independence:

> And for these rights and these principles they are as ready
> as any other colonists have been in any other time and in

> any other country, to meet any struggles and to make any
> sacrifices, to which they might be called upon, as others
> before them, to pledge their lives, their fortunes and their
> sacred honour.[2]

The *Herald* pressed this line of attack on the new Constitution throughout January and February of 1856.[3] It was a great risk for the newspaper and, with their considerable legal expertise, the editorial committee must have been aware of its magnitude. The newspaper had gone beyond calling for reforms that it was in the power of the existing legislature to effect. It was desperately attempting to goad the British Government into action.

The members of the editorial team at the *Herald* were not alone in their accusation that the Parliament at London had usurped the power that belonged to the Colony of Victoria. In April, the *Age* attacked the new Constitution, particularly for the 'absurd property qualification for the members of both Houses', and for the likelihood that it would 'prolong and intensify political agitation in the Colony'. It called on colonists of all classes to meet together and draw up a fresh Constitution based upon 'British feelings and British principles' in conformity with the political sentiments of the colonists.[4] In September 1855, the *Argus* had protested the 'mutilation' of the Constitution Bill that had been drafted by the Victorian legislature, and complained of 'the coolness of the Colonial Minister and the obedient Parliament [which] proceeded to cut and carve upon the rights with which constitutionally, they had no power to interfere'. It called upon the Governor to demand 'the full powers and privileges to which, as British subjects, the Colonists are entitled'.[5]

The new goldfields representatives, including the nominee Dr Owens, added great strength to the Opposition in the Council. In swift succession, these new members moved motions for improved facilities on the goldfields. Benson moved and Grant seconded a motion for the establishment of a thirteen-member Select Committee to clarify the powers and procedures of the new courts of the goldfields.[6] In response to a grievance in the Creswick district between diggers and a landowner, Pyke moved for the creation of a

Select Committee to clarify the law relating to mining on private property.[7] Another grievance aired was that some landowners demanded payment from miners who intended to mine for gold on their land. Grant and Lalor pressed the Government for a prompt clarification of the law, with Lalor warning the House that 'the diggers would brook no delay whatever'.[8] Pyke presented a petition from the diggers of Forest Creek (Castlemaine) calling for vote by ballot.[9]

Most audaciously of all, the goldfields representatives moved for the redress of grievances associated with the battle at Eureka. They sought compensation for injuries sustained during the military and police operations. They also demanded to see all of the dispatches between the Governor and the Secretary of State regarding the military operation at Ballarat.[10] Lalor moved an amendment seeking the tabling of all dispatches and communications from the resident commissioner and authorities at Ballarat. Humffray seconded the amendment.[11] The Governor found himself besieged, as never before, with demands for accountability. His Minute stipulating that the Ministry must enjoy his confidence, and that all measures must meet his approval before their introduction into the House, may have reflected his determination to assert his authority in the face of an imminent challenge to himself, his Government and the new Constitution from an increasingly numerous and bold opposition.

Doubtless, Stawell also felt great apprehension at the influx of goldfields representatives. Like Foster himself, he must have been shocked to learn that his cousin had lost his bid to be declared as a candidate for the electorate of Villiers-Heytesbury, in the Western District. At a public meeting of the electors, a motion had been moved proposing the Colonial Secretary as the candidate to represent the constituency, but since no person present was prepared to second the motion, it had failed.[12] Stawell knew that he would have to face the coming storm without the customary, loyal support of his cousin. Moreover, his opposition in the Council now included the nominee Dr Owens, a fearless, seasoned and popular campaigner for reform who had publicly called upon him to resign during the hiatus in the trials of the Eureka prisoners. It may have been these considerations that prompted him to reinforce the loyalty of his other trusted colleagues in government by ensuring that they received enhanced pensions and that they faced the coming election with the advantage of the status of Government Ministers.

Following this first constitutional crisis, Higinbotham commenced his long battle to elevate the principle of responsible government to a secure place in the political culture of Victoria. In his editorial for 4 December, he warned that the inauguration of the new Constitution foreshadowed the beginning of a new and more formidable struggle against official corruption and arbitrary power. He called attention to a public meeting of the Reform Association, scheduled to occur that evening at the Mechanics Institute of Prahran, to discuss the issue. He advised that 'known and sterling liberals from other parts' would join the local reformers of South Bourke and that the meeting would protest against the 'extraordinary proceedings' of the Executive Council, and the 'still more extraordinary views of Sir Charles Hotham with regard to his own powers under the new Constitution'.[13] He declared that the time had come 'to remind our representatives that the trust reposed in them, and their manner of discharging it, will be watched and scrutinised with unsparing vigilance'. He called on the readers to join the Reform Association and to attend meetings in their own areas, and he called for a central league to be formed 'for promoting the great object of CONSTITUTIONAL REFORM'.[14]

The representatives of the diggers had proven themselves as an effective parliamentary force. Within a few days of entering the Council, they had exacted from the Ministry and the entire legislature an affirmation of the principle of responsible government. Their strategy was to hold the Government members to their professed eagerness for this principle to be observed, however tokenistic that commitment might be. They had succeeded in breaking the nexus between the autocratic Governor and the compliant ministry. As at Eureka, although the representative members had lost the battle, they had won a tactical victory. They had emboldened their fellow Councillors to reject Hotham's views of 'popular responsible government'. They had forced a debate upon a key constitutional principle that had been left undefined in the Constitution. They had forged an alliance with the constitutional lawyers Chapman and Grant in the Assembly, and Higinbotham and Michie in the press. The battle lines over the issue of responsible government were now drawn and the stage was set for four decades of conflict over the issue.

The meaning of 'responsible government'

Twenty-seven months earlier, in August 1853, the Duke of Newcastle, as Secretary of State for the Colonies, had directed the Governor-General, Sir Charles FitzRoy, that the new Australian constitutions were to prepare the colonies for responsible government. However, as noted, in its final form the 1855 Constitution made no express statement affirming the principle of responsible government in Victoria. Higinbotham and others saw this omission as a fundamental betrayal of the legitimate expectations of the colonists. It allowed for ambiguity and disagreement about the essential political principle underlying the Constitution, and opened the way for the current Governor, or any successor, to claim powers *vis-à-vis* the legislature that arguably were incompatible with the principle of responsible government.

The legal historian Charles Parkinson has criticised the Constitution Bill as 'disorganized and totally unsystematic', and he adds that 'exactly how Stawell envisaged the operation of the governor's role under the new constitution at this early stage is not entirely clear'.[15] Indeed this ambiguity with respect to the principle of responsible government was the underlying cause of the constitutional crisis of 1855. The urban radicals, goldfields representatives and the long-standing Opposition members in the Legislative Council in late 1855 all championed the principle of responsible government (in its modern sense). Fearing that his Government was losing control, Hotham unwisely reacted by claiming powers that were not only autocratic but unconstitutional.

The different views of Higinbotham and Hotham regarding 'responsible government' reflected two opposing strains of contemporary

British political thought about the appropriate model for devolving power to colonies such as Victoria. In 1854–55, Higinbotham and the editorial committee of the *Herald* supported the view of Sir William Molesworth of the Philosophical Radicals and their associates in the Colonial Reform Society in London. The Philosophical Radicals adopted a progressive liberal philosophy on a range of contemporary issues.[16] They advocated parliamentary reform, the separation of church and state, individual freedom, women's rights and divorce law reform. They also opposed slavery, the death penalty and physical punishment.[17] They took a particular interest in the issue of devolution of power to Britain's colonies. Their leader was Sir William Molesworth, the Member for Southwark.

To them, the meaning of the term 'responsible government' was that the locus of power in a British colony such as Victoria should reside in a democratically elected legislature, with only limited and specific powers reserved to the Imperial Parliament in Britain. In his speeches to the House of Commons in 1850, Sir William Molesworth had vigorously advocated the need to devolve power to the colonies. He had called for new constitutions to be drafted after genuine consultation with the population through elected representatives. By contrast, Hotham's view of what he termed 'popular responsible government' was largely consistent with the views of Henry George Grey, the former Secretary of State for the Colonies. Grey was prepared to concede a more democratically elected colonial legislature, but insisted that the locus of real power in the Colony must remain with the Governor, for he was ultimately responsible to the British Government. At issue was the question of whether, under the new Constitution, the colonial government was to be responsible to the British Government or to the elected representatives of the colony.

On 9 December 1853, John Foster, as Chairman of the Select Committee that drafted the Victorian Constitution, reported its recommendations to the Legislative Council. The *Report* contained no recommendation that the Governor should be guided by the legislature regarding the choice of the ministry. A month later, after the new Constitution Bill had been discussed in the House, Clause 44 had read: 'that the appointment to all public officers in the Colony of Victoria hereafter to become vacant, or to be created, (other than corporate offices) whether such officers be salaried or not, shall be vested in the Governor, with the advice of the Executive Council'. Stawell had led the debate seeking to have the words 'with the advice of the Executive Council' deleted. The Colonial Secretary John Foster, the Surveyor-General Andrew Clark, and William Haines, had all staunchly supported his argument that the Governor alone should have the power to appoint and dismiss Ministers. But they faced opposition. When the matter came to a vote, Stawell curiously changed sides and voted to retain the words that he had earlier sought to have removed. The motion was passed by a majority of one.[18]

The matter did not rest there. In its final form the following words were added to Clause 44 of the Constitution Bill: 'with the exception of the officers liable to retire from office on political grounds, which appointments shall be vested in the Governor alone'. At the time that the Constitution Bill had been introduced into the House, John O'Shanassy had complained of 'a very great discrepancy between the Bill as drawn up, and the report of the Committee'.[19] The *Melbourne Morning Herald* also accused Stawell of inserting clauses on his own initiative, adding that that several clauses of the Bill were directly opposed to the Committee's conclusions.[20] This may have been a life-long habit of Stawell's, for in 1883 a similar complaint led to his resignation from the Council of the University of Melbourne. Other members of the University Council objected that while he was acting as Chancellor, Stawell had decided an issue before the Council had fully discussed it.[21] There were other instances in which people made similar accusations. In December 1853, Dr Alfred Yates Carr reported to the Bendigo diggers that Stawell had ignored certain amendments made at the committee stage of the Management of the Goldfields Bill, and had then, on his own initiative, added a clause that significantly altered the effect of the legislation.[22] Three months later, the squatter member John Goodman complained that 'the Government' had altered the wording of the recommendation of the Select Committee on the Constitution for three-year terms of office and substituted wording providing for five-year terms. The Select Committee, he said, had specifically rejected this provision.[23] The legal historian John Waugh comments:

> Stawell's bill also went beyond the Committee's resolutions in its provisions regarding royal instructions to the Governor (Clause 43), quorums, presiding officers and resignation of members, (clauses 7–11, 19–23), and the power of each house to adopt standing orders (clause 32).[24]

Whether or not Stawell was responsible for the additional words in Clause 44, they created a 'Trojan horse' that gave the Governor the means to re-assert his claim to the exclusive power to dismiss and re-appoint any of the Ministers, by declaring their resignation to be on 'political grounds'. The exact meaning of the phrase was not defined. Though they may not have realised it, the members of the legislature had forfeited to the Governor their right to appoint the ministry in consultation with the Governor. In 1854, very few of the members of the Legislative Council had legal training. Perhaps, trusting in Stawell's misleading assurance that the Constitution enshrined 'responsible government', they may have failed to recognise the danger in the additional words that had been added. As the Chief Law Officer of the Colony, Stawell should have warned Hotham that his Minute was contrary to the Constitution, but instead of that, he was prepared to defend it and to profit from it. When he was questioned in the Legislative Council about the status of the principle of responsible government in the new Constitution, Stawell blustered and dissembled. A leading article in the *Age* called upon the Attorney-General to admit that 'either the Bill was self-contradictory or the Government have acted illegally'.[25]

Two unexpected deaths

Suddenly, Victorian colonists learned that two of the chief protagonists in the struggle over the new Constitution had died. Early in 1856, Victorians received the news that the liberal-minded Secretary of State for the Colonies, Sir William Molesworth, had died in London on 22 October 1855.[26] His widow reported that his last words were: 'the cares of state weigh heavy on my mind'.[27] On New Year's Day, Victorians learned that Sir Charles Hotham had died. He had attended the opening of the Melbourne Gasworks on 17 December, where reportedly he had caught a chill and suffered complications. He died on 31 December.[28]

The aftermath of Hotham's death

Hotham may have been deeply discouraged at his inability to please his ever-changing political masters. There had been six Secretaries of State for the Colonies between 1853 and 1856. In June 1854, the conservative Sir George Grey succeeded the more radical Duke of Newcastle. Sidney Herbert (another radical) succeeded Grey for two weeks in February 1855, when Lord John Russell (a moderate conservative) replaced him. Five months later in July 1855, Sir William Molesworth, the Philosophical Radical, succeeded Russell, but Henry Labouchere, another liberal, succeeded him in late October. The constant changes of expectation took their toll on Hotham. Following the trials of the prisoners from Eureka, Lord John Russell had rebuked him for the decision to charge the prisoners with high treason.[29] His failure to secure convictions against those charged with high treason after the battle at Eureka was humiliating. On seeing him pass by in the street, the crowd at a public meeting subjected him to 'three groans'.[30] There were unrelenting campaigns against him by the Victorian press, which also reached British readers.[31] The *Age* repeatedly called for Hotham's dismissal and argued that the *Herald*, in advocating intervention by the Governor-General in Victoria's affairs, had belatedly adopted its view.[32]

The appointment of Sir William Molesworth as the new Colonial Minister in July 1855 dashed Hotham's expectation that his success in reducing the Colony's debt would find favour. Molesworth reprimanded him for having resorted to 'the expedient of reductions which will be inconvenient to the community'.[33] Now, in the latest humiliation, the Legislative Council had rejected his Minute at the urging of the press. In a personal letter to his brother John, Sir Charles Hotham complained that he had withstood 'a tirade of abuse' for his attempts to deal with disorder and the finances. His letter concluded with a bitter remark about Victoria: 'it is a vile hole and I shall never like it'.[34] In the same dispatch in which he reported that he had proclaimed the new Constitution, he reported that his health had 'materially suffered', and he requested that a successor be appointed.

The death of Sir Charles Hotham was announced in the *Argus* and the *Herald* on New Year's Day 1856, with both reports enclosed in a black border as a sign of mourning. The *Herald*'s announcement made obligatory references to the death as 'melancholy' and 'mournful', with some appearance of sincerity in considering its effect upon Hotham's widow and children, yet beyond this, the tone was one of barely contained jubilation and relief. The paper refrained from any acknowledgement of Hotham's achievements, either during his period as Governor of Victoria or throughout his remarkable naval career. A leading article in the *Herald*, suggestive of the style and views of Higinbotham, made much of the religious axiom that God is the author of Death, and suggested that the Governor's death was 'some great lesson intended by Providence, for those who are ordinarily too obtuse to observe, too callous to feel, or too proud to receive instruction'.[35]

By contrast, the *Herald* deeply mourned the death of Sir William Molesworth. An editorial observed:

> To more than one individual connected with this paper, the death of that distinguished man was a personal affliction. We enjoyed his friendship for years. We co-operated with him in his early struggles for colonial reform. We can bear testimony to the noble simplicity and disinterestedness of his character, and we can estimate the loss that has been experienced in his untimely death by all the colonies of the British Empire.[36]

The editorial committee of the *Herald* knew that Molesworth's death spelled the end of their hope of intervention from London to reform the Victorian Constitution. Despite the Constitution's shortcomings, it was apparent that the Colony would have to live with it and the reformers would have to deal with its inadequacies when opportunities arose.

Higinbotham protests Westminster 'interference'

James MacPherson Grant and Higinbotham took a different view at this point. Grant told the House that the majority of the population believed that the Constitution 'would never accomplish what was intended', yet he believed in the possibility that 'those who were elected to the new legislature could improve it'.[37] But Higinbotham maintained his view that the Constitution had not been validly enacted and that it ought to be redrafted with input from a popular congress. He made a last powerful appeal to the British Government to accept this plan.

The legal historian John Waugh writes that the new constitutions of Victoria and New South Wales were 'in an awkward position'. He notes 'the Victorian Legislative Council never formally agreed to the amendments made in London'. He suggests that the British Government wanted to avoid a full debate which would 'insult the colonies' since they had been told that they could write their own constitutions, and that the option of returning the amended bills to the colonial legislatures to pass the amendments made in the British Parliament would have been too time-consuming.[38]

A plan such as Grant's, to reform the new Constitution by successive amendments as opportunities arose, presented a problem. If, as Higinbotham argued, the Constitution had not been validly enacted, then any reforming amendments in the future would face the same objection, and might be nullified by a future challenge to the legal validity of the *Constitution Act*. To solve the problem, Grant moved and Owens seconded a motion in the Council calling upon the Acting Governor, Edward Macarthur, to direct the law officers of the Crown to provide the House with their written opinion as to whether the Constitution Bill possessed 'the force of law in this Colony'. When asked why this was necessary, Grant referred particularly to the campaign in the *Herald* questioning the validity of the *Constitution Act*. He said that the *Herald* was 'the legal journal *par excellence*' and therefore its arguments deserved serious consideration. He was repeatedly pressed to name the lawyers who were responsible for these opinions, but Grant replied that, 'he did not consider himself bound to do so'.[39]

After a delay of four months, William Stawell, as Attorney-General, and Robert Molesworth, as Solicitor-General, responded to the motion of Grant and Owens with an opinion that they tabled in the Legislative Council. They declared that:

> The Bill passed by the Legislature of Victoria, as amended in the schedule to the Act of Parliament, 18 & 19 Vict. Cap:55 possesses the force of law in this Colony. We attribute its efficacy not to the power of the Colonial but of the Imperial Legislature, and the assent given by Her Majesty to the Bill as amended, such assent having been made by the Imperial Legislature a condition precedent to the measure coming into operation.[40]

The *Herald* scoffed that Stawell and Molesworth 'did not dare to give their reasons'. The editorial writer maintained that the British Parliament had intended that the Bill, after consideration in the British Parliament, should have been remitted to the colonial Parliament for its amendments to be adopted.[41] Failure to do this was a 'blunder', which had a fortuitous benefit in that it 'still leaves us a loophole, to escape from the most fearful calamity that can befall a free people – that of having an irresponsible oligarchy fastened about its neck'.[42]

Condemning the 'extravagant and prodigal' Governor's Civil List, the *Herald*'s editorial writer or writers argued that the Victorian *Constitution Act*:

> If it derives its validity from the imperial Parliament alone … has none at all; for it is a money bill, and there is no principle more clear and indubitable than this — that Parliament cannot and will not pass a bill that has clauses to tax the colonies having legislatures of their own.[43]

Judge Redmond Barry never forgot Higinbotham's challenge to the Constitution's validity that had prompted Grant's motion and forced this declaration from the most senior law officers of the Crown. Nor did he forget that Higinbotham, in his 'Summary for Europe' of 30 January 1856, had dared to charge the British Parliament with 'usurpation' and 'tyranny'. Many years later, he discussed a proposal for a parliamentary history of Victoria. Regarding Higinbotham, he declared, 'the historian will want to know what sort of man he was that challenged the Constitution, and – and the Empire'.[44]

The affair of Hotham's Minute proved that bold and determined leadership could force the autocratic Governor and his craven ministry to bend to popular feeling. Higinbotham – the man who enjoyed the challenge of handling a refractory horse – saw that it would involve a fierce and protracted battle of wills, and he primed himself for the task.[45] He expressed his resolve to challenge the complacency of the House in his own characteristic style:

> Our legislature is one that it is not sufficient to ignore, if you would rouse it to resentment; nor will you succeed by spitting in its face. You must cudgel it into the sensibility of shame and flagellate it into the irritability of self-respect; and even then, the chances are that it will prefer the sluggish stupor of subjection to the lively vigilance of freedom.[46]

It has long been assumed that Higinbotham's strong view about responsible government developed in response to the constitutional crises of 1865 and 1867.[47] But his writings in the *Melbourne Morning Herald*

(1854–56) reveal that this view was discernible much earlier. It clearly motivated his leading role in the press campaign around the Minute and the pensions affair. Hotham's death brought an unsatisfactory end to the Governor's autocratic claims, for there was no clarification of the question of whether in fact the new Constitution enshrined the principle of responsible government in the modern meaning of the term. Higinbotham suspected that the newfound commitment of the Government members to the principle of responsible government was merely a face-saving tactic. He believed, as did Lalor, that in future those who upheld responsible government would need to watch and scrutinise with 'unsparing vigilance' the behaviour of their Government Ministers to ensure that the principle was not violated again. This was to become a watchword of his political career.

8

HIGINBOTHAM, DUFFY AND THE IRISH LEGACY

In early 1856, an immigrant arrived in Melbourne who was to change the dynamics of Victorian politics. The Irish nationalist Charles Gavan Duffy arrived with his family to a hero's welcome from his countrymen in Victoria. Duffy had faced five trials under the *Treason Felony Act* for his part in the failed 1848 Uprising in Ireland, but eventually he had been acquitted. The Irish Protestant community (including Higinbotham) was immediately on high alert. Duffy's status as the leader of the Young Ireland movement guaranteed instant popularity with Irish sympathisers in Victoria. His publication of a book of Irish ballad poetry endeared him to some Irish Protestants as well as Catholics. He was friendly with many of the leading writers and statesmen of England and Ireland. His organisational abilities, his skills as a publicist, his knowledge of the law and his political experience as a recent member of the House of Commons made him overnight a figure of great standing in the Colony.

The Irish Protestants, Stawell and Foster, who had insisted upon the exclusive property qualifications for candidature for the new Legislative Assembly, had done so with an eye to deterring candidates whom they regarded as opportunists.[1] Now they looked on in dismay as Duffy's supporters easily raised a subscription of £5,000 to finance a fitting residence for him in the Melbourne suburb of Hawthorn, and enable him to meet the property qualification required for candidature for the new

Victorian Legislative Assembly. Addressing a dinner of two hundred guests presided over by John O'Shanassy, Duffy defiantly declared, 'I am still an Irish rebel to the backbone and to the spinal marrow ... because tyranny has supplanted law in my native country'.[2] It was a remark that his political opponents would seize upon as evidence that he was an unrepentant traitor.

Duffy was born in Ireland in 1816 into a Catholic family in County Monaghan. Despite the difficulties under which Catholics laboured, his resourceful parents managed to ensure that their promising young son received a good education. As he grew to manhood, he studied Irish history. He learned that Ireland had endured centuries of misrule from the fourteenth century Statutes of Kilkenny to the harsh Penal Laws of the seventeenth and early eighteenth centuries. These laws were designed to disenfranchise the native Catholic population from all power, both political and economic. They forbade Catholics from receiving an education (including sending a child overseas to be educated), from holding any public office, from receiving an inheritance or gift from a Protestant, from being the guardian of a child, from residing within five miles of a corporate town, from buying or leasing land, or from engaging in trade or commerce.[3] Duffy's indignation at these historic injustices was further sharpened by the British Government's tardy response to Ireland's plight during the famine years.

The famine and the Repeal movement

Throughout the 1840s, European potato crops suffered from the blight *Phytophthora infestans*. In Ireland, political, economic and social factors combined to make the effects of the blight particularly devastating. Between 1845 and 1849, Ireland lost between one-fifth and one-quarter of its population through starvation, disease and forced emigration.[4] Amongst the Irish Catholic majority, the British Government's failure to intervene to alleviate the famine of the late 1840s amplified the popular agitation for repeal of the *Act of Union*. It was this Act, which had deprived Ireland of her own legislature.

More than forty mass meetings for Repeal were held throughout the spring and summer of 1843. At a 'monster meeting' at Drogheda, Daniel O'Connell, who led the movement for Repeal, told the crowd that the alternative they faced was 'to live as slaves or die as free men'. The Prime Minister, Sir Robert Peel, met O'Connell's challenge, declaring, 'Depreciating as I do all war, but above all, civil war, yet there is no alternative which I do not think preferable to the dismemberment of this empire'.[5] The British Government was on high alert to an impending Irish rebellion, and it was assisted in its efforts to curb rebellion by the Orange Order, a society dedicated to the protection and furtherance of Protestant interests.

The Orange Order staunchly supported the monarchy (during Protestant succession), the maintenance of a Protestant monopoly of government office, and the exclusive right of Protestants to bear firearms. It organised to protect Protestant clergy and gentry from the attacks from Catholic secret societies that often followed disputes over the enforcement of tithes and rents.[6] The Orange Order was a bulwark of conservatism in British politics. It had opposed the *Catholic Emancipation Act* of 1819. The Reform Bill of 1830 aimed to remedy some of the worst abuses in the British electoral system, but the Orange Order had forbidden its members to vote for any candidate for the British House of Commons who supported it.[7]

Since its foundation in 1797, the Orange Order had experienced a stormy history. Thomas Verner, a first cousin once removed of George Higinbotham, was the Master of the largest and most prestigious of its lodges, the Dublin Grand Lodge.[8] It had been briefly dissolved in 1828, and then permitted to re-establish. It membership comprised Church of Ireland clergy and prominent people associated with Dublin Castle, the seat of the United Kingdom's administration in Ireland. Among its 130-odd members, this Lodge included two earls, several prominent landed magnates, and a number of members of the Irish Parliament before its abolition by the *Act of Union* of 1801. As head of the Irish Treasury before the *Act of Union*, George Higinbotham's great-uncle Andrew Higinbotham had been a member.[9]

When the failure of the potato crop in Ireland was under discussion in the House of Commons in 1846, the Member for Armagh, Colonel Sir William Verner, a cousin of George Higinbotham's father, denied that there was a crisis. He admitted to his fellow members of the House that 'distress prevailed in many parts', however he declared:

> The potato crop, – divested of the diseased portion – was still an average crop, and there was more grain of every description in the country at that season of the year, the month of March, than had been for several years previous.

He attributed the rising prices for foodstuffs to hoarding and speculation. He opposed the repeal of the Corn Laws, which, by imposing a duty on imported grain, exacerbated the famine in Ireland. Instead he called for strong measures to control political agitation.[10] At the time, Higinbotham was living in County Tyrone and attending the Dungannon Royal School for his secondary education. As the school was located nearly 100 kilometres from his mother's home in Bray, it is likely that he was staying with Sir William Verner, whose grand estate named Churchill was located a short distance from the school on the shores of Lough Neagh. Verner was the Member for Armagh in the House of Commons, and a deputy Grand Master of the Armagh Orange Lodge.

During the Napoleonic Wars, William Verner had distinguished himself in the Iberian Peninsular Campaign of 1808–09, and subsequently fought in five battles with the Duke of Wellington, including the battle of Waterloo. He retired with the rank of Colonel.[11] He inherited the Verner family's property, comprising a three-storey mansion and about 700 acres. The property was known as Churchill (previously Church Hill), and located near the southern shore of Lough Neagh at Verner's Bridge, Armagh, only a few miles east of Dungannon in County Tyrone.

Over successive generations, the mansion had been enlarged and elegantly furnished. The *Newry Telegraph* described it in 1828 as 'chastely beautiful and classic', and the gardens as 'tastefully laid out pleasure grounds'.[12] Verner had married an heiress named Harriet Wingfield. Their family consisted of eight daughters and two sons who had survived beyond infancy.[13]

William Verner's role in sectarian politics in Ulster came under investigation in 1835 when the British Parliament became so concerned at reports of a series of violent incidents in County Armagh that it appointed a Parliamentary Select Committee to enquire into the Orange Order.[14] The Orange Order's members claimed that the Order was a purely defensive and religious organisation. They stressed its respect for the law, including the *Act of Union*. They professed that, while strenuously opposing the 'fatal errors and doctrines of the Church of Rome', they would abstain from all uncharitable words, action or sentiments towards their 'Roman Catholic brethren'. But opponents alleged that the Order was behind a campaign known as 'wrecking', by which Catholic householders in some districts were violently harassed and driven from their homes.[15]

The Select Committee investigated allegations against the Orange Order including infiltration of the army, condoning of drunkenness, misuse of government-issued firearms, and perversion of the judicial system to the disadvantage of Catholics.[16] Colonel William Verner, whose own conduct was under investigation, was a witness before the Select Committee, and he strenuously defended the Orange Order from such allegations.[17]

One of the deponents to the Select Committee, a Quaker named James Christie, declared that the campaign of 'wrecking' had originated in 1794 on the estates administered by James Verner (brother of William and Thomas), and had continued through to 1797.[18] The Select Committee examined a magistrate named Louis Perrin, who had investigated the violent attacks, house-burning and pillaging of property in the Catholic neighbourhoods of Marghery and Tanderagee in Armagh in 1830. Perrin had been unable to convict anyone of the offences because of the evasiveness of witnesses. His remarks were strongly critical of the role played by Colonel William Verner, particularly for his failure to preserve the peace by dispersing 'the persons there tumultuously and unlawfully assembled'. He concluded that 'he is liable to be prosecuted at suit of the

Crown by information for such (as it seems to me) criminal neglect of his duty'.[19]

Like Magistrate Perrin, the Select Committee found it impossible to establish the truth. From the implausibility of witnesses' accounts it was obvious that a code of silence was operating, and that even the authority of the Parliament could not break it.[20] The fact that no person had been convicted for the serious attacks at Marghery and Tanderagee in 1830, and other offences, showed that the law was being flouted with impunity in Ireland, by the gentry, the clergy, the tenantry, the labourers and even by some of the magistrates.[21]

In 1836 the British Parliament condemned the Orange Order, and legislated for its dissolution. This created dismay and dissension within the Order, and consternation in the Verner family. Thomas Verner, as Grand Master of the Dublin Lodge, declared in a public statement that the accusations against the Order were malevolent falsehoods, and he declared that 'We regard every loyal citizen as our friend, be his religion what it may ...'[22] James Verner, as Grand Secretary of the Orange Lodge, asserted that 'The Orange Association, as now constituted and regulated, does not in anywise militate against the law of the land'. But he urged his Orange brethren to 'live soberly and righteously in Christian charity with all their fellow subjects, and in constant obedience to the laws of their Creator and of their country'.[23]

As a Member of Parliament, Verner commuted between his northern home in County Armagh, and his residence in Belgravia, close to the Parliament in London. In the mid-1830s, he took a third residence in Dublin. It is likely that his business in Dublin involved the Loyal Orange Order, for Verner, with his close links to the Armagh gentry, was one of its three Deputy Grand Masters.[24] His residence in Dublin in 1836 suggests that he may have been engaged in consultations with his brothers to manage the damage to the Orange Order in the short term, and to plan for its eventual re-instatement. With an eye to the future, he may have become aware of the potential value of the promising ten-year-old son of his cousin, Henry Higinbotham. Just as he himself had been selected at a tender age to be educated by his great-uncle Thomas (who later appointed him the heir to Churchill), so he may have taken a particular interest in George Higinbotham's education.[25] It is likely that George spent time on the Churchill estate with his Verner relatives. As Sir William and Lady Harriet Wingfield had married in 1819, several of the couple's ten children were probably living at home during the period of George's secondary education at the nearby Dungannon Royal School.

Perhaps it was on the broad acres of the Churchill estate, under Verner's tutelage, that Higinbotham, as a boy, learned the skill of breaking in horses at the same time as he imbibed the stories of the battle of Waterloo and the gallantry of the Duke of Wellington.[26] Colonel Verner was a man who so loved the mare Constantia that he had ridden in the battle of Waterloo, that he called one of his daughters by the mare's name. In 1835, when George Higinbotham was nine years old, the mare died. Verner built a monument over the mare's grave and inscribed a poem in tribute to it.[27] It is likely that Higinbotham's life-long love of horse riding, rowing and boating dated from boyhood days spent not in his mother's cottage at Lota, but on the Churchill estate by the waters of Lough Neagh.[28] These relaxing activities would have been welcome interludes in the life of a family that was otherwise earnestly engaged in Orange affairs, and that recruited its younger members to the cause.

The choice of the Dungannon Royal School, ninety kilometres distant, would seem an unlikely one for a Dublin boy, considering that most of his older brothers had attended school in Bray. Perhaps there was a stage between the 'very careful early training at home' that Morris noted, and George's entry into the Dungannon Royal School when he received schooling from a governess on the Verner estate in the company of his Verner cousins.[29] Transport from there to the nearby Dungannon Royal School for his senior schooling would have been easily managed, and would have given George a base for school holidays, and ensured that his progress and welfare could easily be monitored by family.

During Higinbotham's adolescence, despite the official disbandment of the Orange Lodges, the prominent Irish Protestant families maintained their social networks. They watched with alarm the mobilisation of millions of the Catholic Irish urging Repeal of the *Act of Union*. Ports were watched for possible shipments of arms to Ireland. Chartist demonstrations were watched for signs that an outbreak of civil disturbance in England could have been a ruse to divert military resources at the time of an uprising in Ireland. It is likely that there were expectations placed upon George Higinbotham to play his part in defending Protestant interests.

Duffy's experiences were a mirror image of those of Higinbotham. Despite the marked contrast in their religious and political allegiances, the two had a curious connection through Higinbotham's second cousin, Jenny Verner. During the years that Higinbotham was probably living at Churchill, Jenny, a niece of Sir William Verner, resided there.[30] She was the daughter of Captain James Verner, William's elder brother.[31] When George was eleven, Jenny, aged fifteen, commenced at a school for young ladies in Newry. At about this time she met John Mitchel, a young Trinity graduate, who was the son of a Presbyterian minister. A few months later, Jenny caused consternation when she eloped to England with him. Colonel Verner pursued the couple and brought them back. Mitchel spent eighteen days in Kilmainham Gaol on charges of abduction that were subsequently dropped. Jenny's parents opposed the young couple's wish to marry, but a second elopement succeeded and the couple married in 1837.[32]

Higinbotham may have known Jenny from childhood. He would have been acutely conscious of the embarrassment her elopement caused to the Verner family – an embarrassment that intensified over the following decade when Mitchel came to national prominence as the radical face of the Young Ireland movement. This movement attracted people who sympathised with Daniel O'Connell's nationalist goals but were frustrated by his reliance on peaceful protest, and impatient for more decisive action. In powerful prose, Mitchel drew heart-rending images of the famine of 1845–49. In a description of his travels through the famine districts of Ireland, he wrote:

There is a horrible silence; grass grows before the doors; we fear to look into any door though they are all open or off their hinges, for we fear to see yellow, chapless skeletons grinning there; but our footfalls rouse two lean dogs that run from us with doleful howling, and we know by the felon gleam in their wolfish eyes how *they* have lived after their masters died.[33]

He accompanied his reports of the famine with blistering attacks on the failure of the British Government to respond to the suffering, and he demanded repeal of the Union. So incensed was Mitchel that he advocated guerrilla warfare, including railway sabotage, to promote the Repeal movement.[34] For a time he worked closely with Duffy, who published his articles in *The Nation*, the organ of the Young Ireland movement. Through the friendship, Duffy would have learned of the militantly Protestant atmosphere in which Mitchel's young wife, Jenny, had been raised on the Verner estate. This would explain his deep suspicion of Higinbotham, who was, he declared, 'influenced and controlled by the prejudices which an Irish Protestant boy rarely escapes'.[35]

In one of his last editorials for the *Herald* before departure for the *Argus,* Higinbotham expressed his concerns about Duffy's entry into Victorian politics. The editorial commented on a letter from the Congregationalist, John Fawkner, which the *Herald* had published the day before. Fawkner's letter attacked Duffy for having described Victorian colonists in his newspaper, *The Nation,* as 'Irish in population and feeling'. More significantly, Fawkner asserted that the elaborate preparations that O'Shanassy and the Catholic clergy had made for Duffy's reception proved that 'he had been sent for by the priesthood here'. He declared that 'two Celts have wrested this gold colony from England and laid it at the feet of the Bishop of Rome'.[36]

The next day, in a leading article, Higinbotham took issue with some of Fawkner's more extreme statements. It may have been a collaboration with Aspinall, for the later parts were written in Aspinall's typically satirical style, yet the earlier parts showed the intellectualism, earnestness and poetic turns of phrase that characterise Higinbotham's style. Higinbotham began by drawing a clear distinction between the Catholic and non-Catholic Irish. He further distinguished between the majority of Irish Catholics whose loyalty could be relied upon, and the extremists who might pose a danger. He agreed with Fawkner that 'the narrow prejudices and religious bigotry of the sacerdotal and Ultramontane party' constituted a threat. The Ultramontane movement within nineteenth-century Catholicism looked 'beyond the mountains' to the Pope in Rome as the source of authority in the Church, rather than to the local bishops. This movement foreshadowed the declaration of Papal Infallibility, which was made at the First Vatican Council in 1870. Employing the powerful imagery that was a hallmark of his style, Higinbotham wrote:

> The old world – with its gothic ruins, its barbaric monuments and its yet lingering darkness of intolerance and superstition – may be for some time longer the haunt of such spectres, and the midnight rendezvous of such fiends as delight in the orgies of fanaticism or in the still more dreadful horrors and frantic rites of persecution. It is ours on this new continent … to guard ourselves against the introduction of anything so likely to prove fatal to our peace and prosperity.[37]

These images derived not from paranoid fantasy, but from historical reality, for Europe had been racked for centuries by religious wars. The Spanish Inquisition – a byword for fanaticism, intolerance and cruelty since it began in 1478 – had claimed its last victim as recently as 1826 when it sentenced a Spanish schoolteacher to be burned to death for refusing to instruct his pupils in the tenets of the Catholic faith.[38]

Although the Inquisition was finally abolished in 1834, the fanatical persecution of 'heretics' that it had conducted for centuries left a long legacy of fear and mistrust of the Catholic hierarchy amongst religious minorities, particularly those who lived in predominantly Catholic countries. The historian Paul de Serville has characterised Irish Protestantism as 'the strictest caste in Europe'.[39] Bitter memories of the persecution of Protestants in Europe, and Spanish support for the 1798 Uprising in Ireland, had produced a strong defensive reaction. The Irish Protestant Ascendancy prepared its sons for their role in fighting for the glory of Empire and the defence of the Sovereign and the Protestant religion. The 1848 Uprising and the more recent attempt on the lives of 800 Protestant passengers on a train at Trillick reinforced the long-standing fear among Irish Protestants of Catholic conspiracies against them. Mitchel's advocacy of guerrilla warfare, and Duffy's willingness at first to publish Mitchel's articles, raised in Protestant minds the suspicion that he too covertly condoned violent extremism.

In his autobiography, Duffy defended himself from such accusations. He described how Mitchel's growing extremism led to a bitter breach between them, and he noted that afterwards Mitchel left *The Nation* and established his own publication, the *United Irishman*.[40] To Duffy, Fawkner's accusation that he was an emissary of the Pope must have been galling, for one of the reasons that he had despaired of achieving reform in Ireland was that Dr Paul Cullen, the Catholic Bishop of Armagh and later Cardinal of Ireland, had denounced him to the Pope. Cullen likened Duffy to the Italian radical, Giuseppe Mazzini, who had spearheaded uprisings in support of a unified Italian state.[41] So great a supporter of papal authority was Cullen that in 1870, it was he who proposed the wording of the declaration of Papal Infallibility at the First Vatican Council. Although Duffy was a committed Catholic, he was convinced that Catholic and Protestant Irish could work together for the good of the country. Duffy, unlike O'Connell a decade earlier, sought to recruit the Protestant middle class to his reform campaign, and did so with some success. Ironically Duffy was more a victim than an agent of the same 'sacerdotal and ultramontane party' within Catholicism that Higinbotham and Fawkner feared.

Conversely, Duffy's deep suspicion of Higinbotham was based largely on what he knew of his origins and associates, for as he wrote in his autobiography:

Top

George Washington at Princeton
by Charles Willson Peale

This portrait was a gift from
George Washington to Joseph
Wilson, the grandfather of
George Higinbotham. In
1906 the portrait was sold
to Princeton University
and it is now displayed in
the Princeton Library

Bottom

Sir Charles Gavan Duffy
(1816–1903)

Photo courtesy of the
Parliamentary Library
of Victoria

Sir William Stawell
(1815–1889)

Detail from a portrait by
Ludwig Becker,
c.1855– c.1860.

Image courtesy of the
State Library of Victoria

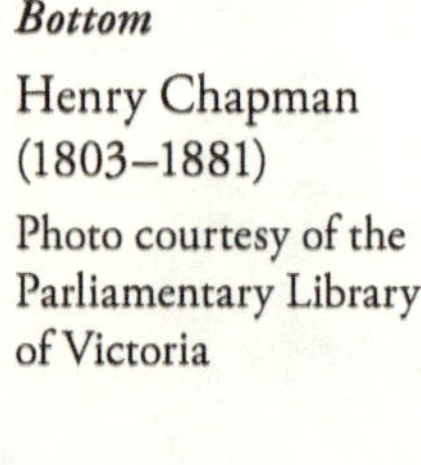

Henry Chapman
(1803–1881)

Photo courtesy of the
Parliamentary Library
of Victoria

> He was not a conscious bigot, but he had for allies all those
> who had transplanted the secret conspiracies and rancorous
> bigotry of the old world to the new.[42]

Duffy would have been aware that Higinbotham was a Verner descendant through his paternal grandmother, Jane Verner. But Duffy may have known less about Higinbotham's mother's family, the Wilsons, who were a major influence on his childhood. The Wilsons belonged to a Unitarian congregation with a long tradition of supporting both religious and political reform. It was a source of tremendous pride to Higinbotham's mother, Sarah, and her brother, Thomas, that their father, Joseph, had fought with George Washington. After the victory, Washington had bestowed upon his friend a full-length portrait of himself painted by Charles Willson Peale. This heirloom had pride of place in his Uncle Thomas's house in Dublin, where it served as a reminder to the family of the sacredness of the principle of self-government, and their family's close involvement in the struggle to achieve it. During Higinbotham's early childhood there would have been occasions when he would have seen the full-length portrait of Washington that now hangs in the library of Princeton University, for it had been given to his grandfather as a gift from Washington, and subsequently bequeathed to his Uncle Thomas.[43]

Upon Joseph's death, his son Thomas Wilson also received his books, watch and revolutionary firearms.[44] No doubt as a child Higinbotham had examined these heirlooms at his uncle's house, for it was located only a few doors from his own, and in the same street. No doubt he also had absorbed the stories, told by his mother and uncle, of Washington's heroic armies who had fought for the rights of the colonists against a tyrannical king. This early exposure to the legends associated with the American Revolution and of the ideals underlying the Declaration of Independence inspired him and stayed with him throughout his life.

The ideals of the American Revolution went beyond mere resistance to tyranny. They included an assertion of the rights of man and advocacy of a democratic system of government answerable to the people. These ideas gained popularity during the eighteenth-century Enlightenment. Philosophers such as Jean-Jacques Rousseau and John Locke challenged the long-held assumption that the right to govern followed the fact of conquest. Instead they argued for the notion of a 'social contract' by which the legitimacy of government rested upon the consent of the governed. Higinbotham supported this new democratic philosophy, including its advocacy of religious toleration. The challenge was how to apply such precepts to Ireland. The bitter history of the last three centuries had so poisoned relations between the communities that any sudden devolution of power to the Catholic majority would bring the risk of reprisals against his own Protestant community. Similarly in Victoria, the dilemma that he contemplated was how to promote democracy without endangering the interests of Protestantism.

It was true, as Duffy charged, that Higinbotham had attended a privileged Protestant school for his secondary education. Yet his headmaster at the Royal School, the Reverend John Darley, an ordained Church of Ireland minister, earned the respect of Protestants and Catholics alike for his broadminded Christian outlook that anticipated modern ecumenism. After retiring as headmaster, Darley ministered to famine victims and he was noted for his kindness and consideration to all, regardless of religious affiliation.[45] These early broadening influences exposed Higinbotham during his formative years to an interpretation of Christianity that emphasised charity and tolerance. As he matured, he developed political views that were unusually liberal for Irish Protestants of his class.

During his years in London, Higinbotham prepared himself for the Bar and worked as a parliamentary reporter for the liberal *Morning Chronicle*. Several references in editorials in the *Melbourne Morning Herald* and later in the *Argus* suggest that, during these years, Higinbotham associated with some of the leading members of the Philosophical Radicals.[46] In the months before the passage through the British Parliament of the *Australian Colonies Act* in 1850, the Philosophical Radicals took a particular interest in the relationship between Britain and her colonies. Mindful of the lessons of the American War of Independence, Molesworth advocated a form of colonial constitution based upon democratic principles that he believed were compatible with the structure of the British Empire. He saw the press as having a vital role to play in guiding the process of devolution of power to Britain's colonies in such a way as to ensure both ongoing loyalty to Britain and the implementation of democratic values via a consultative process.

Through this group, Higinbotham's political horizons were greatly broadened and he encountered the new philosophy of Jeremy Bentham and the Utilitarians. This was a secular philosophy that was not founded upon a view concerning religious truth or the afterlife. It taught that the basic duty of the state was to create the conditions necessary for human happiness and improvement in the present. In time, Higinbotham developed distinctly liberal views of his own on a range of issues including land reform, women's rights, public education, capital punishment, responsible government and law reform. He embraced Molesworth's distinctive view about the need for Britain to allow self-government in her colonies while maintaining control of those external matters that affected the Empire. Though the Irish Protestant community staunchly upheld the value of group loyalty, it contained a spectrum of political beliefs. By the time he had formed his adult political views, Higinbotham had moved to occupy the opposite end of that spectrum from Sir William Verner.

9

THE *ARGUS*, DUFFY AND THE 1856 ELECTION

In September 1855, Higinbotham found his position at the *Herald* under threat, for a new editor was appointed. Dr George Evans, aged fifty-three, was an English-born classical scholar, a lawyer, an ordained Congregational minister and a political conservative. On the morning of the third, readers of the *Melbourne Morning Herald* discovered that the familiar banner heading on the front page of their newspaper had changed to read simply '*The Herald*'. The London printing firm of Levey, Robson and Franklyn had bought the newspaper. The new managers were Francis Burdett Franklyn and the brothers George, William and Oliver Levey.[1] By changing the appearance of the columns and employing different fonts, they had created a new look. Poetry was included and there was greater coverage of plays, musical events and horse races. The *Herald*'s editorial explained to its readers that the newspaper's former proprietors had been shocked to discover that the newspaper was suffering from a 'pecuniary crisis'. The new management had initiated major economies to resolve the difficulty.

At first the new team assured the readers that there would be no slackening of the *Herald*'s determination to act as the public's conscience.[2] They promised that the *Herald* would engage in no polemics regarding religion, although they declared support for the 'The Great Cause of Protestantism', and for the National System of education over the Denominational System.

They pledged their opposition to 'the encroachment of sacerdotal power … upon the functions of the state'. But it soon became clear that, despite denials, the tone of the *Herald* was changing, and the editorial committee had become divided on a range of issues. A crudely anti-Catholic sentiment now emerged in its columns. Jubilation at the news of the successes of the Sardinian allies in the Crimean War was coupled with the fervent hope that they would undertake 'the exorcism of Rome', and deal with 'The Triple Tyrant'.[3] A rollicking, satirical poem by a new contributor named Peter Perfume told of a French Abbot who drank himself to death in a vat of beer, and was subsequently canonised by the Pope as 'Saint Beeriemanne'.[4] Frederick Sinnett, in his new guise as 'Mr Punch', lashed the *Herald* for its 'loud and loose leaders'. He slated Franklyn for his autocratic style, and identified him as 'the sole dictator in all questions of criticism; musical, dramatic, literary, artistic or otherwise'.[5] Indeed Franklyn may have written a number of the editorials that Sinnett criticised, for the writing style of the new editor, Evans, was more laboured and aloof.[6]

In mid-October 1855, the new management at the *Herald* accepted a lengthy paid advertisement promoting the case of the squatters regarding their leases.[7] An editorial appeared in early November describing the formerly censured John Foster as 'a scholar and a gentleman', and supporting his candidacy for the new Legislative Council.[8] Two days later, a similar article praised him as 'that good man and suffering patriot'.[9] The issue of 12 November revealed a striking difference of opinion amongst the editorial writers. The leading article praised the Australian people for 'calmly deliberating on the Constitution, and the complexion they shall give to their future empire'. By contrast, the editorial in the adjacent column called for further debate and reform of the Constitution.[10] Editorial consistency was shattered, and the credibility of the *Herald* as 'the mind and conscience of the public' had evaporated.

All of this was discouraging to Higinbotham, but fortunately a new opportunity presented itself. The editor of the *Age* brought an action against Edward Wilson, the editor of the *Argus*, for a provocative leading article it had published, entitled 'The Wickedness of the *Age*'. Wilson engaged

Michie, Chapman and Higinbotham to defend him. The *Age*, as plaintiff, gained a pyrrhic victory, for the court found in its favour, but the court also indicated its disdain for the *Age*'s case by awarding damages of only one farthing.[11] For Wilson, Michie and Higinbotham, their 'loss' was a cause for celebration. Perhaps in the afterglow of success, the irritation that the editors of the *Herald* and the *Argus* had vented from time to time against each other may have been forgotten. Wilson and Higinbotham may have discovered that, despite certain differences, they shared similar views on a range of issues. For some months, Wilson had been looking for a new editor for the *Argus* as he planned to travel to England for his health. In the junior counsel he had at last found the man for the position.

In the following month, August 1856, Higinbotham commenced work as the editor of the *Argus*. It may have been the first paid journalistic work for five months, and was therefore very welcome. In March 1856, Higinbotham had received an invitation from Acting Governor Edward Macarthur, on the advice of the Attorney-General, William Stawell, to accept an appointment as a Justice of the Peace. Higinbotham had accepted the offer, perhaps with a view that it would lead to a salaried position. The offer needed the authority of the new Governor, Sir Henry Barkly, before it could be gazetted, but before Barkly arrived, Higinbotham had accepted Wilson's offer and commenced work at the *Argus*. In order to defend himself and Stawell from any suggestion that Stawell's invitation was a politically motivated offer from a Government Minister to a newspaper editor, Higinbotham published a letter in the *Argus* explaining the circumstances and the timing of the offer.[12]

There may have been further significance to the timing of Higinbotham's departure from the *Herald*. In late July 1856, six months after the 'Summary for Europe' editorial of 30 January, an edition of the *London Illustrated News* arrived in Melbourne. An article in it vehemently denounced the 'disloyalty' of the *Herald*'s editorial in which Higinbotham had lashed the British Government for usurping the authority of the local legislature regarding the new Constitution.[13] It denied that the views expressed represented the views of the majority and it warned, 'so fierce a tone is apt to inflame discontent into sedition'.[14]

This was a charge calculated to alarm a newspaper owner. The previous year, Henry Seekamp, the editor of the *Ballarat Times*, who had called on his fellow-countrymen for a 'vengeance deep and terrible' for the 'foul massacre' at Eureka, was convicted of sedition for his remarks and sentenced to six months in prison.[15] The denunciation in the *London Illustrated News* must have shocked all those employed at the *Herald*. Apart from the disgrace, a charge of sedition, if proven, could have resulted in heavy penalties, including fines and imprisonment for the management and journalists alike. Perhaps Franklyn, the Levey brothers and Evans were relieved that Higinbotham was no longer on the *Herald*'s staff. He too must have been relieved that his days at the *Herald* were over. His new position as editor of the *Argus* was publicly acknowledged, and he enjoyed a handsome annual salary of £900. Aspinall and Michie both expected to enter the new Legislative Assembly at the first elections under the new Constitution. With a high income and a platform on which he may have expected that he could communicate his own views to the readers, Higinbotham knew that, before long, he too could stand for election to the Legislative Assembly.

The *Argus* and editorial policy

It was to be an uneasy alliance between the proprietors of the *Argus*, Edward Wilson and Lauchlan Mackinnon, and their new editor. Wilson may have been aware that it was Higinbotham who wrote the editorial that had created such embarrassment for the *Herald*. Conversely Higinbotham would have been well aware that although Wilson's *Argus* had encouraged the goldfields' population to campaign for their rights, when the military engagement at Ballarat was imminent, the *Argus* had urged the Government to take a 'stand' in order to prevent 'anarchy and confusion'.[16] More recently, in the days leading to the North Bourke by-election of 1855, the *Argus* criticised one of the candidates, Dr Thomas Embling, because of his public support for the cause of the diggers following the conflict at Ballarat in December 1854.[17]

Historians have been puzzled to account for the conservative nature of *Argus* editorials during the time that Higinbotham was the editor, for they contrast with views that he expressed in word and deed in later life. A leading article in September 1856 praised the new Constitution as 'the most liberal in the world' – a view which Higinbotham certainly did not share – and spoke disparagingly of Archibald Michie's conduct during his time in the old Legislative Council, which he left in 1853:

> As a legislator, Mr Michie has not shone. He sat as nominee for several months but was neither very consistent in his attendance nor very useful when he did attend ... Mr Michie seems rather to look upon the legislature as an agreeable lounge after the dry details of Court business are concluded, than as a place for serious occupation. He lounges in leisurely, cracks a few jokes upon the subject then under discussion, then walks off to dinner with his digestive faculties invigorated by the slight interlude of the fun of law-making ...

Higinbotham did not arrive in Melbourne until March 1854, and was most unlikely to have written such an attack on his current colleague at the Bar and former employer and mentor at the *Herald*. As the article describes Michie's shortcomings as if from direct observation, it is also unlikely that Wilson was the author, for he was never a member of the Legislative Council. Suspicion must fall upon the *Argus*'s co-proprietor, Lauchlan Mackinnon, who was a member of the Legislative Council concurrently with Michie in 1853.

Mackinnon joined the *Argus* in 1852 with Edward Wilson and James Gill and remained associated with it until 1876.[18] As the former representative of a squatting electorate, Mackinnon had reason to attack Michie whose memorable terms of abuse of the squatters for their 'wealthy ruffianism' and 'squattocratic impudence' may have offended him.[19] Moreover, through the *Herald,* Michie had led the campaign against the squatters' claims to pre-emptive rights of purchase of the runs, and to the property qualifications for the proposed new Houses of the Parliament, which were designed to protect the interests of landholders.[20]

Lauchlan Mackinnon was born in 1817 in Skye, Scotland, the son of a Presbyterian minister. He arrived in Melbourne in 1840. He took up squatting in a succession of locations and represented the Port Phillip District in the New South Wales Legislative Council and later, the constituency of Belfast (Port Fairy) and Warrnambool in the Victorian Legislative Council. Mackinnon had the reputation of being a liberal in his political views. He did not sympathise with the squatters' claims to long leases and pre-emptive purchase rights. He was active in opposing transportation of convicts, and in the campaign for separation of Victoria from New South Wales. However, in 1843, when sectarian rivalry flared in relation to the election campaign of the 'Father of Separation', Edward Curr, for the seat of Melbourne in the New South Wales Legislative Council, Mackinnon prioritised sectarian feeling over political conviction and threw his support behind the Protestant campaign that saw Curr defeated. Mackinnon's biographer, Jacqueline Templeton, describes him as 'a fiery and outspoken orator', and notes that he had a reputation for 'immoderate speech-making'. She quotes William Westgarth, his friend, who said of him that 'he could never take a subject of deep interest to himself quietly'.[21]

An incident that took place five days before the military conflict at Eureka shows the level of Mackinnon's political activism. On 29 November 1854, Mackinnon wrote to Sir Charles Hotham's private secretary, Captain Kay, drawing his attention to the *Argus*'s editorial of that day. It featured a brutal attack on the character of the Chief Secretary, John Foster, whom the *Argus* accused of misappropriating the Immigration Fund and then expecting the Legislative Council to sanction his action retrospectively.[22] The *Argus* explained: 'the Fund is secured by act of Parliament to a distinct object, and it is not in the power of the Council to alter it'. It denounced the misappropriation of the fund as 'robbery'. It absolved Sir Charles Hotham from responsibility, arguing that he would never have sanctioned it, 'had his advisors laid the matter properly before him'. The following day, the *Melbourne Morning Herald* followed with its own attack on Foster for abuse of his position, and continued its attack on 2 December.[23] Within the week, Hotham dismissed Foster.

The tone of the letter of 29 November suggests that Mackinnon and the Governor had planned the attack, and that Mackinnon was collaborating with the Governor in his plan to oust Foster. In the letter, Mackinnon reported that he was lobbying members of the Legislative Council for a vote of no confidence in Foster in order to gain public support for Hotham's plan to dismiss him. Mackinnon wrote to Kay:

> I have to beg that you may convey to His Excellency the Governor my own and Mr Wilson's best thanks for his kindness in causing the Minutes in question to be sent to me. You see we have opened our batteries on the Ministry. I am moving energetically among the representative members on the subject of a vote of a want of confidence, and the idea is being taken up with avidity among them and will be discussed at a meeting to be held today. I doubt that they may have the pluck to move in the matter. If they do act on the idea, Sir Charles' cause will be an easy one.[24]

Though Hotham was undoubtedly convinced that Foster had misled him concerning the Immigration Fund, he may have had a second motive for dismissing him. His plan may have been to sacrifice an unpopular official in order to deflect the unpopularity that he would incur from the coming military clash at Ballarat in which lives inevitably would be lost. Mackinnon's eagerness to oblige the Governor by leading the press attack on Foster, as well as the *Argus*'s editorial the following day, in which the Governor was urged to 'take a stand' against the diggers, suggest that on occasions, it was Mackinnon who directed editorial policy at the *Argus*.

During Higinbotham's time as the editor, there were other leader-writers as well, including James Smith, the theatre and literary critic, who became a firm friend, and Moses Wilson Gray, who was a close friend of Duffy and a prominent advocate of radical land and electoral reform.

According to the journalist William Astley, a warm friendship existed between Gray and Higinbotham. Astley reported:

> Gray's connection with the *Argus* was severed from considerations of delicacy. The tone and policy of the *Argus* were conservative while Gray belonged to the advanced liberals.[25]

Higinbotham's feeling for Gray was evident in the tribute that he paid to him at the opening of the Trades Hall Chambers in 1882. On that occasion, he described Gray as 'the most stubborn, uncompromising politician I ever met', and added, 'I wish I could say the same for myself'.[26] Given the esteem in which he held his friend, it is unlikely that in 1857, Higinbotham, as the newly appointed editor, made the decision to terminate Gray's services. It is more likely that either Wilson or his partner Lauchlan Mackinnon did so. This incident suggests that the management of the *Argus* strictly enforced the newspaper's conservative stance.

The *Argus* and the 1856 election

Victoria's first election under the new Constitution was a time of great political uncertainty. The novelty of allowing those in possession of the new Miner's Right to vote made the outcome of the election particularly uncertain. There were high hopes at the same time as deep forebodings. Would the voters understand what was required of them in order to cast a valid vote? Would the squatters allow the passage of legislation for a land policy that was in the public interest, or would they act purely in defence of their own interests? The political instability in New South Wales augured poorly for Victoria, which had modelled its Constitution largely on that of New South Wales. Looking to the future, there was the fear that deadlocks might emerge between the Houses of the Legislature, for the Legislative Council was endowed with substantial powers to block legislation from the

Legislative Assembly, and the Constitution provided no means of resolving a deadlock.

There were anxieties as to how religion would fare under the new broader franchise. The new Constitution provided for a government grant to churches, but this was not available to non-Christians such as the Jews, nor was it available to all of the Christian sects, for some were conscientiously opposed to accepting money from Government. This issue exacerbated tensions between the Anglicans and the non-episcopal Christian sects. It served as a wedge between those who wanted immediate and thorough reform of the Constitution and those who believed it should have a 'fair trial'. As Catholics and Anglicans both stood to gain from the grant, some members of these long-antagonistic churches discovered a common interest in keeping the clause that provided for the grant.

Amidst this hotbed of fervent aspirations and anxieties, Duffy announced his candidature for the Legislative Assembly. For the *Argus*, this raised alarming possibilities. Would the voters be easily swayed by demagogues or hoodwinked by unscrupulous candidates? Would interested parties use bribery and corruption to promote their candidate? On 27 October, the *Argus* reported Duffy's success at the election for the Western Victorian seat of Villiers-Heytesbury that covered Warrnambool and Belfast. A leading article in the *Argus* began with a warning about the 'clannish party spirit which sometimes induces Catholics and Irishmen to vote for unfit candidates'. In the next paragraph, the writer grudgingly welcomed Duffy's victory and acknowledged his high character and great abilities. It then snidely referred to his win as an addition to 'the many circumstances of self congratulation which have attended his entry into colonial public life'. Then the *Argus* cuttingly enquired:

> Will he be one of those to form unholy alliances and cliques
> – to become a party man, and, as such, to be the champion
> of his own adherents however despicable, and the assailant
> of his own opponents, however worthy? To such conclusions

must he come at last if he fall into the trap of attempting
either to lead or to join an 'Irish party'.[27]

Duffy, in his autobiography quoted a letter from his Irish friend Edward
Whitty who suggested that it was the new editor (Higinbotham) who
was responsible for this offensive article.[28] Given the similarities between
Mackinnon's blatantly sectarian treatment of Edward Curr in 1843 and the
Argus's treatment of Duffy, it seems likely that it was Mackinnon who was
responsible for the article.

In the weeks before the election of 1856, the *Argus* had published a
succession of editorials warning against 'the unspeakable evils of party'.[29] As
this was a characteristic view of Higinbotham's that he long maintained, it
is certainly possible that he was the author of this series, although the views
expressed were also typical of Wilson's *Argus* even before Higinbotham's
employment there.[30]

'Party' tactics

Higinbotham used the term 'party' in the usual sense of an organised
political grouping. But reflecting the contemporary Irish usage of his
day, the term, as he used it, was overlain with pejorative connotations
of partisan conduct or sectarianism. The explanation for Higinbotham's
intense feelings about 'party' and its link with sectarian animosity may lie
in political events in Ireland a decade earlier.

In a leading article in the *Argus* three months before the 1856 election,
an article written in a style that was recognisably Higinbotham's painted a
damning picture of pre-election activity in an unnamed English borough.
In this election, the two main parties, the Blues and the Reds, used bribery,
corruption and intimidation on a massive scale to secure success for their
respective candidates. Higinbotham described the liberal use of alcohol
to fuel ill-feeling between the Blues and the Reds, 'who scowl and "bite
their thumbs" at one another when they are sober and fall to fisticuffs and

bludgeon blows when they are drunk'. He spoke of an 'invisible dispenser of unlimited hospitalities', and described the operation of a system of bare-faced bribery:

> In the back parlour of the headquarters of the Blues sits a sallow attorney whose bank balance at the Blue Bank has been suddenly swelled to a magnificent figure by a draft from some anonymous prodigal in London. Through this back parlour passes a file of voters, each of whom enters the room singly, with an expression of cupidity in his eyes, and departs from the chamber with a grin of satisfaction upon his face, and certain medallion faces of his sovereign firmly inclosed in his tenacious palm.
>
> Strange to say, in the back parlour of the Reds, sits another sallow attorney who also gives a mysterious audience to the free and independent electors of the borough, and dismisses them from his presence one by one with a smirking smile of an uniform pattern stamped upon the countenance of all.

On the day of the election:

> Partisans ... drive frantically about the borough, in cabs and coaches, to bring up inebriate, doubtful or reluctant voters to the poll ... (or) to spirit away a wavering or hostile elector; to lock up a drunken opponent until the clock has struck the hour of four ...[31]

This description may seem far-fetched for an English borough, and indeed, Higinbotham's experience of English life had been largely limited to London. But if the scene depicted in the editorial is transposed to the city of Dublin, and if the party names 'Orange' and 'Green' are substituted for 'Reds' and 'Blues', it well describes the 1847 General Election in the seat of Dublin that took place during the time that Higinbotham was an undergraduate of Trinity College.

At that election, the famine was in its third year and the political atmosphere was charged to flashpoint. Two days previously the revered leader of the Repeal movement, Daniel O'Connell, had died while on a pilgrimage to Rome. The funeral was scheduled for the day following the election. Between 1843 and 1846, he had led the Repeal movement involving millions of Irish Catholics. He was imprisoned after being convicted of conspiracy in a trial that was later acknowledged to have been unfair. Imprisonment in harsh conditions weakened his health and may have hastened his death. There was a natural outpouring of sympathy, particularly from many Catholic electors who regarded O'Connell as the man who had liberated Catholics from the worst of the penal laws and brought hope to millions of his countrymen.

Higinbotham's experience of party politics at the time of the 1847 General Election in Dublin would have been a rude awakening for an idealistic lad. In the months preceding it, British politics was in a volatile state with the defection of the followers of Sir Robert Peel (known as 'the Peelites') from the Conservative Party, partly over Irish issues. As the famine intensified, the British Parliament passed the *Crime and Outrage Act*, which further restricted freedom of speech and assembly in Ireland. It imposed a curfew in some areas that were deemed particularly susceptible to rebellion.[32] The Act inflamed widespread resentment. Despite the famine and the heightened tensions, the Orange side of politics largely ignored the desperate conditions that motivated the widespread dissent in the lead-up to the election of 1847.[33] Sir William Verner made no reference in his election speech to the desperate plight of the famine-stricken population, but stressed his unswerving support for the *Act of Union*.[34]

A Repealer named John Reynolds unexpectedly nominated for election in the Conservative party stronghold of Dublin. The two sitting Conservative members, Edward Grogan and Sir William Gregory, were Protestants who had defied extremist Protestant opinion and subscribed their names to the Irish Party pledge. By this pledge they committed themselves, along with Smith O'Brien and over thirty other Irish Members of Parliament, to abstain from 'all considerations of party or prejudice' in order to present a united front, 'in the cause of our afflicted country'.[35] Gregory had voted for the repeal of the Corn Laws, and some therefore accused him of betraying the interests of the Protestant landowners.

A surprisingly strong show of popular support made it possible for Reynolds, though a man of modest means, to assemble the necessary funds – he estimated £2,500 – to mount his challenge. On 30 July 1847, Sir William Gregory delivered his election speech, emphasising that what Ireland needed was not Protestant Ascendancy but unity among Irishmen. The recently reinstated Orange Order took umbrage at this and announced that 'under no circumstances' would they vote for him.[36] They counted on there being no risk that the seat of Dublin would fall to a Repealer, but in using this tactic they overplayed their hand. A wave of sympathy for O'Connell assisted Reynolds' electoral chances, but at least as important was the high percentage of Conservative supporters who simply abstained from voting in view of the Orange Lodge's denunciations of both Protestant candidates. When the votes were counted, Reynolds had won the seat.[37]

The two Protestant candidates had been widely expected to win, but money from an external source and crafty tactics enabled Reynolds, though a political novice, to turn the unwise decision by the Conservative Party to his own advantage and to claim victory. Gregory was known to have been sympathetic to O'Connell and the famine victims. He was responsible for significant input into the famine relief laws that were belatedly passed, yet it was he who lost his seat to Reynolds. The lesson that Higinbotham is likely to have drawn from the 1847 election was that a corrupt party system, animated by extreme sectarianism, awash with money from unknown sources and employing shady practices, had ruined the chances of a candidate who had made a patriotic and principled stand in the interests of the whole country in its hour of greatest need. Throughout his life, Higinbotham denounced 'party' and urged the view that a representative must exercise his own judgement.

The depth of his conviction suggests that he may have been personally involved in assisting one or both of the two Conservative candidates for the seat. Edward Grogan was a Trinity graduate who had served as the Member for Dublin City since 1841. Higinbotham might well have met him during his undergraduate years through his membership of the committee of the College Historical Society, for Grogan maintained an interest in this Society. On at least one occasion during Higinbotham's time on the committee, the minutes show Grogan was in attendance.[38]

At the time of the 1856 election in Victoria, Higinbotham may have feared that Duffy and O'Shanassy would lead a large 'Irish party' using the tactics that had worked so well for Reynolds in Dublin in 1847. He was alarmed at the ease with which the Irish Catholics raised an electoral fund for Duffy. Two years earlier, in the *Melbourne Morning Herald*, he had denounced a similar outpouring of largesse when Smith O'Brien, the leader of the ill-fated 1848 Irish Uprising, had visited Victoria. The editorial attacks on 'party' in the lead-up to the 1856 election in Victoria may have been covert attacks on Duffy, for Higinbotham and Mackinnon might have been aware of Wilson's regard for Duffy. By contrast, the *Argus*'s attack on O'Shanassy was blatant, venomous and personal.[39] It is difficult to identify the writer with certainty. Morris denied that such a personal attack was in Higinbotham's nature.[40] Its harsh, judgemental tone was in keeping with that of the 'Where Are the Ninety?' series, which Duffy attributed to Wilson, but may have been written by Mackinnon. The campaign by the *Argus* against Duffy and O'Shanassy made little difference to the outcome of the election, for both Duffy and O'Shanassy were easily returned, but it may have further stoked the fires of sectarian enmity in Victoria and divided the reform movement. Higinbotham may have found that he had less editorial licence than he would have liked, for Mackinnon had determined that the *Argus* would be no friend of either religious tolerance or of political reform.

Winning the secret ballot

The fear that the Victorian election of 1856 would degenerate into an ugly 'party' contest did not eventuate. As editor of the *Argus*, Higinbotham wrote of his delight at seeing that responsible government had at last been inaugurated by the election of the new Parliament:

> Responsible Government spreads happiness and safety, wealth and comfort, cheerfulness, enjoyment and improvement amongst and throughout a people … cheers the path of the politician, and supports the men who strive after great reform under a thousand rebuffs, delays, miscarriages and mortifications.[41]

He noted that the vote was conducted 'in a quiet, business-like and unexcited manner'. With evident satisfaction, he commented that 'the unequivocal success of the experiment in Victoria' would advance the adoption of the secret ballot in Britain, as reformers had long striven for.[42]

While some of the credit for the 'unexcited' conduct of the first Victorian election may have been due to the newness of the process, and to restraint on the part of both the Irish Catholic and the Protestant church hierarchies, even more credit was due to the introduction of the secret ballot in the previous year. If a vote was secret it could not be bought, as the buyer had no means of ascertaining if the voter kept his side of the bargain. As soon as the goldfields candidates gained entry to the old Legislative Council in late 1855, the campaign for the introduction of the secret ballot began in earnest.

It was the barrister Henry Chapman who was chiefly responsible for the introduction of the secret ballot into Victoria. He had come to prominence when he and Butler Cole Aspinall had successfully defended John Joseph, the first of the prisoners to be arraigned for high treason following the battle at Eureka. Subsequently Chapman won the metropolitan seat of South Bourke after campaigning on the issue of responsible government. During Higinbotham's time as editor, the *Melbourne Morning Herald* enthusiastically supported Chapman's candidacy, detailing his long and distinguished service in London with the Philosophical Radical Party in its battles for Catholic emancipation, parliamentary reform, municipal reform and free trade.[43]

After gaining the seat, Chapman built a consensus amongst Opposition members that the secret ballot was 'the key to political progress'.[44] When Haines's Law Officers refused to draft the clauses regarding the secret ballot into the Electoral Bill, Chapman volunteered to do so.[45] He masterminded the detail in the Bill that overcame some of the perceived difficulties in designing a workable secret ballot system. On 19 December 1855, William Nicholson, the Member for the metropolitan seat of North Bourke, introduced the Electoral Reform Bill. Attorney-General William Stawell fiercely opposed it, arguing that a secret ballot would appear furtive and anti-British, undermine accountability and promote corruption.[46] Chief Secretary Haines declared that the Bill, if passed, would amount to a motion of no confidence in the Government. The Bill passed by a majority of seven, and the Government resigned.

The news was reported to Hotham who, although he was ill, immediately wrote a dispatch to the Secretary of State for the Colonies. In it he paid tribute to William Haines whom he described as 'an able assistant and above all, a gentleman', without whom he could never have coped.[47] He authorised William Nicholson to form a new ministry. His final vexation occurred on 27 December when Nicholson informed him that he was unable to form a new ministry. Hotham's biographer, Shirley Roberts, notes that 'the news distressed Hotham greatly, but he was now too ill to be able to take any action on the matter'.[48] Three days later, his condition deteriorated, he lapsed into a coma and died on the last day of 1855.

The secret ballot was, as Chapman argued, the essential first step in the process of democratising the political system of the Colony. It was not supported by either of the long-standing Opposition members, O'Shanassy and Fawkner. Its success was a tribute to the combined efforts of the mining population and their representatives in the old Legislative Council working with the urban reformers and the Philosophical Radicals in both the legislature and the press.

10

METAMORPHOSIS

The historian Geoffrey Serle observed of George Higinbotham that 'he provides the unusual example of the man who becomes more radical over the years'.[1] Jarlath Ronayne, in his book about the influence of Trinity graduates in early Victoria, described Higinbotham as 'the most radical and the most complex of all the men educated at Trinity College who held the stage in Victoria'.[2] The complexity was especially apparent in the radical yet conservative nature of his political views. Like many of his contemporaries in Victoria, Higinbotham was deeply loyal to the monarchy and intensely respectful of the rule of law and Parliament. But as the battle at Eureka and subsequent political instability showed, disenchantment was growing with the workings of these institutions in Victoria. There was a widespread aspiration for more equitable laws and for a modern political system that better reflected the aspirations of the population. What was distinctive about Higinbotham's staunch support for the traditional institutions was his insistence that they could be and must be fully consistent with advanced democratic principles and full responsible government.

It is during his years as editor of the *Argus* that we see Higinbotham at his most conservative. Partly this was because the ethos of the *Argus* was more conservative than that of Michie's *Melbourne Morning Herald* when he joined it in 1854. It was also because he feared the prospect of a powerful Government led by Catholics. Early in the life of the first Parliament, Charles Gavan Duffy and John O'Shanassy worked together as a united team. Higinbotham's delight in seeing the new Parliament was tempered by the ingrained Irish Protestant fear of a Catholic majority with powerful leadership. He need not have worried, for before long the threat abated when a bitter rivalry grew between O'Shanassy and Duffy.

Victoria's first Parliament

Charles Gavan Duffy described the atmosphere on the day that Victoria's first Parliament under the new Constitution met:

> The day was proclaimed a holiday. The soldiers of the 41st Regiment, the Volunteer Artillery, and Rifles paraded; flags ... were drawn out. Flags and banners streamed the houses in the line of procession, bands enlivened the scene. The corporation, headed by the Mayor, the Judges in their robes, the Town Councillors in their uniforms, the Foreign Consuls looking as like ambassadors as they could contrive to do, and the Governor ... escorted by volunteer cavalry, arrived at a Chamber crowded with ladies.[3]

Victoria's long-awaited new Parliament had assembled. Geoffrey Serle remarks on the array of professional talent in the new Parliament, for among the new members there were doctors, lawyers, miners, wholesale traders and squatters. William Stawell, William Haines, John Foster and Hugh Childers, the Ministers from the previous Government, were returned. Duffy attributed their support to 'the squatters who relied upon them to protect their tenure of the public lands, and the bankers who thought they were the only bulwark against a democratic-digger administration'. In fact the diggers were not well represented in the Legislative Assembly, partly because of the property qualification and partly because of the unfair electoral boundaries that left the goldfields under-represented. As Serle observed, 'a squatter's vote was worth five times a Melbourne resident's and seven times a digger's'.[4] The sectarian partisan effect was less marked than

Higinbotham feared, but he may have viewed this as a mixed blessing. Duffy proudly reported to a friend: 'they fought for me like lions in the name of the poor old country … Protestants as well as Catholics'.[5]

Even before his election, Duffy had made his presence felt in the old Legislative Council. His visit to St Patrick's Hall coincided with the introduction of a Bill to regulate the admission of barristers. The Bill included the requirement for every applicant to the Bar to take the Oath of Supremacy. For over a century, Irish and English Catholics had refused to take the oath in the form prescribed in the Bill, and in consequence were disqualified from practice. Duffy took credit for the fact that, by drawing the attention of members to the significance of the requirement, he managed to have the Bill withdrawn.[6]

As soon as he was elected, Duffy seized the reform initiative. He proposed a motion from the Opposition benches to abolish the property qualification for members of the Assembly. He argued that possession of landed property was not required for candidates to the House of Commons, and pointed out that in Victoria it debarred many competent and deserving candidates from seeking office. He claimed credit for having been 'the first to lead the Opposition to victory against the Government, and the first to get a Bill carried through all its stages'.[7] In January 1857, he successfully proposed the appointment of a Select Committee to consider the question of federation of the Australian colonies. From his experience in the House of Commons, Duffy also found himself in a position to advise on British parliamentary procedure, for under the new Constitution, British standing orders were to apply until local ones were adopted. But his abundant advice was sometimes resented. In a rare apologetic note in his autobiography, he admitted that he was sometimes 'too peremptory and brusque'.[8]

William Haines, the former Chief Secretary, formed the first ministry, but it was to be short-lived. Stawell suggested to the serving Chief Justice, Sir William a'Beckett, that the time had come for him to stand down.[9] In December 1856, a'Beckett announced to the ministry that he wished to resign. Stawell then succeeded him as Chief Justice. Childers left the Colony expecting to take up the position of Victorian Agent-General in

London. Under a plan developed by the Assembly, he would have had great influence over immigration policy and loan negotiations for railway works. Unfortunately, the Legislative Council did not approve the plan and Childers did not receive the appointment.[10] The ministry, which had relied heavily upon Stawell's advice, quickly fell.[11]

In March 1857, O'Shanassy approached a number of experienced members of the former Legislative Council with a view to forming a new ministry to be led by Duffy and himself. One can only imagine the dismay and recriminations that must have taken place behind closed doors amongst the Irish Protestant community in Melbourne as they contemplated the political vacuum caused by the departure of Stawell and Childers, and the prospect of a new Government to be led by O'Shanassy and Duffy. An editorial in the *Argus* suggested that Stawell and Childers had been 'driven into retirement'. It condemned the vote of no confidence that had brought down the Government as a *'coup d'état'*, and argued that it would be 'unquestionably for the worse'. The writer was probably Higinbotham, for the powerful word picture drawn was typical of his style. He scolded:

> You have no right to remove your best men from private
> pursuits, and get them to devote themselves, body and mind,
> to the study of public business, – to be kicked over like
> ninepins for the amusement of parliamentary schoolboys. It
> is not by such treatment that the services of your best men
> can be secured. It is by just such treatment that they are
> driven into retirement, and that the hungry and unprincipled
> adventurer is left sole master of the situation.[12]

Duffy would later complain that throughout Higinbotham's time as editor the stance of the *Argus* was 'pro-Government' and 'shamefully unfair' in its coverage of events.[13] This was true, but after Higinbotham's time as editor, worse was to follow.

O'Shanassy invited a number of members of the Legislative Assembly to join his ministry but received repeated rebuffs. As Duffy commented,

'Nobody had ever seen Irish Catholics in Cabinet under the British Crown … and they were not prepared to countenance so startling a novelty'.[14] In an effort to include experienced members from the former Government, O'Shanassy invited John Foster, the former Colonial Secretary, to join his ministry. Michie, who had assisted O'Shanassy to bring down the Haines ministry, refused to join the new ministry because it included John Foster.[15] Dr John Owens also conveyed the objections of the goldfields representatives to the inclusion of Foster, whom they regarded as 'so justly detested by the miners for his past policy'.[16] On 29 April 1857, this new ministry resigned after only fifty days in office, with little accomplished. Indeed, the instability continued during the life of the first two Parliaments, for there were seven ministries between December 1856 and December 1861. As Duffy observed in his autobiography, 'public life was often a perpetual guerrilla warfare of surprises, ambuscades, plots and single combats'.[17]

The influence of Thomas Higinbotham

Higinbotham's apparent retreat into conservatism at this stage of his life may have been further reinforced by the arrival in Melbourne of his older brother Thomas, in late 1857. The two brothers had very different childhoods. In the Higinbotham family there were eight siblings, of whom George was the youngest. Thomas, born in 1819, was the fourth child. During his early childhood, his parents, Henry and Sarah, had lived a genteel life in Dublin, where Henry operated a successful business as a general trader. Henry had embarked upon a particularly ambitious business venture that required share capital, but in 1826, a few months before the birth of George, the venture had failed disastrously.[18] In an effort to save the situation, Henry embarked upon financial measures of questionable propriety, but to no avail. The failure brought serious financial losses to its shareholders, and debt and disgrace upon Henry Higinbotham and his family.[19]

Over the next three years, the lease on the family home was sold, Henry's business was sold, the lease on the Higinbotham property in

County Cavan was sold. Henry's name was removed from the official listing of nobility and gentry of Dublin and from the list of merchants and traders.[20] At some point it seems likely that husband and wife separated, for they gave different addresses, but both stayed in the environs of Dublin for some years.[21] Following the financial debacle, Sarah's family, the Wilsons, played a significant role in supporting the family financially, and they may have provided significant psychological support as well.[22] Morris, in his biography, reports that George Higinbotham's early schooling (unlike that of his brother Thomas) took place 'at home'. During these years, Sarah and her young son may have been drawn into the orbit of the Wilsons, for even after the sale of the lease on their home, they did not live far apart, and the two families had children close in age. Sarah's brother, Thomas Wilson, was a prominent member and benefactor of the Strand Street Unitarian Congregation. Sarah may have reverted to attending Unitarian services with her brother and his family, possibly taking George with her.

As he matured, George Higinbotham would have learned that this Unitarian Church congregation valued freedom of religious expression highly, and advocated the use of reason in interpreting the scriptures. It also promoted liberality in political ideas. The French and American Revolutions were upheld as beacons of progress. Since the time of Cromwell, when the congregation had met in private homes, it had welcomed leading liberal thinkers in religion and politics from England, Scotland, France and America.[23] Among the leading figures associated with this church were Francis Hutcheson and Thomas Paine, whose writing influenced the American Declaration of Independence; Archibald Hamilton Rowan, a Scottish aristocrat who led a march through Dublin to commemorate the first anniversary of the French Revolution; Dr William Drennan, who conceived the plan for a secret society of radical reformers that became the Irish Volunteers; Robert Emmet, who led the 1803 Uprising in Ireland; George Brown, who steered the anti-slavery legislation through the Pennsylvania State legislature, and John Toland and Joseph Priestley, who advocated the emancipation of the Jews. George Higinbotham would later espouse many of these liberal values. As an intelligent boy, conscious that within this congregation, his mother's family were prominent and respected people, he may have taken these reformers as role models for himself.

When George attended the Royal School in Dungannon for his secondary education, it seems that the Verner side of the family exerted a strong countervailing influence. Loyalty to the sovereign and the Anglican Church, as well as pride in Britain's military victories were upheld as cardinal virtues. Rebellion was regarded with horror. But George, unlike his brother Thomas, had been exposed to liberal ideas at a formative time. Years later, after much thought and study, he developed his own philosophy, drawing upon the contrasting worlds of Orange conservatism and Unitarian liberalism. From time to time he experienced the pull of one world more strongly than the other.

Thomas, being six years older than George, had a more privileged early childhood. He was already attending school when the family's fortunes collapsed, and he may not have spent so much time during his formative years in the company of his mother and the Wilson family. Unlike George, Thomas's vocational training was in engineering. His views as an adult were more typical of the conservative Irish Protestant of his day. Thomas developed great expertise in railway technology at the height of railway expansion in Britain. He served in senior executive positions on several major British railway projects. On arrival in Melbourne, he was appointed Chief Engineer of Roads and Bridges in the Colony. Thomas was unmarried and lived with George and Margaret in their house at Emerald Hill. By 1861 he was Engineer-in-Chief of the Victorian Railways.

In late 1860, Thomas and George combined their savings and purchased a large beachfront block at Brighton. Here Thomas designed and built a new house and established a garden. George Higinbotham's son-in-law, Edward Morris, who was a frequent visitor to the house, recorded:

> The house was built in villa fashion, with a single floor and a broad verandah running round three sides. A lawn with openings through tea-tree scrub separated the house from the beach, and a beautiful avenue of trees connected it with

the road, by the side of which there was a large and pleasant garden.[24]

The historian Susan Priestley records that on the other side of the road, St Kilda Street, there was a ten-acre paddock where several sheds and a dairy were located. Here the Higinbothams kept cows, horses and ponies. She notes that there was an orchard in which 'prolific varieties of Kentish apples' were grown, perhaps reflecting Margaret's upbringing in the Kentish countryside.[25] Thomas, George, Margaret and the infant Edith Sarah, who was born in 1859, moved into the house. The remainder of George and Margaret's children were born in this house: Alice Mary in 1863, George Robert in 1865, Edward in 1869, Maud in 1870, and Ethel, who died in infancy, in 1872.[26]

This was to remain George and Margaret's home until 1887 (seven years after the death of Thomas), when they moved to the inner-city suburb of South Yarra. Morris records that during the twenty-three years that the brothers spent together, 'the colony was distracted by the fiercest party feeling on political questions, and the sympathies of the brothers were enlisted on opposite sides'.[27] Yet he denies that this ever caused 'the slightest ruffle' in their friendship.

The brothers did not move in the same social circle. In 1864 Thomas was elected to the Melbourne Club. In 1839 an older second cousin of the Higinbotham brothers, named William Verner, had been its first president.[28] This Club was the preserve of the wealthiest and most influential men of Melbourne society. In order to join the Club, an applicant for membership first had to be elected by the members, and then to pay an entrance fee of forty guineas (£42). The English barrister Stanley Leighton, who visited the Colony in 1868, had attributed George Higinbotham's absence from the Melbourne Club to defensiveness about Margaret Higinbotham's low social status.[29] Though Leighton's remarks need to be seen in the context of his anger at being rebuffed for a political appointment that he hoped for, there may have been a grain of truth in his accusation that Higinbotham avoided society. Morris explained that George Higinbotham 'never went into society' because Edward Wilson advised him not to do so as editor. He adds that the advice was 'in itself palatable' to George Higinbotham, who afterwards found the habit of utmost value during his political life.[30]

Morris provides a hint regarding one particular issue that divided the brothers. He reveals that Thomas left his entire estate to George's family in his will, along with a request that the family name be changed to 'Verner', and he notes that George declined this request.[31] This suggests that George did not share Thomas's admiration for the Verner family. At some point he had rejected the extreme sectarian values that Sir William Verner upheld, but Thomas may not have done so. The daily presence of Thomas in the home must have acted as a constant reminder to George of the views and expectations of the conservative members of the Irish Protestant community.

Thomas served as the Engineer-in-Chief of the Victorian Railways for nearly two decades, and was responsible for the design, construction and superintendence of all the Victorian lines not already under construction before his arrival. As such he was responsible for meeting budgets for the expenditure of millions of pounds of loan money borrowed on public credit. It is likely that this responsibility influenced his perspective on the industrial relations conflicts of his day, and George may have seen some of these issues, initially at least, through his brother's eyes.

Higinbotham and the unemployed

During Higinbotham's time at the *Argus*, Victoria underwent a period of fundamental economic readjustment as the easily accessible gold veins became exhausted. Those who had flocked to the goldfields seeking a life of independence and self-sufficiency faced the inevitability of looking for employment to survive. The shift from self-employment to waged employment required a transition during which capital could be formed and enterprises established. Many of the diggers resented the formation of companies to invest capital in machinery for gold extraction via quartz crushing, for they feared a return to the odious 'master and servant' labour relationships of Britain. The cost of labour in Victoria had risen sharply during the gold rushes, but as the labour market became saturated, jobs with good wages became scarce, and the number of unemployed workers escalated. At first the development of agriculture and industry, and the building of roads, wharves, bridges and public buildings masked these effects. Improved communications and more produce also brought a reduction in the cost of living. However, these economic advances were insufficient to provide employment for the many thousands who had returned from the goldfields, and the thousands of new migrants who continued to arrive. Serle commented:

> Melbourne saw processions of a thousand or more unemployed men carrying placards and shouting slogans – 'We want bread! Give us work!' – and sending deputations to the government … Beggars – an unwelcome feature of the old world – became part of the everyday scene.[32]

Industrial conflict, strikes, deputations and organised protests multiplied. In some industries employers who were determined to reduce wages and conditions resorted to importing 'scab' labour and to other exploitative measures. The workers formed unions and strove to maintain or improve their wages and conditions.[33]

The extent of public frustration over the issue of land reform grew. At a series of public mass meetings in 1857, delegates were elected to a mass organisation known as the Land Convention, which developed and advocated a platform of radical land reform policies. The members proclaimed their demands in frequent public demonstrations in order to maintain pressure on the Government to prioritise land reform. The historian Stuart Macintyre describes their method:

> Their meeting place was a hotel opposite Parliament House, set up to resemble a legislative chamber with its banner (a

flash of lightning, inscribed *vox populi* passing through a Southern Cross) hung above the speaker's chair (which was occupied by the radical lawyer Wilson Gray). Their amphitheatre was the Eastern Market, a row of long, open arcades half way down the hill on the site now occupied by the Southern Cross hotel, where leading members harangued the crowds that congregated in flickering torchlight at the end of the working day.[34]

As the numbers of unemployed grew, the *Argus* under Higinbotham at first denied the scale of the problem, insisting that it was a seasonal effect that would soon right itself. At a meeting of 2,000 unemployed men in mid-August 1857, the *Argus* was repeatedly attacked for having painted a rosy picture of employment prospects to British readers. It was said that this false information had induced many to emigrate, only to be bitterly disappointed on arrival.[35] To his credit, Higinbotham published full reports of these speeches but, as the attacks on the *Argus* continued, he denounced the leader of them as a 'charlatan' and refused to report his speeches any further.[36]

In 1857, Higinbotham's colleague at the *Argus*, Moses Wilson Gray, was elected as the president of the Land Convention. At about the same time, Gray was dismissed from the *Argus*. Higinbotham defended him in an editorial. While critical of the utopianism of the Land Convention, and of its claims to represent public opinion more accurately than the Legislative Assembly did, Higinbotham conceded that 'they have it in their power … to achieve a great deal of good'.[37] He argued that although the Convention included some 'mere scamps and vaporers', it also included men 'well known to command respect for any body they join'. He singled out their president, Moses Wilson Gray, 'a reformer with whom we are frequently compelled to disagree, but of whose earnestness and sincerity we never have had a doubt'.[38]

A compromise over electoral reform

Geoffrey Serle noted that, from 1857 onwards, 'almost all important reforms were blocked. The Assembly was powerless.'[39] Higinbotham suspected that the Legislative Council was deliberately destabilising Governments in order to defeat attempts at electoral reform, with the aim of delaying the passage of a land reform act. He wrote to Chapman:

> I believe this to be the design of the squatters … they hope by breaking up the Government to delay or defeat the Reform Bills, and thus to postpone the evil day … I will do all I can to maintain the Government in office and to defeat what seems to me to be an unprincipled conspiracy.[40]

The Government's strategy was to prioritise electoral reform in order to pave the way for land reform. In 1858, O'Shanassy's Government re-introduced the Electoral Reform Bill that had previously been rejected by the Council. Anticipating another rejection, the Government capitulated and accepted significant dilution of its reform proposals. Serle noted:

> Higinbotham accepted the coup with no complaint, claimed that the Bill was 'greatly improved', suppressed reports of the howl of execration from the goldfields, and finally wrote: 'We have established perfect political equality. Every man is secured in the enjoyment of his political rights.'[41]

Serle struggled to reconcile Higinbotham's apparent capitulation to his known advocacy of democracy. He commented:

> For one who had known the gross discrepancies in the value of the votes in 1856, it must have seemed a great achievement to raise the value of the individual digger's vote to more than half that of the rest of the community. Yet such recognition

of necessity cannot be squared with his reputation for integrity.[42]

Higinbotham may have justified the compromise to his conscience as a tactical retreat in order to advance the land reform program on which the livelihoods of thousands of aspiring farmers depended.

By December 1857, Higinbotham had ceased to deny the scale of the unemployment problem. He urged the Government to create public works and to provide assistance to the unemployed to relocate to areas where work was available.[43] By September 1858, he also recognised that employers in some industries were taking advantage of the glut of labour to reduce wages and conditions. He expressed sympathy for the strikers on the Geelong–Ballarat railway:

> A few contractors ... become wealthy at the expense of their workmen, a portion of whose just claims is altogether repudiated, and whose fairly earned wages are wrongfully withheld.[44]

He called for a Government Inquiry, or even for the works to be stopped. In this, as in other editorials on the subject, Higinbotham expounded first one case and then the converse. Typically, after conceding some justification to each contention, he concluded with a compromise position that he thought best represented the public interest. Reading such editorials, it is not hard to imagine that an after-dinner conversation on a topical issue between George and Thomas Higinbotham may sometimes have provided the material for an editorial the following day.

Again, it may have been their different experiences of life that led to the differences in outlook between the two brothers. As a student at Trinity College during the famine years, George Higinbotham would have travelled regularly through Dublin streets crowded with thousands of famine-ravaged men, women and children who were desperately seeking alms, work, shelter, or passages on ships. Higinbotham was always sensitive to human suffering. His friend James Smith said of him:

> A tale of wrong stirred him to the quick, a narrative of injustice roused a fierce feeling of indignation within him; and when his sympathies were excited, he displayed an almost womanly tenderness of emotion.[45]

The increasing distress and destitution in Melbourne between 1857 and 1861 may have revived painful memories of the tragic scenes that he had witnessed in Dublin a decade earlier. Thomas, who had moved to England in 1839, had been spared this direct and daily confrontation with profound human misery during the famine years in Ireland.

By December 1858, Higinbotham had become seriously concerned at the scale of the unemployment problem. He regretted his earlier judgemental editorials. In a leading article, he announced:

> Hitherto it has generally been inferred that those who have made the Post Office verandah their nightly lair belonged to the disreputable class of 'loafers', and that the vagabond life they led was less a matter of necessity than of choice. We now learn with mingled feelings of satisfaction and regret that this hypothesis is at variance with fact … The painful fact of the present existence of much actual and severe destitution must be dealt with and cannot brook delay.[46]

He repeated the call for the Government to provide food and shelter in the short term, along with public works, until the longer-term remedies were available. As he saw it, the long-term solution to the plight of the unemployed would come with the issuing of contracts for major railway works, and the availability of land for agriculture at an affordable price. The Land Bill that had been introduced by the Haines Government in 1857 passed the Legislative Assembly only to be rejected in its entirety by the Legislative Council. Although Higinbotham had criticised the Bill, he had hoped that, with some improvements, the Council would accept it. He was aghast at the peremptory manner in which the Legislative Council rejected it at the outset. He described the rejection as 'the fruit of nine months of legislation by the Assembly blighted in a single night by the breath of the five thousand pounders'. He particularly blamed the Government leader in the Council, the squatter William Mitchell, for this 'ruinous waste' of the Assembly's time.[47]

Although he had earlier warned against workers having unrealistic expectations, by late 1858 he wrote positively about the 'eight-hour movement'.[48] This movement had been formed two years earlier with the aim of reducing the hours of work to a maximum of eight hours per day, and already it had achieved some successes in the building trades, and amongst quarrymen, saddlers and harness-makers.[49] Prominent in the eight-hour movement was Dr Thomas Embling, who had chaired a public meeting in Melbourne in December 1854 that expressed support for the miners at Eureka.[50] It was clear that Higinbotham's conservatism was under challenge, but his liberal principles were put to a further crucial test.

Dispute with Wilson

Following the short-lived O'Shanassy Government, a Government led by William Haines took office at the end of April 1857. Haines introduced three Bills to reform the *Electoral Act* by shortening the duration of Parliaments from five years to three, increasing the number of Members of Parliament, and altering the electoral boundaries to make the numbers represented in each seat more equal. Higinbotham enthusiastically supported these democratic reforms but Edward Wilson was adamantly opposed to them. In a lengthy 'Letter from Europe' addressed to the editor of the *Argus*, he argued that 'representation upon the population basis leads inevitably to monopoly of power … class legislation and intolerable tyranny'.[51] In place of representation on the basis of population, Wilson advocated that 'the great principal interests' comprising landowners, squatters, agriculturalists, miners, merchants, manufacturers, house owners and labourers should each have 'six or eight members' in the House. This, he believed, would constitute 'true democracy' rather than mere 'government by crowd'.

In line with the position adopted by Sir William Molesworth and other Philosophical Radicals, such as Henry Chapman and Archibald Michie, Higinbotham was opposed to such a proposition. He had come to Victoria fired with democratic ideals. Like Molesworth, he believed that the role of the press was to guide the formation of loyal democracies in the colonies of the British Empire. He had been bitterly disappointed with the final form of the Constitution of 1855, but had pinned his hopes on reforms such as the current Haines Electoral Reform Bills. In May of the previous year, Wilson had written a similar letter, and Higinbotham had written an eloquent rebuttal:

> We hold that the great end of all electoral systems is as far as possible, to secure justice and good government to every individual; that no amount of wealth gives anyone an extra claim to these matters; that a community is not a commercial company in which a man should have a voice potential in proportion to the number of shares he is able to buy ... that all men who live in a country have as large an interest in its good government and as equal a stake in it, that their mere pecuniary possessions are as dust in the balance.[52]

Wilson was unmoved by Higinbotham's rejoinder. The intent of this new letter was clearly that, as proprietor, he was instructing his editor to oppose this key principle of the Reform Bills. Higinbotham saw that his position as editor hung in the balance but he would not assist in destabilising the Haines Government, nor would he be deterred from guiding the Colony towards democracy. He published Wilson's letter, but in the adjacent column he expounded a lengthy rejection of Wilson's view. He chided:

> It is startling to find a man with all the experience and acuteness
> that Mr Wilson possesses propounding views like these.[53]

This exchange portended the end of Higinbotham's employment as editor of the *Argus* in the following year. Four days after the publication of his letter in the *Argus*, Edward Wilson wrote to Henry Parkes, the editor of the *Sydney Morning Herald,* complaining about the influence of 'mobs' in Victorian politics. He wrote:

> It is a bitter pill for me and particularly so as the *Argus* is an aider and abettor. Higinbotham is a most estimable man, but occasionally wild in his opinions and stubborn in adhering to them.[54]

Morris noted in his biography that 'Mr Higinbotham would brook no interference in his work as editor'.[55] In fact Higinbotham's hand may not have been as free as Morris believed. Compared with the political stance of his earlier writings for the *Melbourne Morning Herald* and his later speeches in the Parliament, many of the *Argus* editorials seem uncharacteristically conservative. This suggests that, as editor of the *Argus*, he was significantly constrained by the expectations of the proprietors. It seems to have been at the time of this dispute over the principles of representation that Higinbotham's 'stubbornness' became intolerable to Wilson. David Blair and Wilson Gray had left their employment at the *Argus* after finding themselves ideologically opposed to the views of the proprietors. Now it was the turn of Higinbotham. In 1859, following a frank but civil exchange with Wilson, Higinbotham resigned his position as editor and applied himself more fully to his career at the Bar.

Nicholson's Land Bill

In late October 1859, William Nicholson became the new Chief Secretary. In January 1860, his Minister, James Service, the President of the Board of Land and Works, introduced a new Land Bill. It conformed to a number of the principles that the Land Convention advocated, although it failed to address the thorny issue of the squatting tenure. After lengthy discussion and several amendments, the Bill passed the Legislative Assembly with a majority of 44. In May 1860, the Bill was considered in the Legislative Council. There it was stripped of most of the provisions for the key reforms that it was intended to introduce.[56] Rather than accept the amendments, the ministry resigned, and the Land Convention members applauded it for its principled stand. The Governor attempted to find a new ministry, but failing to do so, he urged Nicholson to return to office and to proceed with the Land Bill.[57] To the fury of many members of the Land Convention who feared a complete capitulation on land reform, Nicholson agreed.

On 28 August at about 5 p.m., 500 people assembled outside the Parliament building. They followed the tradition established by the Bendigo miners in 1853 of wearing red ribbons as a symbol of their solidarity. They attempted to enter the building but were prevented. During the dinner break, Moses Wilson Gray emerged from the Parliament and led the crowd away to the Eastern Market where he addressed them. He then returned to the Parliament. However, many of the protesters followed him back to the Parliament. It is unclear how the violence began, but at some point protesters threw stones at the windows. The police used their truncheons, and some in the crowd threw stones at the police. About fourteen injured police officers and one reporter were taken inside to the parliamentary Smokers' Room, which became a temporary hospital. Police reinforcements arrived and charged the crowd again, beating them with batons. Most of the protesters dispersed, but some remained. The Mayor arrived and read the *Riot Act*. It took until 11 p.m. for the area to be completely cleared so that the parliamentarians could leave the building safely.[58]

Serle commented that 'the left had overplayed its hand for a strong public and parliamentary reaction followed'.[59] He argues that this made it easier for Nicholson to proceed with the much-mutilated Land Bill, and in mid-September 1860 it was enacted. The Legislative Council had triumphed, and the hopes of thousands of families to buy land for a farm at an affordable price were dashed.

Since 1856 when he had first become editor of the *Argus*, Higinbotham had witnessed a number of reforms. The first of these was the introduction of the secret ballot under the former Legislative Council. In 1857, he had witnessed the concession of manhood suffrage for Assembly elections (though plural voting provisions remained). In 1858, triennial Parliaments replaced the original five-year terms. However, the reform process had stalled. The sticking point had been the principle of 'one vote, one value', which the Legislative Council had firmly rejected, and which was not fully obtained in Victoria until 1950.[60] Higinbotham had closely observed the political process to date, and well understood where the obstacles to progress lay. The time had arrived for him to become an active participant.

Higinbotham enters the Legislative Assembly

In May 1861 the Treasurer, Charles Hotson Ebden, the Member for Brighton, resigned his seat. Higinbotham seized the opportunity to represent the constituency at the by-election. The principal issues on which he stood were: universal suffrage, public education, land reform, support for strong and stable Government, and state aid to religion.[61] He told the electors of Brighton that the two highest priorities were land reform and public education. He insisted that 'every individual in a free country who contributes to the taxes of the State ought to enjoy a vote in the selection of those who legislate for the State'. He opposed the frequent changes of Government of recent years, arguing that 'they have so exasperated the minds of members of Parliament against one another, and so distracted their attention from the business of legislation, that legislation in the House of Assembly is at the present time … at a stand-still'.[62]

On 17 May he was sworn in at the table of the Legislative Assembly. Morris noted:

> The honourable and learned member was warmly congratulated by the occupants of the Treasury benches,

including the Chief Secretary (Richard Heales), the Attorney General (Richard Ireland) and Messrs Grant and Brooke. He then took his seat below the gangway on the Opposition side of the House.

The position in which he chose to sit indicated his political stance. The seats in the Legislative Assembly were arranged as three sides of a square. The Government sat on one side facing their Opposition, while the unaligned members sat on the third side known as 'the corner'. From time to time the unaligned members signalled a change in their support for a Government by moving closer to or further from its side of 'the corner'.

It was a particularly anarchic period in colonial politics. The Government of Richard Heales was in the last months of its life. It was the sixth ministry to hold office in the five years since the inauguration of the new Constitution. As political parties were yet to develop, personalities and factions formed an ever-changing kaleidoscope of short-lived alliances in the period. Morris noted that Higinbotham soon became noted for 'the persuasiveness of his speech and the fire of his oratory'.[63] He included a comment from a letter written about the new member that foreshadowed his future impact on the Legislative Assembly:

His high character and talent are a phenomenon in the House; he holds the Ministry in awe. I do not think they like him, but they fear him – which is better; and the Opposition respect him, which they do not any other member of the governing party.[64]

11

THE MEMBER FOR BRIGHTON

At the age of thirty-five, Higinbotham was now in his second career – that of parliamentarian – in which he was to make his most significant and memorable contributions to Victorian history. At the outset, he was determined to be neither a supporter of the Government nor of the Opposition, but his own man. Yet his reputation had preceded him, and it was the liberal members James Macpherson Grant and Richard Heales who welcomed him warmly into the Legislative Assembly. Another who did so was John Henry Brooke, who represented Geelong. In November 1860, Brooke had been appointed President of the Board of Land and Works, and Crown Lands Commissioner. A radical democrat with strong links to the Land Convention, Brooke discovered an exploitable gap in the existing *Land Act* under which he began issuing annual 'occupational licenses' for agricultural settlement. This daring move – though later challenged in court and disallowed – alarmed the Council, and increased the Government's popularity with electors at the following general election of 1861.[1] To the alarm of many conservatives, the Government won overwhelming support on the goldfields, and eight activists from the Eureka period were returned, five of whom became Ministers in the new Government.

Higinbotham's inauguration as a member occurred only seven weeks before the scheduled end of the parliamentary session. In the seat of Brighton, the general election of 1861 was fiercely contested. Because of Higinbotham's declared independence from either side of the political divide, both sides contested his candidacy. The Opposition candidate at that election was William Adams Brodribb, a New South Wales squatter who had recently retired to Melbourne. During his nine months in the Legislative Assembly, Brodribb had opposed moves to reduce both the property qualifications and the terms of office of Legislative Councillors, and he had opposed a proposal for payment of Members of Parliament.[2] In the electorate, 710 votes were cast and Brodribb defeated Higinbotham by 65. However, in early 1862 he resigned the seat to take his family on a trip to Britain, thereby causing a second by-election for the seat of Brighton. Once again, Higinbotham stood for election for the seat of Brighton.

The Government candidate was fifty-three-year-old John Goulson Burtt, a British Chartist. As a twenty-one-year-old he had accompanied the leading Chartist, Thomas Attwood, to the House of Commons in 1839 to present the great petition signed by 1,280,000 people urging wide-ranging political reform. After settling in Victoria in 1858, Burtt prominently supported the Eight-Hour movement. In later years Higinbotham paid tribute to his former opponent as a man of unsurpassed 'liberal instincts' and 'fearless character'.[3] The fundamental policies on which Higinbotham campaigned at this election were support for stable government, and land reform. He told the electors of Brighton:

> He believed that the common sense of the majority of the people in this colony was decidedly opposed to the system which had hitherto prevailed, viz, that of turning out government after government at intervals of about fourteen months.[4]

On land reform, Higinbotham was more cautious. The most contentious issue of the day was the Government's Land Bill. It was the product of many months of work by Charles Gavan Duffy, who had carefully studied and compared the land systems of the British Isles and of the United States. The legislation was designed to make ten million acres (four million hectares) of land available for purchase by selectors for agriculture and housing. The Bill divided Victoria into thirty-seven counties, and each of these was surveyed into 2,914 parishes. The Act established a mechanism for surveying, advertising and recording the sale of land from the Crown to selectors. As a compromise, it proposed to grant the squatters ten years of further occupation of their existing runs. Principally because of this last provision, Higinbotham did not commit himself to support the third reading of the Government's Land Bill.[5] The *Argus* reported his speech to the electors:

> He believed that part of the Land Bill that related to agricultural settlement contained many excellent provisions. (Cheers). There was, however, another part of it from which he entirely dissented, viz., those clauses that gave the squatter a continuance of tenure for ten years longer. (Applause. A voice – 'we must have the little man in!' and cheers.)[6]

In his speech to the electors of Brighton, Higinbotham made a reference to his having displeased a conservative group known as the Victorian Association. He described it as 'a clandestine political association' that worked to overturn governments and thereby prevent legislation from enactment.[7] Higinbotham's opponent at the 1862 by-election was William John Clarke, a pastoralist, philanthropist and member of the Melbourne Club who later built the mansion Rupertswood at Sunbury.[8] This time 690 votes were cast and Higinbotham won the seat by 98.

In June 1862, during his first months as a member of the Legislative Assembly, Higinbotham supported Richard Heales' *Common Schools Act*. Until the passage of this Act there had been two systems: the National System of Government-owned schools and the Denominational System of schools owned and operated by the various religious denominations. The latter received some government aid, and both systems competed for a limited amount of government funding. The distribution of schools favoured towns over country areas, and the mechanisms for accountability for government funding were inadequate. The *Common Schools Act* was designed to create a single Board with representatives of the various denominations. The Board members were expected to devise and apply an agreed formula for meeting the educational needs of all the Colony's children, and of apportioning government aid according to this formula, and ensuring accountability for its use. The Catholic Church and Anglican Church opposed the Bill through their leading representatives, but as the current system was wasteful and failing thousands of children, the Act was carried.

On 14 November 1862, Higinbotham gave notice of a Bill to amend the law relating to conveyancers, for nine of them had lost their livelihoods as a result of recent changes to the law.[9] Concern for working people whose livelihoods were damaged by political events over which they had no control would prove to be a recurring theme of Higinbotham's political career. His Bill passed the Legislative Assembly but was voted down without a division in the Legislative Council.[10]

The *Argus* and 'contempt of Parliament'

Behind the conflict over the possession of land and political power in colonial Victoria, there loomed a battle of political ideologies. In the small community of Melbourne, Higinbotham stood out as one who had challenged conservative ideology. Despite the convention of writing anonymously for the Melbourne *Herald*, it is likely that his conservative opponents would have identified him as the lawyer-journalist who had led the press campaign against Hotham's Minute and the pensions affair in 1855. His role in that press campaign and the controversial *Herald* editorial of 30 January 1856 marked Higinbotham as an adversary. In that editorial, he had declared that the Australian colonial legislatures were sovereign in the realm of domestic affairs, and that their rights and privileges were no less than those of the British Parliament. He accused the British Parliament of 'usurpation' and 'tyranny' for its refusal to recognise the right of the local

Victorian legislature to decide the provisions of its own Constitution.[11] He had prefaced his declaration with the following bold assertion:

> The Australian people will not submit to any badge of inferiority, neither in themselves to the inhabitants, nor in their legislatures to the Parliaments, of England. They claim in both cases an ABSOLUTE EQUALITY. They are willing and anxious to hold, directly and immediately of the Crown. But they repudiate and protest against the interference of the Parliament at Westminster as a usurpation and a tyranny. They assert their rights as co-equal and co-ordinate.[12]

The assertion of the rights of the Victorian legislature was destined to be one of the first of the battles that the young Colony would face.

In late April 1862, the month that Higinbotham regained the seat of Brighton, a leading article in the *Argus* raised constitutional arguments contrary to those that he had expounded six years earlier in the controversial *Herald* editorial. The *Argus* article followed an earlier leading article that was published in the *Argus* on the day that Higinbotham had made his pre-election speech to the electors. This earlier article was a savage and scurrilous attack on William Frazer, the Member for Creswick.[13] In style, it was similar to the *Argus*'s ferocious personal attacks on O'Shanassy and Duffy in the late 1850s, but this time the motivation was not sectarian. The *Argus* was campaigning against certain members of the Legislative Assembly who were, it claimed, 'men of inferior class', 'public nuisances', 'skunks', 'murderers of the Queen's English' and blasphemers. It accused them of 'making representative government a farce'.[14]

As well as Frazer, the *Argus* particularly attacked Charles Jardine Don, the Member for Collingwood. Don was a stonemason who, at one period, worked on the building of the Parliament House by day and sat in it as a member by night.[15] He was an avowed advocate for the working class, who had played a prominent part in the movement for the eight-hour day. The *Argus* denounced Don as an 'arrant simpleton' and accused him of making 'querulous complaints against imaginary oppressors, and puerile protests against fictitious wrongs'. Another working-class advocate was George Elliott Barton, the Member for North Melbourne. The *Argus* derided him as 'the most ridiculous little caricature of a democrat there ever was … a noisy little fellow doing patriotism in that very Irish manner'.[16] Another was Louis Lawrence Smith, an enterprising medical doctor and former ship's surgeon who scandalised conservative opinion by producing, advertising and selling medical information and advice to the general public.[17] Perhaps an additional irritant was the fact that Smith urged the Government to provide services for the destitute. Another of the 'men of inferior class' was the former Chief Secretary, Richard Heales, a coachbuilder who also identified as a workingman's representative.[18]

The affair began on 3 April 1862 when William Frazer, in his capacity as Chairman of a Select Committee of the Assembly that had been appointed to inquire into the management of the Police Force, raised the case of two sergeants of police who had sent a petition to the Chief Secretary lodging complaints against the Chief Commissioner of Police.[19] The men were subsequently accused by the Chief Commissioner of insubordination and were called to face a Board of Inquiry. In the Legislative Assembly, Frazer had questioned the impartiality and the legality of the proposed Board of Inquiry.[20]

The article in the *Argus* accused Frazer of deliberately fostering discontent within the Police Force, and then constituting himself as 'a court of appeal to every malcontent policeman in the Force'. It alleged that Frazer was a 'privileged ruffian' whom accident had 'pitchforked into the House'. It accused him of being the puppet and the rude instrument of a certain 'well-known influence'.[21] Though the malign 'influence' was not defined, it may have referred to the quest for political rights of Frazer's goldfields constituents. Frazer had formerly been a miner at Ballarat at the time of the conflict at Eureka in 1854. Later, he had been elected to the Ballarat local court and had served on the Ballarat Mining Board. Though he was not qualified as a lawyer, he had some knowledge of the law. The drafters of the Victorian law relating to mining partnerships drew heavily upon his thorough knowledge of the practicalities of mining.[22]

Frazer raised the matter of the *Argus*'s attack in the Legislative Assembly and moved that the article be declared 'a scandalous breach of the privileges of the House'.[23] His call resonated widely, not only because of the affront to the Legislative Assembly, but perhaps because a number of members had suffered personal attacks by the *Argus*, and because the representatives from the goldfields well remembered the *Argus*'s betrayal of the miners' cause at Eureka in 1854. The Assembly voted to call the *Argus*'s general manager, George Dill, to the bar of the House. Dill chose to ignore the summons, and the House therefore found him guilty of 'contempt'. He was then arrested by the sergeant-at-arms and brought before the bar of the House to answer questions. The *Argus* argued that the appropriateness of its earlier denunciation of certain members of the Assembly as 'privileged ruffians' was amply demonstrated by 'the exultation, ribald laughter and cowardly jibes' that some members made when Dill finally appeared at the bar of the House.[24] When asked to name the writer of the article attacking Frazer, Dill refused and was committed to the custody of the sergeant-at-arms for one month. The *Argus*'s indignant report of Dill's confinement in the parliamentary 'dungeon' bordered on a lampoon with bitterly comic references to the enormous size of the padlock used to secure the cell.[25] Dill brought an action before the Supreme Court seeking damages for wrongful imprisonment. A writ of *habeas corpus* was served and Dill was released on his undertaking to present himself to the Court. The full court of the Supreme Court of Victoria heard the case.

The affair raised the question of the powers of the Legislative Assembly to deal with cases of contempt of Parliament, and this highlighted the clash of ideologies. The Government attempted to pass a Bill claiming that both Houses of the Victorian Parliament were entitled to the privilege of the House of Commons to act as a court in such matters. The *Argus* conducted a campaign of frenzied opposition, and received support from several regional Victorian newspapers whose editors were alarmed at the prospect of any restriction on the freedom of the press. Though the issue of freedom of the press had long been regarded as a radical cause, the *Argus* sought to harness the concern about press freedom to its crusade against the increasingly democratic composition and purposes of the Legislative Assembly. It argued that the claim of the Legislative Assembly to the privileges of the House of Commons constituted a grave threat to press freedom.[26] Quoting extensively from legal and constitutional authorities, the writer of a subsequent editorial in the *Argus* fumed:

> The attempt of the Victorian House of Assembly to arrogate to itself the powers of the English House of Commons, must be regarded as one of the most monstrous and flagitious usurpations which can be made on the liberty of the subject in a free British community … It is no answer to say that the House of Commons itself possesses these privileges, and, therefore they may exist with safety to the Constitution … To pretend that any legislative assembly in this age … can assume, by a stroke of the pen, all the prerogatives that belong to the House of Commons, is surely the most astounding proposition that can be submitted to a people born under the constitution of England and having a reverence for British law.[27]

Despite the *Argus*'s campaign, the full court of the Supreme Court found in favour of the Legislative Assembly's privilege to deal with cases of contempt of the Parliament. The decision was confirmed on a subsequent appeal to the Privy Council. It was another hard-won victory in the battle for democracy in Victoria.

Dill's case raised a number of complex and conflicting legal and constitutional principles. The saga had arisen in the context of an attack on the Government and had developed into a long-running *cause célèbre* that snowballed until it threatened to destabilise the Government and to ruin the chances for land reform. At this early stage of his parliamentary career, Higinbotham decided upon a policy of discretion. There were personal considerations, for he had recently worked with Dill during his years at the *Argus*. As a former anonymous journalist himself, he could not demand that others who (like himself) had written anonymously should have their identity forcibly revealed. Neither could he wholeheartedly support the *Argus*'s cry of 'freedom of the press' when it equated freedom with indulgence in shameless personal attacks. It was likely that these considerations restrained Higinbotham from playing a prominent role on this occasion.

However, in 1869 a similar issue arose regarding the Parliament's right to try the landowner Hugh Glass for 'breaching the privileges of the House' (in this case paying bribes to members). This time Higinbotham played a very prominent role.[28] He initiated the motion in the Legislative Assembly to issue a warrant to bring Glass before the House. Glass challenged the legality of the warrant. Stawell, as Chief Justice of the Supreme Court, declared that the Parliament lacked the right to define its own privileges (in this case, to issue the warrant for Glass's arrest). Higinbotham urged the Speaker of the House to contest the judgment before the Judicial Committee of the Privy Council. The Committee declared that 'the full privilege and power (of the House of Commons) has been transferred to the Colony entire' under its *Constitution Act*. This decision affirmed the Victorian Parliament's right to bring individuals before it for breaching the privileges of the House without the supervision of the courts.

The cases of Dill and Glass were important milestones in defining the powers of the Victorian Legislative Assembly outside the *Constitution Act*. The first was won in 1862 through the initiative of the members, particularly William Frazer, the Member for Creswick. Frazer recognised that the editorial attack upon himself for acting in the role that the House had conferred upon him constituted a breach of the privilege of the House, and he called upon the Legislative Assembly to use its powers to deal with the matter. The second case in 1869 was won largely through the leadership of Higinbotham, who urged the Speaker of the House to contest the decision of the Supreme Court, which he believed to be wrong.

The bathing hut dispute

Local political tensions may have been a factor in a dispute that flared in 1862 between Higinbotham and the local municipal council. The dispute concerned the Higinbotham brothers' property in West Brighton. The property had originally been a part of a 'Special Survey' of ten square miles, which the first purchaser, Henry Dendy, had negotiated directly with the British Government. Like many of the properties later sub-divided from the Special Survey, its western boundary extended to the high-water mark on the beach. Higinbotham discovered that a local man named Mark Hollow had constructed a bathing hut on his property, above the high-water mark, without permission. He insisted that it be removed, but Hollow appealed to the local council to support his right to build there. Council informed Hollow that it would consider a permit if the building was relocated below the high-water mark. Under this proposal, the Higinbotham family would still have suffered some loss of amenity.

The matter came to the attention of Duffy as President of the Board of Land and Works. The council sent a deputation to urge Duffy to allow the construction of the bathing hut below the high-water mark adjacent to the Higinbotham property. To Higinbotham's relief, Duffy informed the council that they had no right to authorise any building on the beach.[29]

It is possible that the council's vigorous support of Hollow's right to build his bathing hut close to the beach boundary of the Higinbotham property might have been motivated by a desire to embarrass George Higinbotham in the local area. The president of the local council at the time was George W. Rusden, who currently served as Clerk of the Parliaments. The chairman of the municipality was R.K. Hammond, who had proposed the nomination of William Clarke, Higinbotham's opponent at the April by-election.[30] Rusden was a man of conservative instincts who, in a letter to Charles Dickens in 1868, likened Australian voters to 'unthinking machines'.[31] He was deeply indebted to the conservative side of Victorian politics for he was one of those who had benefited from the generous 'compensation' that the 1855 Constitution allowed to him for the loss of his position when the former Legislative Council terminated. At the time that the Draft Constitution was being considered by the Victorian Legislative Council, the proposed retirement allowance to Rusden as Clerk of the Legislative Council was two-thirds of his salary of £5,000, less the amount of any future government salary.[32] This exceeded the annual salary of a Supreme Court judge. An editorial in the *Melbourne Morning Herald*, probably written by Michie, had condemned the proposal as an example of the 'feathering' of official 'nests'.[33] Various members of the former Legislative Council had opposed the retirement allowance to Rusden, objecting that the amount was 'exorbitant' and (in one case) condemning it as a 'bribe'.[34] Rusden was not unemployed for long, for upon the inauguration of the new legislatures in 1856, he was appointed as Clerk of the Parliaments.

In the lengthy 'Summary for Europe' in the *Herald* of 30 January 1856 (the same editorial whose tone had so shocked the *London Illustrated News*), Higinbotham had reported that in 1854, many payments to officials (not including the payment to Rusden) were made improperly. He charged that 'house rent and exorbitant pay' were given to 'the whole circle around the Government out of the moiety of the Land Fund'.[35] The Land Fund was derived from 50 per cent of the proceeds of the sale of government land, and designated for the purpose of bringing immigrants to Victoria. This was a serious accusation, but he was not the first to make it. In the lead-up to the dismissal of the Colonial Secretary, John Foster, in December 1854, the *Argus* had accused the Government of improperly spending the Land Fund.[36] Indeed, correspondence between Lauchlan Mackinnon, co-proprietor of the *Argus* and Captain Kay, Hotham's private secretary, suggests that the source of the revelation may have been Governor Hotham himself.[37] Just over a year later, Higinbotham had repeated the accusation in the *Herald*, adding further charges about anomalies in the finances of the Colony. In accusing the previous Government of widespread patronage, that was not only extravagant but illegally obtained, Higinbotham may have excited Rusden's ire. If Higinbotham's accusations were true, it is likely that Rusden, as Clerk of the Council, would have played a role in administering the scheme. This may explain the deep-seated dislike of

Higinbotham that Rusden displayed in a partisan colonial history that he wrote in 1897.[38] In his history, Rusden attacked Higinbotham as 'a theoretical enthusiast, steeped in a mixture of the ideas of John Stuart Mill and the French iconoclasts of 1789'. It may have been a personal animosity towards Higinbotham that motivated Rusden to take Hollow's side in the bathing hut issue.

The failure of Duffy's *Land Act*

The bathing-hut issue may have thawed relations between Duffy and Higinbotham, but the effect was short-lived. Despite the hopes that both Duffy and Higinbotham held for the *Land Act* as the means of settling small farmers on good agricultural land, the squatters promptly discovered loopholes in the legislation that enabled them to exploit it. Many squatters employed 'dummy' selectors who were prepared to perjure themselves. While purporting to buy land for their own use, the 'dummy' bidders were in fact purchasing it as agents of the squatters. This process undermined the central principle of the Act, which was to restrict the sale of agricultural land to those with a genuine intention to settle upon the land and to farm it. The Act had the opposite effect to that intended, for it allowed the squatters to acquire vast freehold estates for grazing and speculation. The Act became law in June 1862, and within a few months, 110 squatters managed to purchase 932,000 acres (377,167 hectares) of the land that the Government had intended for small selectors.[39]

In his autobiography, Duffy attributed the failure of the Act to defects in its legal structure. He implicated some of the leading Irish Protestants in the Act's downfall, particularly Richard Ireland, the Attorney-General.[40] Ireland was a barrister who, in his youth, had been associated with radical causes in Ireland. He came to prominence in Victoria for his outstanding defence of seven of the Eureka prisoners, but since those days he had become conservative.[41] Ireland had engaged a fellow Irish Protestant, William Hearn, a former Professor of Law at the University, to draft the Land Bill.

Duffy considered that the agreed fee of £500 for drafting the Bill was 'unusual' and, when compared with the annual salary in 1862 of £610 for the Secretary of the Law Department and £600 for a Crown Prosecutor, the fee does seem to have been generous.[42] Hearn was one of four Foundation Professors of the University who had been actively recruited for his position, and he received the high salary of £1,000 and accommodation. He was a man of conservative leanings who was keen to participate in the political process. Despite the indignation of the Chancellor of the University, Redmond Barry, Hearn stood for the Legislative Assembly in 1859.

Whether it was intentional or not, a series of legal loopholes in Hearn's drafting of the *Land Act* had allowed the squatters to evade the intentions of the Act with impunity.[43] Higinbotham denounced the 'numberless loopholes through which unscrupulous persons might find the means of evading the provisions of the Act'.[44] This criticism of the drafting might have encouraged Duffy to believe that Higinbotham would be prepared to assist with advice on rectification of the problem provisions of the Act. If so, he was disappointed. Duffy recorded that following the Act's failure:

> I insisted on submitting the opinion which the law officer sent for my guidance to a barrister unconnected with office, and I sent it to Mr Higinbotham, who advised that I was bound to follow the opinions of the legal officers of the Government.[45]

In 1867, Ireland would admit that he knew of the Act's defects at the time of the enactment of the legislation, but did not alert his colleagues.[46] Duffy moved an amendment to the *Land Act* aiming to rectify the problems in drafting, but the damage was done. The Government's land reform initiative had lost credibility, and support from the independent members had dwindled since the passage of the Act. Debate upon Duffy's amendment was underway when Richard Ireland unexpectedly entered the chamber and took advantage of the state of the House to call for a division. With insufficient supporters present, the amendment was lost, and the squatters cemented their victory. Higinbotham subsequently wrote to Duffy apologising that he had been unprepared for the sudden division that ended the debate, for otherwise he would have defended him. Perhaps unconvinced, Duffy transcribed the letter in his autobiography without further comment.[47] Regardless of Higinbotham's explanation that his failure to support Duffy at the critical time was unintentional, Duffy may have concluded that the Irish Protestants had collaborated to engineer his downfall by ensuring that he could not resuscitate his *Land Act*. Five years later, when Ireland admitted his prior knowledge of the loopholes in the legislation, Duffy took satisfaction in the public reaction, which he described in his autobiography:

> Mr Ireland had not much character to lose, but that little was lost forever. His election committee immediately sent him notice that he need not return to Kilmore, which he then represented, and though he tried another constituency when the opportunity came, he was never, during the remainder of his life re-elected to Parliament – a signal instance of public justice.[48]

The incubus of the Council

The difficulty of government in the period arose from many sources. Sectarianism was a continuous source of friction in Government as well as in colonial society. In addition, there was a division of support between the rival Catholic leaders, O'Shanassy and Duffy. The two men had quarrelled bitterly in 1859, and although the Catholic hierarchy had negotiated a reconciliation, the relationship thereafter was tenuous at best. There was also competition between different sections of the economy, such as gold mining, agriculture, business, banking and the pastoral interests. In addition, localities competed for roads, bridges and other public works. Differences of view between free trade supporters and those favouring tariffs to protect local industry became increasingly significant and, as always, the personal ambition of members complicated the business of government. Yet beyond all of these political challenges, nothing contributed so much to the instability and the paralysis of Government in the period as the fraught relationship between the Legislative Assembly and the Legislative Council.

Significant legislative achievements were very few. Geoffrey Serle commented that despite long, drawn-out sessions lasting eight or nine months of the year, Parliament 'contributed almost nothing to the solution of the supreme problem of the day – how to hold migrants in Victoria by developing the economy'.[49] The problem was a structural one arising from the provisions of the Victorian Constitution of 1855. Unlike Victoria, which had an elected Upper House, New South Wales had a nominated Upper House. There a Lower House could, in extreme circumstances, threaten to 'swamp' a recalcitrant Upper House by appointing additional members to alter the political balance. The historian Robin Gollan commented that although this 'safety valve' was rarely used, 'the fact that it existed made for more amiable relations between the Houses'.[50]

Under the Victorian Constitution of 1855, a high property franchise restricted membership of the Legislative Council to those who possessed property valued at £5,000, or a property leasehold that returned £500 annually. The electors of the Upper House were themselves required to be holders of property to the value of £1,000, or of a leasehold that returned £100 per annum. Accordingly, the Upper House represented the interests of the propertied class. The Council had the power to amend Bills emanating from the Lower House except for Appropriation Bills. These it could reject but not amend. In the case of a rejected Appropriation Bill, the Constitution provided no means of resolving a deadlock between the two Houses. Writing in 1865, the influential British journalist and political analyst Walter Bagehot noted that Victoria was an example of 'the evil of two co-equal Houses' in a constitution, for 'each House can stop all legislation and yet some legislation may be necessary'.[51] During the constitutional drafting process in February 1854, Michie had warned via an editorial in the *Melbourne Morning Herald* that restricting the membership of the Upper House to a small but wealthy elite would lead to 'agitation and strife that would probably last for years'.[52] Unfortunately for Victoria, the drafters of the 1855 Constitution did not heed his warning.

The Constitution denied a voice to women, foreigners who had not been naturalised for a period of five years, those convicted of certain offences, those who were illiterate, those who owed rates or taxes, those who were not in receipt of £100 annually, and those who had not resided for six months in the electorate in which they had registered to vote. Though the Miner's Right made it possible for many miners to vote, this last provision particularly disadvantaged gold miners who moved from rush to rush. Aborigines were not specifically excluded, but few would have met the criteria.

At the time of the drafting of the Constitution in the old Legislative Council, the government members had sought to reassure the representative members that the powers of the new Lower House *vis-à-vis* the Upper House would be conducive to smooth and effective government. John Foster, the Colonial Secretary, told the House:

> The purse-strings would be entirely within the control of the lower house. This would give to the lower house, thus constituted, all the power possessed by the British House of Commons as far as the state of society in the Colony will admit of our making it so.[53]

Hugh Childers, the Auditor-General until November 1853, and thereafter Collector of Customs, made a similar claim in the Council:

> The Lower House would have control over the money bills, while the Upper House would have hardly a voice in the matter. The House which was elected would have the control over the entire funds of the Colony – a power granted by the Home Government without being asked for by the Legislature.[54]

By 1861, the hollowness of these promises had become apparent. A succession of Governments of different political complexions had found that obstruction of their key Bills by the Legislative Council made it impossible to keep faith with their constituents. This failure caused widespread dissatisfaction with the political system. Graham Berry, the recently elected Member for Collingwood, declared that Victoria had an 'unworkable constitution'. In 1878, Berry, as Premier of Victoria, would lead a delegation to London to urge the British Government to implement constitutional reform in order to resolve the continued constitutional impasses. He added:

> The Constitution had given them an Upper House which would do nothing itself, and would prevent the Assembly from doing anything – an Upper House composed of men determined to hold the land at all hazards against the people of this country.[55]

Seventeen months before he entered Parliament, Higinbotham wrote in the *Argus*:

> The present Assembly is in a state of utter demoralisation. It is a mere rabble of political desperadoes ... Every man is for himself, and parliamentary life has degenerated into a mere scramble.[56]

It was rumoured that the machinations of the Victorian Association brought about the defeat of the Heales ministry on 12 November 1862. Writing in 1883, the Victorian barrister John Quick observed that the defeat was a victory for the Victorian Association, which had bought the votes of certain members of the Legislative Assembly in the interests of the squatters. He wrote:

> The Ministry were defeated by needy schemers, notorious renegades, apostates and traitors, who, for place, pay, power

and patronage sold themselves and their constituents and brought into contempt the representative institutions of the country.[57]

In February 1856, Higinbotham had written lyrically of 'the pride and magnanimity that distinguished the assemblies of the public men in North America'.[58] He had contrasted this vision of orderly debate and earnest concern for the national interest with the debased state of the Victorian legislature of the time, and he had hoped for improvement. But the intervening years since the inauguration of the new Constitution of 1855 had delivered only a further deterioration in the conduct of colonial politics. Higinbotham had declared in 1856:

> Our legislature is one that it is not sufficient to ignore, if you
> would rouse it to resentment; nor will you succeed by spitting
> in its face. You must cudgel it into the sensibility of shame
> and flagellate it into the irritability of self-respect … [59]

Having briefly served in the Legislative Assembly in 1861, and then more firmly having established himself in 1862, Higinbotham was ready to do battle with the demoralised 'scramble', to harness it, to imbue it with a sense of direction and purpose, and to force it to address and resolve the problems facing Victoria.

12

ATTORNEY-GENERAL GEORGE HIGINBOTHAM

At home in Brighton, Higinbotham's family was growing with the birth in 1863 of a second daughter, Alice Mary, and the arrival in 1865 of his son, George Robert. But it is doubtful if he found much time for the duties and delights of fatherhood during the years 1863 to 1868. These were some of the most important of the years in which he made his mark on Victorian political and constitutional development.

In June 1863, the Haines–O'Shanassy Government attempted to amend the Duffy *Land Act* to increase the squatters' rents. The Government proposed to base the rents on an assessment of the capacity of the runs to carry stock. This had become necessary because the amount of revenue collected in lease rentals was well below the anticipated sum. The Bill was defeated and the Government resigned. A new ministry under James McCulloch took office with Higinbotham as the Attorney-General. Born in Scotland in 1819, McCulloch was the president of the Melbourne Chamber of Commerce, the local director of the London Chartered Bank and a noted philanthropist. At the time, his firm was engaged in purchasing squatting runs in north-eastern Victoria, and it is therefore unlikely that he would have regarded Duffy's *Land Act* favourably, especially with its proposal to raise squatting rents. Despite his own conservative inclinations, McCulloch bowed to popular feeling by including in his cabinet some liberal-minded Ministers. Amongst these were the former Premier, Richard

Heales, who was appointed President of the Board of Land and Works; twenty-nine-year-old George Verdon, who had been an elected member of the Land Convention and who became Treasurer; Archibald Michie, who was appointed Minister of Justice; and George Higinbotham. The other Ministers were Thomas Howard Fellows, Postmaster-General; James Sullivan, Minister of Mines; Matthew Hervey (MLC), Commissioner for Public Works; and James Goodall Francis, Commissioner for Trade and Customs.

The results of the election in November saw the Government increase its numbers to 47 of the 78 seats in the House. The *Argus* bemoaned the 'class of persons' who had come forward as candidates. It celebrated the defeat of some of the more radical members of the previous Parliament, but lamented that 'a new race, not less noisy, greedy or shameless' had arisen to fill their seats.[1] It attacked McCulloch's cabinet as a 'mongrel administration'.[2] But McCulloch had chosen his ministry carefully. It included liberals and conservatives, and advocates for both free trade and for protection to local industry. The inclusion in the ministry of men of known liberal opinions was necessary to reflect the popular feeling. By contrast, some members of the Legislative Council may have been relieved to see that, as well as McCulloch himself, the ministry included a second squatter in Matthew Hervey. In the eighteen months between March 1861 and November 1862, Hervey had been the Acting President of the Legislative Council.[3] In McCulloch's ministry, the liberal Heales and the squatter Hervey shared responsibility for the Board of Land and Works as President and Vice-President respectively.

The composition of McCulloch's ministry suggested that, like the previous 'coalition' ministry, it too would soon suffer division and collapse. Indeed, its hold on power was always precarious.[4] But the McCulloch ministry defied these gloomy expectations. It proved to be a most united, successful and long-lived ministry. This was due, in large part, to the influence of George Higinbotham. A fellow parliamentarian described Higinbotham as 'the brains, the heart and the right hand' of the ministry.[5] Disunity and personal ambition had been the undoing of previous administrations, and Higinbotham had repeatedly expressed his resolute opposition to the destabilising of governments. This reassured McCulloch that he could rely upon Higinbotham to oppose any attempt at a breakaway by dissident members of the cabinet. The ministry met in Higinbotham's legal chambers in Chancery Lane, Melbourne.[6] According to the Treasurer, George Verdon, much of the success of the cabinet was attributable to Higinbotham's leadership. He acknowledged his 'kindness, gentleness and forbearance' towards his colleagues, and he commented:

> He made allowances for others which he never would make in his own case, and his unselfishness, devotion to duty, and kindness gained for him the love of his colleagues and the devotion of all who served under him.[7]

The issue of land reform was of the highest priority, but the ministry found that, despite the inclusion of the two squatters, at first it could make no headway against the determined opposition of the Council. In 1863 and 1864, Heales had introduced into the Legislative Assembly two Bills seeking to amend Duffy's *Land Act* so that it would operate, as originally intended, for the benefit of the small agriculturalist, and also to increase government revenue by a charge upon the stock-carrying capacity of the leased land, but the Legislative Council rejected both. Heales became ill with tuberculosis and took leave of the Assembly in April 1864, two months before his death. James Macpherson Grant succeeded him as President of the Board of Land and Works and Commissioner of Crown Lands and Survey.

As the lawyer who had successfully defended seven of the Eureka prisoners, and taken a prominent role in opposing Hotham's Minute, Grant had a reputation as a radical, but he was also a realist. He introduced a Land Bill that was essentially conservative. McCulloch's ministry argued that the Duffy *Land Act* was a 'contract' that had been negotiated between the squatters and the rest of the population. The 'contract' guaranteed tenure of the squatters' land at an agreed rental for nine years in return for making some of the land available for Crown grants to intending agriculturalists.

Confederate Cruiser *Shenandoah* in Hobson's Bay, January 1865
Walter Hart: Engraver
Image courtesy of the State Library of Victoria

Her Majesty's Colonial War Steamer *Victoria* dressed in flags to mark the visit of
the Duke of Edinburgh to Melbourne in 1867
Image courtesy of the naval Museum, HMAS Cerberus, Crib Point

George Higinbotham (1826–1892)
Electric Photo. Engraving Co., photographer, 1892
Image courtesy of the State Library of Victoria

The ministry did not wish to provoke a confrontation with the squatters by re-opening the entire basis of that agreement. However, in the lead-up to the election of October 1864, Higinbotham warned that if the Council should reject the Government's proposal to amend the Duffy *Land Act* so as to remove the abuses of it, 'I will be no party to any further compromise or delay'. He threatened that the Government would immediately repeal the *Land Act* of 1862 and sell the squatters' leased lands.

The Government insisted that the land reform proposal was essentially to tighten conditions of eligibility for a Crown land grant and thereby restore the original intention of making land available to the deserving small agriculturalist. To achieve this, the Government proposed amendments that would close off loopholes that had been exploited by non-genuine selectors. The Government did not seek to increase the squatters' lease rentals, even though that meant foregoing much-needed revenue. The income to the Government from the squatting leases remained at 1¼d (one penny farthing) per acre, and did not include a charge on stock. This was approximately a quarter of the cost of a daily newspaper. It was also about one-nineteenth of that proposed for the selectors, who would pay rent of 2s (two shillings) per acre for their probationary leases.[8] But by allowing the leaseholders' rents to remain so much lower than those to be imposed on the selectors, the Government faced the criticism that it favoured the squatters.

In January 1865, Grant succeeded in passing his new amending Land Bill through the Legislative Assembly. Despite the conservatism of the Bill, it took protracted negotiations with the Council and finally a conference between the Houses before it became law. In the process, the squatters gained one of their objectives, which was to have more freehold land available for purchase at auction. Two million acres of land that had previously been reserved for Crown grants under the terms of the Duffy Act became available for purchase at auction under various conditions.[9] From Higinbotham's view, the determination of the Council to promote the interests of the squatters had, once again, frustrated the good intentions of the Government to provide the small agriculturalist with access to suitable and affordable land. Like Duffy's *Land Act* of 1862 and Nicholson's *Land Act* of 1860, despite some gains by the selectors, the main beneficiaries were the squatters.

In his speech to the electors of Brighton in October 1864, Higinbotham revealed his intense frustration with the Council when he called it 'a permanent obstruction to wise legislation', and 'a standing menace to all governments'. He continued:

> There is a crafty design which aims at the aggrandizement of a few by a monopoly of the public property, and of the exclusion of the mass of the people from political privileges. Well gentleman, I am sorry to say that the Legislative Council represents this body in the community.[10]

He threatened that if the Council continued to obstruct legislation, he would introduce a Bill to reform it. The effect of that reform, he said, would be to 'strike a blow at a very dangerous class – the wealthy lower orders'. This was the language of class turned on its head. His attack on the Legislative Council resonated with the gathering, who applauded with enthusiasm. The phrase 'wealthy lower orders' became forever associated with Higinbotham's attack on the squatters as a class whose self-serving behaviour reduced them to the social rank of criminals and ruffians. It was also Higinbotham's public announcement of his determination to bring the squatters to account if they should again fail to consider the public interest or to abide by the expressed popular will.

A key innovation in Grant's *Land Act* was the principle of probationary leases before purchase was approved. During the period of probation, the intending purchaser was required to provide material evidence, such as fencing, clearing or building works to a prescribed value, to show that he was genuinely intent on farming the land. If he failed to do so within three years, he forfeited the opportunity to purchase the land and pay for it in instalments, and it could be sold at auction. This and other safeguards were put in place to ensure that Crown land grants were accessible only to bona fide agriculturalists. But this Act, like Duffy's *Land Act*, largely failed to achieve its objectives. In the first place, insufficient land was made available for selection for agricultural purposes.[11] Secondly, many dummy bidders purchased leases on selections with no intention to meet the requirements regarding material improvements. In the words of the legal historian Sir John Quick:

> The land racket, commenced under the Duffy Act was continued with aggravated energy ... Taverns were kept open for the accommodation of gangs of dummies and stage coaches were, with unblushing effrontery, engaged from day to day to carry the dummies from sale to sale.[12]

The Act required that selections that failed to meet the requirements would be forfeited. Once forfeited, the land became available for sale by auction. This gave the squatters what they wanted: the opportunity to purchase more land with a freehold title.[13] Quick noted that much more land was sold at auction under the Grant *Land Act* than under either of the two previous *Land Acts*.[14] He commented:

> The conditions of probationary leases were as severe upon bona fide settlers as they were favourable to dummies, whose object was to secure the forfeiture and sale of selections by auction.[15]

Many bona fide selectors forfeited their selections because they could not afford both the rent and the cost of the required improvements while saving for the purchase price deposit and instalments. Their land was put to auction and they were not entitled to receive compensation for improvements.[16]

Higinbotham had supported strong ministerial powers in the Act to determine eligibility for the Crown grants, rather than totally relying on legislation, and this principle became incorporated into the Grant *Land Act*. He told the House:

> It is idle to say that the land legislation can meet and defeat the various contrivances of fraud … if men are tempted by strong inducements of avarice and are provided with legal means to effect their object, the State will be defrauded and the poor men for whom you wish to legislate will be utterly defeated.[17]

Quick commented that this expanded role of the Minister was another feature of the Grant *Land Act* that proved its value and was included in the subsequent reforming *Land Act* of 1869.[18]

But while some small agriculturalists benefited from the Grant *Land Act* of 1865, the squatters as a class were the main beneficiaries. They kept their low-lease rentals and they gained the opportunity to purchase a great deal of freehold land at auction. As at the time of Eureka, the wealthy avoided paying a fair share of the government revenue and the burden fell heavily upon working families. To Higinbotham and many colonists, the Act fell short of the expectations of voters, and provided a further example of the Legislative Council's indifference to the public interest.

The arrival of CSS *Shenandoah*

While the issues of land policy were continuing to be debated, the attention of the entire colony was temporarily distracted by an unexpected event. The American Civil War between the Northern Union and the Southern Confederacy, which had begun in 1861, presented a dilemma for McCulloch's Government when, on 26 January 1865, a man-of-war, announcing itself as the Confederate Steamship *Shenandoah*, suddenly arrived in Hobson's Bay, Melbourne. The captain, James Waddell, requested of the Governor, Sir Charles Darling, permission to effect repairs to the ship. Waddell also requested permission to provision the ship with coal and supplies of food and beverages.[19]

The *Shenandoah* was the latest of three famous privateer ships that the Confederacy had surreptitiously obtained from British shipyards and used to harass Union shipping and to disrupt the blockade of Southern ports. Officially, Britain was neutral in the American conflict. Nevertheless, certain British individuals collaborated with Southern Confederate agents to obtain fast ships suitable for use as commercial raiders. The collaborators acted on behalf of British mill interests who favoured the continuation of slavery in order to ensure the supply of cheap cotton for British mills. To evade detection by British authorities, the ships were disguised as merchant ships until they had left British ports. When each ship reached an appointed position in open waters, a supply ship met it. The Union Jack was hauled down; the privateer ship was refitted with armaments, renamed and assigned a Confederate crew to enable it to raid Union shipping.[20]

When an even more daring Confederate plan to commission ironclad battleships in British shipyards was detected, the US Ambassador, Charles Francis Adams, threatened war with Britain.[21] The plan was abandoned, but the collaborators purchased, as one last privateer ship, a steam-powered merchant sailing vessel named the *Sea King*, which featured several aero-dynamic and hydro-dynamic innovations to maximise speed and manoeuvrability. They converted it at sea off Madeira into an eight-gun man-of-war and renamed it CSS *Shenandoah*.

The first of the privateer ships, the CSS *Florida*, seized thirty-seven 'prizes' before the USS *Wachusett* captured it in October 1864. The second was the *Alabama,* the most feared of the privateer raiders, which sank nearly 100 ships.[22] The *Alabama* was destroyed in a naval battle with the Union's sloop-of-war *Kearsage* in Cherbourg harbour, in June 1864. Some of its crew were re-assigned to the *Shenandoah,* which commenced its depredations of Union shipping in October 1864. *En route* to Melbourne, the *Shenandoah* captured eight ships and took prisoners.

The arrival of the *Shenandoah* created a sensation in Melbourne. Captain Waddell noted in his diary:

> A little before sunset she dropped her anchors in Hobson's
> Bay, cheered and surrounded by steamers densely crowded
> … I was prepared for the reception. It was from generous

and brave hearts who believed in the righteousness of the Southern cause. The pilot had said, 'You have a great many friends in Melbourne'. [23]

About 7,000 sightseers visited the *Shenandoah* and were warmly welcomed by the crew. [24] The Mayor of Melbourne welcomed the Captain. The *Argus* bemoaned the re-election of President Abraham Lincoln, and expressed the hope that the Civil War would see the 'fortitude' of the South in resistance defeat the 'obstinacy' of the war-mongering President and his cabinet. [25] Some of the citizens of Ballarat arranged a ball in honour of the 'Officers of the CSS *Shenandoah*'. The Melbourne Club hosted a banquet with the Confederate officers seated at the president's table. Many judges, businessmen, government officials and most Victorian parliamentarians attended the banquet. [26] But the gaiety masked a sinister reality. The battle of Gettysburgh, the turning point in the war, had been reached in July 1863 and the Confederate cause itself was sinking fast. It soon became clear that the damage to the ship's propeller and hull required the use of a maritime slip to bring the ship out of the water for repair. As Britain and her colonies were ostensibly neutral in the conflict, such major material assistance to the Confederate cause would arguably be in conflict with their neutral stance. If the Union should prove victorious, how would such assistance to the Confederacy be viewed?

William Blanchard, the United States Consul in Melbourne, insisted that the *Shenandoah* was not entitled to the benefits accorded to a belligerent ship under the rules of warfare, for it was not a ship of the Confederate Navy but a pirate ship of British origin. He threatened that the British Government would pay for all later depredations caused by the *Shenandoah* if the Captain's request for repairs, fuel and provisions should be agreed to. He demanded that the ship be impounded. But despite being forced to rely on her sails for speed, the *Shenandoah*'s armoury was substantial. It was equipped with eight cannons, including four of the innovative Whitworth rifled cannons that were capable of being elevated and which fired both specially designed bolts and shells with great accuracy. The *Age* commented, 'the guns, all new, are magnificently mounted and are in excellent order'.[27] The crew were well practised in naval warfare. HMCSS *Victoria*, which protected the Colony, was launched in 1855. It had been subsequently refitted and carried eight 32-pounder guns and three smaller bore guns.[28] It had been designed for a range of duties such as survey and tendering to lighthouses and assisting at shipwrecks. At 580 tons, the displacement of the *Victoria* was about half that of the *Shenandoah*.[29] The *Victoria*'s supremacy in a conflict with the *Shenandoah* could not be assumed. Politically, too, any threatening move against the *Shenandoah* would have been extremely unpopular in Victoria. Any attempt to imprison or otherwise threaten the Captain or crew while on shore would have invited hostile retaliation, for these were desperate men, dedicating their lives to reviving the fortunes of the South. They knew very well that if they should fall into Union hands, they would face the death penalty as privateers.[30] The Governor sought advice from his Law Officers, Higinbotham and Michie, and his entire Executive Council as to how he should respond to the Captain's request.

Michie and Higinbotham advised Sir Charles Darling that there was no evidence of any act of piracy having been committed by the crew of the *Shenandoah*, and that it should be accorded the rights of a ship of war belonging to a belligerent power.[31] The legal historian John Bennett is highly critical of this advice to the Governor, which he regards as evidence of their ignorance regarding British maritime and international maritime law. He argues that Blanchard's analysis of the legal position should have been accepted.[32] Indeed, the advice given by Michie and Higinbotham was clearly inconsistent with the facts. Visitors to the *Shenandoah* reported that the livery of the *Sea King* was visible on the ship's crockery, and that the lettering of the name 'Sea King' was still faintly visible on the ship's stern. There was also abundant evidence of the *Shenandoah*'s piracy provided by prisoners who had escaped from it and who provided detailed testimony to the US Consul, which he had forwarded to the Governor.

Bennett argues that the correct procedure would have been 'to detain the *Shenandoah* until the pleasure of the Colonial Office could be ascertained'.[33] But it is unlikely that Captain Waddell and the crew would have submitted to a detention of some weeks with no progress. They were determined to waste no time in resuming their activities, and were well aware that, any day, a battleship of the Union Navy could arrive to capture them.

Within the confines of Port Phillip with its narrow opening to the sea, they were vulnerable to attack should this occur. Even while the *Shenandoah* was anchored in Hobson's Bay, sympathisers of the Union carried out a daring attempt to destroy it. Under cover of night they attached explosives to its hull, but the fuse failed to ignite properly. Though this plan miscarried, Waddell knew that other attempts were inevitable. He also knew that to gain his objectives in Port Phillip, his greatest asset was the public sympathy for the cause of the South among people of influence. To that end, he graciously accepted the invitations extended to himself and the officers. He played to perfection the role of a man of honour fighting for the freedom of the South from the tyranny of the North. He knew that he was in no position to demand repairs to his vessel. He also knew that the public sympathy in Victoria was predominantly for the Southern cause, and by extension to himself and his officers and crew. Public opinion was slowly but inexorably exerting pressure on the Governor to accede to his request. So, by a combination of political astuteness, charm and deception, backed by the firepower of the *Shenandoah,* Waddell achieved all of his objectives in Victoria.

By 18 February, the *Shenandoah* was repaired and re-provisioned. It was refuelled from a ship named the *John Fraser* that had sailed from Liverpool, the headquarters of the collaborators, to deliver to it a load of Cardiff coal. This grade of coal burned without producing smoke, and was therefore highly prized by raiding vessels as it gave them the advantage of seeing their victim's smoke before their own was visible.[34] The rendezvous must have been planned many weeks earlier, and this suggests that the Captain had planned to call in at Melbourne before the damage to his vessel occurred. The most likely reason was to recruit additional crew members. Despite giving his word 'as a Southern gentleman' that he would not contravene Britain's *Foreign Enlistment Act* by taking on British citizens as crew, Captain Waddell did, in fact, secretly recruit forty-two crew members while in Melbourne. Though the Government had reports of this, the Captain refused permission to have his ship searched, and the Government was unwilling to provoke a confrontation over the issue.

The *Shenandoah* left Port Phillip with a full crew on 19 February to resume marauding Union shipping in the Pacific. After General Lee surrendered on 9 April, the *Shenandoah* continued to attack Union ships until it surrendered in Liverpool on 2 August. About thirty ships of the Union's Pacific whaling fleet were captured, many after the close of the war.

The Governor's dilemma was that, although Britain had declared an official policy of neutrality in the Civil War, it operated an unofficial policy of tacit support to the Confederacy. As the loyal servant of the Empire, which policy was the Governor to follow? If he had strictly followed Imperial law regarding neutrality, as Blanchard demanded, it would have involved Victoria in attempting to seize the ship, for, as Blanchard argued, legally it was not a ship of the Confederate Navy and had been engaging in acts of piracy. An attempt to seize the ship may or may not have succeeded, but inevitably would have involved bloodshed, loss of life, and possibly the loss of HMCSS *Victoria*. Perhaps in order to provide an excuse to the Colonial Office for the Governor's non-compliance with Blanchard's request for the Government to impound the ship, Higinbotham and Michie provided a 'white lie' regarding the evidence of the *Shenandoah*'s true status. This lent a respectable appearance to the Governor's decision to refuse Blanchard's request.

Given the support for the Confederacy in Victoria, the firepower of the *Shenandoah* and the imminent end of the Civil War, it may have seemed to the Governor and the Executive Council that the simplest and safest response was to accede to Captain Waddell's request and to have the *Shenandoah* depart as quickly as possible. They knew that Britain risked being held to account for the compensation that would be demanded later, but none could have foreseen that Waddell would continue to attack Union shipping for four months after the South had surrendered.

The Secretary for the Colonies, Edward Cardwell, wrote to Darling informing him that 'Her Majesty's Government are of opinion that you acted with propriety and discretion'.[35] Clearly, Darling had made the right choice in their view. But, as Blanchard had warned, Washington demanded that the British Government recompense the United States Government for the losses to Union shipping caused by the three privateer ships. Following the Treaty of Washington on 8 May 1871, a tribunal of five arbitrators was established at Geneva to decide the matter. The arbitrators represented Britain, the United States, Brazil, Italy and Switzerland. By a majority of one, the Tribunal decided that Britain should recompense the United States $15,500,000.[36]

In 1873, Higinbotham defended himself before the Legislative Assembly from the accusation that it was his advice to the Governor that had cost Britain so dearly. Regardless of the wording of the Victorian Constitution, he had always taken the view advocated by Sir William Molesworth that a colonial Governor should act on the advice of his Ministers in domestic affairs, but not in matters affecting the Empire. Here, he believed, the Governor acted as the servant of the British Government. At least on this score, Higinbotham's own conscience was clear. In his view, neither he nor Michie nor any other of the Executive Councillors had given their advice regarding the *Shenandoah* in their capacity as Ministers of the Crown, for matters of Empire, such as relations with foreign governments, lay outside their field of responsibility. From Higinbotham's point of view, the Governor was under no obligation to accept the advice of the Ministers on this matter. 'Whatever advice was given', he said, 'was given not as Ministers of the Crown'.[37]

The *Shenandoah* incident focused attention on the vulnerability of Melbourne to hostile shipping in the new age of steam. It also highlighted the complexities and limitations of Molesworth's doctrine. The distinction between domestic and Imperial matters was not always clear in practice. Co-ordination between entities such as the owners of the maritime slip, the water police, the army and the railways had made possible a coherent response to the challenge on this occasion, and harm to the Colony had been averted. If the Governor and the Colonial Government had disagreed about their goals, the result might have been confusion or even tragedy. The incident also highlighted the impracticality of Molesworth's doctrine because of the distance of the Colony from London, and the delay in exchanging information and receiving instructions. Further, the incident demonstrated that the interests and security of the Colony were separate from those of Britain. It was clear that henceforth Victoria needed to take more responsibility for its own safety. In 1866, the Treasurer, George Verdon, visited London and obtained from the Colonial Secretary the training ship HMS *Nelson*, and the sum of £100,000 towards the cost of the armour-plated monitor ship HMVS *Cerberus*.[38]

Bringing the judiciary under responsible government

Higinbotham's most famous dispute during his time as Attorney-General was with Justice Redmond Barry. It began in January 1864 and continued for more than three years. Barry applied for leave of absence to Governor Charles Darling instead of to Higinbotham as Attorney-General. In doing so, he attempted to assert a privilege of Supreme Court judges to communicate directly with the Governor. The Governor referred the judge's letter to Higinbotham, who famously replied:

> The Attorney-General cannot permit any officer in his department – no matter how eminent the position of the officer may be, or how independent the law may have made him in the exercise of his official functions – to place himself outside the limits of the system of responsible government, and communicate with the Attorney-General on an official subject by means of letters addressed to the Governor in person.[39]

Higinbotham later admitted that he regretted the use of the term 'officer' to describe the status of a judge – not because it was inaccurate, but because it had given the erroneous impression that the Executive did not respect the independence of judges. 'A more unfounded impression never existed', he protested, and added that he believed it was 'one that had been sedulously cultivated in order to disguise and conceal the true relations of this question'.[40]

To Higinbotham and the Governor, the point in dispute was that the correct protocol under responsible government for all judges, whether of the Supreme Court or County Courts, was to apply for leave to the elected Government, not to the representative of the British Crown.

The legal position regarding judges' conditions of employment was complicated, because three Acts of Parliament dealt with the subject. Under the *Supreme Court (Administration) Act* of 1852, the Governor and Council could suspend any judge of the Supreme Court 'who shall be wilfully absent from the colony without a reasonable cause'. Barry contended that the later *Constitution Act of 1855* (18 & 19 Vict. c.55) had effectively repealed this Act by implication. Under this later Act, a judge could be removed by the Governor on receiving addresses from both Houses of the Parliament. This effectively gave great bargaining power to the Legislative Council, since it could withhold co-operation from the elected Government of the day.

In late 1853 and early 1854, when the Constitutional Committee of the Legislative Council had been engaged in framing provisions for the Constitution Bill, Dr Augustus Frederick Adolphus Greeves had moved that the judges of the Supreme Court should only be removed on the presentation of a joint address from both Houses of the legislature. His motion was lost without a division being called for.[41] Despite this, the proposal was reinstated in the Victorian *Constitution Act*.

The oldest of the three acts in force was the Imperial statute of 1782, known as the *Colonial Leave of Absence Act*. This Act had been drafted before the advent of colonial self-government. It provided that the Governor and his Executive Council (which at this stage was not elected but appointed) could dismiss a judge who was absent without having sought and received permission from the Governor.

The four justices of the Supreme Court – Redmond Barry, William Stawell, Edward Williams and Robert Molesworth – held that the 1852 and

1782 Acts no longer applied. They therefore denied that the Government of the day had the constitutional power to dismiss them. They argued that only the Governor, after receiving addresses from both Houses of the Parliament, could dismiss a Supreme Court judge. They did not extend this argument to the judges of the lower courts, but sought only to defend what they regarded as the personal rights and privileges of the judges of the Supreme Court.

Higinbotham and Michie contended that all three Acts were still in force, so that there were, in effect, three methods by which a judge could be removed. One of these was by the Governor in Council. At the time that the 1852 *Supreme Court Act* was drafted, the Governor's Council consisted of those Councillors whom he nominated, but in an era of self-government, the term 'the Governor's Council' had come to mean the Ministers of the elected Government. From the point of view of Higinbotham and Michie, this was as it should be, for it was an essential feature of responsible government that the elected Government of the day should have power over judges' salaries and conditions of employment. Beyond the issue of the privileges of the Supreme Court judges loomed the larger constitutional issue of responsible government which, they believed, was essential for the future peace and good government of the colony.

The dispute became a lengthy saga that Morris described as a four-act play.[42] It involved the Legislative Council, the Judicial Committee of the Privy Council, the Secretary of State for the Colonies and the British Law Officers. In April 1867, the affair ended with Higinbotham's and Michie's position vindicated.

The failure of the Bill to reform the Legislative Council

Following the departure of the *Shenandoah*, the Constitution Act Amendment Bill (alternatively entitled 'A Bill for Reform of the Legislative Council') came before the Legislative Council. It aimed to reduce the property qualification of members and of electors for the Legislative Council, and to reduce the terms of office of members from ten to five years. McCulloch's Minister, Matthew Hervey, introduced the Bill into the Council and spoke eloquently in favour of its principles. He argued that it was essentially a conservative measure because 'a great reduction had taken place in the value of land since the *Constitution Act* came into existence', and this had reduced by about a half the number of people who met the property requirements to vote for members of the Legislative Council. He argued that reducing the property qualification would help to overcome the current difficulty of finding candidates for seats in the House. He pointed out that neither Tasmania nor South Australia had a property qualification for candidates for membership of their Upper Houses.[43]

Those opposed to the Bill invoked the spectre of democracy. Eighty-one-year-old William Henry Hull, the Member for Central Province, reminded members of the French Revolution and warned of the dangers of 'ultra democracy' in the Legislative Assembly, arguing that Victoria was particularly vulnerable because the Victorian goldfields had attracted 'the tag-rag and bobtail of the world'. He accused Hervey of being an 'ultra'.[44] He quoted indignantly from Higinbotham's election speech in which he had attacked the Council for obstructionism. 'Was such language to be endured?' Hull asked rhetorically. Next, McCulloch's former Minister, Thomas Howard Fellows, prominently attacked the principles of the Bill in the Council. The Pastoral Association had retained Fellows as its standing counsel, and he had resigned from McCulloch's ministry over ideological differences. He expressed regret that the Council had not been *more* obstructive. 'It would have been an excellent thing', Fellows said, 'if the Council had kicked manhood suffrage out'.[45]

There may have been a personal element behind Fellows' motivation for attacking the McCulloch ministry's reform proposals. In June 1854, Fellows had stood as a candidate for the Loddon District in the (old) Legislative Council. A lengthy article in the *Melbourne Morning Herald* had attacked him for doing so while maintaining his position as the standing counsel to the Pastoral Association. Though the article was anonymous, the writer was probably Michie. He had argued that in accepting the position of a legislator while being retained as advocate to 'a small class interest inimical to the welfare of the rest of the community', Fellows occupied 'a debased and contemptible position'.[46] When McCulloch's Reform Bill was put to the vote in the Legislative Council, the numbers for and against were equally divided, but as a clear majority was required for any change of the Constitution, the Bill was declared lost.

The Government had taken three key policies to the election and received strong popular support. It had negotiated exhaustively with the Council in order to pass the Grant *Land Act*. But the Council had driven such a hard bargain that the resulting Act benefited the squatters more than the intended class of small farmers. The Bill for Reform of the Legislative Council had been lost. Only the Tariff Bill remained. It therefore came before the Parliament against a background of polarised and mounting popular feeling, orchestrated by the rival newspaper proprietors. Although a relatively mild measure in itself, the Tariff Bill had come to assume great symbolism as a critical point in the contest for power between the McCulloch Government and the Legislative Council.

In his nine years in Victoria, Higinbotham had seen how indifference to the public welfare had played out in the maladministration of the goldfields, the dilatoriness and deception in the drafting of the Constitution, the brutal attack on sleeping families at Eureka, the scandalous misuse of public funds for private purposes, and more recently, the heartless indifference to the needs of the unemployed. It was in this same light that he saw the inexorable determination of many of the wealthy landowners and squatters to deny access to affordable, agricultural land to families struggling to sustain themselves. It was man's inhumanity to his fellow man that filled him with outrage. It had done so during his youth in famine-stricken Ireland, and would continue to do so until the end of his life.

He knew that he could not change human nature, but he believed that the political process was capable of a higher purpose than outcomes determined by the power of vested interests. He believed that the parliamentary process must be made to operate within the framework of respect for the public interest. If the Upper House could be made to see its role as a house of review that was respectful of the expressed will of the electorate, there was hope that the Constitution could yet be made workable.

But to reach this point he now saw a need to force the issue by precipitating a crisis of such magnitude that it would shake the Council out of its complacency and cause it to feel the full force of the public hostility that was gathering against it. If the Council should block the combined Tariff and Appropriation Bill, and thereby starve the Government of funds, such a political crisis would ensue. He gambled that the public alarm that this would generate would bring the Council to a realisation that it must modify its obstructionism.

13

THE STRUGGLE FOR THE PUBLIC PURSE

The gestation of the constitutional crisis that was to shake Victorian society for fifteen years had its origins in the drafting of the new Constitution of 1855, but the struggle between the Upper House and Lower House began in earnest in spring 1864 with a proposal for a reform of the tariff. By then it was apparent that the inability of successive Governments to implement the policies of land reform and electoral reform that the electorate demanded was caused not so much by a lack of will as by a lack of political power. Despite promises to the contrary at the time of drafting, by 1864, the popularly elected Lower House had come to realise that it could not govern effectively because major reforms were repeatedly obstructed by the Upper House. The electors of the Legislative Council numbered about 8,500 in a population of approximately 600,000, and were predominantly pastoralists and merchants.[1] About one-seventieth of the population wielded power out of all proportion to their numerical strength.

At the election of September 1864, McCulloch announced that the Government would embark on a reform of the tariff. David Syme, the publisher and editor of the *Age* newspaper, welcomed McCulloch's proposed tariff reform. In editorials and news columns, Syme had argued passionately for a tariff policy to protect Victoria from cheap imports, hoping thereby to stimulate the development of native industries. Since taking over as editor and publisher in 1860, Syme had halved the cost of the newspaper to threepence and would subsequently reduce it to twopence. The increase in its circulation that resulted expanded the influence of Syme's ideas. He maintained the radical stance that the *Age* had taken since its establishment in September 1854, and his editorials appealed to a nascent colonial patriotism. As well as protection of native industry, he strongly supported land reform and electoral reform. 'Cheap land, abundant labour and fiscal protection must go hand in hand in this country before it attains to the prosperity of which it is so eminently capable', he declared.[2]

In the early 1860s, the Victorian economy was stagnant.[3] A population eager for employment was naturally attracted to the idea that the protection of native industry offered the promise of economic development. McCulloch denied that the proposed change to the tariff constituted protectionism, claiming that its purpose was merely to distribute duties across a range of commodities more equitably. The export duty on gold was to be abolished, and duties on certain products would be reduced, while others would incur new duties. In September 1864, in his election speech to his constituents at Cranbourne, McCulloch urged voters to support the ministry because its current legislative program would prepare the way to attend to unspecified 'important matters that had been delayed for years past'.[4] In time it became apparent that one of these 'important matters' was education reform. He argued that there was 'nothing inconsistent with free trade principles in changing the duties from tea and sugar to other articles of import'. But he also claimed that the intention of the proposed change was 'to equalize our tariff with those of the neighbouring colonies'.[5] In an effort to appeal to the advocates of protection, McCulloch argued that free trade should not be 'pushed to such an extent as to offer bonuses and to give protection to other countries at our own expense'.[6] The *Argus,* which strongly opposed protectionism, attacked the muddled messages in McCulloch's speech and warned voters that 'the Ministry may turn protectionist at the first opportunity'.[7] Higinbotham, who had identified as a free trade supporter at the election of 1861, also denied that the proposed reform was protectionist.[8] He told the Legislative Assembly on 31 January 1865 that the purpose of the new tariff would be to cast the burden of taxation 'upon classes who had not hitherto borne their fair share of it'.[9]

In November 1864, the Governor, Sir Charles Darling, had written to the Secretary of State for the Colonies, Edward Cardwell, reporting the results of the recent election, and advising him of the popular support in Victoria for protection of native industry. In February 1865, he received Cardwell's reply. Cardwell declared that 'it would be a subject of sincere regret to Her Majesty's Government' if the principle of protection of native industry should be implemented in Victoria.[10] Despite the implied instruction that the Governor should take steps to inhibit the implementation of protection, Darling took the view that it was the duty of a colonial Governor to act on the advice of his Ministers, and kept his own counsel.

One week before the *Shenandoah* entered Port Phillip, the Treasurer, George Verdon, had presented his budget and outlined the Government's new rates. As was customary, the new duties schedule was circulated to ports and implemented immediately. But rumours circulated that the Legislative Council was planning to block the Tariff Bill. Indeed, since the inauguration of the Parliament ten years earlier, the Legislative Council had blocked fifty-nine Bills.[11] On 2 March, in an attempt to prevent the Council from doing so, McCulloch took the advice of Higinbotham and arranged for the Tariff Bill to be combined with the Appropriation Bill in what became known as a 'tack'. Under the Constitution of 1855, the Council was empowered to reject but not to amend money bills. By combining the two Bills, Higinbotham and McCulloch expected that the Council would have to allow the new tariff, for to reject the combined Bill would leave the Government without money to function, and thereby create a serious crisis. Higinbotham defended the legitimacy of the arrangement by arguing that the Tariff Bill and the Appropriation Bill were alike in that both were money bills, and that there was nothing in the Constitution against the 'tacking' of bills.

Four and a half months later, the combined Appropriation and Tariff Bill passed the Legislative Assembly by 38 votes to 19, and was then presented to the Legislative Council.[12] During the debate in the Legislative Assembly, some members opposed the Tariff Bill as not being truly protectionist, while others objected to the abolition of the gold export duty. The historian Gwyneth Dow argues that McCulloch feared that his critics would turn against the Government and that this motivated him to provoke a conflict with the Council, convinced that the strength of their indignation with the Council would win them to his side.[13] By contrast, she argues that Higinbotham 'saw it as a mission to which he was dedicated'. She adds that 'it released the passionate political energy which was to establish both his authority and his reputation'.[14]

Upon receiving the combined Appropriation and Tariff Reform Bill, the Council appointed a committee to examine it. The committee reported that the 'tack' was unconstitutional. The Council therefore 'laid aside' the entire Bill and made no report to the Legislative Assembly. In effect, the Bill was rejected. The new duties continued to be collected, but the Government could not access the revenue because the Appropriation Bill had not passed the Legislative Council. McCulloch moved four resolutions in the Legislative Assembly, that were probably drafted by Higinbotham, claiming that the Lower House alone had the right of granting aid and supplies to the Crown. The last resolution demanded that the Legislative Council adopt the tariff and thereby acknowledge 'the rightful control of this House over taxation and supply'.[15] The Council refused to do so.

The Colony in turmoil

On 28 July 1865, the *Government Gazette* announced that payments to government employees were suspended. The following day, McCulloch tendered the resignation of his ministry to Sir Charles Darling, but the Governor declined to accept it. Instead an irregular arrangement was negotiated with the London Chartered Bank, of which McCulloch was a director. The Bank agreed to advance short-term loans to the Government. When the Government failed to repay each loan, the Bank sued the

Government. When the Governor received a court document from the creditors showing that the money was owed to the Bank, he authorised the payment from consolidated revenue. By this method the Government obtained £880,000 to meet its requirements.[16]

The Governor reported to the Colonial Office what had happened. He advanced his own view that the Council had been trying to force the ministry to resign because of the 'honesty and good faith' they had shown in carrying out the provisions of the *Land Act*.[17] In October, the Legislative Council called upon the Governor to forward to the Queen a petition largely composed by Thomas Fellows. The petition requested Imperial intervention to maintain 'the Constitution, as by law established'.[18] It argued that it was illegal for the Governor to borrow money without the sanction of both Houses of the Legislature. It described the current arrangement as 'not only collusive but unconstitutional, if not revolutionary'.[19] The Chamber of Commerce forwarded its own petition to the Queen, with twenty thousand signatures. In December, twenty-two Executive Councillors also petitioned the Queen, complaining of 'illegal acts' that 'could not have been committed, much less persisted in, if His Excellency, the Governor, had not given them the sanction of his authority'.[20] The Executive Council included Ministers from both the current and former administrations, many of them opposed to the current Government.

Darling forwarded the Executive Council's petition, but he accompanied it with a lengthy dispatch in which he defended his actions. He characterised the conduct of the Executive Councillors who had signed the petition as 'highly discreditable'. He pointed out that their arguments 'suppressed every material fact and circumstance upon which it is well known that my justification of the proceedings they impugn is based'.[21] It is likely that Higinbotham assisted in the drafting of this dispatch.[22] Darling made a tactical mistake when he attacked the characters of the Executive Councillors who had signed the petition and added that he would not be prepared to work with them in the future.[23] This would provide the grounds for the Colonial Secretary to declare that Darling had favoured one side in the dispute and thereby disqualified himself from continuing as Governor.

The Supreme Court also became embroiled in the dispute. A case brought before it involved the issue of whether certain duties on goods that had been paid were in fact owed, or whether (as the plaintiffs argued) the duties had not been 'lawfully imposed'. The Chief Justice, William Stawell, considered that the resolutions of the Legislative Assembly on which the collection of the new duties was based 'are not equal to an Act of Parliament, and that nothing but an Act of Parliament can have the effect of imposing taxation'.[24] However, the Government's counsel had advanced a second argument that was not decided. They had argued that under a privilege that the Legislative Assembly had inherited from the House of Commons, the Legislative Assembly was entitled to impose and collect the customs duties until the end of the session in which the resolutions were passed. On this view, the duties were lawful. It claimed that the evidence for this privilege was to be found in the journals of the House of Commons. Regarding the status of the House of Commons journals as evidence of the existence of the claimed privilege, Stawell commented that the question 'is one of some difficulty, and we will further consider it'.[25] Higinbotham then announced that the Government would appeal to the Privy Council, and in the meantime, the Government continued to collect the duties while the matter was awaiting determination.

The conflict had now reached grave proportions. On one side of the dispute, the Chamber of Commerce, the pastoralists, the Supreme Court, most of the banks, the Executive Council, the Legislative Council and a section of the press were aligned. On the other side, the Government and a substantial majority of the electors aligned. The Colonial Office in London became alarmed at the mounting crisis. Sir Frederic Rogers, the Permanent Under-Secretary to the Colonial Office, was either unaware or chose to ignore the fact that the matter of law was to be considered by the Privy Council. He attacked Sir Charles Darling for following the advice of his legal officers. Edward Cardwell, the Colonial Secretary, rebuked Darling for 'continued violation of the law, with the concurrence of the Queen's representative'.[26] Pre-empting the decision of the Privy Council, the petitioners argued that the Supreme Court had asserted that the matter of the collection of duties 'was not warranted by law'. They further complained that 'the Governor still allows the pretended duties to be collected as if no judgement had been pronounced'.[27]

The legal historian John Bennett comments that 'the Colonial Office seems not to have seen the judgement or realized that the proceedings were interlocutory'. He notes that Rogers reported that the Government was 'disingenuous', and that the Governor was at fault, 'because he persisted in acting on the opinion of his legal officers after an adverse judgement of the Supreme Court'. In Bennett's opinion, the facts did not warrant these accusations.[28]

Meanwhile, the Legislative Assembly had passed the Tariff Bill as a separate measure and re-submitted it to the Legislative Council. But the separated Tariff Bill was rejected by a majority of fourteen.[29] It was no more acceptable to the Council than the tacked Bill had been, for this time it included a preamble in which the Assembly asserted its exclusive right to grant supply.[30] Following the Council's rejection of the Bill, Darling announced that the collection of duties under the new tariff would cease, and the amounts already received would be refunded. The ministry called upon the Governor to dissolve Parliament. On 28 November, the Governor prorogued the Parliament, and in the course of his speech he declared that 'the vital principle of representative institutions is the enlightened will of the community'. The Government members cheered when they received the news of the Governor's declaration.[31]

In the lead-up to the election of December 1865, McCulloch told his constituents that their vote at the coming election would decide:

> Whether the right of taxation is vested solely in that branch of
> the Legislature which represents all classes of the community
> ... or whether the people ... are to submit to the dictation
> of the other branch of the Legislature in whose election they
> have no voice, and over whose actions they have no control.[32]

At the election, the Government received increased support from the electors. Opposition numbers were reduced to 20 in a House of 78. Michie, who had been subjected, along with Higinbotham, to months of frenzied personal attacks by the *Argus*, lost his seat in the wealthy constituency of St Kilda. At Brighton, Higinbotham was returned, though his majority was reduced to 46 votes out of 746.[33] Higinbotham's opponent was James Wilberforce Stephen, a Law lecturer at the University of Melbourne who had the support of the Free Trade League. In his election campaign material, Stephen claimed that the principle of free trade was at stake. He asserted that Higinbotham had misinformed the electors about his stance on that issue. He drew a comparison with the issue of the payment of members, which Higinbotham had previously opposed but subsequently supported.[34] Higinbotham hit back, arguing that a person who was opposed to the principle of the payment of members on the grounds that a candidate for the Assembly ought to be financially independent, could not conscientiously accept payment from an organisation such as the Free Trade League which would expect him to 'carry out the purposes of that particular association'.[35]

On 12 February 1866, the Parliament reconvened. The Tariff Bill passed the Assembly, and was again rejected by the Council. Once again, the Council objected to a preamble asserting the principle of the Assembly's exclusive right to grant supply. Higinbotham defended the preamble in the Assembly. He argued that the drafters of the Constitution had never intended to give the two Houses equal powers with respect to money bills, but to grant to the Lower House, as the more representative House, the right to raise taxation and tariffs. In this he was correct, for when the draft Constitution was under consideration in the (old) Legislative Council both the Colonial Secretary, John Foster, and the Collector of Customs, Hugh Childers, had assured the members that, under the draft provisions of the new Constitution, the Lower House would have control over money bills.[36]

With the failure of his third attempt to have the Council pass the Tariff Bill, McCulloch resigned. This left Darling in a predicament because no alternative ministry could be found among the few remaining Opposition members in the House. He appealed to McCulloch to continue. The McCulloch ministry returned to office, still insisting that the Council must yield in order for the country to be governed. Once again, the Tariff

Bill (reconstituted as the Customs Bill) passed through the Assembly and was presented to the Council. The members of the Legislative Council proposed a conference with seven delegates from each House. Higinbotham was not included among the representatives of the Legislative Assembly. He continued to hold that the preamble was necessary, 'to serve as a perpetual reminder to this House of its own rights'.[37] The conference arrived at an agreement by which the Assembly agreed to modify the preamble and the Council agreed to pass the Customs Bill. However, before the Council had voted upon the Bill, news arrived on 17 April that the Colonial Office had recalled Governor Darling.

The shock announcement foreshadowed a new stage of the conflict, and was destined to prolong it for another twenty-seven months. The recall of Darling meant not only that he would lose his salary and his right to a pension, but that he was disgraced. Edward Cardwell, the Colonial Secretary, accused Darling of colluding in illegal acts, and of showing partisanship in the dispute between the Houses.[38] In particular he commented that by attacking the Executive Councillors, Darling had rendered himself ineligible to serve as the Colony's Governor in the future.[39] But with the agreement between the Houses now achieved, the two Bills with an amended preamble passed both Houses.

The Darling grant controversy

While the petitioners may have felt vindicated by the Colonial Office's recall of Darling, the response from London served to further inflame political tensions in Victoria. It engendered a new wave of indignation against the Opposition, and an outpouring of sympathy for the Governor and his family. In the weeks before his departure and even after it, there were many petitions to the Queen in support of Darling.[40] The Legislative Assembly acknowledged his service in a formal address to the Queen. As Colonial Office regulations did not allow a serving Governor to accept a gratuity, they proposed a grant of £20,000 to Lady Darling.

On 2 May 1866, Higinbotham delivered a lengthy speech in the Legislative Assembly. He said that he felt deeply 'the injury done to Sir Charles Darling', and he urged that the House should not allow him 'to leave these shores ruined in fortune or in reputation'. He urged a vote of confidence and thanks to Sir Charles, and also compensation to him for 'the heavy pecuniary loss, which, in addition to his injured reputation, he will have to endure'. He added that the dispatches from the Colonial Office 'threaten danger to the public liberties of this people', for they constituted interference with the domestic affairs of the Government of the Colony. He warned of the existence of a powerful class in the Colony that was 'hostile to the continuance of responsible government'. When a member objected, Higinbotham instanced the Opposition's tactic of appealing to Britain and endeavouring 'to secure by English interference, the object which might be legitimately sought for by colonial action'. He concluded with an appeal to the Assembly to 'place upon record ... by a significant act, our firm determination to maintain in their integrity the self-governing rights of independence in this country'.[41]

By now the struggle had become multi-faceted. It had long been a struggle for power between the Houses. In the eyes of many, it was a struggle to establish democracy. Now, with the recall of Darling, the issue had become personalised. With the interference by the British Minister, the struggle had taken on elements of a dispute about nationhood.

Sir Charles Darling left Victoria on 5 May 1866. Cheering crowds accompanied him to the wharf and there were emotional scenes as he departed. When Darling arrived in London, the Secretary of State for the Colonies had changed. The new incumbent was the Fourth Earl of Carnarvon, Henry Herbert. Darling lobbied for an inquiry that would clear his name, but was unsuccessful. Over a period of nine months, he appealed in vain to Carnarvon for some financial assistance, but his appeals were contemptuously rebuffed. The historian John Bennett believes that, unlike his predecessor, Carnarvon disapproved of Darling's handling of the *Shenandoah* incident and that this may explain his repeated curt dismissals of Darling's pleas.[42] A letter from Darling requested the Victorian

Legislative Assembly to delay progress on the gift until he knew if his plea for an inquiry would be granted.

In February 1867, the Speaker of the Assembly received a reply from Carnarvon stating that it was 'impossible' for him to advise Her Majesty to assent to such a proposal. He added that if Sir Charles Darling, while in the service of the Colonial Office, were to accept the proposed gift, it would be regarded 'as a final relinquishment by Sir Charles Darling of that service, and of all the emoluments or expectations attaching to it'.[43]

In April 1867, with all avenues exhausted and his finances depleted, Darling resigned from the Colonial Service. When the news reached Victoria, the Assembly prepared to proceed with the grant. In late July the new Victorian Governor, Sir John Henry Manners Sutton, agreed to make the customary formal request to the Assembly to raise a money grant. Privately he wrote to the Colonial Office that this did not signify his approval of the measure. Nevertheless his decision to comply with the Government's request angered his superiors. Ten months later, Sir Roundell Palmer, a former Attorney-General in Lord Russell's Liberal Government, tabled a motion that the House of Commons should condemn Governor Darling's conduct.[44] In Victoria, the Assembly included the grant in an Appropriation Bill and presented it to the Council. This revived the dispute about the right of the Legislative Assembly to control money bills and the issue of 'tacking' bills. On 20 August, the Council rejected the Bill and the Government was left without money to pay its civil servants and suppliers.

The situation was now as it had been in 1865 except for the fact that Manners Sutton negotiated a Temporary Supply Bill with the Legislative Council.[45] This provided an interim solution to the problem of the finances, but not to the issue of the Darling grant. McCulloch asked Manners Sutton to prorogue Parliament briefly so that a new session could be declared, and the Appropriation Bill with the grant included could be again presented to the Parliament. When the Governor declined, the ministry again resigned.

On 10 September 1867, the Governor prorogued the Parliament and reconvened it a week later. The McCulloch ministry presented the Appropriation Bill, including the Darling grant, to the Council. On

16 October, the Council again rejected it. The House was dissolved on 30 December. The historian Henry Turner recorded that in late 1867 there were numerous public meetings where the speakers were 'riotously unanimous for sweeping away the obstructive Council'.[46]

Manners Sutton wrote to Richard Temple-Grenville, Duke of Buckingham and Chandos, who in March 1867 had replaced Henry Herbert as Secretary of State for the Colonies. He warned that 'a conflict such as that now in progress strains the Constitution ... I cannot assert that the Constitution will endure the strain much longer.'[47] However, in a dispatch written on 1 January 1868, Buckingham instructed Manners Sutton that he:

> ought not again to recommend the vote to the acceptance of the Legislature ... except on a clear understanding that it will be brought before the Legislative Council in a manner which will enable them to exercise their discretion respecting it without the necessity of throwing the colony into confusion.[48]

Ironically, two months later, the Colonial Secretary dispatched a contradictory instruction, but it arrived too late to be implemented. The ministry had resigned yet again, and the deadlock had resumed. The Governor was unable to find an alternative ministry and, in the circumstances, no parliamentary business could be transacted. For two months, the members met and, in the absence of a ministry, adjourned the House. As McCulloch was unwell, Higinbotham regularly moved the motion for adjournment. In a confidential dispatch to the Secretary of State for the Colonies, Manners Sutton appealed to Buckingham to issue an 'authoritative' announcement that if the Council continued to oppose the wishes of the majority, it must be held responsible for a situation in which the Queen's Government could not be carried on. Buckingham, Rogers and the Parliamentary Under-Secretary of State for the Colonies, Charles Adderley, considered that this request should be refused. They informed Manners Sutton that to accede to his request was 'impossible'.[49]

The Sladen–Fellows Government

On 6 May 1868, the Governor convinced Charles Sladen to form a Government. Sladen was a lawyer and sheep grazier who represented the Western Province in the Legislative Council. On 29 May, the Governor re-opened the Parliament. Thomas Howard Fellows, who had transferred to the Legislative Assembly to strengthen the conservative team in that House, became the leader of the new Government in the Assembly. On 9 June, the new Sladen Government lost a vote of confidence in the Legislative Assembly but, as there was no alternative ministry, it continued in office. Fearing that unless it made some overture towards the Opposition, the Sladen Government would be stymied, Fellows offered to re-introduce the Darling grant in a separate Bill.

Fellows reached an agreement with the Council that they would pass the Bill provided that there was no preamble or 'tack'.[50] With such an understanding, he might have planned to tempt the majority in the Assembly to agree to support this course of action. This would drive a wedge between those in the Assembly who were prepared to settle for achieving the grant to Darling, and those who were determined not to surrender the fight until the Council agreed to acknowledge the Assembly's claims to control of the public revenue. He might have hoped that by convincing the Legislative Council to allow the passage of the Darling grant, the Council could fend off the attack on what it insisted were its rightful powers regarding money bills. If his scheme worked, his Government would have achieved a victory and might have been able to gain the confidence of the Assembly.

Whether the 'wedge' would have succeeded will never be known, for news arrived of an extraordinary turn of events in London. Sir Charles Darling had applied to withdraw his resignation from the Colonial Service, and this had been accepted. It was later revealed that the Secretary of State for the Colonies had invited him to do so.[51] Darling received £2,000 from the Colonial Office. He notified the Legislative Assembly that he was now unable to accept a grant from the Victorian Government. Darling provided an explanation that may have served to save face for the British Government over its dramatic change of attitude. He said that he had been under 'a misapprehension as to the views entertained by Her Majesty's Government' when he had tendered his resignation, but that the matter had since been resolved. Darling's livelihood and pension entitlements were restored; the serious charge that, as Governor, he had repeatedly connived in illegal acts was apparently forgotten. The issue of the grant was now irrelevant.

The end of the deadlock

Perhaps it was the strain of the years of Darling's life in Victoria, culminating in the unjust and capricious treatment of him by his superiors, that took a toll on his health, for he died in January 1870, aged sixty. From the time of his arrival in Victoria in 1863, he had served two Secretaries of State for the Colonies: Henry Pelham Clinton, the Fifth Duke of Newcastle, and Edward Cardwell. Colonial policy was contested in Britain, and it was important for a colonial Governor to know the mind of the Minister of the day. But like Hotham before him, Darling had to rely on dispatches carried by ships. He often had to make decisions in rapidly changing circumstances and inevitably there were times when he risked incurring the wrath of his superiors. He had also tried to meet the expectations of the Colonial Office's permanent staff. As Governor of the Colony and a man of liberal convictions, he had considered it his duty to take the advice of the elected Government regarding domestic affairs. But in the turbulence of the protracted constitutional struggle, it had proven impossible to satisfy all of his masters. Following his death, both Houses of the Victorian Parliament agreed to grant Lady Darling the sum of £5,000 for the education of her children and a pension of £1,000 per year.

In Victoria, despite the long and taxing struggle, the issue of the control of money bills was as far from resolution as ever. The Lower House's claim to control money bills was not vindicated. The Upper House was not vanquished. Twice the British Government had intervened just as the struggle between the Houses was reaching a point where the Council was on the brink of giving ground. In both instances, the Colonial Secretary had adroitly moved his chess piece – the Governor – in such a way as to snatch victory away from the Legislative Assembly in its dispute with the Council.

The historian Gwyneth Dow remarked that, during the long constitutional struggle, Higinbotham had become known as 'the most adamant defender of the powers of the popular House, and as the most uncompromising opponent of the Council and of Imperial interference in domestic affairs'. She added that he was 'probably the most hated and the most loved man in Victoria'.[52] The conservative historian Turner – who was no admirer – said of Higinbotham that by his passionate oratory, 'he exercised a sway over the House which in Victoria has never been equalled'.[53] But his failure in the constitutional struggle affected Higinbotham's relationship with McCulloch, who would, in time, view him as a liability.

The Colonial Office and colonial democracy

The role of the Colonial Office during the Victorian constitutional crises of 1865 and 1867 was a continuation of a pattern of behaviour that was observable as far back as 1854, when the Victorian Legislative Council forwarded its draft Constitution to London. In the thirteen years between 1854 and 1867, when the second deadlock was ended by Governor Darling's re-instatement, ten incumbents from four different parties had held the office of Secretary of State for the Colonies. The portfolio was immense and the incumbents did not stay in office long enough to master it. Inevitably each relied on the advice of his permanent staff. The Colonial Office staff were therefore extremely influential not only in administering policy but in advising as to what that policy should be.

The Colonial Office had long distrusted democracy, which it saw as tending to republicanism, and the constitutional struggle in Victoria seemed a case in point. In 1854 Sir Frederic Rogers had warned that 'responsible government, once established, the dissolution of the Empire becomes a matter of time'.[54] At the time of the passage of the new Constitution of 1855, Rogers had justified the anti-democratic nature of the Constitution by mendaciously noting in his report on the draft Constitution that the Legislative Council in Victoria had adopted the scheme, 'with little popular remonstrance'.[55]

This was untrue, for there had been a great deal of 'popular remonstrance'. In recent years new evidence has come to light that, from as early as 1853, the diggers on the goldfields were concerned about their lack of political rights. In the 1980s, a petition, thirteen metres in length, was discovered in a rubbish dump. Its preservation for over 130 years was a surprise. The petition contained over 5,000 names of diggers from five goldfields, and had been presented to Lieutenant-Governor Joseph La Trobe on 1 August 1853.[56] The petition had been edged in green silk; an indication that the women of the goldfields who sewed the edging cared about the issues as well as their menfolk. The petitioners reminded the Governor that, 'although they contribute to the Exchequer more than half the revenue of the Colony, they are the largest class of Her Majesty's subjects in the Colony unrepresented'.[57]

The historian Graeme Tucker notes a public meeting of 800 people on the Ovens goldfield in April 1853 at which there was a call for political representation for the diggers, and another at Sandhurst (Bendigo), attended by 6,000 people on 16 July 1853, which also protested the lack of representation.[58] This widespread feeling of political powerlessness among the goldfields population arose initially in response to issues about the gold licence and to grievances about the administration of the goldfields. By December 1853, at both Ballarat and Bendigo, the diggers movement had begun to develop an organisational structure and to articulate an agenda. These developments coincided with the framing of the new Victorian Constitution, for the diggers discovered that the public had been excluded from the drafting process.

How strongly people felt can be gauged from the resolutions of a public meeting at Bendigo on 31 December 1853, attended by 1,500 people. They declared:

> A free people can only assume a Constitutional Government through chosen representatives, informed of the interests, circumstances and desires of their correspondents, deliberately adopted in open and independent communication in national convention – we hereby, in full public assembly, make solemn declaration that the Legislative Council has usurped the people's authority, and does not represent, express or recognize the public opinion …

The meeting even threatened civil disobedience to the proposed Constitution:

> Any such measure emanating from the Council would be regarded by the people as a violation of their inherent and inalienable rights, and without the force, the dignity and the obligation of constitutional law.[59]

This meeting was sympathetically reported in the London-based publication, the *Australian and New Zealand Gazette*.[60]

In Bendigo in mid-January 1854, Dr John Downes Owens accosted the Colonial Secretary John Foster on behalf of the goldfields population and urged him to allow popular consultation in the drafting of the new Constitution. Foster replied that the 'correct method' was to send a petition to the Legislative Council.[61] A petition to the Legislative Council was composed and based upon the resolutions of the public meeting at Bendigo of 31 December 1853. The petitioners boldly charged that 'the Legislative Council has usurped the people's authority'.[62] When the Bendigo diggers' delegates subsequently presented this petition in February, the Council declined to accept it. John Pascoe Fawkner moved a motion supporting the aims of the petition but this was defeated.[63] The *Australian and New Zealand Gazette* reported to its British readers that they were:

> very much disgusted with the refusal of the Legislative Council to hear Doctors Owens and Wall at the bar of the House against the new Constitution bill.[64]

In early 1854, when the recommendations of the Constitutional Committee were considered in the Legislative Council as a whole, the goldfields population's concern about their lack of political rights quickly translated into alarm at the revelation in the newspapers of what they had feared: the provisions of the draft Constitution were strongly anti-democratic in flavour. The *Melbourne Morning Herald,* of which Archibald Michie was the principal shareholder in 1854, took a particular interest in the provisions of the new Constitution. Its editorials were critical of some key provisions of the draft, particularly concerning the property qualifications for voting, and the extensive powers of the Governor *vis-à-vis* the legislature. More so than its rivals, the *Herald* featured reports from its correspondents on the goldfields of the public meetings and their resolutions. Yet, until recently the *Melbourne Morning Herald* has not been systematically studied for its reports of these meetings on the goldfields.[65] They reveal that, far from being politically apathetic, or as Stawell charged, too busy 'a money-making', the people of the goldfields – including professionals, teachers, shopkeepers, bankers and tradespeople – engaged in every legal form of public 'remonstrance' that was available to them to protest the provisions of the draft Constitution.

The anti-democratic provisions of the proposed Constitution became one of the grievances that precipitated the conflict at Eureka in December 1854. A public meeting at Bendigo of 26 August 1854 illustrated the mounting alarm of the population. Those present complained of 'their almost total exclusion from the rights of free men under the proposed new Constitution', adding that 'the meeting respectfully claim their right to a voice in the framing and passing of laws that may vitally affect their interests'.[66] A month before the conflict at Eureka, the principles and objects of the Ballarat Reform League were passed at a public meeting. In its opening sentence, the resulting document asserted 'the inalienable right of every citizen to have a voice in making the laws he is called upon to obey'. It declared that the League's object was 'to place the power in the hands of responsible representatives of the people to frame wholesome laws and carry on an honest government'. It objected to the proposed property qualifications for members and electors and called for 'full and fair representation'.[67]

On 28 November, at what was to be the final meeting before the dawn attack at Eureka, Sir Charles Hotham, the Attorney-General and the Colonial Secretary met with three delegates of the goldfields population. Their grievances were discussed, including the denial of political rights under the proposed new Constitution. The Governor, William Stawell and John Foster adamantly refused to concede on the issue.[68]

It is not plausible that Rogers was unaware of the political grievances that formed a large component of that dissent, or that he sincerely believed that the undemocratic provisions of the new Constitution were justified by a lack of 'public remonstrance' against them. The protest meetings, petitions, memoranda and delegations seeking consultation and representation for the goldfields communities were reported in British newspapers. The major metropolitan newspapers of Victoria were also circulated in Britain through the post. The *Australian and New Zealand Gazette* had regularly documented the dissent simmering on the Victorian goldfields over many months, and had featured an editorial on the defects of Victoria's new Constitution draft.[69]

Rogers had served three Colonial Secretaries as the Permanent Under-Secretary over the past nine years and had become the guiding spirit of Colonial Office policy. As a constant figure serving a succession of Ministers, he had long warned against ceding too much power to the colonies, particularly instancing the danger that the colonies might introduce 'very high prohibitory duties on our own cotton and woollen goods'.[70] In Canada in the mid-1850s, large debts from railway expansion led the Government to introduce a tariff designed to raise revenue. Before long, the tariff had changed such that its effect was to protect native industries from foreign imports.[71] It is likely that Rogers feared that McCulloch's Tariff Bill might lead to a similar development. He was also unwilling to see the Victorian Upper House, which had been designed as a brake on democracy, overborne by popular activism. The Victorian example might be repeated in other British colonies where Lower Houses came into conflict with

Upper Houses. In Rogers' view, democratic pressures must be resisted if the Empire was to keep control of her colonies.

From the point of view of both the British Government and the Colonial Office, it was essential to demonstrate control. Darling's repeated requests for an inquiry to clear his name were declined possibly because of what it might reveal. An inquiry might have drawn attention to the questionable way in which the Colonial Office and two Colonial Ministers from two different parties had handled the constitutional crisis in Victoria. A large gift from the Victorian Government to Sir Charles Darling was an even greater threat, for it would have constituted an intolerable snub to the Minister and the Colonial Office who had accused the Governor of illegal actions. This may explain the decision to invite Darling back into the Colonial Service with a barely plausible, face-saving explanation. The long-term welfare of the Victorian population was sacrificed to the Minister's need to avoid the embarrassment that would ensue if the proposed grant from the Victorian legislature were to succeed. The move disrupted the process, which was showing signs of causing the Legislative Council to make concessions in response to the mounting public pressure.

In November 1869, Higinbotham would reflect on all that had transpired, and make a caustic observation that has been often quoted. He would tell the Legislative Assembly:

> The million and a half of Englishmen who inhabit these colonies, and who during the last fifteen years have believed they possessed self-government, have been really governed during the whole of that time by a person named Rogers.[72]

But it was not merely the personality of Rogers that was the cause of the problem. Following the pensions affair and Hotham's Minute ten years earlier, Higinbotham's youthful, idealistic expectations that the British Government would be prepared to facilitate an enlightened system of self-government in Victoria had given way to a jaundiced view of the entire colonial system as being fundamentally a deception:

> The Governor, only the sham of a sham; himself only a
> servant of a Downing Street Clerk; the Downing Street
> Clerk only the minister of the hour, – the minister of the
> hour swayed by every wind of baleful influence, home faction
> or jobbing could bring to bear on dispensers of patronage.
> What wonder that such a hotbed of absurdities and follies
> and dishonesties should break down in the working and
> make colonial government synonymous with the thimble rig,
> or with any other equally skilful machinery for deceiving the
> public eye, and emptying the public pocket.[73]

His friendship with Sir Charles Darling may have caused him to resile from such a cynical view for a time. It may have renewed his hope that, with a liberal-minded Governor, a workable democratic system could yet be salvaged from the flawed Constitution of 1855. But recent events proved to him that the Colonial Office, regardless of the popular will, was determined to buttress the oligarchical system it had imposed in 1855, and to oppose the efforts of the popularly elected House to take control of the public purse.

For Victoria, Darling's recall ensured that the disagreement between the Houses remained an open sore for years to come. The unresolved dispute would lead to a further damaging and bitter deadlock in 1878, under the ministry of Graham Berry. Indeed, it would be well into the twentieth century before the undemocratic aspects of the 1855 Constitution were erased. This happened partly by amendments of the Constitution, partly by changes to the Governors' instructions by the British Government, and partly by the establishment of political practices. Ironically, given Higinbotham's views, the growth of the party system also played a part in countering the oligarchical nature of the Constitution.

14

THE AFTERMATH OF THE STRUGGLE

The recall of Governor Darling dealt a devastating blow to the campaign that Higinbotham had waged to establish the right of the popularly elected House to control Victoria's finances. He saw this principle as fundamental to responsible government, but recent events confirmed what Higinbotham had long suspected: that the Minister of State for the Colonies, and his advisor, the Permanent Under-Secretary of the Colonial Office, still held ultimate power in the land.

Another deep disappointment to Higinbotham arose from the abandonment of his Education Reform Bill. Under the existing system, approximately half the children in the Colony did not regularly attend school. Some families could not afford fees; others lived in districts where no local school existed. In some larger towns, there was a costly duplication of schools as the various religious denominations built schools to serve their flocks and competed for government aid.

On 4 September 1866, the McCulloch ministry established a Royal Commission, with Higinbotham as the Chairman, to investigate a workable system of public education.[1] Representatives of all the denominations were represented on it, although the Catholic representative, Henry Archer, was not an official representative because of the refusal of Archbishop Goold to appoint one. During the latter stage of the constitutional struggle, the Royal Commission met on fifty-two occasions, examined a great many expert witnesses and debated many proposals. It completed its work on 29 January 1867 with a unanimous *Report*.[2]

It recommended that education should be made compulsory, that a responsible Minister be appointed, and that a training school for teachers be established. It recommended that fees for education should continue for most children, but that in rural areas, special grants should be available for the education of Aboriginal children, Chinese children and underprivileged children. There were two highly controversial recommendations. The first was that 'sectarian' religious teaching should not be permitted in the new government schools, although 'religious' teaching would be encouraged. The second was that the expense associated with the building program and the employment of teachers should be financed via a tax on land.[3]

In addition, the Royal Commission produced a draft Education Bill.[4] But without the revenue that the proposed tariff or an unmodified *Land Act* might have returned, the expense could not be met, except by the imposition of another new tax. McCulloch knew that this would inevitably revive the conflict with the Council, and he was unwilling to precipitate another deadlock. Because of the issue of funding, and also because of the opposition of some of the churches, particularly regarding religious teaching in the schools, the Government decided against proceeding with its Education Bill for the time being. This was a very deep disappointment to Higinbotham, who had invested an immense amount of time and energy into the process. To him, education was essential, not only for the intellectual and moral development of each child, but also because a modern democracy required an educated electorate.

Throughout the deadlock, Higinbotham's old friend and neighbour, Captain George Cole, supported him in the Council and at the election meetings in Brighton, but other friendships suffered. Higinbotham deeply regretted that the struggle he had led had destroyed the career and reputation of the Governor, who had become a friend.

As a young journalist with the *Melbourne Morning Herald*, he had endured the dark days of Eureka with Butler Cole Aspinall, his colleague from the *Morning Chronicle* in London. Occasionally, they had composed editorials together. But Aspinall could not forgive McCulloch for supplanting the radical Heales ministry in which he had served as Attorney-General, nor Higinbotham for taking over his office. After all, it was he whose brilliant defence had saved the black American, John Joseph, from the gallows, and that victory had opened the way for the acquittal of all the other Eureka prisoners. Aspinall saw himself as the rightful incumbent who had been displaced by a rival.[5] He became a vigorous opponent of the ministry and accused it of dissembling over the question of protection. He denounced the proposed tariff as 'framed by a committee of commercial ministers so as to please the others', and quipped that it was 'neither fish, fowl, red herring nor pilchard'.[6] This anti-Government stance in a mining electorate at a time when the abolition of the gold duty was part of the proposed tariff reform may have contributed to the loss of his seat.

Archibald Michie, who had given Higinbotham the opportunity to write for the *Melbourne Morning Herald* within days of his arrival in Melbourne, lost his seat in December 1865, although he remained Minister of Justice until July 1866. Michie's gravitas as an older parliamentarian of long standing, his indomitability in debate, his reputation as one of Melbourne's leading lawyers, his voluntary work as counsel for three of the prisoners from Eureka and his personal popularity in Melbourne society had contributed much to the Government's appeal and strength. After Michie's defeat and with McCulloch unwell for a period in early 1868, Higinbotham had led the campaign to force the Council to concede the Assembly's right to control the finances. His fierce determination won him passionate admirers and equally passionate enemies.

He became the primary target of the conservative press and the Opposition. They assailed him with relentless personal attacks, particularly in the weeks before the election of 1866. The *Argus* decried him as 'the most mischievous man who ever attained public distinction in Victoria'.[7] He was – the newspaper asserted – a violator of the law; his conduct was fraudulent, treacherous and reckless; he was motivated by pride and arrogance; he misunderstood political and constitutional history; he was deluded or insane.[8] He was furthermore said to be 'outrageous, unscrupulous and utterly dishonest … in the service of the mob … the worst tyrant there is'.[9] Outwardly he treated the barrage of vilification from his opponents with indifference, but inevitably the insults took a toll on him.

His former adversaries did not miss the opportunity to even old scores. Duffy mischievously suggested that the constitutional struggle would be solved if Higinbotham were to fall asleep for forty-eight hours.[10] Despite Richard Ireland's role in the failure of the Duffy *Land Act*, one of Higinbotham's first acts as Attorney-General had been to appoint him a Queen's Counsel. Ireland's experience and achievements, including acting as counsel for eight of the Eureka prisoners, justified the elevation. But during the constitutional struggle, Ireland had become an implacable foe of the McCulloch Government. Under attack from Ireland in the House, Higinbotham lost control and accused him of representing the views of 'the very vilest faction by which this country has been cursed'.[11] One unexpected ally was the Speaker of the Legislative Assembly and former Speaker of the old Legislative Council, Sir Francis Murphy. Having received a rebuff from his electorate of Murray Boroughs in late 1865, Murphy successfully contested the seat of North Grenville against Aspinall and another candidate. He told his constituents that, although he had striven to act with impartiality throughout the dispute, he had privately agreed with the Government's stand on the rights of the Assembly.[12]

Jones, Glass and the bribery scandal

Another 'friend', Charles Edwin Jones, did enormous damage to Higinbotham's reputation by his unprincipled conduct. Jones was a tailor who was active in the temperance cause and initially a supporter of free trade. His outspoken attacks on Irish Catholics won him the support of the Orange Order in Ballarat, though the Melbourne Orange Lodge expelled him in 1867. After McCulloch ousted the O'Shanassy ministry in June 1863, the Orange Order in Ballarat supported Jones for the seat of Ballarat East at the 1864 election. Jones succeeded, and won the confidence of the ministry, which appointed him to the position of Government Whip. As Whip, he rendered valuable service to the Government by managing to keep the free trade supporters and the protection supporters from uniting to threaten the Government's majority.

Jones may have expected that his services would be rewarded with an invitation to join the ministry, but if so, he was disappointed. It may have been his history of vociferous anti-Catholicism that prevented it. With the intention of achieving agreement among the churches for education reform, the Government hoped to engage the Catholic hierarchy in its Royal Commission and subsequent plan to create a new system of public education. It could not afford to have as a Minister a man who was known for his fiercely anti-Catholic rhetoric. Before long, rumours began to circulate that Jones had been soliciting funds from both the free traders and the pastoralists on the understanding that he was secretly working to defeat McCulloch. The scale of the funds that he solicited from the pastoralists was said to be scandalously large. He defected to the protectionist Opposition in October and lost his seat at the election of 1868. Shortly afterwards, he regained the seat. On 22 December 1868, the McCulloch Government withdrew its Education Reform Bill after the second reading. Jones reconciled with the Government and in April 1870 he received an appointment to McCulloch's second ministry.

The appointment of Jones to the ministry proved disastrous. Substantial evidence of the bribery scandal came to light via court cases and a parliamentary inquiry. Jones vigorously protested his innocence and Higinbotham, who at first refused to believe the charges against his colleague, acted for him as counsel. But as the evidence mounted and Jones' guilt became irrefutable, Higinbotham was forced to recognise that the man whom he had believed to be an honourable friend was indeed guilty.

The *Argus*, which had previously defended Jones, now attacked Higinbotham and the McCulloch Government for elevating Jones to the ministry, 'in spite of his having deserted them two years previously … and in spite of the ugly and well-founded rumours that were in circulation about his character and conduct'.[13] It also attacked Jones for his membership of the Orange Order, which it described as 'a political society with secret signs and watchwords organised for the purpose of transplanting to Victoria the religious and national animosities which have been the curse of Ireland'.[14] It argued fulsomely that the revelations of Jones' reprehensible conduct proved that the *Argus* had been right all along in its campaign against the Government, and its argument that the McCulloch ministry was responsible for 'lowering the whole tone of political life in this colony … and demoralising the representative body'.[15] While not excusing Jones, Higinbotham believed that he had been suborned by others who were the real instigators of the corruption that had dishonoured the Legislative Assembly and the Government. The *Argus* denounced this argument as 'claptrap'. Higinbotham became determined that those who had funded the bribery should be identified and suitably punished.

Higinbotham may have been particularly sensitive to the *Argus's* comments about the Orange Order. The remarks about importing Irish animosities into Victoria may have been designed to carry a warning to Higinbotham, who was Irish, rather than Jones, who was Welsh. In Ireland, the Orange Order had a reputation for condoning violence and for requiring its members to swear an oath of secrecy that extended to shielding other members from the obligations and sanctions of the law where they conflicted with Orange business. Judge William Fletcher, before a grand jury in County Wexford, denounced 'those societies called Orange societies' for 'the pernicious effect of such oaths of silence on the justice system', declaring that 'they poison the very fountains of justice'.[16]

On his father's side, Higinbotham was descended from the family that had established the Orange Order in 1797. During his secondary education at the Dungannon Royal School, it is likely that he stayed at the nearby stately home of Colonel William Verner, his father's cousin, who was the Deputy Grand Master of the Orange Lodge in County Armagh.[17] However, Higinbotham's son-in-law, Morris, hints in his biography that, by his early twenties, Higinbotham had drawn apart from Verner. He reveals that the issue of feeling for the Verner family was a lifelong point of difference between George and Thomas Higinbotham.[18]

Regardless of his current feelings about Sir William Verner, there is some evidence that, in the past, Higinbotham and his mother Sarah had been the beneficiaries of Verner's generosity. Higinbotham may have been apprehensive at the prospect of a revelation of his link with Colonel Sir William Verner. In 1835, the British Parliament had appointed a Select Committee to inquire into the Orange Order, which heard a range of serious allegations against Verner linking him with outbreaks of sectarian violence and associated illegality.[19] Following the investigation, the Whig Government condemned the Orange Order and legislated for its dissolution. A decade later, the Conservative Party returned to power and reversed the ban. Perhaps in the expectation that Verner would deliver votes for the Conservative Party at the coming general election of 1847, it elevated him to the Baronetcy.[20] Verner had also misled the British House of Commons about the seriousness of the crop failure in Ireland at the time of the famine. Higinbotham may have read the *Argus*'s comments about the Orange Order as a warning that it might air these murky affairs involving members of his extended family and Orange politics for the purposes of mounting a new assault on his character. He may have seen in the *Argus* article an implied threat to link his previous defence of Jones with the Orange Order's well-known practice of protecting fellow members who broke the law in the pursuit of Orange business. Any such revelation would destroy his reputation for personal integrity, and cast into doubt his impartiality as Chairman of the Royal Commission into Education and author of its subsequent *Report*.

An inquiry by the Legislative Assembly revealed that a land magnate named Hugh Glass was the principal organiser of the bribery fund that Jones had administered. The money had been donated by pastoralists and used to suborn members of the Legislative Assembly to vote according to their interests.[21] Glass was reputedly Victoria's richest man. He had gained much of that wealth through acquiring freehold land via dubious means, including trading in land certificates. These government-issued certificates were intended to compensate the poorer landowners who had been adversely affected by the operation of the Duffy *Land Act*. They entitled the holder to buy freehold land under the more advantageous terms that subsequently applied. But the certificates became a negotiable currency and fell into the hands of squatters. Glass also employed approximately 300 'dummies' and used their services to amass freehold land that successive Governments had set aside for genuine agriculturalists.[22]

Glass and his accomplice, John Quaterman, were brought before the bar of the House and both confessed to some of the charges, though Glass denied that he had ever intended to corrupt anybody. They were taken into custody by the sergeant-at-arms and delivered to the Melbourne Gaol on the authority of the Legislative Assembly. When the question arose in the House as to how long the two men would be imprisoned, Higinbotham insisted that 'a real and substantial punishment' was called for to serve as a warning to others.

Glass's lawyer claimed that the warrants for his client's arrest were incorrectly drawn and applied to the Supreme Court for his client to be released under a writ of *habeas corpus*. William Stawell, the Chief Justice, heard the case. Richard Ireland, who represented Glass, argued that the Legislative Assembly did not have the right to send a man to gaol. The opposing counsel, Archibald Michie, refuted this argument and contended that the faults in the drafting of the warrants were too minor to invalidate them. Stawell decided, and his brother judges, Edward Williams and Redmond Barry concurred, that it was a matter for the Supreme Court to determine the extent of the powers of the Legislative Assembly, and that in this case the warrants provided insufficient information to the Supreme Court for it to determine whether the limits of the powers had been exceeded. To the jubilation of his supporters, Glass was discharged.[23]

In the Assembly, Higinbotham condemned the Supreme Court's decision. According to the *Argus*, he was in a 'white fury'. He denounced the decision as 'hasty and unconsidered'. He contended that it was wrong that Stawell, who had drafted the law, was also construing it. He argued that 'honest and uncorrupt administration of the affairs of this country' could best be achieved by punishment of the perpetrators. He urged an appeal.[24] The Legislative Assembly established a Special Committee to consider the matter, and the Committee recommended an appeal to the Judicial Committee of the Privy Council. Throughout this period, Glass remained at liberty, but his health deteriorated.

The appeal was heard on 31 January 1871. The Judicial Committee confirmed that the Legislative Assembly had the right that it claimed to commit a person for contempt of the House according to its own judgment of the offence, because 'the full privilege and power (of the House of Commons in 1855) has been transferred to the colony entire'.[25] This was the second time that the power of the Legislative Assembly of Victoria to deal with cases of contempt had been considered by the Privy Council. The earlier attempt in 1862 involved the *Argus*'s printer, George Dill, who had defamed William Frazer, the Member for Creswick.[26] Having already considered the matter of the privileges of the Victorian Legislative Assembly, the Judicial Committee barely disguised its irritation. It pointedly criticised Stawell for his decision and made very explicit the reasons for reversing it. This was the last attempt by the Supreme Court to exercise control over the Legislative Assembly in the exercise of its privileges.[27]

Glass meanwhile had become very ill, and died before the Legislative Assembly could again attempt to imprison him. Had he been punished in 1869 when he had first been brought before the bar of the House, while still in good health and flaunting the lifestyle that his misdeeds had made possible, the lesson would have seemed entirely appropriate and would have received public support. But the long delay occasioned by the need to appeal Stawell's decision meant that the moment was lost. There was nothing to be gained by making an example of a dying man. The bribery scandal therefore ended in an anti-climax. It is doubtful that the voting public gave Higinbotham much credit for his leading role in having the Legislative Assembly recognise and apply its powers to deal with the corruption, or that they appreciated the significance of the Privy Council's confirmation of the Legislative Assembly's powers.

The scandal had shaken public confidence in the Assembly and in the ministry. What may have lingered in the minds of many was the venality and duplicity of Jones, and the fact that Higinbotham had initially defended him. The scandal tarnished the image of the Legislative Assembly and the Government as well as the perpetrators. At the election of 1871, both Higinbotham and Jones were to lose their seats.

The five resolutions of 1869

In the wake of the constitutional struggle in Victoria, the question of the relationship between the Australian colonies and the British Empire was extensively debated in the British House of Lords. Early in November 1869, nine months after he had resigned from the ministry of James McCulloch, Higinbotham gave a marathon speech in the Legislative Assembly over five nights, in support of five resolutions dealing with the Victorian Constitution. He did so in response to the news that a group of Victorian *émigrés*, some of whom were known to hold conservative views, were planning a conference in London to discuss the topic of the relationship between Britain and her Australian colonies. The organisers had invited the Victorian Government to send a representative to the conference. George Verdon, the former Treasurer who was serving as Victoria's Agent-General in London, cautioned against doing so. Higinbotham suspected that the motivation for the conference was to censure the Victorian Government for its stance in the recent struggle. Accordingly he argued against dignifying the conference with official attendance from the Victorian Government.

Higinbotham told the Legislative Assembly that on reading a report of the recent debate in the House of Lords, his eyes had been opened to the extent of anti-democratic and anti-colonial sentiment that some of the Lords harboured. He had been dismayed to discover that most of the speakers had agreed with Lord Salisbury's contention that it was wrong for a colonial Governor to be 'a mere mute person ... who is to do ... whatever the Ministers who happen to be seated in his council chamber may bid him'. The exception had been the Lord Chancellor, Sir Hugh Cairns, who had argued:

> If it was to be laid down as a rule that the Secretary of State
> at home was to hold in leading-strings the Ministry of the

Colony, then the pretence of free colonial institutions was simply a delusion and a mockery.[28]

Higinbotham felt compelled to confront the House of Lords with an expression of the indignation of the colonists of Victoria.

Perhaps inspired by the historical example of Martin Luther, whose ninety-five theses nailed to the door of the Wittenberg Cathedral in 1517 sparked the Protestant Reformation, Higinbotham drafted five resolutions for debate in the Legislative Assembly. The resolutions encapsulated his political philosophy and challenged the members to declare themselves as supporters or opponents. The first of Higinbotham's five resolutions committed the Legislative Assembly to declining the invitation to send a delegate to the London conference because it was the initiative of 'a self-constituted and irresponsible body of absentee colonists'.[29] The Chief Secretary MacPherson unsuccessfully proposed an amendment but the motion was carried.

The next four recommendations concerned political principles. The second resolution declared the right of the Victorian population to self-government, affirmed that Victorians wished to remain 'an integral portion of the British Empire', and acknowledged the obligation of Victorians to provide for their own defence, 'by means furnished at the sole cost and retained within the exclusive control of the people of Victoria'. Again MacPherson unsuccessfully proposed an amendment, but the motion was carried.[30]

The third resolution protested against 'any interference by legislation of the Imperial Parliament with the internal affairs of Victoria'. No amendment was proposed and the motion was carried. The fourth resolution objected to 'advice, suggestions or instructions' from the Secretary of State for the Colonies to the Governor. It condemned such instructions as 'a violation both of the principles of responsible government and of the constitutional rights of the people of this Colony'. The Government opposed the motion, but it was passed by 39 to 19 votes. The last resolution committed the Legislative Assembly to support the Government 'in any measures that may be necessary' for the purpose of securing the recognition of the right of the Victorian Government and the Queen 'to make laws in and for Victoria in all cases whatsoever', and to prevent the 'unlawful interference' of the Imperial Government in Victoria's domestic affairs. This motion was carried without comment.

In the course of his speech on the resolutions, Higinbotham told the Legislative Assembly:

> We all know, though we don't like to say it, that responsible government does not exist. We don't govern ourselves, and we know it. We are all ashamed of it, though we don't care to say it. The same sense of a want of respect extends to our constituents, and I believe that in time it will tend to degrade the national character by extending this sense of shame and want of respect for our constitution.[31]

To Higinbotham, 'the Englishman's sense' of the term 'responsible government' covered both the scope and the manner of government. He reminded the Legislative Assembly that the wording of the *Constitution Act* made clear that, subject to Royal Assent, the two Houses had been given the power to make laws 'in all cases whatsoever'. To him, the fundamental principle was that 'the head of the Executive shall be independent of all influences except the advice of his advisors who shall be responsible to Parliament'.[32] He reasoned that Victoria did not enjoy the kind of government envisaged in its Constitution because the Colonial Office continually issued instructions to the Governors, and because the Colonial Office 'has always in practice steadily, persistently and designedly disregarded the existence of responsible government'.[33] He argued that self-government logically implied responsible government, for 'if you make the governor dependent on anyone except his responsible advisors for advice, what becomes of the power of self-government to the people?'[34]

The successful passage of all five resolutions proved that Higinbotham's views about responsible government could not be dismissed in London or in the Legislative Council as those of a single, eccentric member or even of a minority of members. The resolutions amounted to a landmark declaration that the Legislative Assembly of Victoria claimed the right of the elected colonial Government to govern independently of the interference of the Colonial Office or the British Government.

In the course of his speech, Higinbotham alluded to William Stawell's leading role in the drafting of the 1855 Constitution and noted that the recent discussion in the House of Lords regarding the 57th Clause of the Victorian Constitution had thrown new light on the process of its drafting. He explained that Lord Lyvedon, who under his previous name Vernon Smith served as the Under-Secretary of State for the Colonies, had told the House of Lords:

> The object of the 57th clause of the Constitution Act was to prevent the governor – whoever he might be – doing exactly what Sir Henry Sutton had done, proposing any vote of money against the opinion of the Legislative Council and the Secretary of State.[35]

This contradicted Stawell's declaration in 1854 to the (old) Legislative Council that responsible government was a 'main principle' of the Constitution, and also the assurance of Childers that 'the Lower House would have control over the money bills, while the Upper House would have hardly a voice in the matter'.[36] It suggested that, despite these assurances, they had been acting in close co-operation with the Colonial Office in drafting the Constitution to prevent responsible government by ensuring that no Governor could allow the Legislative Assembly to raise a grant of money unless it was approved by the Legislative Council and the British Government. Higinbotham acidly remarked:

> I commend this opinion to … the learned Chief Justice of the Colony. The next time that learned functionary is called upon to give a judicial decision of the meaning and intention of the

framers and draughtsmen of our Constitution Act, I venture
to think that he will find in Lord Lyveden's opinion a source
of the most new and wonderful views of our constitution.[37]

Higinbotham explained that these revelations, emanating from the debate in the House of Lords, had precipitated his resignation from the previous McCulloch ministry. As Attorney-General, he had considered that the views expressed in the House of Lords favouring tighter control by the Colonial Office should have been prioritised for discussion in the Victorian Legislative Assembly at the commencement of the Parliamentary session, but that he had been prevented from bringing them forward. He declared that he would not return to ministerial office until he could do so, 'with colleagues, who, with the full approval of the House, will take office for the sole or principal purpose' of pursuing the issue of responsible government.[38] His explanation implied criticism of the previous Chief Secretary, McCulloch, and the current Chief Secretary, MacPherson, for their unwillingness to do so.

But as well as the resolutions, Higinbotham also suggested a bold plan to circumvent Colonial Office interference. He did not ask the Assembly to vote upon it but merely to consider it. He suggested that the Chief Secretary should immediately write to the Lord Granville, the Secretary of State for the Colonies, and inform him of the passage of the resolutions. He should also say that henceforth the Victorian Ministers would deal directly only with their British counterparts. They would not communicate with the Colonial Office and:

> No official communication addressed to Her Majesty's
> representative on any subjects relating to Victorian affairs,
> except the reference of bills home, would be entertained by
> Her Majesty's advisers …

He suggested that if the British Government refused to accept this plan, the Victorian Government should be prepared to break off diplomatic relations.

He argued that 'the English Government will first feel the inconvenience of it'. He added that the neighbouring colonies would be sure to follow Victoria's lead. This, he believed, would mean that 'we shall be establishing the rights and liberties of all these Australian colonies'.[39]

The successful adoption of the resolutions signalled a consensus on which Higinbotham hoped to build a continuation of the struggle, and it sent a signal to supporters to come forward and declare themselves. Although the majority agreed to the resolutions, the plan that Higinbotham had outlined required the leadership of the Chief Secretary, but neither MacPherson nor McCulloch was prepared to undertake the task. Having achieved the passage of his resolutions, Higinbotham could do no more. His bold plan did not come to fruition.

Nevertheless the five resolutions were significant, for they indicated that the Legislative Assembly concurred in his vision of the Victorian Government's right to govern independently of Colonial Office or Westminster interference. At Higinbotham's urging, the members had found the courage to declare their conviction formally. Already the lesson of the Victorian deadlock had led Lord Carnarvon, in 1867, to ensure that the Constitution of the Dominion of Canada would not lead to deadlock between the Upper and Lower Houses.[40] The report of the Victorian resolutions in Britain would answer the views expressed during the debate in the House of Lords by Lord Salisbury, Earl Grey and the Duke of Argyle, who had called for the Colonial Office to exert its control over the Colony. Though Higinbotham's suggested path was more confrontational than the members were prepared to accept, the five resolutions clarified what the ultimate constitutional goals should be. The next few decades would see Victoria still plagued with conflict between the Houses of the legislature, but experimenting with various methods of working towards the goal of responsible government.

The *Education Act*

In the week before the general election of 1871, Higinbotham addressed the electors of Brighton. He spoke of the recent deadlock and the 'illegal act' of the Secretary of State for the Colonies in instructing Governor Henry Manners Sutton not to allow the Appropriation Bill to be presented to the Legislative Council if the Darling grant was joined to it. He said that 'a new epoch in our national life' could have begun with that moment. He reminded the electors of 'the sustained and noble feeling' that the colonial population had shown a few years earlier, and said that the present apparent indifference was due to 'the apathy of those who ought to lead the people'.[41] But in criticising the leaders, he seemed to have lost confidence in his own ability to lead. His opponent, the young colonial-born Thomas Bent, shrewdly worked the electorate in the course of his duties as the local rate collector. He concentrated his attack on Higinbotham's failure to pursue local issues and concerns. Helped by the damage to Higinbotham's reputation from his association with the disgraced Jones, Bent won the seat of Brighton by 14 votes.[42]

For the next two years, Higinbotham concentrated on his practice at the Bar. During his absence, both Houses passed an *Education Act*.[43] The decision, which had been repeatedly deferred for years, was precipitated by a legal challenge to Regulation 63 of the Common Schools Board. The Board had relied on this regulation for the power that it claimed to withdraw funding from any school that did not comply with its requirements, and to transfer the funding to another nearby school that did comply.[44] Representatives of the Catholic Education Committee and the Anglican Church who sat on the Common Schools Board were behind the challenge. Regulation 63 had been an essential element in the strategy of the McCulloch Government to progress steadily towards a system of common schooling. The administrative powers of the Board were used to discourage the wasteful proliferation of schools in the more populated and wealthy areas, and to force schools to accept their share of underprivileged children. But when Charles Gavan Duffy became Chief Secretary in 1871, the moment to strike had arrived. The legal challenge succeeded and signalled the defeat of the Board's power to enforce its regulations by the threat of the withdrawal of aid.

This threw the entire system into chaos, for without the Board having the power to enforce its own regulations, the education system came close to reverting to the wasteful and chaotic system that had prevailed before 1862. In addition, the Supreme Court's decision threatened to unleash a barrage of legal suits from school committees that might claim compensation for lost government aid. Both Houses of the legislature recognised that a new education plan was required immediately. The Government of James Goodall Francis replaced the Duffy Government in June 1872. It drew heavily upon Higinbotham's 1867 Bill that had been withdrawn, but omitted some important safeguards that the 1867 Bill had included. It made provision to allow religious teaching to be organised outside normal school hours by 'boards of advice' that would be elected from the local community. Fearing legal challenges, the Parliament gave unassailable powers to the Minister of the day under the new Act. In time, this would lead to abuses that were roundly condemned by a Royal Commission in 1877.[45] Non-government schools were on notice that, over the next five years, grants would gradually be withdrawn. In an effort to attract a supply of good teachers to the new government school system, the Government promised better conditions than those enjoyed by teachers outside the system.

It must have been galling for Higinbotham that he could only look on as a spectator while his former political rival, James Wilberforce Stephen, introduced the Bill and became the Minister who inaugurated the system that he had largely devised. But a larger sorrow occupied his mind at the time. In December 1872, the month that the *Education Act* was enacted, he and Margaret lost their eleven-month-old baby daughter, Ethel, who died of whooping cough.[46] They buried her in the nearby cemetery of St Andrew's Church, Brighton. Eight years later, her Uncle Thomas was buried in the same gravesite.

15

LAST YEARS IN PARLIAMENT

During his last four years in Parliament, Higinbotham still hoped that it might be possible to achieve a fundamental reform of the Victorian Constitution with a view to ensuring that it truly conformed to the principle of responsible government. But at the election of 1873, his concern for working people emerged as another prominent theme. He also lent his support and the prestige of his good name to the cause of women's rights. He tried to ensure that teachers would be compensated for the income they had lost in transferring to the government system. But bitter political divisions in the Legislative Assembly escalated the parliamentary warfare to heights never previously known.

In May 1873, Higinbotham stood as a candidate for a by-election in the electorate of East Bourke Boroughs. His previous electorate of Brighton comprised market gardeners in the eastern section along the Elster Creek, and wealthy owners of seaside villas in its western section. By contrast, East Bourke Boroughs was a suburban seat with a high proportion of wage earners. In addressing the electors at Brunswick on 12 May 1873, Higinbotham concentrated on constitutional issues. He told the voters that 'self-government is said to exist here. It exists by law. It does not exist in fact.' He reminded his audience that, prior to the 1855 Constitution, Governors were issued with 'a long list of instructions', prescribing in detail how they were to conduct the affairs of the Colony. He declared that despite the granting of self-government through that Constitution, 'the instructions, with only a few literal alterations … continue in substance and in fact to govern the conduct of those governors to this day. They were never absolutely altered or recalled.' As a result, Governors were still required, as in 1855, to remit monthly despatches to the Secretary of State for the Colonies 'in respect of every local measure which is deemed of sufficient importance', and that if their handling of these matters displeased the Colonial Secretary, they might be rebuked, 'or even recalled'. He said that the recent crisis involving Governor Darling was evidence of the continuing interference in Victoria's internal affairs.[1] He cited the system of bestowing Imperial honours on colonial politicians as a particular instance, arguing that it constituted 'an illegal means of perpetuating illegal interference'.[2]

Higinbotham also discussed the issue of the Legislative Council. He argued that a second chamber of the legislature was 'wholly unnecessary', but acknowledged that it would not be abolished in his lifetime. He could tolerate it, he said, provided that the Legislative Assembly was allowed 'the sole and exclusive control of all the public finances'. He pointed out that this was the customary right of the House of Commons in England.[3]

In addressing the electors at Brunswick, Higinbotham also dealt with issues affecting the lives of ordinary people. He said that the population was currently asleep, but that one day it would wake up and 'follow the example of the workers in Dorsetshire and Essex who were forming societies for raising their miserable wages'.[4] He announced that he no longer supported assisted migration because the economic circumstances of the country had changed, and continued use of public revenue to bring impoverished wage earners from Britain to Victoria would tend to reduce the wages of working people in Victoria. He expressed confidence in the *Education Act* to provide Victoria with 'a system of public education unequalled in any other country' and promised that, if elected, he would give his 'hearty support' to James Wilberforce Stephen, the Minister for Public Instruction. He called on the electors to reward teachers 'liberally' for their noble work.[5] Higinbotham won the seat against a local candidate, Allan Staley, with 716 votes to his opponent's 478.[6]

The *Argus* was appalled at the prospect of the old enemy re-entering the fray. It warned the electors that he was a tyrant who enjoyed creating conflict, and was chronically inconsistent in his views.[7] Higinbotham began his new term by calling for a leasing system and a land tax to make more land available to those of modest means. He recognised that a land tax would create another trial of strength with the Legislative Council, and he believed that this time the Legislative Assembly would succeed in asserting its right to control the finances of the Colony.[8] But with no party structure to support him and without the support of his former ally McCulloch, who was serving in London as Agent-General for Victoria, his plan did not proceed.

Educational grievances

In June 1873, Higinbotham denounced the injustices in the administration of the new *Education Act*. He told the Legislative Assembly that the salaries of 442 teachers had been 'absolutely lowered' and that the reductions were 'very considerable'.[9] Indeed, most teachers lost between one-tenth and one-eighth of their income when they entered the government service. Hundreds of them accepted the Government's offer because they took James Wilberforce Stephen at his word when, in the second reading speech on the Education Bill in 1872, he promised that they would be placed 'in the same position as civil servants and will be entitled to the same retiring allowances'.[10] In fact it was deceptive to entice teachers to join the government service with this promise, for Section 22 of the *Education Act*, which provided for retirement allowances, relied on supplementary legislation that was not enacted until a decade later.[11] This became a major grievance of the Victorian Institute of Teachers, which worked with some of the Protestant Members of Parliament for the fulfilment of the promise.

In time, the grievance was largely redressed for the male teachers, through the *Public Service Act* of 1883, which extended the retirement allowance to many of them. But the same Act drove a wedge between male and female teachers in the Institute, for it entrenched the inferiority of women teachers with respect to pay, promotion and retirement allowances. In 1882, the ministry introduced the *Married Women's Property Act Amendment Act*.[12] This amendment to the earlier *Married Women's Property Act* of 1870 allowed women to make claims on friendly societies and provident funds. It was not the boon that women teachers might have expected, for thereafter the Department required women teachers to provide for their own retirement with life insurance policies.

Women's rights

Higinbotham's progressive views about women's right to vote first came to the public attention on 1 March 1865, when he supported an amendment to the *Electoral Act* that closed the franchise to women. He said that he supported women's right to vote but that it had not been the intention of the framers of the Bill to enable it, and that 'the privilege should not have been conferred on them inadvertently'.[13] During the campaign for the election of February 1866, the *Argus* attempted to discredit the constitutional principles that Higinbotham advocated in his election speech to the electors. It ridiculed him as an inventor of 'political novelties', and sarcastically suggested a new novelty that he could announce for the coming election:

> He could announce that the radical consideration of woman's
> rights could no longer be delayed, that the slavery of one half
> of the human race was a subject that could not be trifled
> with, and that, however his motives might be misrepresented,
> he intended to bring in a bill for conferring the franchise on
> females, introducing them into Parliament, and making at
> least one third of the Executive Council consist of that sex.[14]

Another attack on Higinbotham for his support for women's rights came from *Punch*, whose editor, Frederick Sinnett, had previously worked as the business manager for the *Melbourne Morning Herald* until a dispute with Michie about the newspaper's ballooning debt ended his association with it.[15] Sinnett's *Punch* abounded in derogatory stereotypes of Irish people, and he had a particular antipathy to Higinbotham. Following the end of the deadlock and Higinbotham's resignation from the ministry, he published a satirical poem about Higinbotham, ending with the following stanza:

> *From 'woman's right' to insurrection*
> *Upholding each in turn*
> *(To gratify his self-affection,*
> *What* would *he* not *have done?)*[16]

In April 1869, the *Argus* published a letter from an anonymous writer who signed her name as 'ADA'. Susan Priestley, the biographer of Henrietta Augusta Dugdale, who was an early advocate of women's rights, identifies Dugdale as the writer of the letter.[17] Dugdale was born in London in 1827, married at fourteen and became the mother of three sons. From an early age she took a keen interest in public affairs and well remembered the Chartist rallies in England seeking democratic political reform. After her arrival in Victoria in 1852, her first husband died and she later remarried. She wrote and lectured about women's issues, became the president of the Woman's Suffrage Society when it formed in 1884, and was a strong advocate for legislation entitling women to own property in their own name.

In 1869, when the letter was published, the British Parliament was preparing to enact such legislation. Seeing that the British *Married Woman's Property Act* was imminent, Higinbotham advocated an equivalent Victorian Act. In March 1869, he had introduced a Bill to amend the law relating to the property of married women and this was finally enacted on 29 December 1870.[18] The Victorian statute allowed married women for the first time to be the owners and managers in their own right of money and property that they earned or inherited. It also enabled them to purchase property in their own name, and to be free of responsibility for the debts and obligations of their husbands. Dugdale argued in her letter to the *Argus* that a Bill to secure property to women is 'but a poor and partial remedy to a great and crying evil'. Referring to the wider question of women's rights, she urged Higinbotham to 'lay the axe to the root of the tree'. She particularly urged that women be permitted to divorce when marriages failed through their husbands' desertion, drunkenness, cruelty or infidelity; and that women should be entitled to study at university, to vote and to enter Parliament.

No doubt Dugdale was aware that the editor of the *Argus* had previously scorned Higinbotham for his support for women's rights, but she framed her letter as a criticism of Higinbotham. She may have done so with the wily expectation that the editor would be enticed to publish her letter by seeing in it an opportunity to ridicule Higinbotham by again associating him with the cause of women's rights. Dugdale concluded with an appeal to the editor, indicating a naiveté that was probably feigned:

> If you have any influence with Mr Higinbotham, try and
> induce him to take a wider view of the married relationship
> and make his remedy complete.[19]

In the week before the letter was published, Higinbotham was absent from the Legislative Assembly because he was recuperating from an ankle sprain that had occurred while he was on a trip to the Ovens district of Victoria.[20] He may have spent some of his recuperation time in discussion with Dugdale about the promotion of a Victorian equivalent to the British *Married Woman's Property Act*, and they may have jointly agreed on the form and tone of the letter to the *Argus*.

Far from being critical of Higinbotham, Dugdale greatly admired him and was extremely appreciative of his support for her cause. His early life experiences make it likely that Higinbotham was utterly sincere in his support for women's rights, and Dugdale would have sensed this. A few years before his birth, his father, Henry Higinbotham, had initiated an ambitious business enterprise involving many shareholders. An economic downturn in 1826 meant that some shareholders failed to pay for their shares and the project fell into financial trouble. A few weeks before George Higinbotham's birth in 1826, the banks refused further credit and the failure of the project was announced in the newspapers.[21] The losses were enormous and the ramifications cast a pall over George Higinbotham's childhood. His mother, who was an heiress, lost her inheritance to her husband's creditors. The family's prosperous lifestyle ended abruptly, forcing them to leave their fashionable and comfortable townhouse in central Dublin. It seems likely that Higinbotham's parents, Henry and Sarah, separated following the financial debacle.[22] Henry lived for a while with his own elderly mother in Dublin.[23] His wife Sarah moved to a cottage near Bray that was owned by Henry's relatives. Higinbotham's older sisters, Rosanna and Jane, lost their dowries, which limited their marriage prospects – Jane remained a life-long spinster. Henry managed to survive on his entitlement to half-pay as a former officer in the British Army with twelve years' service. Fortunately, Sarah's father had left money specifically to her children, and an entitlement for her to the interest of the sums allocated for the children until they came of age.[24] George's brother William, who seems to have suffered some kind of psychiatric disability, may have been particularly vulnerable. Stuart Macintyre noted that a son of Higinbotham's daughter Maud had reported to Gwyneth Dow in 1955 that the brother of his grandfather had been confined to an asylum.[25] William survived George and, in her will, Margaret left money to her children, while charging them with the responsibility to continue a fixed remittance to their Uncle William for his upkeep.[26]

Higinbotham would have been particularly conscious of his mother's anguish at the loss of her inheritance, for her world crumbled and she found herself reliant upon the charity of her in-laws.[27] In her will, Sarah left £3,200 solely to her two daughters with directions to her executors to invest the money. She stated that the profits were to be paid to her daughters in equal shares, and were for their use 'as they shall think fit and proper'. She specified that in the case of either daughter marrying, she was to receive 'the interest and profits of her equal share in the said sum of £3,200, to her sole and separate use, free from the control and interference of her husband'.[28] The family's experience must have made Higinbotham particularly conscious of the unfairness of the law regarding the property of married women.

Morris commented several times on his father-in-law's respectful attitude towards women.[29] He instances the following quote from an editorial in the *Argus* that Higinbotham wrote:

> A model woman according to a very prevalent conception of the character is little better than an amiable idiot; and any woman who evinces strength of mind and vigour of intellect becomes an object of derision and a butt for the feeble sarcasm of the mentally destitute of the other sex.[30]

It is likely that Higinbotham had friendships with several women with 'strength of mind and vigour of intellect'. Lady Andalusia Molesworth, the wife of Sir William Molesworth, leader of the Philosophical Radicals, may have been one such acquaintance. The Molesworths were a childless couple who kept an open house at their home in London and invited friends and eminent people to participate in political discussions. Their house was located next to the London home of Sir William Verner, and, it may have been through Verner that Higinbotham met Molesworth. As both Molesworth and Verner were Baronets and members of the House of Commons, they may have moved in a similar social circle, yet their political views were markedly dissimilar.

Lady Andalusia Molesworth was a former singer who overcame prejudice against her humble origins to achieve fame as a society hostess. Among the guests who attended the couple's dinner parties were the historian T.B. Macaulay, the writers W.M. Thackeray and Charles Dickens, and leading politicians. A contemporary recalled that Andalusia possessed 'a mysterious power of drawing out clever people and making them talk'.[31] While little is known for certain of this period of Higinbotham's life, there are occasional hints in his journalism that he had a warm friendship with Sir William Molesworth. It is likely that as a young man far from home, with an intense interest in politics, Higinbotham spent considerable time enjoying the hospitality and intellectual stimulation provided by the Molesworths.

Another woman of similar qualities who had a life-long influence on Higinbotham was the mother of a friend. While a student at Trinity College Dublin, Higinbotham became friendly with Henry Brougham, a fellow student who joined the Historical Society with him and participated in its debates. Both friends were awarded the College's distinction of 'Trinity Scholar' as a mark of their high academic achievement.[32] Forty-nine years later, upon hearing the news of the death of Henry Brougham's mother (and only six months before his own death), Higinbotham wrote a letter of condolence to his friend Henry, who had become the Anglican Dean of Lismore in Ireland. 'She was the oldest and most steadfast and the most revered friend I had the unmerited happiness to possess in this world', Higinbotham wrote.[33] Mrs Brougham, who was christened Catherine Anna Mona Macartney, had been born in 1804 into an illustrious Irish Protestant family. Her great-grandfather was the Honourable Robert Fitzgerald, who, after the Battle of the Boyne in 1690, presented the keys of the city of Dublin to William III.[34] In 1826, the year of George Higinbotham's birth, she married the Reverend Henry Brougham, Rector of Tallow, County Waterford.[35] Five years afterwards, he died, leaving her with two young sons: Henry, born in 1827, and John in 1829.

After Higinbotham's own death in December 1892, Henry Brougham sent a letter of condolence to Morris on the death of his father-in-law. In it, Brougham reminisced about his friendship with Higinbotham at Trinity. He related how, in company with five other students (all of whom subsequently progressed to academic or professional careers), they used to meet once a week at his mother's home. The students prepared for these sessions by writing papers, in prose or verse (as the College's syllabus required), and signed them with fictitious signatures. His mother would read them aloud. Afterwards the papers were discussed and criticised.[36] It appears that Mrs Brougham's role was that of a supplementary tutor to a group of her son's friends. Such an arrangement was not uncommon. Alone among British universities at the time, Trinity College Dublin allowed students to qualify for their degrees purely by passing the examinations, and they were not required to attend lectures at the University. Many students saved money by making private arrangements for their own tuition, often involving family, friends or a local clergyman.[37]

Mrs Brougham's tutorials followed a common format used at that time in English-speaking countries to assist students to improve their written English expression, to overcome speech impediments, and to eliminate provincial accents and idioms. Higinbotham greatly appreciated what he learned in these sessions and always retained a great admiration for Mrs Brougham. He communicated with her by letter for the rest of his life. In his letter of condolence to Henry Brougham, Higinbotham added:

> Neither time, nor long separation, nor the known diversity of our thoughts and interests appeared to change her kind disposition to me, from the first time I had the privilege to know her more than forty-five years ago. Her memory will be precious to me, as to you, for the rest of my life.[38]

Mrs Brougham was clearly a highly educated woman, and the reference in Higinbotham's letter to 'the known diversity of our thoughts and interests' suggests that the topics in Mrs Brougham's discussion group were wide ranging. Morris, relying on his father-in-law's memories, wrote, 'she was a woman of singular liberality of thought, openness of mind, and greatness of character'.[39] Higinbotham's admiration for these qualities reveals his appreciation of Mrs Brougham's intellect as well as her admirable personal qualities.

He may have appreciated similar qualities in Henrietta Dugdale. They shared an interest not only in women's rights but also in rebutting the attacks by religious conservatives on the modern geological discoveries about the age of the world.[40] At the inaugural general meeting of the Victorian Women's Suffrage Society in 1883, Higinbotham, who had been appointed to the bench of the Supreme Court, donated three guineas

(£3 and 3 shillings), and declared his support for the movement. In the same year, Dugdale published a book entitled *A Few Hours in a Far-Off Age*, imagining a future society based upon the ideals of her early feminist philosophy. It featured a frontispiece with an elaborate dedication to Higinbotham. In the book she honoured him for his integrity and bravery and promised that 'women will never forget his fearless endeavour to gain justice for them'.[41] It appears that Higinbotham's wife felt similarly about women's rights. In 1891, when the Victorian Women's Suffrage Society presented a petition to Parliament, one of the leading signatures was that of Margaret Higinbotham.[42]

In later years, as Chief Justice of Victoria, Higinbotham became a trustee of the Queen's Fund, which aimed to help women in distress. In addressing the ladies who promoted the fund, he praised the fact that the Fund was to be invested and the proceeds administered 'chiefly – I wish I could say exclusively– by the women of Victoria'. He added:

> I don't think we ought to regret that the age of chivalry, with all its foolery is passed; but I don't think that any of us would say – would that we could – that the age of true honour for women, of true respect and reverence for women, has yet fully come …[43]

Political instability increases

As long ago as January 1866, Higinbotham had asked the members of the Legislative Assembly whether they should tolerate a situation whereby

> Particular classes and particular interests shall have the power year after year to excite Parliamentary dissension, to turn out one government after another, for the purpose of procuring delay or overthrowing legislation in the interests of the body politic, to maintain it in the interests of a class or clique.

The interests that he alluded to were those of the squatters. Later the political situation became more complex and unstable, particularly in 1873 as the scheduled withdrawal of government aid to the denominational schools commenced. It was no longer only the squatters who destabilised Governments. The future Australian Prime Minister, Alfred Deakin, commented that it became the policy of the Catholic hierarchy after 1872 'to eject ministry after ministry in the hope of one day finding a Government sufficiently weak to purchase their aid'.[44] The divisive issue of grants to the denominational schools opened a new front in the parliamentary war and presaged a new level of political instability.

At the time of the 1872 *Education Act*, proponents argued that many Catholic children, especially those in sparsely populated areas, would have the opportunity for a free education that had been unavailable under the previous system. But to gain access to it, their parents would have to consent to their being educated side by side with children of other faiths, for it was impractical for Government to subsidise schools specifically catering to each of the different faiths that might be present in any given area.

Under the previous Common Schools system of 1862, many schools had been established by religious denominations that still owned the properties. They had been entitled to government aid so long as they met the requirements of the Common Schools Board. These largely related to the hours of instruction time provided, the keeping of attendance records, and the state of the facilities; but they also related to the distance from the nearest neighbouring school in receipt of government aid. The religious hierarchies had been free to determine the religious content of the curriculum and to choose and supervise the teachers. However, the system was fraught with conflict. There were numerous court cases involving three-way disputes between teachers, their church hierarchy and the Common Schools Board. Frequently these involved an ageing or sick teacher who sought to continue working because there was no sick leave or retirement allowance. There were frequent disputes about the accuracy of attendance records, which were often falsified in order to maximise government aid.

With the announcement that henceforth instruction would be secular during school hours, the influence of the church hierarchies in the selection and supervision of the teachers and curriculum would cease in all schools receiving government funding. With the additional promise that the teachers would become civil servants, the religious-owned Common Schools faced an exodus of their staff. The Catholic Schools Board declared that 'the most objectionable feature' of the Act was that 'it made the teachers civil servants, thus removing them from the control of the Church'.[45] Within the government schools, although no religion was to be taught during school hours, the elected local Boards of Advice were free to make their own arrangements for religious instruction outside of school hours. This arrangement was not acceptable to the Catholic Bishops, who believed that all instruction should take place in a religious context. Moreover, the requirement that Boards of Advice be elected from the local community effectively excluded the Bishops unless they happened to reside locally.

John O'Shanassy and Charles Gavan Duffy were the leading Catholic politicians in Victoria, but the rift between the two had never been healed. Despite Archbishop Goold's efforts to enforce unity, the Catholic vote remained divided. In 1874, O'Shanassy, who had received a papal knighthood from Pope Pius IX for his services to education, resigned his seat in the Legislative Council and sought a seat in the Assembly. His first attempt to take the seat of Kilmore failed because he had expected the sitting member, Lawrence Burke, to retire for him, but Burke refused to do so, and a three-way contest resulted.[46] O'Shanassy then attempted to assert his pre-eminence as the leading Catholic representative by contesting Duffy's seat of Villiers-Heytesbury in western Victoria, but he was defeated. His aim was to introduce an amendment to the *Education Act* that would restore government grants to the Catholic schools. Some leading Protestant politicians reacted by insisting that if this should happen, they would demand the introduction of biblical instruction into the curriculum of the government schools. This further alarmed the Catholic community, which feared that the new government schools would be used for Protestant proselytism. The Catholic Archbishop, James Alipius Goold, condemned compulsory education in his pastoral letter of June 1872 as 'downright persecution for conscience sake'. He directed his flock to refuse their votes to 'those who are in favour of a scheme of godless compulsory education'. Although the *Education Act* made a significant improvement in school attendance rates, it deepened the sectarian divide, and worsened political instability.

McCulloch denounces Higinbotham

In July 1874, George Briscoe Kerferd became the Chief Secretary in a new conservative Government. His legislative program suffered from constant obstruction. In August 1875, when his budget passed by only one vote, Kerferd requested a dissolution of the House. During the absence of Governor George Bowen, the Chief Justice, William Stawell, was the Acting Governor. Although his Government had not suffered a defeat, Kerferd had reason to think that his planned taxation proposal might fail unless he could demonstrate a clear majority for his ministry. Stawell refused Kerferd's request for a dissolution, on the grounds that while the ministry still held the confidence of the House, to grant a dissolution would be 'unconstitutional and expedient', and that he feared it would create a new precedent.[47] Kerferd's ministry then resigned. Stawell approached Graham Berry, the leader of the liberal Opposition, to form a ministry.

Although he did not command a majority, Berry took office on 7 August 1875 and introduced a new Bill for a progressive taxation scheme based largely upon land values. In early September, Stawell dined with James McCulloch, who had recently returned from London where he had served as Agent-General and had been appointed a Knight Commander of St Michael and St George. Stawell confided to McCulloch that he had reservations about the Berry ministry. Eleven days later, McCulloch proposed an amendment to Berry's finance bill. On 29 September, McCulloch joined with supporters of the former Kerferd ministry, which he had recently helped to overthrow. On 6 October, the new alliance defeated the Berry ministry on the floor of the House. Stawell was so confident that this would happen that, some hours before it occurred, he wrote to the Secretary of State for the Colonies to inform him that he expected it to happen, and that he had great confidence in Sir James McCulloch who would form the next ministry.[48]

Berry requested a dissolution from Stawell. He supplemented his request with fifty-two petitions from public meetings in support of the ministry to indicate that the mood of the electorate had changed and needed to be reflected more accurately by a new election. Stawell refused Berry's request, arguing that it had been made 'under similar circumstances' to Kerferd's. In reality, the circumstances were quite different since Kerferd had not suffered a parliamentary defeat. Nevertheless, Stawell argued that to grant to Berry what he had refused to Kerferd would appear as 'foul play'.[49]

In a dispatch to the Colonial Office, Stawell referred to Berry's parliamentary colleagues as 'a dreadful set of men' in whose principles he had 'no faith'. As the legal historian Charles Parkinson notes, Sir Charles Darling had been recalled to London, ostensibly for making a similar comment, but this time there were no repercussions.[50] As he had done earlier at the time of the drafting of the new Constitution, Stawell dismissed the views of the petitioners. He argued that they did not truly reflect general opinion, and that to yield to them would create 'a most injurious precedent'. The Colonial Office refrained from making any formal announcement of its approval of Stawell's decision, but Sir Archibald Michie, who was serving as Agent-General for Victoria, unofficially reported that the Colonial Office was pleased that Stawell had denied Berry a dissolution.[51]

Since the Berry Government had resigned, McCulloch resumed office. Higinbotham criticised Stawell in the Assembly for refusing Berry's request, but Stawell had anticipated that he would do so. In a letter to his wife, Stawell recorded that, on 5 September 1875, he had dined with McCulloch, and indicated to him his anxiety about Higinbotham's growing influence in the House. Parkinson suggests that the topic may have been a part of a larger discussion about McCulloch leading the next ministry.[52] McCulloch may have taken the conversation as a signal that if he wanted favourable consideration from the Acting Governor, he should sever all connection with Higinbotham. He did not need much encouragement to follow this course of action. For him, Higinbotham had outlived his usefulness as a political ally. When Higinbotham addressed the House, criticising Stawell for his refusal of a dissolution to Berry, McCulloch decided that the moment had arrived. The historian Turner continues:

> Suddenly, Sir James McCulloch rose and delivered a scathing indictment of Higinbotham: he accused him of 'placing sham motions on the notice paper to bring about an unsatisfactory state of matters with the Imperial Government'; charged him with being the cause of all the disorganization that had ever arisen in the Assembly; and declared that, if he should direct the next government, Higinbotham should sit in direct opposition, for he would countenance no schemes for embroiling the Colony with the Imperial Government. [53]

A member who was present that day reported to Edward Morris that the calm language as reported in Hansard conveyed 'but little idea of what took place'.[54]

So the powerful partnership of Higinbotham and McCulloch of the mid-1860s exploded in a dramatic scene before the astonished members of the House. McCulloch's vehement denunciation of his former right-hand man signalled the end of an era. Higinbotham's challenge to McCulloch to continue the struggle with the Colonial Office and the Legislative Council had became burdensome, and McCulloch may have been stung by Higinbotham's public criticisms of colonial politicians who accepted Imperial honours. Until that moment, Higinbotham had failed to grasp how far McCulloch had changed. To what extent McCulloch had ever been sincere about the convictions that he had professed in his election speeches and during the struggles in the House in the mid-1860s remains a mystery. But it was clear that they no longer mattered to him.

Without McCulloch's support, Higinbotham's 'no-party' doctrine left him isolated and politically impotent. Relations between McCulloch's governing party and the Berry Opposition had become poisonously bitter, because Berry considered that he had been wrongly denied a dissolution. In retaliation, he determined that no government business would proceed. In a policy that became known as the 'stonewall', his supporters spoke at inordinate length to delay the Government's business and to disrupt its program. McCulloch's Government responded by gagging debate, a device known as 'the iron hand'. After ten weeks in Opposition during this trial of strength in the House, Higinbotham could bear no more. In a letter to his electors he rejected Berry's 'stonewall' tactics and said that could not co-operate with them. He wrote:

> I concur with the Opposition that there should be an
> immediate dissolution of the Parliament and an appeal to the
> people, but I am unable to approve the course that it intends
> to pursue for the purpose of obtaining that object.

In an intensely polarised Assembly in which almost no business could proceed, the only role available to him was that of spectator. But, as he told the voters:

> It is not permitted to a member of Parliament to be a mere
> onlooker in a parliamentary war. It is his first duty to take
> his place and bear his part in the strife on the one side or the
> other ... I have therefore resigned my seat.[55]

On 25 November, James Service, a future Premier, attacked McCulloch, describing him as a man of no convictions who had wrecked two ministries and who was 'a mere pirate'. Addressing the House, he asked, 'Is there not one voice in the Assembly to say that Sir James McCulloch was justified?' There was silence. He asked the question once more, and again was met with silence.[56] McCulloch's days as Chief Secretary were numbered. The opportunism behind his making and breaking of alliances, the betrayal of his former loyal comrade-in-arms and the shallowness of his commitment to those constitutional principles that he had once vigorously advocated, were all now starkly revealed. In the election of May 1877, McCulloch suffered a humiliating defeat, and Graham Berry formed a new ministry with a very large parliamentary majority. Within seven months, Victoria would reel under its bitterest constitutional crisis ever.

16

SUPREME COURT JUDGE

On 8 January 1878, a day that became known as 'Black Wednesday', more than three hundred civil servants were shocked to learn that the Government of Graham Berry had dismissed them at a day's notice. They included heads of government departments, senior officials, judges, magistrates, coroners, office staff and inspectors of the Education Department. Fifteen days later, another hundred officials suffered the same fate. The dismissals were ostensibly forced upon the Government by the Legislative Council's refusal to pass its Appropriation Bill. The Legislative Council had refused to do so because the Government had 'tacked' to it a Bill for the payment of members of the Legislative Assembly. In fact there was no immediate financial crisis, and the sackings were designed to demonstrate the Government's determination not to be obstructed. Berry later acknowledged that the dismissals were reprisals against the Council. 'It was blow for blow', he said, 'and the consequences fell on those whom the Council would dearly have liked to have saved'.[1]

Berry was a Londoner who arrived in Victoria in 1852 and kept a general store in South Yarra. He had been a juryman on one of the trials of the Eureka prisoners. In 1855, he had become secretary of the Prahran Reform League, where he gained exposure to the broader ideas of seasoned political reformers. He opposed the concentration of power and wealth in the political system, and during the period of agitation by the Land Convention he addressed public meetings in company with speakers such as Charles Don and Moses Wilson Gray.[2] Throughout the period of the struggle with the Legislative Council over the tariff and the Darling grant, Berry supported the stance of McCulloch and Higinbotham.

The previous Kerferd ministry's tariff reform remitting certain duties on imported goods alarmed some local manufacturers, especially of footwear and clothing, who feared increased foreign competition. In the manufacturing centres of Collingwood, Richmond, Emerald Hill, Footscray and Ballarat, the Protection movement joined forces with Berry's Reform movement to form the National Reform and Protection League. The League soon had 150 branches across Victoria, and included trade unionists, selectors and miners. It drew up its own platform and selected candidates for election who were pledged to uphold the League's policies.[3] At the election of May 1877, Berry's party won a landslide victory, which incidentally strengthened Protestant representation in the Legislative Assembly.

In 1878, Berry was fighting on many fronts. His success in forcing through a land tax in the previous year made enemies for his Government in the Legislative Council.[4] As leader of the National Reform and Protection League, he was at war with the pastoralists, bankers and merchants, as well as all those who were opposed to reform of the political system. Berry had opposed the 1872 *Education Act* when it had been debated in the Assembly, and this had raised the expectation of many Catholic and Anglican voters that he might be prepared to restore the grants to denominational schools. But among his supporters in the Assembly were many staunch Protestants who were equally determined to resist such a measure, and some were determined to promote the introduction of biblical instruction into the curriculum of the government schools. The *Education Act* of December 1872 had set a 'five years' grace' period for the withdrawal of all grants to the denominational schools. The expiration of the deadline brought to boiling point the issues of grants, biblical instruction and the fulfilment of the promise of retirement allowances. The Victorian Institute of Teachers was agitating vigorously for the promised retirement allowances. O'Shanassy, who had gained the seat of Belfast (Port Fairy) in the Legislative Assembly, was determined to restore the grants. Berry needed a strong and united backbench to prepare his Government for the great battles looming ahead.

Few of Berry's supporters in the Assembly were independently wealthy. Although payment of members had been introduced as a trial measure in 1870, there was apprehension that the Council would refuse to continue it. Berry's first priority was to keep his supporters from breaking up into factions, and he saw that a bold move for the continuation of payment to members would unite his supporters behind him. Determined to have the measure succeed, Berry embarked on the dismissals of government employees as a retaliation against the Council after it rejected the legislation to authorise parliamentary salaries. This confrontation revived the heady sense of solidarity that had motivated the Legislative Assembly in the earlier struggles of McCulloch and Higinbotham to assert the primacy of the popularly elected body over the oligarchical Legislative Council.

The dismissals were spread across the entire government bureaucracy. This masked the fact that they were particularly aimed at the Education Department, where a number of people who had been outspoken on the educational controversy were selected for dismissal. The vacancies so created allowed for the stealthy introduction of a number of political appointees into senior positions in the Education Department. The Minister of Education, William Collard Smith, hinted at this motivation when he told a public meeting at Ballarat to which about five hundred of Berry's supporters had been transported by a special train:

> The needed reductions in the Civil Service could never have been made except under pressure of this excitement … He had begun in the Education Department at the top of the tree, and he would stake his reputation as a public man that in a few months he would effect such a change that the Department would give more satisfaction than ever it had done before. If the gentlemen now placed in charge were not competent, they would have to go also … No doubt some competent officers had been included in the dismissals, especially at the Education Office, but he felt that he could

not dispense with part only, or he might find in those left an obstruction to the carrying out of necessary reforms.[5]

Whatever course of action was to be implemented regarding the deadline for the withdrawal of grants, there was sure to be opposition, and Berry's Government was determined to suppress dissent and ensure conformity with the Government's policy.[6]

The standoff with the Council continued. In December 1878, Berry and his parliamentary colleague, Professor Charles Henry Pearson, embarked upon an 'embassy' to London, aiming to persuade the British Government to empower the Victorian Legislative Assembly to reform the Constitution without the agreement of the Legislative Council. Pearson advocated the case in the British press and lobbied politicians for intervention to end the chronic obstruction of legislation by the Victorian Legislative Council. The embassy failed, since the Secretary of State for the Colonies, Sir Michael Hicks-Beach, a Conservative Member of Parliament, opposed its request for assistance. However, Hicks-Beach privately warned the Legislative Council that if it were to persist in rejecting 'reasonable' reform, the Imperial Government might have to consider action. By April 1879, a compromise was negotiated between the Legislative Council and the Legislative Assembly. Payment of members was extended after a separate Bill was introduced. About 340 of the 400 of those dismissed were reinstated. Some, but not all, of those who were not reinstated received compensation.[7]

Appointment to the Supreme Court

One of those dismissed in January 1878 was the Engineer-in-Chief of the Victorian Railways, Thomas Higinbotham. He was not greatly inconvenienced. Because of his extensive experience and because he had recently completed a tour of the United States to study the latest railway technology, he was eagerly recruited by the Governments of

South Australia, Tasmania and New Zealand to report on their railway systems.[8] Even so, George Higinbotham took offence at the Government's treatment of his brother. A year later, following the death in April 1878 of Judge Thomas Howard Fellows, the Berry Government offered him an appointment as a judge of the Supreme Court; but despite the urging of his friends, he refused the offer because it came from the Government that had peremptorily dismissed his brother.[9]

In 1880, under the new ministry of James Service, an old friend from his early days in Emerald Hill, Higinbotham was again offered an appointment as a judge of the Supreme Court. At first he rejected the offer, because he was strongly opposed to a policy of Service's Government. The policy was to introduce a Reform Bill that would expand the Council's franchise and include a proposal for resolving deadlocks between the Houses of the legislature. The Bill proposed that in a situation where the Council had twice rejected a Bill that had passed the Assembly in two consecutive sessions, there would be a dissolution of both Houses. There would then be a joint sitting of the two Houses, and if the Bill was passed at the joint sitting, it could then be enacted as law.[10] Though he was no longer in Parliament, Higinbotham strongly disapproved of the plan, which was, he argued, 'subversive of the foundations of our Constitution'.[11] A part of him still hoped for more fundamental constitutional reform.

The Reform Bill was narrowly defeated and Higinbotham then accepted the appointment. He told a friend who congratulated him, 'I shall never cease to be a politician in the sense in which you and I have understood the term, to my life's end'.[12] It is noticeable that Chief Justice Stawell made no objection to Higinbotham's appointment. For two years, the bench had been in need of a new member. Higinbotham, as an experienced barrister and former Attorney-General, was undeniably well qualified. In 1971, Geoffrey Serle commented that, in 1880, Higinbotham 'could easily have taken the leadership of the Liberal party instead of Berry'.[13] Ninety years earlier, many Victorians, probably including Stawell, held that expectation. Stawell may have reasoned that in the Parliament Higinbotham still posed a threat, but that his influence as a judge would be limited since he would be outnumbered by other members of the Court. As Parkinson noted, until this time the Supreme Court had demonstrated 'an ideological unity' under Stawell. But with the death in 1880 of Sir Redmond Barry (shortly after passing sentence of death on the bushranger, Ned Kelly), and the accession of Higinbotham, the ideological battle between Higinbotham and Stawell that had previously been fought out in the Parliament was now transferred to the bench of the Supreme Court.[14]

Parkinson commented that Stawell and Higinbotham represented two extremes in judicial ideology; 'Stawell stood for judicial power against the Parliament and the executive; Higinbotham for Parliamentary supremacy and an expansive view of executive power'.[15] Higinbotham believed that under responsible government, the Parliament was the guardian of the interests of the citizens. Stawell, however, believed that judicial oversight of government was necessary in order to safeguard the interests of the citizenry. When it came to statutory interpretation, Parkinson noted that Stawell preferred to employ a literalist interpretation whereas Higinbotham typically gave statutes a broad reading to maximise the Government's discretion.[16]

The prerogative of mercy

A difference of view between Higinbotham and Stawell arose with respect to the Governor's prerogative of mercy. According to the instructions from the Secretary of State for the Colonies, the Governor was obliged to require that the judge who had passed a death sentence on a prisoner provide him with a report that he could use to determine whether to issue a pardon or to commute the sentence. The judge could also be required to attend a meeting of the Executive Council to produce his trial notes and discuss the report. At the outset of his appointment to the Supreme Court bench, Higinbotham declared that he found this instruction objectionable because it undermined the independence of the Colony's judiciary and thereby contravened the principle of responsible government. He insisted that he would 'officially and openly refuse to comply with the requirements contained in the so-called instruction' unless those requirements were conveyed to him by 'Her Majesty's Advisers for Victoria'.[17]

Between mid-April and mid-July 1884, Stawell served as the Acting Governor in the interval between the departure of the former Governor, the Marquess of Normanby, and the arrival of Sir Henry Loch to replace him. During this interval, Higinbotham had occasion to pass sentence of death on Henry Morgan, who was convicted of murder. Higinbotham wrote to George Kerferd, the Attorney-General, pointing out that the relevant instruction to the Governor had not changed since the time when Victoria was known as the Port Phillip District of New South Wales, and that it had 'ceased to be warranted'.[18] Kerferd responded that the matter of the instruction to the Governor was one for the consideration of the Imperial Government, but he attempted to defuse the issue by undertaking that, for the future, the Ministers of the Crown would issue the invitation to the judge in a capital case to attend a meeting of the Executive Council.

As Acting Governor, Stawell confidentially forwarded ten letters about the matter, which had been exchanged between Kerferd and Higinbotham, to the Secretary of State for the Colonies. The officials of the Colonial Office discussed the correspondence. The Law Officers were consulted and, since the letters had been forwarded without Higinbotham's knowledge, the decision was made to take no action.[19] They may have reasoned that if they were to take any action against Higinbotham, it would tend to confirm his argument about Colonial Office interference.

In December 1885, the issue was revived by another case in which Higinbotham passed a sentence of death. On this occasion, Higinbotham released a letter to the press. In it he stated his intention, 'to withhold my personal attendance from any meeting of the Executive Council called to consider a capital case', and he added: 'I shall decline to communicate, by report or otherwise, with that body'. But he offered to communicate with the Attorney-General or a Minister of the Crown in advising the Crown regarding the case.[20] The publication of the letter outlining his objection to the Governor's prerogative was designed to raise public awareness of this aspect of the role of the Governor under responsible government and its implications for the independence of the judiciary.

Two years later, as Chief Justice, Higinbotham wrote to the Secretary of State for the Colonies explaining his objection to the fact that the Governor was required, by virtue of his instructions, 'to decide either to extend or withhold a pardon or a reprieve according to his own deliberate judgement whether the members of the Executive Council concur therein or otherwise'. This instruction, Higinbotham argued, was 'flagrantly illegal'; therefore it was the duty of the judge to refuse to comply with it.[21] Perhaps referring to the public protests at the execution of the bushranger Ned Kelly in 1880, Higinbotham referred to the invidious position created for the Governor by the instruction:

> The representative of the Crown is sometimes exposed to the gross indignity and the very painful embarrassment of being compelled on the eve of the execution of a criminal to apologise – at one time to a crowd collected from the street, at another time to an equally ignorant crowd of clergymen and laymen – for his Ministers in allowing the law to take its course, and refusing to transfer to incompetent and irresponsible persons the most delicate and responsible duty connected with the exercise of this prerogative.[22]

In his early years as a journalist, Higinbotham had written about the death penalty in terms that revealed his strong, personal revulsion at the execution of a criminal by hanging. To him, the necessity of passing a sentence of death was a painful and weighty matter that needed to be based firmly upon the law. He felt that the Governor's instructions, by giving the prerogative of mercy to the Governor, and not requiring his decision to be accountable, undermined the judicial process in the Colony and thereby the principle of responsible government.

The Working Men's College

As well as his long-standing interest in promoting the practice of responsible government in his years on the Supreme Court, Higinbotham also continued his interests in religion, and in social and educational progress. During the early 1880s a proposal to set up a Working Men's College in Melbourne took shape. In time, it would become the Royal Melbourne Institute of Technology, and then RMIT University. Its first Vice-Principal in 1885 was Benjamin Douglass, a former prominent trade union leader, and a founding member of the Council of the College.

The pastoralist and philanthropist, Francis Ormond, made an initial donation of £5,000 on condition that the Government donated a suitable piece of land and that other individuals matched his contribution. Ormond wished to make technical and practical education available to workingmen, and argued that this would improve manufacture in Victoria.[23] He intended that the College would be 'non-sectarian, non-political and open to all'. He said that the London Working Men's College was the inspiration.[24] This statement may have led Higinbotham to expect that the Melbourne initiative would follow the Christian Socialist philosophy of Frederick Denison Maurice, the founder of the London Working Men's College. Maurice's philosophy was based upon the teaching of Jesus. He denounced the greed that underlay capitalism and urged sympathy for the poor.

Maurice was born in 1805 and ordained as a minister of the Church of England in 1835. He served as Professor of English Literature, History and Theology at King's College, London, until dismissed in 1853 on religious grounds. Between 1846 and 1860, Maurice also served as chaplain of Lincoln's Inn.[25] Higinbotham enrolled there to train for the Bar in 1848, so it is very likely that he would have known him personally.[26] Maurice was a prolific writer, a scholar and an inspiring preacher. His influence on twenty-three-year-old George Higinbotham may have been considerable. Some of the sermons from Maurice's time at Lincoln's Inn have been collected and printed, and are among a lengthy list of his published works. His teachings were, in some respects, unorthodox. His *Theological Essays* precipitated his dismissal from King's College. They anticipated the ecumenical movement, and denied aspects of the Church's traditional teachings about hell. Maurice's leadership of the Christian Socialist movement was a further departure from traditional Anglicanism. To this day the American Episcopalian Church honours Maurice with a feast day on its liturgical calendar, and credits him with awakening Anglicanism to the needs of society.[27]

Maurice, like Higinbotham, had a strong social conscience that arose from his religious convictions. In 1854, he founded the first Working Men's College in London, and became its first principal. It is likely that during his time at Lincoln's Inn, Higinbotham developed the deep respect for Maurice's theology and good works that he expressed in his speech at the inauguration of the Melbourne Working Men's College. The dismissal of Maurice in 1853 may explain Higinbotham's lifelong irritation with the hierarchies of the Christian churches, including his own Anglican Church. His admiration for Maurice's theology may also explain his high hopes for the Melbourne Working Men's College.

In June 1882, at the inauguration of the Victorian project, Higinbotham was the first guest speaker. He praised Ormond for his generous gift and welcomed the College as a boon to the Colony. However, he argued for a more liberal education to be made available that would 'improve and elevate the mind of the worker', for he saw the opportunity to create an institution that would offer the workingman a higher type of education than was offered by the mechanics' institutes. He instanced the study of politics, theology and metaphysics. He said that the workers must learn to build an economy based upon co-operation rather than competition between labour and capital, and that workingmen should see each other as fellow-workers, not rivals.[28] He also expressed a strong preference to see the governance of the College largely in the hands of the workingmen themselves. He pointed out that Victoria's workingmen had proved their effectiveness at organisation because they had made substantial progress in their aim to establish the eight-hour day. 'It would be just and also expedient that the working men ... ought to have the main and principal control and management of this College through their representatives', he declared.[29]

However, it soon became obvious that the major donors wanted more traditional governing arrangements and were interested in providing a more narrowly vocational curriculum.[30] Perhaps disappointed that the Working Men's College was not to be closely modelled on Maurice's philosophy, or perhaps because he became extremely busy with other matters, Higinbotham gradually withdrew from the project. Had he known that in time the Working Men's College would become a fully-fledged university, and that future Governments would offer loans that would enable working-class students, both male and female, to embrace a wide range of academic pursuits, he would undoubtedly have been pleased.

17

CHIEF JUSTICE HIGINBOTHAM

In 1886, Stawell retired through ill-health. The Government of Duncan Gillies and Alfred Deakin offered to appoint Higinbotham as Acting Chief Justice. He replied, reminding them of his earlier stated objection to co-operating with any 'illegal instructions issued to the Representative of the Crown by the Imperial Government'. Indeed, he added:

> It would be my duty to use the increased responsibility and possible large opportunities of that position to secure the independence of the Queen's Representative in this Colony, and to expose and resist the illegal interference of the Colonial Office in our domestic affairs.[1]

Perhaps taken aback by this response, the Government then offered the appointment to eighty-year-old Sir Robert Molesworth. In September, the Government made a new offer to Higinbotham, this time the appointment as Chief Justice. Henry Wrixon who was Attorney-General, and with whom Higinbotham had a warm friendship, took pleasure in making the offer.[2] Higinbotham, now sixty years of age, and showing early signs of heart disease, decided to accept, but with a proviso regarding the 'dormant commission'. This referred to a practice whereby the Chief Justice of the Supreme Court would take the role of Acting Governor in the case of a temporary vacancy in the office of Governor. The new Governor, Sir Henry Loch, was concerned that to appoint Higinbotham in circumstances where he had refused to co-operate in what he regarded as Imperial interference would be to concede that he was correct.

Loch invited Higinbotham to write to the Secretary of State for the Colonies, Sir Henry Holland, who became Lord Knutsford in February 1888, and he suggested that he should outline the grounds of his complaints against the Colonial Office. Whether he realised it or not, Loch had offered Higinbotham the opportunity to communicate as a possible future Acting Governor of Victoria with the man who had been the legal advisor to the Colonial Office from 1867 to 1870 – the period when Higinbotham had led the struggle between the Legislative Council and the Legislative Assembly in Victoria. Although Lord Knutsford had been appointed Colonial Secretary only as recently as January 1887, he had long been associated with the Colonial Office. In 1870, following his period of service as legal advisor, he was appointed assistant Under-Secretary of State for the Colonies. He left the Colonial Office in 1874 and was elected to Parliament as a Conservative member. Thirteen years later, he was appointed Secretary of State for the Colonies.[3]

Higinbotham wrote to Lord Knutsford in a letter that extended to approximately 6,500 words. He said at the outset, 'I address you in your private capacity as an English politician interested in colonial affairs, and not in your character of Her Majesty's Secretary of State for the Colonies'. His first letter examined the history of British colonial policy towards Victoria from the point of view of constitutional philosophy. He objected to the interference of the Colonial Office in local affairs. He argued that the instructions to Governors ignored the change in the status of the Colony since the Constitution of 1855 and the existence of responsible government.[4] He charged that the policy of the Colonial Office over the last thirty years had probably arisen from 'the natural but very censurable desire of irresponsible subordinate officers to retain for their department by a stratagem a power which they know has been taken away from it by law'.[5]

He particularly charged the Colonial Office with interference at the time of the struggle between the Houses of the Victorian Parliament:

> It is a fact within my personal knowledge that Colonial Office influence was strenuously exerted ... in Victoria from about the year 1864 to the year 1868. At that time, the Colonial Office first endeavoured by means of instructions to the Governor to check and prevent legislation on the subject of the tariff. When that question led to a contest between the two Houses of the Victorian Legislature, the Colonial Office influence was exerted in favour of one House as against the other House, and against the will of the great majority of the people repeatedly expressed at several general elections. It was owing solely to the influence of the Colonial Office that the claims of the Legislative Assembly to the exclusive control of the public finances received at that time a decisive check, from which they have never since recovered ...[6]

The response to the letter took over a year, and during this time Higinbotham received an offer of knighthood. But Higinbotham was not to be diverted as easily as McCulloch and Michie had been by such an inducement. He courteously declined the offer.[7] He then wrote a second letter to Lord Knutsford that was more confronting. In it, Higinbotham objected to 'the sinister and clandestine policy, which the office over which you preside has successfully pursued for the third part of a century'.[8] His objection therefore harked back to the years of the Eureka conflict and the drafting of the Constitution. Lord Knutsford replied, objecting to the use of these words. Higinbotham's letter implied that the staff of the Colonial Office had knowingly betrayed the interests of the colonial population by failing to ensure that the new Constitution of 1855 reflected the aspirations of the colonial population as a whole. Higinbotham had always viewed this denial of political rights as one of the principal causes of the conflict at Eureka.

Higinbotham also objected to the term 'Executive Council', denouncing it as misleading since it 'ignores altogether the existence of responsible government'.[9] Indeed, since he had left the Parliament he had resigned his membership of the Executive Council and declined to be addressed as 'the Honourable'. He attacked the practice of bestowing Imperial honours on colonial politicians, 'as the prize of personal or party intrigue', and recommended instead that the granting of honours should be a prerogative of 'the colonial Governor to be exercised upon the advice of colonial advisors of the Crown and upon the recommendation of both Houses of the colonial Parliament'. He released his correspondence publicly, and this last point drew an indignant response from seventy-six-year-old Sir Archibald Michie, who accused Higinbotham of exceeding what Sir Henry Loch had asked of him, and writing 'a solemn, didactic and all-round lecture to Lord Knutsford'. He ridiculed Higinbotham's suggestion for Australian honours and satirically suggested some of his own inventions, such as 'the Duke of Donnybrook', 'the Marquis of Moonee Ponds' and 'Baron Bendigo'.[10]

The immediate result of this lengthy and acrimonious correspondence between Higinbotham and the Secretary of State for the Colonies was that Higinbotham was not chosen to serve as Acting Governor during his period of office as Chief Justice of Victoria. When Sir Henry Loch decided to visit England, arrangements were made for Sir William Robinson, the retiring Governor of South Australia, to take the role of Acting Governor of Victoria. Higinbotham's campaign to require the Governors to abide by the advice of their Ministers on matters of local interest was resisted by successive Secretaries of State for the Colonies. But in July 1888, the Colonial Office was forced to back down when a crisis arose in Queensland.

A man named Benjamin Kitt was sentenced to three years' imprisonment for stealing three pairs of boots. The Queensland Government recommended to the Governor that Kitt be released, but the Governor, Sir Anthony Musgrave, refused to take its advice. The Ministry then resigned. The Premier, Thomas McIlwraith, protested that the Governor's refusal to accept the advice of the Ministry constituted 'a grave departure from the principles of responsible government'. On this occasion the Colonial Office gave way, perhaps reluctant to embark upon a confrontation with another Australian colonial government over the issue of its instructions to Governors. It overruled Musgrave, who died in early October from a heart attack.[11] Shortly before Higinbotham's death in 1892, Sir Henry Loch, the Governor of Victoria, entered into negotiations with the British Government regarding proposed amendments to the Letters Patent and the Governor's Instructions. He discussed these with the Premier, Duncan Gillies, Alfred Deakin and the Attorney-General, but withheld them from Higinbotham. The Letters Patent and Instructions to Governors of the Australian Colonies were subsequently revised to make them compatible with the principle of responsible government in its modern sense.[12] Higinbotham may have died without knowing that his decades of labour had borne fruit.

Consolidation of the statutes

While Higinbotham's views about the 'dormant commission' may have raised questions in the mind of members of the Government about the suitability of his appointment, they were soon won over by a work of great importance that he performed during his time as Chief Justice. When he had first become Attorney-General in 1863, he had consolidated the statute law of Victoria. This involved collecting all the provisions in statutes relevant to a particular legal topic, removing obsolete sections, updating where appropriate, and condensing them into a single draft statute, which was then to be enacted by the Parliament. These enactments were then organised and indexed and printed in volumes.

Twenty-five years later, the statutes again needed to be consolidated. Though it was an immense task involving five to six hundred statutes, and lasting nearly thirteen months, Higinbotham undertook it without payment. On weekdays he worked after the Court rose, as well as on Saturdays and throughout the legal vacation.[13] He chose as his assistant forty-year-old

Donald Mackinnon who, like himself, had been a journalist and barrister, and whose knowledge of the law and capacity for hard work he highly respected.[14] As with the earlier consolidation, the subsequent enactment by the Parliament of the new consolidated statutes relied heavily on the legislature's confidence in the mastery of law and the personal integrity of the consolidators. Bennett observes that there were disagreements over Higinbotham's consolidations but concedes that they were 'rare', and he notes that the process of legislating the new consolidated Acts 'produced a sense of parliamentary achievement absent from the constant disagreement over more contentious legislative programs'.[15]

The consolidation not only organised and clarified the statutes, but saved money for practitioners and their clients by reducing the need for expensive copies of multiple Acts to deal with each legal subject. All the Victorian statutes were now contained within seven volumes. On 16 December 1890, at the conclusion of the work, Higinbotham was invited to attend both Houses of the Parliament to receive the thanks of the entire Parliament. The publication of the seven volumes of statutes took two years and was not completed in Higinbotham's lifetime. After his death, Morris recorded that the President of the Legislative Council and the Speaker of the Legislative Assembly presented a set of the 'splendidly bound' volumes to his family.

Healing a divided legal profession

The Supreme Court Justices must have been apprehensive at the appointment of Higinbotham, for over the years he had come into conflict with a number of them and their predecessors. With Michie he had fought Judges Redmond Barry, William Stawell, Edward Williams and Robert Molesworth over the issue of their status under responsible government. He had clashed with Thomas Howard Fellows in the Parliament over the 'tacked' bills. He had opposed James Wilberforce Stephen's candidature for the seat of Brighton. In 1862, he had acted successfully for Molesworth's estranged wife in an application for alimony from the judge pending a suit for judicial separation from him on the grounds of cruelty.[16] Yet even before Higinbotham's arrival in Victoria, there were tensions among the judges, and between them and the barristers and solicitors.

From March 1854, when Higinbotham first enrolled at the Victorian Bar, he found a fragmented legal profession in which the Supreme Court Justices were intensely watchful of their power and privileges *vis-à-vis* the judges of the lower courts, and all were inclined to be dismissive of the rights of the humbler legal practitioners. One of Higinbotham's first leading articles in the *Melbourne Morning Herald* appealed to the judges to make awards for legal costs in litigation according to a scale of fees that fairly recognised the work of the 'attorneys' who did much of the background legal work but were poorly paid.[17]

Shortly before his arrival, a new courthouse had been built in Melbourne at a cost of £1,200, but Justice Redmond Barry declined to sit in it when he found that the judges of his court were expected to share the new building with the judges of the County Court. One of these was judge Robert Pohlman, who preferred to be addressed as 'your Honour' rather than by the traditional address 'your Worship'. Barry complained to Governor Hotham that the Supreme Court Justices were compelled to share tenure of the court with a gentleman who has 'assumed their title', and who now intended to 'usurp their seat'. He advised that he would present a requisition for 'some suitable place in which I can sit without a compromise with the station which I have the honour to hold'.[18]

A *cause célèbre* in late 1854 highlighted the Governor's lack of respect for the office of County Court judges. Judge Robert Pohlman was simultaneously a nominee member of the Legislative Council and a member of the Denominational Schools Board. At a time when the Government was keen to reduce expenditure, Pohlman placed a notice of motion on the notice paper of the Legislative Council proposing a vote of money for the denominational schools. He did so without first seeking leave of the Governor and the members of his Executive Council. Annoyed by this, Hotham instructed his secretary to write to Pohlman and threaten him with dismissal from his judicial position. A copy of the letter came into the hands of the editor of the *Melbourne Morning Herald*, who expounded the constitutional implications of Hotham's threat, pointing out that it did not pertain to the performance of the judge's duty and that it indicated the danger of allowing a Governor who did not respect the judiciary to appoint and dismiss them.[19] Pohlman managed to keep his judicial appointment but took care to preserve his independence from the Governor by resigning his nominee membership of the Legislative Council and standing successfully as an elected member.

With the passing of the first generation of Supreme Court judges who had been active protagonists in the dispute over their status under the new Constitution, the preoccupation with asserting a privileged status above the County Court judges abated. Higinbotham saw an opportunity to heal the wounds of the past and create a more co-operative and collegial feeling within the judiciary. As Chief Justice, he received £500 more annually than his brother judges, but he set this amount aside to entertain members of the legal profession at annual gatherings. To these gatherings he invited the judges of the Supreme Court and County Court, the chief officers of the court, and many of the barristers and solicitors. As the numbers were large, he divided the total into four and hosted four dinners at the start of each legal year. Despite his reputation as a man of ascetic habits who was unused to entertaining large numbers of people, Higinbotham undertook these gatherings with the intention of bringing the legal profession together in a friendly way. Morris, who was now a member of the family, having married Higinbotham's eldest daughter Edith in 1879, may have formed his own first-hand impressions of such occasions. He noted that Higinbotham was 'a genial and kindly host', and that the aim of the social gatherings succeeded, for 'feuds, perhaps more than one or two, were healed at these dinners'.[20]

Higinbotham's dissident opinion re *Toy v Musgrove*

In the 1880s anti-Chinese sentiment escalated in the Australian colonies, largely led by unionists in industries such as furniture-making where

Europeans competed with Chinese workers.[21] The promoters pointed to reports of disturbances in California and warned that the same could happen in Australia if the Australian colonies did not follow the lead of the United States and restrict Chinese immigration.[22] The editors of some newspapers, such as the *Bulletin*, wrote articles about the Chinese in Australia that showed the influence of the new theory of Social Darwinism. The theory suggested that the struggle between animal species for survival was mirrored in humans by a struggle between 'superior' and 'inferior' races and nations. Accordingly, Australia needed to protect itself from being over-run by 'inferior' races such as the Chinese.[23]

In May 1888, Sir Henry Parkes, the Premier of New South Wales, imposed a tax of £100 per head on Chinese immigrants and introduced other restrictions on their liberty. This defied Imperial authority. The Chinese Ambassador in London responded with a remonstrance to the Foreign Office and reminded him that the British Government retained the power to veto the colonial legislation. The Secretary of State for the Colonies, Lord Knutsford, wrote to the Governments of the Australian colonies pointing out that the proposed exclusion of the Chinese from Australia constituted 'a serious international difficulty'. Despite this, Parkes refused entry to the next Chinese arrivals.[24]

In the previous month, A.W. Musgrove, the Victorian Collector of Customs, had refused admission to Victoria to all the Chinese passengers on the ship *Afghan* when it arrived in Hobson's Bay. This was in conformity with the *Chinese Act* of 1881 that imposed a tax of £10 per head, to be paid by a ship's captain for each Chinese citizen he landed in Victoria. The number of immigrants for each ship was also restricted. The *Afghan* was only entitled to bring fourteen Chinese immigrants but it brought 268.[25] A citizen of China named Chun Teon Toy, who was a passenger on board the *Afghan*, brought an action for damages against Musgrove.

The case provoked much interest as it raised debate about the powers of the Colony *vis-à-vis* the Imperial Government. A point at issue was whether the Ministers in Victoria had the legal right to legislate to exclude foreigners, or whether it was the prerogative of the British Crown to admit or exclude foreigners. The full bench of the Supreme Court of Victoria, consisting of Justices Holroyd, a'Beckett, Wrensfordsley, Kerferd, Williams and Higinbotham heard the case. Justices Higinbotham and Kerferd (two former parliamentarians) took the view that the Victorian Government had the right to exclude foreigners. Higinbotham argued that the Constitution gave the Victorian Government all the powers of the British Government, including the authority to exclude aliens. He took a broad view of the *Constitution Act*, arguing that the intentions behind the Act could be deduced from the circumstances at the time of its enactment. He contended that Stawell's undertaking to the Legislative Council in 1854 that responsible government was a 'main principle' of the Act was relevant to understanding the subsequent Act, and that the 1855 *Constitution Act* granted full responsible government to Victoria. However, the four other Justices took the view that the Constitution had granted only 'an instalment of responsible government'.[26] Higinbotham found to his dismay that the majority view of the Supreme Court bench contradicted his own view.[27]

Damages and costs were awarded to Toy, the plaintiff. The defendant, Musgrove, appealed to the Privy Council in England. Its subsequent decision in 1891 reversed the Victorian decision, but it based its decision largely on other grounds and made no determination on the constitutional question. In the interval of time between the arrival of the *Afghan* in April 1888 and the Privy Council's decision in 1891, both Victoria and New South Wales introduced even more stringent legislation to restrict Chinese immigration. It was regrettable for the future of relations between Australia and China and for inter-racial harmony within Australia that the issue of Chinese immigration had become entangled with the aspiration for responsible government.

Nearly a century later, the former Governor-General of Australia and High Court Justice, Sir Ninian Stephens, commented:

> Higinbotham's interpretation of the Constitution Act ... may not have been correct as a matter of law, but as a prophetic statement of what would be, and should be, the position in

Britain's self-governing colonies it proved by the end of the century to be fully justified.[28]

This is a paradox that has struck several historians and constitutional lawyers who declare that Higinbotham was wrong in his understanding of the law, while conceding that he was proven right by the course of historical events. The legal historian Charles Parkinson, noting that Higinbotham's view was in the minority, comments that 'time, however, has been with Higinbotham on this issue'. Geoffrey Serle writes that 'whatever Higinbotham's legal eccentricity, his view of what should be the case in domestic self-government had history on its side'.[29] Robin Gollan makes a similar point and adds a pertinent observation:

> As a statement of present law, Higinbotham's view was mistaken. But as a statement of the rights of self-government, it was unexceptionable. By the end of the century, Higinbotham's views had been established by convention. In this process, his assertion of rights as law was a compelling factor in having them established as law.[30]

At a personal level, finding himself outvoted on the bench must have been a bitter blow to Higinbotham, for it meant that a lifetime of efforts had been based on a view of the legal position that the majority of the bench now declared to be incorrect. Throughout his career as journalist and politician, he had sought to foster the principle of responsible government, and he had always maintained that the Constitution provided for it.

The Supreme Court's decision raised disturbing questions. Had the brave speeches and resolutions in the Legislative Council in support of that principle at the time of Hotham's Minute in 1855 been pointless? Was Sir John O'Shanassy right when he declared in 1855 that talk of responsible government was 'all a delusion and a sham'?[31] Had the post-Eureka strategy of progressing the diggers' causes through parliamentary means been a mistake? Had he misled the Legislative Assembly in 1869 when he persuaded a majority of the members to the view that the Colony had been granted responsible government? Doubtless, he remained committed to his view, but the defeat was humiliating.

Higinbotham and the Maritime Strike

The prosperous 1880s in Victoria were followed by the great depression of the 1890s. Though the economy was still buoyant in 1890, the ranks of the unemployed in Melbourne swelled by early winter with an influx of out-of-work agricultural labourers, and the resources of charities were stretched. Meetings of the unemployed sent deputations to Government Ministers but were routinely rebuffed, and the police were instructed to break up gatherings using the 'Move On Clause'. Delegations of the unemployed visited the Governor, the Mayor and the Anglican and Catholic Bishops imploring them to use their influence with the Government Ministers to provide relief, but the Government showed little inclination to help. On 30 July 1890, a delegation visited Chief Justice Higinbotham, who assured them of his sympathy. They noted that he treated them with 'that genuine cordiality that places peer and peasant on an equality'. He expressed the view that it was the duty of the Government to start relief works 'of a varied character in order that the robust and their weaker brethren should share in the privilege of keeping body and soul together'.[32]

In Sydney in mid-August, the Mercantile Marine Officers' Association declared its intention to strike for better pay and conditions. The Melbourne members sought to affiliate with the Trades Hall Council, but the Ship Owners' Association dismissed all those who refused to give up this affiliation. To strengthen its bargaining power, the Marine Officers' Association sought and received the support of a Maritime Labour Council, which included seamen and wharf labourers. Australia-wide industrial action on the waterfront followed the lockout of the Marine Officers. Other unions, including shearers and coal-miners, joined the struggle. In late August 1890, gas stokers refused to handle coal that had been mined and delivered by non-union labour, and walked off the job. This left Melbourne without gas for industry and street lighting.[33] By September, 50,000 Australian workers were out of work as industry was impacted. The strike extended to New Zealand where another 8,000 were also out of work.

The historian Stuart Svensen has extensively researched the Maritime Strike. He declares that it was the biggest event of its kind in Australian history, and characterises it as labour and capital 'on strike against each other'.[34] Svensen highlights the significance of the changing structure of capitalism in the period between 1886 and 1890, and its consequences for industrial relations. He notes that amongst the industries that were principally affected by the Maritime Strike, the majority were joint stock companies in which ownership was divorced from management. Compared with traditional owner-managers, the new generation of managers, who were employed by companies, were not risking their own money if they provoked strikes.[35] He argues that a small clique formed which was determined to control industrial relations policy. Since 1886, when the Employers' Union first formed, they had begun to organise and plan for a major offensive against the unions.

Svensen also highlights the important role of Alfred Lamb, a member of the Legislative Assembly of New South Wales and vice-president of the New South Wales Employers' Union. Lamb's 'masterstroke' was to unite the warring factions of shipowners and enlist their support in the struggle.[36] Once they combined, the shipowners were well placed to spread the dispute and engage the unions on many fronts throughout Australia. But Svensen also holds some unionists to blame, noting that poor tactics and disorganisation by the Australian Shearers' Union and the Labour Defence Organisation contributed to the unions' ultimate defeat.[37]

James Service, a veteran member of the Victorian Legislative Assembly, who had recently become a member of the Legislative Council and who was himself a shipowner, urged the Ship Owners' Association to arrange a conference with the unions. At first they agreed to meet, but under the influence of the Employers' Association, they changed their minds. As more unions joined the strike in sympathy, the shipowners retaliated by taking advantage of the large number of unemployed non-union workers to break the strike. In Port Adelaide, police used batons to control disputes on the waterfront.[38] In New South Wales and Victoria, the Governments called out their permanent military forces to intimidate the strikers and their supporters.

On 29 August, the Government ordered that 2,000 special constables be enrolled. In Melbourne, Colonel Tom Price, Commander of the Victorian Mounted Rifles, received orders to bring detachments from country districts into Melbourne in time for a mass meeting of union sympathisers scheduled to occur two days later. In 1857 Captain John Price, the father of Colonel Tom Price, had been an inspector of convicts who had earned a reputation for cruelty. A number of convicts who were kept on a prison ship moored at Williamstown saw their opportunity for revenge. While on shore duty, they hurled stones at Captain Price and killed him. In 1890 his son, Colonel Tom Price, paraded his troopers through the streets of Melbourne to strike fear into the union sympathisers. He famously instructed his men that when he gave the order to fire, he expected them to 'fire low and lay them out', though he later denied that this was an instruction to kill.[39]

Irish-born Francis Longmore, a former gold miner at Ballarat and veteran member of the Legislative Assembly, told the House:

> I knew Price long ago. I knew his father; I knew what he was when he was in charge of the convicts and seven of them were hanged for killing him because he was such a tyrant. This officer to whom I have been referring would have followed his father's footsteps at the Maritime Strike if he had had the chance.[40]

Longmore's chilling description of Price's propensity for brutality was echoed by the authors of the *Report* of the Finance and Control Committee of the Trades Hall Council. They feared for those attending the mass meeting of 31 August, noting:

This vast assemblage of the people was overshadowed by a military force of a thousand soldiers armed and equipped with 40,000 rounds of ball cartridges in their cartouche cases; that the lives of the Executive Committee had already been compassed and their names inscribed upon the rifle bullets, and that not only the manhood of the country, but our helpless women and children, were in a reckless moment to be given over to the mercy of a man filled 'from the crown to the toe top full of direst cruelty'.[41]

To Higinbotham, the intimidating parade of the armed troopers through the streets of Melbourne must have evoked disturbing memories of earlier protests in which protesters who assembled peacefully were met with the threat of a military onslaught. He would have remembered that in 1843, when he was a seventeen-year-old lad about to commence study at Trinity College Dublin, a gathering of several thousand people was expected to assemble in the suburb of Clontarf to hear an address from Daniel O'Connell and to support his call for repeal of the *Act of Union*. The British Government responded by sending 3,000 men on warships to Dublin Harbour with orders to 'cut the people down' if they should dare to assemble. Like Longmore, he remembered the dawn raid at Eureka in 1854 that occurred in response to a mass campaign for political rights and the redress of valid grievances; and he remembered that it was a mounted trooper who carried out the cold-blooded shooting of his fellow journalist, Frank Hasleham.

By September, Sir Bryan O'Loghlen, the Member for West Bourke, who would be Premier of Victoria within a year, called for a conference of employers and employees to resolve the situation, but the Minister of Customs, James Patterson, countered that 'No Government can afford to be neutral when a question of law and order is concerned'.[42] On 15 October, O'Loghlen proposed a motion regretting that the Employers' Union would not meet with the Trades Hall in an unconditional conference.[43]

Benjamin Douglass, the trade union leader who had worked with Higinbotham on the Working Men's College project, encouraged him to donate to the strike fund.[44] Higinbotham presented the president of the Trades Hall Council with a cheque accompanied by a letter stating:

> The Chief Justice presents his compliments to the President of the Trades-hall Council, and requests that he will be so good as to place the amount of the enclosed cheque of £50 to the credit of the strike fund. While the United Trades are awaiting compliance with their reasonable request for a conference with the employers, the Chief Justice will continue for the present to forward a weekly contribution of £10 for the same object.[45]

Higinbotham knew that he broke protocol by associating his office with the donation, but he did so to maximise the public impact of the gesture. He hoped to encourage a conference between the parties, thereby averting bloodshed and bringing the dispute to an honourable conclusion. He continued his donations for a further ten weeks. He also wrote to a group of women who organised a fund-raising bazaar to assist the families of the strikers. He urged them to remain positive, adding:

> I think it is clear that the recent defeat has been caused by the want of more extended union amongst the classes that labour, and this lesson, if well understood and remembered, will provide greater benefit to labour than present victory.[46]

The conference never took place. The strike collapsed and the employers were everywhere victorious. The shipowners required the marine officers to apologise for their temerity as a condition of re-employment.

In an obituary to Higinbotham, the journalist Price Warung noted that his donation to the strike fund in his official capacity as Chief Justice infuriated some people. He added that one capitalist had declared that he wished that 'a company of the permanent artillery should haul the Judge from the Bench, put him against a wall and shoot him'.[47] Higinbotham's gesture failed, but it won for him personally the lasting gratitude of the maritime workers of Victoria. Writing in 1972, Gwyneth Dow noted, 'to this day the Seamen's Union lays a wreath on his statue on each anniversary of his death'.[48]

CONCLUSION

The heart condition that had affected Higinbotham for several years became increasingly troublesome. He suffered from shortness of breath and recurrent attacks of angina pain. Throughout his life he had sought to maintain fitness by rowing and exercising, but, though he and his medical advisor would not have known it, his long-standing habit of smoking cigarettes, especially when combined with over-work, may have undermined his health and contributed to his death at the age of sixty-six. In September 1892, three months before his death, he attended the funeral of Mr Justice Webb and, as Chief Justice, delivered an outstanding eulogy. Morris noted that, despite this, an observer was 'much shocked at his fragile appearance', and that by Christmas his health had collapsed:

> The end came with great suddenness. At half past one in the afternoon, he was talking to his son, who, to his father's great delight, had just come down from the country. Some half an hour later an attack of *angina pectoris* came on with great violence. His wife alone was with him at the end. The paroxysm lasted less than half an hour, but without much to show that it was worse than others. It was nearly half past two when George Higinbotham died on the last day of the year 1892. His last look was an upward glance, apparently of surprised and joyful recognition.[1]

At his own request, his funeral was a strictly private one at St Andrew's Church, Brighton. Only his friend Benjamin Douglass, his former Chief Justice's Associate Gerald Piggott, and his medical practitioner Dr Dunbar

Hooper accompanied the family at the funeral service and the burial in the Brighton Cemetery.[2] It had been his wish to be buried with his brother Thomas and his infant daughter Ethel at St Andrew's Church, Brighton, but that graveyard had reached capacity. Though there was no official ceremony to mark his death, both Houses of the Parliament passed resolutions of regret at his passing and extended their sympathy to his family. Morris noted that 'very interesting speeches were delivered by old friends, younger admirers and old opponents'.[3] A number of church leaders delivered sermons marking the occasion.

Higinbotham's death was major news in the newspapers of Victoria, along with expressions of condolence and reflections upon his contributions to Victorian public life. Some expressed reservations about aspects of his political career.[4] The *Argus*, which had been a merciless critic throughout his time in Parliament, continued to deprecate his political reform agenda, but paid a high tribute to him in death:

> No man in his time played a more conspicuous and more important part in the making of the Colony and no man has cut a deeper groove in its political destinies … He was a leader in journalism, in politics and in law.[5]

The Supreme Court judges, Sir Hartley Williams, Henry Hodges and the new Chief Justice, Sir John Madden, lamented Higinbotham's passing. They praised him for his personal qualities, his thorough knowledge of the common law, his professionalism, his integrity, his industry and his exemplary courtesy. Justice Hodges regretted the 'irreparable loss' and ended his speech with the following tribute:

> Britain may have greater lawyers; Britain may have greater statesmen; Britain may have craftier politicians; but Britain has no son with a stronger, gentler, firmer, more tender, nobler nature than the man who lately presided this court.

Destruction of primary sources

Eighteen years before his death, Higinbotham had instructed his family that, following his death, all of his personal papers should be burned 'without delay'. He repeated the instruction in 1884. It covered all of his manuscript books and accounts, which, he said, none but his wife Margaret should read, and included all diaries, 'political and professional remains' and other papers. His family carried out his wish. Morris confessed:

> With the wish to write the life strong within me, I assisted
> in the burning, knowing that I was destroying material that
> would have been of priceless value to a biographer.[6]

This was the first of three fires that destroyed vital information about Higinbotham's life and times. Nearly thirty years later, during the Irish Civil War in 1922, Michael Collins, the leader of the Provisional Government, used British artillery to end the siege of the Four Courts building in Dublin by militants opposed to a treaty with the British. The resulting fire destroyed the Irish census returns from 1821 to 1851, and the majority of the records of births, deaths, marriages and wills. This loss has hampered the task of tracing Higinbotham's family through Irish public records. Although the originals of the wills of Higinbotham's mother Sarah, and his grandmother Jane Verner, were destroyed, copies had been made of both and these copies miraculously survived the fire.

Nearly four decades later, yet more primary sources were lost when a third fire engulfed St Andrew's Church in Brighton, Victoria, in 1961. Higinbotham belonged to this Anglican congregation and served as the chairman of the vestry. Some of the records that were lost in the fire might have provided further insight into his relationship with the Anglican community in Brighton, as well as his work for education in the local area.

The loss of so much biographical information has made our understanding of Higinbotham incomplete. What little we have known until recently about Higinbotham's early years does not explain the complex and forceful man that he became, nor what drove him to such efforts for constitutional reform, nor how his guiding vision originated and developed. Though several biographical works exist, in the absence of letters, diaries or photographs it has been difficult to discover the private man and to delve into his inner life. Necessarily historians have had to resort to speculation where knowledge has been lost. Fortunately, the Internet, digitised newspapers and computer-assisted microfilm readers have made new resources available to researchers, and some of the long-standing gaps in our knowledge are being filled.

The major source of personal information from one who knew Higinbotham well is Morris's biography, published in 1895. But in deference to the family's wish for privacy, Morris omitted much that he would have liked to include. There are gaps in the narrative, inconsistencies, missing years, and silences about key turning points in Higinbotham's life. Morris does not portray his subject as a son, a father or a husband. Though Higinbotham had five brothers, two sisters, and many cousins, Morris comments upon his relationship with only two of the brothers. There is just the barest description of his wife Margaret as 'a spinster, native of Kent'.[7] Like many nineteenth-century biographies, the principal concern of Morris's *Memoir* is to elevate its subject in the reader's estimation. However, the modern reader expects the writer of biography to seek to understand the subject by placing him in the context of his family and his times, by exploring the philosophical and religious underpinnings of his outlook, by re-creating his worldview, by imagining his feelings, and by offering psychological insight. Though it is a most valuable resource, Morris's biography is limited in these respects.

It was in 1874 that Higinbotham first left the instruction that his papers be destroyed. Historians have long wondered why. The historian Stuart Macintyre wrote:

> George Higinbotham regarded his political career as a failure. He found the business of politics distasteful. He refused to accommodate himself to the exigencies of party

politics. He believed that his time as an elected minister and representative was wasted, that he had achieved none of his objectives and while still in his forties, he withdrew from the Victorian Parliament, never to return.[8]

Higinbotham's decision to retire from politics corresponds roughly with the period in his career when his relationship with McCulloch was becoming strained, and he could see no way to achieve his goal of democratising the Constitution. It was at about this time that he first instructed his family to destroy his papers. It may have been a period of such deep disillusionment that the evidence of his earlier efforts for what now appeared to be a lost cause served as a painful reminder to him of the magnitude of his failure.

Although his diary and personal papers are irretrievably lost, his contributions to the *Melbourne Morning Herald* have survived in other collections. They are vastly more extensive and revealing than was indicated by his son-in-law Morris in his brief reference to them in the *Memoir*, and they provide us with important new insights. Though he wrote anonymously, his distinctive style and themes make it possible to identify his work.[9] The voice that we hear is not that of the older man ruefully reviewing a life devoted to a cause that he mistakenly believed had come to nothing, but of a fervent and determined young idealist who believed he could succeed, and who lived by the motto of the Dungannon Royal School: *Perseverando vinces*.[10]

Higinbotham's journalism for the *Melbourne Morning Herald* before, during and after the military conflict at Eureka may have been a subject of great sensitivity, and this may explain Morris's failure to acknowledge his father-in-law's twenty-seven months of work for this newspaper. Another event that would have occasioned pain was the accusation of sedition made against the *Herald* during Higinbotham's time by the *London Illustrated News*. The accusation was in response to the first of two editorials that Higinbotham wrote accusing the British Government of 'usurpation' and 'tyranny' for failing to allow the Victorian legislature an opportunity to review the changes it made to the Victorian Constitution.[11]

The silences in Morris's biography suggest that there were other areas of sensitivity as well. These included family matters such as his wife's service with the Devlin family, his fraught relationship with the Verner family, his brother William's psychiatric condition, his father's failed commercial enterprise and its effect on his mother and siblings.[12] Higinbotham had experienced the tenacity and spitefulness of his enemies, and may have anticipated that after his death they would eagerly exploit any new opportunities to blacken his name. Rather than burden anyone with the responsibility to put aside the papers relating to the more sensitive issues, Higinbotham may have thought it simpler to destroy everything. His instruction has given rise to speculation that he may have been concerned to hide some shameful secret, but this seems unlikely.

The genesis of Higinbotham's ideas

George Higinbotham grew to adulthood against the backdrop of the widespread agitation for Repeal of the *Act of Union*, the twin scourges of famine and forced emigration, and the 1848 Uprising. These events awakened his interest in many political questions, including the rights of majorities and minorities, the rule of law, loyalty to the sovereign, the relationship between church and state, and the function of Parliament as an institution representing the views of the people. He responded to the distress and turbulence of his times by developing his own political ideals, and using his skills in writing and in oratory to promote them.

His distinctive political ideals marked him out as an atypical member of the Irish Protestant Ascendancy – a class that occupied many of the positions of power and influence in early colonial Victoria. His family background, with its dichotomy between the religious and political allegiances of the maternal and paternal sides of his family, meant that although he was brought up as a member of that class, he was exposed from a young age to a wider tradition of European and American liberal thought than were the majority of his peers. This was reinforced to some degree by his academic studies in history. Higinbotham straddled two worlds: his grandfather Joseph Wilson's American world of sacrifice for the achievement of colonial self-government and democracy, and the world of Irish Protestant loyalty to the British Empire that came down to him from his father's side of the family. He developed his own political philosophy that drew upon both of these traditions. In Sir William Molesworth's ideas of democratic constitutional arrangements within a British Imperial framework, he believed that he had found a solution appropriate to the new Colony of Victoria.

Within his first year in Victoria, Higinbotham's natural predisposition to oppose rebellion against authority came under challenge from his close association with the agitation on the goldfields, which culminated in the battle at Eureka. The link between an unjust political system and rebellion was fully apparent. The realisation of the link increased his anxiety that the new Constitution should provide a workable and just democratic political system. The following year, when the new Constitution arrived from London, it proved to be a bitter disappointment to him as well as to the population of the goldfields and other colonists.

For Higinbotham, the development of a sound Constitution incorporating liberal principles and responsible government within the context of loyalty to the British Empire was essential to the future of the young Colony, and he laboured to achieve it. Had Molesworth remained as Secretary of State for the Colonies, Higinbotham's advocacy of constitutional reform might have borne fruit, but Molesworth's premature death after only three months in office ended this possibility. Later, as a parliamentarian, Higinbotham found that the task of reforming the anti-democratic provisions of the 1855 Constitution faced enormous opposition both from vested interests within Victoria and from the Colonial Office in London. To his great disappointment, he failed to achieve the major reforms that he and many Victorians believed were necessary.

Looking back from the 1970s, Victoria's most eminent historian of the colonial period, Geoffrey Serle, agreed with Higinbotham that the 1855 Constitution was a fundamental problem throughout the post gold-rush period. In his view:

> A grotesque constitution nullified the democratic potential, reduced the parliamentary process almost to futility, and added immensely to class bitterness.[13]

Some historians of the colonial period, especially legal historians, have asserted that the Victorian Constitution as drafted in 1854 stirred little popular interest and provoked no significant opposition.[14] Some argue that the Constitution was liberal and progressive for its times.[15] Some have hailed it as a 'popular', even crediting it with producing Victoria's 'happy state'.[16] Such interpretations perpetuate a rosy view of what was a very flawed drafting process and an ill-omened outcome. The Constitution Bill that emanated from the Legislative Council of Victoria was one of the leading causes of grievance that culminated in the military conflict at Eureka. The *Constitution Act* that resulted in 1855 was at the heart of three damaging political deadlocks in Victoria in its first twenty-three years of implementation.

From 1852 to 1854, the goldfields populations thoroughly explored every legitimate means of seeking redress of their grievances, and one of their constant complaints was that they were practically unrepresented in the legislature. It is also apparent that the agitation on the goldfields was not confined to the diggers, but was a broad-based movement that included mining entrepreneurs, bank managers, storekeepers, theatrical people, press correspondents, doctors, teachers, ministers of religion and prominent lay people. Many were well educated and avid readers of newspapers, yet the majority of them were disenfranchised by the 1855 Constitution. Their aspiration for what they believed to be their rights explains much of the popular support for Higinbotham in the struggles that he led for responsible government in 1855, 1865 and 1867.

The Irish Protestant class in colonial Victoria

Like most Irish Protestants of his day, Higinbotham firmly upheld the *Act of Union*, yet he was discomfited by the knowledge that the lack of an Irish Government exacerbated the desperate plight of Ireland in the mid-

1840s. The Irish members of the House of Commons found themselves to be a relatively powerless minority in a British Parliament preoccupied with other priorities. This dilemma may have sensitised him to the situation of the colonists in Victoria, many of whom wanted to see the Colony as the master of its own destiny while at the same time remaining loyal to the British Empire. Higinbotham believed that this outcome was both desirable and possible. He saw the Empire as an Anglo-Saxon brotherhood of nations, each respectful of the sovereignty of all the others, and having a moral obligation to promote Anglo-Saxon cultural and religious values and material advancement throughout its realm.

Sir William Stawell and his cousin, John Foster, the Colonial Secretary, were Irish Protestants in an arch-conservative mould. The pair exerted a baleful influence over the development of the Victorian Constitution. Stawell advocated a property threshold of £10,000 for the Legislative Council. He urged the Drafting Committee to ignore popular opinion. He stifled debate regarding the principle of responsible government by falsely reassuring the Legislative Council that this principle was already enshrined in the Bill. He attempted to entrench the Constitution via a 'two-thirds' clause to make change nearly impossible. He altered the recommendation of the Drafting Select Committee to set the terms of office of members of the Legislative Assembly at three years, and presented it to the Committee of the whole as five years, and this was subsequently passed. It was probably he who altered the resolution that gave the Legislative Assembly the right to choose the ministry.

As Attorney-General, Stawell opposed any concession of political rights to the goldfields population. In the last hours before the conflict erupted at Eureka, the delegates of the Ballarat diggers met with Hotham, Stawell and Foster in Melbourne in a final effort to avoid conflict. The diggers' representatives pleaded for political enfranchisement, but Stawell advised the Governor that he had no power to grant it, although following the conflict at Eureka and the *Report* of the Goldfields Commission, the Governor did so.[17] His extremism was demonstrated when he charged eight of the prisoners from Eureka with the crime of high treason. When juries would not convict, he meddled in the method of selecting juries. At the time of the inauguration of the 1855 Constitution, Stawell relied upon an unusual definition of the term 'responsible ministers' to obtain increased pensions for some of his appointed government colleagues. This gave the Ministers who were involved an incentive to support Stawell's eccentric definition of 'responsible government' that did not include the concept of Government being answerable to an elected legislature.[18] He also strenuously, but unsuccessfully, opposed the introduction of the secret ballot in 1856.

On his elevation to the Supreme Court bench, Stawell attempted (unsuccessfully) to circumvent the Legislative Assembly's assertion of its privileges in the cases of George Dill and Hugh Glass, who both breached parliamentary privilege.[19] He and the other Supreme Court justices waged a long but ultimately unsuccessful battle to assert their independence of the Government of the day regarding the terms of their employment.[20] As Acting Governor, Stawell injudiciously stoked the fires of political resentment by refusing Graham Berry a dissolution, thereby provoking a bitter attempt by Berry and his supporters to frustrate government business in the Legislative Assembly. The prolonged abuse of parliamentary procedure that ensued so disheartened Higinbotham that he eventually resigned his seat.[21]

Stawell's and Foster's understanding of Government in colonial Victoria owed much to the history and traditions of Ireland. Both were grandsons of John Foster, who was Speaker of the House in the Irish House of Commons from 1785 until its abolition in 1800. The powerful Protestant minority in Ireland had traditionally striven to maintain the infamous penal laws in order to counter what they perceived as the threat from the Catholic majority. Speaker Foster famously upheld the British Government's suppression of those who spoke in the House in support of the emancipation of the Catholic population of Ireland, for he saw himself as answerable to the Government in London rather than the population of Ireland.[22] His son, John Leslie Foster (father of the Colonial Secretary of Victoria) was appointed Baron of the Court of Exchequer in Ireland. He followed his father's tradition of suppressing the Catholic population.[23]

There are traces of this same attitude of contempt and fear of the population in William Stawell's and John Foster's administration of the Government of colonial Victoria, and in their determination to create a Constitution that would frustrate the popular will.

The historian Jarlath Ronayne has identified the pastoralist and member of the Legislative Council, Charles Griffith, as 'the doyen of the Irish cousinage' and it is noticeable that a number of associates of Griffith played prominent roles in the Eureka conflict.[24] Griffith's biographer remarked upon his own 'steely attitude towards the gold diggers' agitations'.[25] The Assistant Colonial Secretary, John Moore, who, at the time of the military conflict at Eureka, issued a proclamation calling on all British citizens 'to render support and assistance to the authorities', was Griffith's former business partner. Hussey Malone Chomley, a sub-inspector of police at Creswick, and second-in-command of a police detachment that was kept in reserve during the Eureka uprising, was his nephew.[26] William Foster Stawell subsequently married Griffith's niece, Mary Greene.[27] To these men, the political agitation at Ballarat was seen through the prism of an Irish Protestant Ascendancy view of rebel movements, which it was their duty to suppress.

As a member of the same class, Higinbotham shared their loyalty to Britain and their concerns for the safety and welfare of the Irish Protestant community. However, his support for the British monarchy was strictly as a constitutional monarchy within a democratic system where the people exercised power through their elected representatives. This democratic interpretation of loyalty to the sovereign reflected the liberal influences that, from an early age, had enlarged his view. Among these broadening influences were his mother's family's pride in Joseph Wilson's involvement in the American War of Independence; the ecumenical spirit of his headmaster, the Reverend John Darley; the outreach to the poor by his chaplain at Lincoln's Inn, Frederick Denison Maurice; and the exposure to ideas for social and political reform of Sir William Molesworth and his circle. Through these influences, Higinbotham came to see that a democratic Constitution and progressive social policies were essential to the future peace and prosperity of the Colony of Victoria if it was to avoid the mistakes that had caused so much misery in Ireland.

Historians debate Higinbotham's legacy

Higinbotham fascinates because he is an enigma. No other Victorian politician excites such polarised opinions about his character, legacy and place in Victorian history. In his own lifetime, both friends and adversaries struggled to understand his complexity. There is a broad consensus among historians that Higinbotham was an exceptional orator, and that his personal reputation was unsullied by any hint of personal scandal or corruption. Although Higinbotham was a man of small stature, and at a personal level an unassuming and courteous man, when stirred by powerful emotions and deep convictions, his oratory carried him to impassioned heights. He grappled with the leading questions of his day: law reform, public education, responsible government, accountability, women's rights, the Empire, and land reform. Some of these issues remain unresolved. His oratory, willpower and burning convictions combined to make Higinbotham a dominating presence in the Victorian Legislative Assembly for fifteen years.

Shortly after Higinbotham's death, a debate about his place in Victorian history began. In February 1895, an anonymous retrospective on Higinbotham's life in the *Imperial Review* reviled him as a man with an 'unbounded capacity for spite and hatred, and a thoroughly unscrupulous idea of politics'. Four months later, a contrasting retrospective on his life in the *Review of Reviews* spoke of his 'crystalline honesty' and his 'high-mindedness'. It added that Victorians cherished George Higinbotham with 'something at least of the feeling that Americans entertain towards George Washington'.[28] Successive generations of historians have continued to disagree markedly in their assessments of him. To this day, historians remain divided into camps of admirers and detractors.

Much of the debate concerns Higinbotham's legacy. For all the turbulence, what did he achieve for Victoria? The legal historian John

Bennett declared that Higinbotham achieved 'virtually nothing' for Victoria, and that his campaign against the interference of the Colonial Office in Victorian politics was 'neither statesmanlike, attractive nor democratic'.[29] However, another legal historian, Charles Parkinson, acclaimed Higinbotham as 'arguably the most influential figure in the development of responsible government in the Colony of Victoria'.[30] New information about Higinbotham's background, motivations and political philosophy provides a fuller context for resolving such arguments when considered in the context of the major political issues of his times.

Some historians have viewed the devolution of self-government and responsible government to the Australian colonies in the 1850s as the expression of a *Zeitgeist* that played out seamlessly and inevitably across the British Empire through the natural extension of home-grown political ideals to British subjects in the colonies.[31] By contrast, some liberal historians contend that it took mass movements to force unwilling governments to concede democratic reforms.[32] Which view we hold about the 1855 Constitution affects our perceptions of Higinbotham, for if its deficiencies are denied, Higinbotham's crusade for political reform is stripped of its context, and thereby deprived of its meaning. His political conduct then becomes explicable only in terms of an aberrant personality. Bennett contends that Higinbotham had 'an aggressive and combative disposition', and he speculates that this resulted from an emotionally deprived childhood. He argues that this – rather than the pursuit of any principles – explains Higinbotham's protracted contests with the Colonial Office, the Legislative Council and the judges.[33]

Victoria's new Constitution of 1855 was notable for the lack of a coherent constitutional basis. It was drafted in 1853–54, seventy-seven years after the Americans had declared independence, sixty-four years after the French had revolted in the name of Liberty, Equality and Fraternity, and five years after the 'Spring of Nations' had taken place with populist uprisings across Europe. In England itself, there had been years of agitation by the Chartists who demanded reform and democratisation of the British system of government, and in Ireland the Repeal movement articulated a profound aspiration for greater political autonomy. Despite this ferment of raised political expectations, the framers of Victoria's Constitution made virtually no concession to the aspiration of many colonists for a constitution that would accord them political rights commensurate with contemporary expectations. The drafters of Victoria's new Constitution scarcely raised liberal principles at all, other than to deprecate them.[34] Indeed, as Archibald Michie pointed out in his report on the drafting of the new Constitution, 'the absence of all guiding principle is painfully striking', and the *Argus* largely concurred.[35]

Michie's powerful and timely campaign through the *Melbourne Morning Herald* may have saved Victoria from some of the most illiberal provisions that the Drafting Committee and Stawell recommended, but it did not save Victoria from all such provisions. The fight for a broadly based, democratic Government consistent with the principle of responsible government in its modern sense was to take decades, and to inflict a heavy toll on Victoria through repeated constitutional deadlocks and associated crises. Had Victoria been blessed with a truly democratic constitution-drafting process from the outset, the conflict at Eureka might have been avoided. The energy necessarily diverted into bitter power struggles with the Colonial Office, between the landholding and landless classes, and between the Houses of the legislature, could have been directed productively. Victoria, blessed with so many natural resources, could have developed rapidly into a fairer, more just society for all.

Among Higinbotham's contemporaries, others such Sir Archibald Michie and Henry Chapman left significant reform legacies. Later politicians, such as Graham Berry, continued the struggle. But Higinbotham's influence was unmatched by any of his contemporaries in its length and intensity. It began with his encouragement of the diggers to pursue their political rights by legitimate means in the months before the battle at Eureka and it continued with his leadership of the attack on Hotham for his Minute in 1855. As editor of the *Argus*, he continued to argue for full democracy and for the principle of responsible government in its modern sense. As Attorney-General, his daring leadership of the constitutional crises of 1865 and 1867 attracted both admiration and censure. Though he did not defeat the Legislative Council at the time, his ideas triumphed, for in November 1869 he won the support of the Legislative Assembly for his five constitutional resolutions. These clearly articulated his vision of responsible government in Victoria, free of Colonial Office interference and free from obstruction of the popular will by the wealthy landed interests of the Colony through their dominance of the Legislative Council. Majority support for Higinbotham's resolutions served notice on the Colonial Office and the Legislative Council that the current arrangements were inimical to the political culture that had emerged in Victoria. Over succeeding decades, the Governor's instructions were reformed and the oligarchical character of the 1855 Victorian Constitution was progressively checked.

Higinbotham had mixed feelings about federation of the Australian colonies. He recognised that federation was inevitable, but feared that it might add a further layer of entrenchment to the undemocratic features of existing colonial constitutions.[36] Had he lived to see the dismissal of the Whitlam Government by the Governor-General, Sir William Kerr, in 1975, he might have felt vindicated. Morris quoted an unnamed 'leading member of the Legislative Assembly' who commented that, in the Convention of 1891 at which colonial delegates discussed constitutional issues relevant to the new Australian Constitution, 'Victorians, one and all flung themselves into the discussions *con amore*, and with the readiness of men experienced in the question'. He added that he attributed this to 'the immense personal influence of George Higinbotham'.[37]

Other achievements

In 1866, Higinbotham chaired a Royal Commission into Education, and subsequently drafted an Education Bill based upon its *Report*. He championed, against great resistance, a universal scheme of government-funded primary education. His Bill was withdrawn before being voted upon, but it paved the way for another public education bill, with similar aims, which became law in December 1872.

Some historians allege that Higinbotham's role in laying the groundwork for the 1872 *Education Act* was animated by either sectarian feeling directed against the Catholic Church (whose schools later lost government aid) or by indifference to religion.[38] Morris assures us that 'deep religious feeling was the mainspring of George Higinbotham's life'.[39] For Higinbotham, religion and politics were entwined. He respected the religious impulse in people of other Christian denominations. However, he argued that much of the opposition on the part of church hierarchies to co-operation on a common educational system was motivated by a competitive urge to amass church property rather than genuine religious considerations. He saw great potential benefits in educating children from different Christian denominations side by side, for 'points of difference between religious bodies might be reduced, as it was desirable they should be reduced'.[40] Dow observed that Higinbotham believed it was not merely a political expedient to bring children of different denominations together for education, but a religious reform, 'desirable in itself'.[41] The *Report* of the Royal Commission in 1867 recommended that broad Christian principles of a non-sectarian nature be included in the curriculum, but the difficulty of reaching an agreement on such principles was so great that Higinbotham abandoned this plan as impractical.[42] In the Bill that he subsequently introduced into the Parliament, he proposed that instruction should be secular during regular school hours, but he did so reluctantly. In J.W. Stephen's *Education Act* of 1872 this principle was established for the government schools.

In the face of derision from some sections of the press and of the all-male Legislative Assembly, Higinbotham's work for women's rights was courageous. It may also have taken courage to act for Mrs Henrietta Molesworth. He would have known that her allegations of cruelty against Justice Robert Molesworth would lead to public scandal, and that to act for her might prejudice his own career by giving offence to a Supreme Court judge. But Higinbotham would have considered that she was entitled to representation. Later, in the Assembly, his timely advocacy ensured that Victoria closely following Britain's lead in passing legislation to reform the laws relating to property and divorce. He was also an early advocate of women's right to vote, which was achieved sixteen years after his death, in 1908.

Higinbotham: too little remembered

Among Higinbotham's contemporaries, some – such as Sir William Stawell, Sir Henry Loch and John Foster – have Victorian towns named after them. The names of the early Governors are familiar to Victorians through place names such as the Latrobe Valley and Mount Hotham. Twenty Melbourne suburbs have a 'Barkly Street', and thirty have a 'Stawell Street'. But in the suburb of Brighton, which Higinbotham represented for a decade, and where he resided for twenty-six years, there are few reminders. There is a 'Higinbotham Street' near the site of the original Higinbotham residence (which has been demolished), and there is 'Higinbotham Hall' in Bay Street, which Higinbotham, during his time as Chief Justice, opened in 1887 as 'The Brighton Free Library'.

A statue of Higinbotham wearing his judicial wig and gown was created by the London-born sculptor Paul Montford in 1937 and is sited outside Melbourne's Treasury building in Macarthur Street, a short distance from Parliament House. It is one of the few tangible reminders of Higinbotham to modern Victorians. But beneath the heavy judicial regalia, the small figure with its smooth, cherubic face and serene gaze does not bring to mind the man of 'dash and daring', of 'courage and rectitude', that the contemporary journalist Price Warung described.[43]

Some evidence of his significance to his contemporaries survives in the Old Council Chamber at Trades Hall in Carlton. Restoration work in 2017 gradually revealed a high frieze on the walls that had been painted over in the 1960s. In 1884, the frieze contained four portraits. In central position high above the speaker's chair was a portrait of Higinbotham.

The other three portraits were of Governor Sir Charles Darling, George Stephenson, British railway pioneer, and Samuel Plimsoll, British politician and social reformer. The inclusion of Governor Darling suggests that those who sought to perpetuate the memory of these two central figures of the Victorian constitutional struggles of 1865 and 1867 well remembered that struggle and understood its significance for the people of Victoria.

The drafting and inauguration of the Victorian Constitution between 1853 and 1855 accelerated the campaign for political rights that had begun earlier on the goldfields, and ignited a long campaign for responsible government in Victoria. The secret ballot was achieved, the franchise was extended, and payment of members was introduced. The issue of responsible government was substantially resolved in terms of instructions to Governors, but it continued to resonate in the dispute about the relative powers of the two Houses of the Legislature that continued until the 1980s. It was not until 1950 that the Legislative Council surrendered its function as the legislative guardian of the rights of property.[44] Until relatively recent times, the Legislative Council blocked even the mildest reforming initiatives of administrations of all political complexions, even conservative ones.[45]

One hundred and ten years after Higinbotham's death, long-awaited constitutional reform came when the Victorian Labor Government of Steve Bracks enacted the *Constitution (Parliamentary Reform) Act* of 2003. This equalised the terms of office of members of both Houses, introduced proportional representation for Legislative Council seats, removed the ability of the Council to block supply bills and brought an improved method of dealing with deadlocks between the Houses. It also committed the Council to recognise the right of an elected Government to implement its specific mandate – 'the policies, promises and initiatives' that it announced in its most recent election campaign.[46]

Of all those who fought for the principle of responsible government in Victoria, none fought so tenaciously as did Higinbotham, nor with such a clear vision of its importance for the Colony's future. In Higinbotham's speeches and writings, we can trace a link to richer European and American traditions of liberal political thought than were known to the principal drafters of the 1855 Constitution. Victoria's current democratic political system was not bequeathed to the population as a gift from Britain. It was achieved via a long struggle. Higinbotham's life story is intimately bound to the story of that struggle for a modern liberal Constitution for Victoria.

Modern Victorians should remember the man whose powerful writing and oratory from 1854 to 1892 played such an important role in the struggle. The people of the goldfields, as well as Higinbotham, Michie, Aspinall, Chapman and those in the liberal press who supported the struggle, also deserve recognition for their vision and steadfastness in the pursuit of democratic ideals.

APPENDIX

Identifying Higinbotham's anonymous writing in the *Melbourne Morning Herald*

George Higinbotham wrote for the *Melbourne Morning Herald* between his arrival in Victoria in March 1854 and his acceptance of the position of editor at the *Argus* in August 1856. These years were notable for the dawn attack at Eureka in December 1854 and the political turbulence around the proclamation of the new Victorian Constitution in November 1855. Higinbotham's writing for both the *Melbourne Morning Herald* and the *Argus* was anonymous, and until recently has not been identified. Even now, it cannot be identified with absolute certainty. His biographer, Edward Morris, provided guidance in identifying some of his contributions to the *Argus*, but he did not do so for the *Herald*.

The fragile condition of the early editions of the *Herald* has meant that researchers have had to rely upon microfilm, but the images were often very difficult, and sometimes impossible to read. Recently, the installation of modern, computer-assisted microfilm readers has made this task possible.

From records of the time, we know that there were four writers of *Herald* editorials in 1854. J.L. Forde, in his 1913 book *The Story of the Bar of Victoria*, records the fact that Higinbotham wrote for the newspaper, and we know that two other barristers, Archibald Michie and Butler Cole Aspinall, also wrote, as did the business manager, Frederick Sinnett, on occasions. Familiarity with the editorials in the period reveals the distinctive 'voices' of the writers. The first 'voice' is typified by a lively style, often using direct speech and a harsh kind of humour that ridicules people for their appearance, their style of dress and manner of speaking. This writer delights in lampoons of senior Government figures. Following the battle at Eureka, he becomes fiercely opposed to the Government. This writer's work, characterised by florid personal attacks, sarcastic humour and an anti-Government stance constitutes the 'voice' of Aspinall. A second 'voice' is that of Frederick Sinnett, the business manager, who sometimes made reference to events and places that linked to his early life in Germany and then South Australia. Sinnett is known to have left the *Herald* in late November 1854 after a dispute with Michie about the paper's mounting debt. He then became editor of the Melbourne edition of *Punch*, where he indulged his talent for humorous writing that was typically irreverent and scurrilous.

A major 'voice' in the *Herald* is that of Archibald Michie, the senior member of the editorial team and the largest *Herald* shareholder. Michie wrote about weighty matters in a style that was lucid, logical and forceful. The dominant theme of many of his editorials was the drafting of the new Victorian Constitution. The fourth 'voice' was that of Higinbotham. Like Michie, he was preoccupied with the constitutional issue, but a number of features distinguish his 'voice' from that of Michie. One of these is his characteristic view of political events from a religious perspective. Unlike Michie, whose outlook was more secular, Higinbotham made frequent use of biblical references and religious arguments and imagery. Also distinctive was his use of literary devices. In contrast to Michie's plainer style, Higinbotham's writing style reflected his classical education. He favoured long sentences, often weaving in several subordinate clauses. He made liberal use of extended similes, metaphors and poetic devices to enhance his writing. In building an argument, he sometimes repeated key words or phrases in a rhythmic fashion, and marked his conclusion with striking imagery.[1] He made frequent use of irony but generally did not stoop to sarcastic personal attacks on individuals.

Morris commented that a feature of Higinbotham's writing was 'his strong feeling for humanity'.[2] He quoted Higinbotham's statement in the *Argus* that 'the treatment of the Aborigines has from the commencement of the settlement of the continent been a standing reproach against the colonists'.[3] This empathy with others was very evident in his writing, and added great effectiveness to his arguments. He had a great sympathy for the young, the vulnerable, the mentally ill and the poor; and he could write about them with compelling pathos. But when faced with instances of deceit, demagoguery, injustice or self-serving opportunism, he declaimed in a thunderous tone.

The reaction of the writers to the conflict at Eureka provides a further clue to the authorship of particular editorials. Michie and Aspinall donated their services to the prisoners from Eureka. For various reasons, Higinbotham did not. The views expressed in the *Herald*'s editorials of the time reflect this division. Amongst the editorials that occur in the *Herald* between March 1854 and July 1856, and in the *Argus* between August 1856 and 1859, there are some that deal with similar themes and advance similar arguments. It is likely that Higinbotham was responsible for these editorials in both newspapers.[4]

A number of Higinbotham's views were distinctive or unusual for their times, as for instance his views on extending the franchise to women, on the proper role of the laity in churches, and on his admiration for the principles of the American Declaration of Independence. We know of Higinbotham's views from the parliamentary records, from his speeches to his constituents and from his judgments.

When we find a corpus of texts in the *Herald* of the period between March 1854 and August 1856 that shows the masterly use of figures of speech, rhythm and powerful imagery, combined with the religious perspective and the known views of Higinbotham, we can assume that we are hearing Higinbotham's 'voice'. Once this voice becomes identifiable, further characteristics of his writing style at this stage of his life also become discernible. He favoured certain phrases and unusual words. Finding these in other editorials helps to confirm his authorship.

An examination of the *Melbourne Morning Herald* for 1853–56 brings to light new facets of the early struggle for political rights and responsible government in Victoria that was the defining context of Higinbotham's political life. It also reveals some previously unknown events and associations in his early life that shed new light upon this important but enigmatic historical figure.

FAMILY TREES

1. **Higinbotham Family**

   This family tree is based on information from several sources, principally Henry Biddal Swanzy, *The families of French and Belturbet and their descendants* (Dublin, A. Thorn & Co., 1908) and E. E. Morris, *A Memoir of George Higinbotham* (London, Macmillan, 1895). Where dates are not provided, the birth order in each family cannot be inferred from positioning on this diagram.

2. **Verner Family**

   This family tree is based on that provided by John Kerr in his article 'Churchill: Home of the Verners', in the *Journal of the Craigavon Historical Society*, Vol. 6, No. 3, with some additional information.

3. **Wilson Family**

   The information in this diagram is compiled from the baptism register of the Dublin Unitarian Church with the kind help of the Rev. Bridget Spain and Mr Rory Delany, and with further information from E. E. Morris, *A Memoir of George Higinbotham* (London, Macmillan, 1895). Where dates of birth are not given, birth order cannot be inferred from position in diagram.

1.

Thomas Higinbotham m. Anne Nixon
d. 1737
Quatermaster: Battle of the Boyne

Ralph   George   William   Thomas m. Mary Nixon   Andrew   Elizabeth   Anne
(Rev.) d. 1795   (cousin)   of Tullymaglowney
(Nutfield)

Robert   Andrew   Lydia   Mary   Henry m. Jane Clark   Jane   Hanna   Catherine
b. 1801   (Irish Treasury)   (Irish Treasury)   (née Verner)   m. Rev. George Horan   m. Andrew Nixon
m. Mary Battersby   d. 1789   2 girls   (cousin) 1793
3 boys, 4 girls

Thomas   Charlotte   Andrew   Mary   Henry m. Sarah Wilson
m. 1800 Jane, daugter of Conway   b. 1765 d. 1845   (Nutfield)   d. 18 Mar. 1861
Benning, Archdeacon of Dromore   Dublin Merchant
2 girls   b. 1789 d. 1851

Henry   Joseph Wilson (Rev.)   Rosanna   Thomas   Jane   William   Robert (Rev.)   George m. Margaret Foreman
b. 1813   b. 1815 d. 1872   b. 1817 d. 1869   b. 1819 d. 1880   b. 1822   b. 1824 d. 1857   b. 1826 Dublin   b. 1836 Kent d. 1910
Engineer-in-Chief Victorian Railways   m. Mary Jones 1834–1916   d. 1892 Melbourne

Edith Sarah Catherine   Alice Mary   George Robert   Edward   Maud   Ethel
b. 1859 m. Edward Morris 1878   b. 1863 m. FitzHugh Annesley Lyon   b. 1865   b. 1869   m. Rev. Charles Darby 1895   b. Jan. 1872 d. Dec. 1872
d. 1896 1 boy, 3 girls   2 boys   4 boys, 3 girls

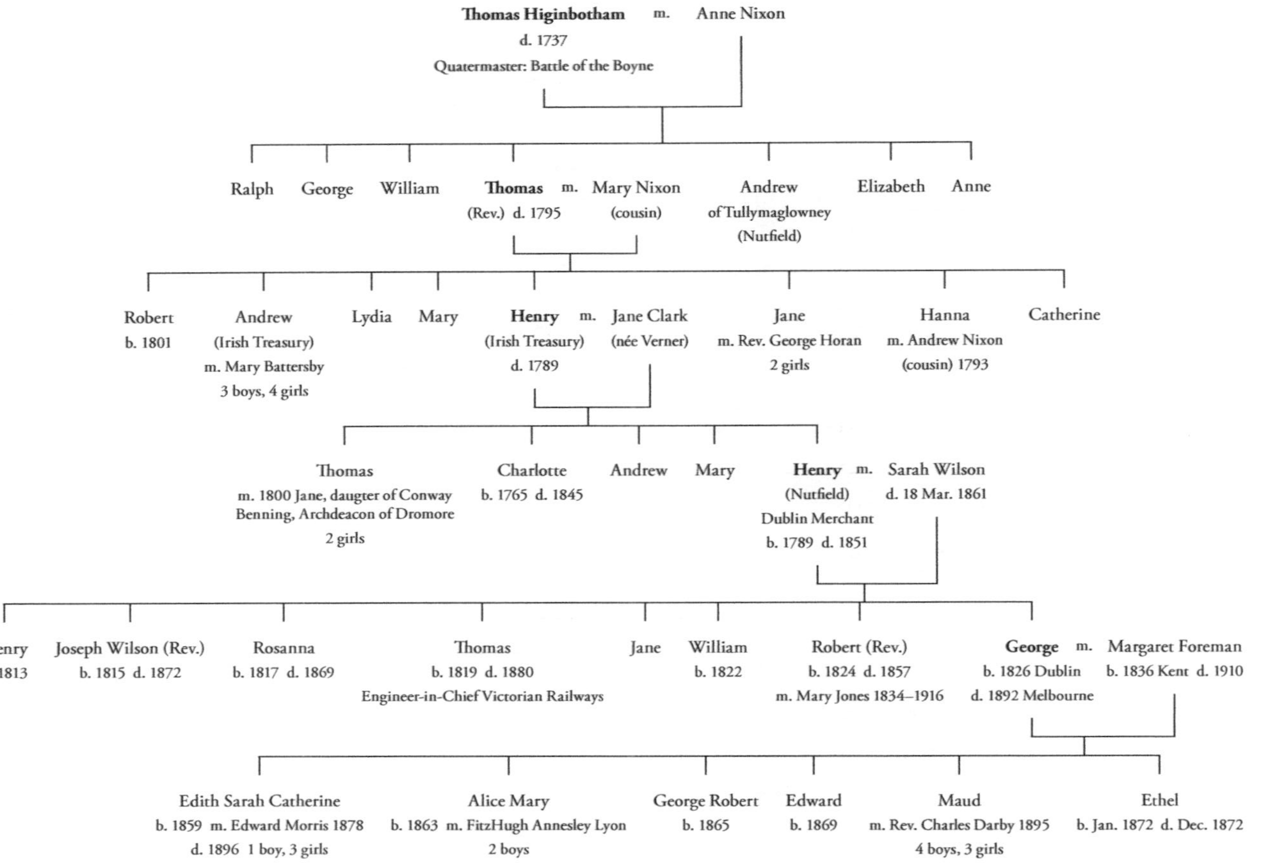

315

2.

Henry Verner   m.   Anne Kerr
d. 1724
Captain of Cavalry, Battle of the Boyne

James   David   m.   Elizabeth Crossle   Thomas   Mary   Anne
1743   of Anahoe
m. Margaret Kerr
Lived at Church Hill
d. 1788 (no issue)

James   m.   Jane Clark   Thomas   Elizabeth   Sarah   Jane   Margaret
b. 1746 d. 1822   1772   d. 1827   d. 1775
M.P. Lived in Dublin   Battle of Bunker's Hill, Boston
Widow of James Dobbin
m. Henry Higinbotham
Grandparents of George Higinbotham

Thomas   James   David   (twins)   John   Elizabeth   William   m.   Harriet Wingfield
(Lt. Col'l) b. 1774   b. 1777   m. Miss Cole   d. 1814   m. Capt. Aldridge   1782–1871
m. Charlotte Elizabeth May   reared at Church Hill as heir, but disinherited   ADC to Lord Cornwallis   The First Baronet and
after quarrel with great-uncle Thomas   Heir to Churchill

William Verner   Jenny Verner
b. 1807   m. John Mitchel
Port Phillip Comm'r for Insolvency
1st President Melbourne Club

William   eight daughters   Edward Wingfield
1822–1873   1830–1899
2nd Baronet m. Mary Pakenham   4th Baronet m. Selina Nugent

William   Alice Emily   Edith   Edward   Sybil   Hubert   Florence   Dorothy
1856–1888   1885–1936
3rd Baronet m. Annie Wilson d. 1888   5th Baronet m. Dorothy Laming   (last direct descendant in male line died in 1943)
(no issue)   Mother of Harry

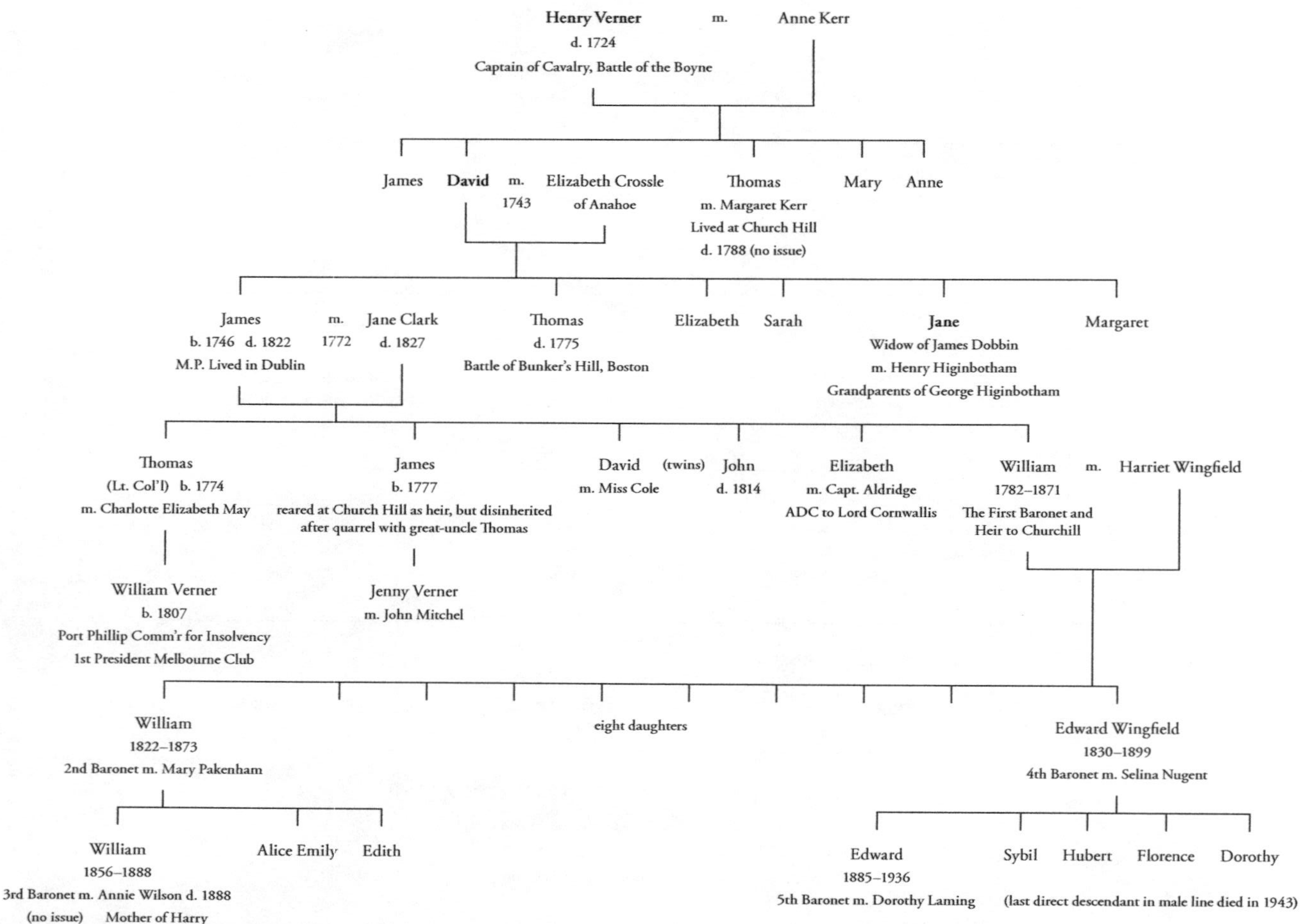

3.

(first wife)
Rose Anne Moore
(Belle of the North)

m.
~1789

Joseph Wilson
d. 1809
reputedly aide-de-camp to George Washington
US Consul in Dublin
owner of Peale portrait of George Washington

(second wife)
Elizabeth

Susannah
Lillias
Robert
James
b. 1807

Thomas
m.
"Mrs E. Wilson"
US Consul in Dublin
Dublin Unitarian
Church Benefactor

Sarah
m.
1811
Henry Higinbotham

Joseph
b. 1818
James
Harrington
Wilson
(inherited portrait
of Washington,
sold to Princeton
University 1906)

Margaret
b. 1819

Rosanne
b. 1820

Robert
b. 1821

Susan
b. 1828

Elizabeth
b. 1831

Thomas
b. 1833

Penelope
b. 1835

James
b. 1836

John
b. 1837

Henry
Brooke
b. 1838

Henry
b. 1813

(Rev.)
Joseph
Wilson
b. 1815

Rosanna
b. 1817
d. 1869

Thomas
b. 1819
d. 1880
Engineer-
in-Chief,
Victorian
Railways
Aus.

Jane

William
b. 1822

(Rev.)
Robert
b. 1824
d. 1857
(plaque
in Derry
Cathedral)

George
b. 1826
d. 1892
Attorney-General
Chief Justice
Victoria Aus.

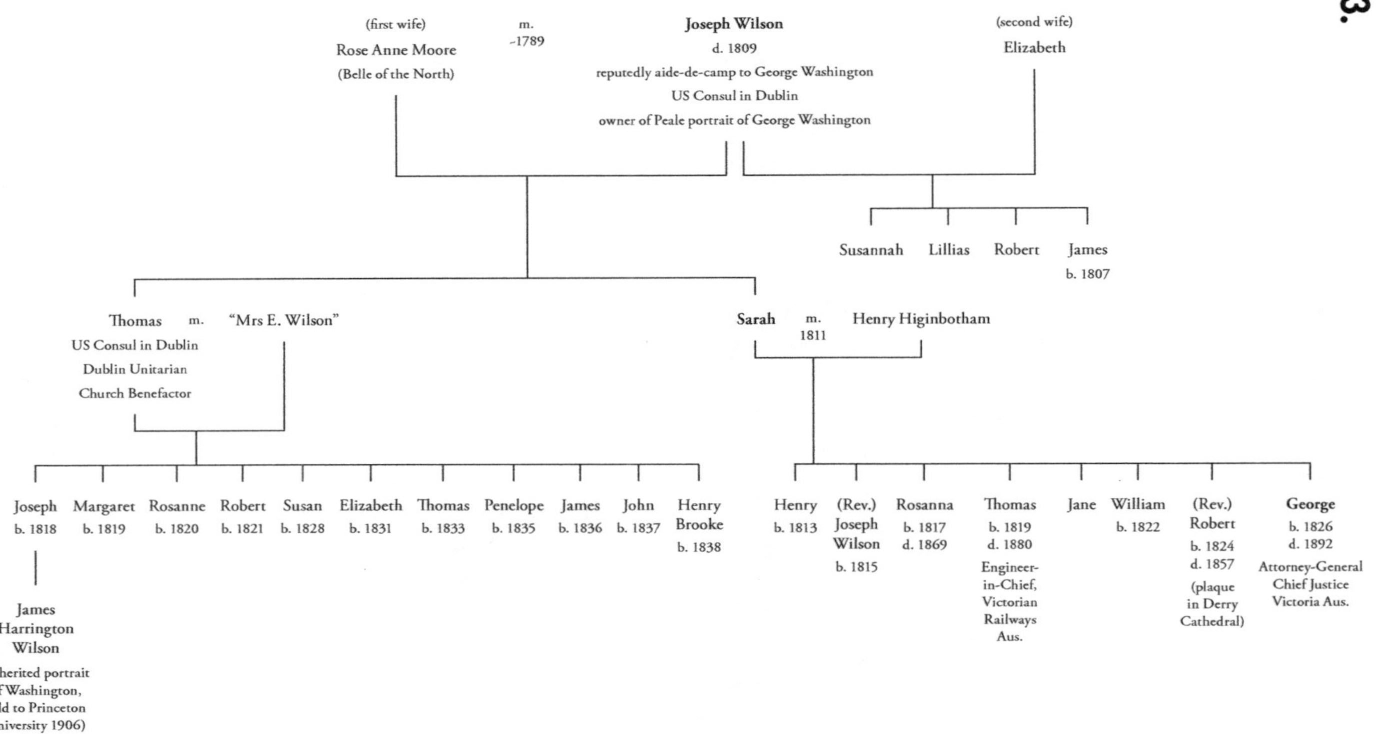

NOTES

Preface

1 Price Warung, 'The Greatest of Australia's Dead', *Bulletin*, 7 January 1893, 9.

2 Geraldine Moore, 'The Young George Higinbotham: 1826–1856'.

3 *Ibid.* Appendix A explains the method by which Higinbotham's contributions were identified.

4 Warung, 'The Greatest of Australia's Dead', 9.

Introduction

1 'The Governor at Geelong', *Melbourne Morning Herald*, 18 August 1854. See also *Argus*, 18 August, 4; *Geelong Advertiser*, 11 September 1854. (Note that articles from the *Melbourne Morning Herald*, the *Geelong Advertiser* and the *Argus* are all available on microfilm from the State Library of Victoria, 328 Swanston Street, Melbourne. The *Argus* is also available online via Trove.)

1: Arrival in Victoria

1 Sir Charles Gavan Duffy, *My Life in Two Hemispheres*, Vol. 2, 134–5. Duffy described Melbourne as he saw it on arrival in 1856.

2 'The Report on the New Constitution' (Leading article), *Melbourne Morning Herald (MMH)*, 29 December 1853.

3 'The Report on the New Constitution', *Argus*, 3 January 1854, 4; 'Report on the New Constitution', *MMH*, 3 January 1854.

4 'The Report on the New Constitution', *MMH*, 12 January 1854.

5 *Argus*, 2 September 1853, 4.

6 'The Legislative Council: 25 January', *MMH*, 26 January 1854.

7 'The Legislative Council: 19 January', *Argus*, 21 January 1854, 5.

8 'Legislative Council: 17 March', *MMH*, 18 March 1854.

9 'The Legislative Council: 19 January', *Argus*, 21 January 1854, 5.

10 'Bendigo: From Our Own Correspondent', *MMH*, 22 December 1853.

11 'Report of the Select Committee of the Legislative Council on the New Constitution', *MMH*, 10 December 1853. Recommendation 58 of the Select Committee on the Constitution read: 'All patronage of the Government should vest in the Governor'. Compare this with *An Act to Establish a Constitution in and for the Colony of Victoria*, 25 March 1854 (reserved), Section XLIV.

12 'The Legislative Council', *Argus*, 15 February, 5. Leading article (unnamed),

MMH, 15 February 1854. *An Act to Establish a Constitution in and for the Colony of Victoria*, 1854, Section XLIV. See also Chapter 6.

13 *Australian Constitutions Act 1850* (UK), s.4.

14 'General Summary for the *Chusan*', *MMH*, 25 March 1854.

15 'His Honour Justice Higinbotham', *Bacchus Marsh Express*, 11 September 1880, 4.

16 Edward E. Morris, *A Memoir of George Higinbotham: An Australian Politician and Chief Justice of Victoria*, 67. Higinbotham's speech as a Member of the Legislative Assembly (undated).

17 Elizabeth Morrison, 'The Contribution of the Country Press to the Making of Victoria: 1840–1890', 72.

18 'Mr Michie's Reply to Mr Sinnett', *MMH*, 25 August 1855.

19 'Removal of the Herald Office', *MMH*, 23 December 1853.

20 'Postage on Newspapers', *MMH*, 12 April 1854.

21 Leading article (untitled), *MMH*, 23 December 1853.

22 'The Diggers' Congress' (Editorial), *MMH*, 23 December 1853; 'Bendigo: From Our Own Correspondent: 14 December', *MMH*, 22 December 1853.

23 'The Diggers' Congress' (Editorial), *MMH*, 23 December 1853.

24 'Bendigo: From Our Own Correspondent', *MMH*, 22 December 1853.

25 'Bendigo: From Our Own Correspondent: 25 June 1854', *MMH*, 29 June 1854.

26 'Bendigo: From Our Own Correspondent', *MMH*, 24 July 1854; 'Mr Smith O'Brien' (Leading article), *MMH*, 25 July 1854; Sean McConville, *Irish Political Prisoners 1848–1922: Theatres of War*, n. 199, 96.

27 *Ibid.*

28 Shirley Roberts, *Charles Hotham: A Biography*, Chapters 3–6; 'The New Governor' (Editorial), *MMH*, 15 February 1854.

29 Editorials, *MMH*, 26, 30 June and 1, 3, 14, 18, 26 July and 11 August 1854.

30 *Report of the Royal Commission Appointed to Enquire into the Goldfields of Victoria*, 1855, Minutes of Evidence, Question 3728; Roberts, *Charles Hotham*, 115–16.

31 'Country News: The Governor at Geelong', *MMH*, 18 August 1854; *Argus*, 18 August 1854, 4; *Geelong Advertiser*, 11 September 1854.

32 'Country News: The Governor at Geelong', *MMH*, 18 August 1854; *Argus*, 18 August 1854, 4; *Geelong Advertiser*, 11 September 1854; 'Our Governor' (Leading article), *MMH*, 28 December 1854.

33 'The Legislative Council' (Leading article), *Argus*, 24 July 1854, 4.

34 'Bendigo: From Our Own Correspondent', *MMH*, 16 January 1854; *MMH*, 2, 7, 23 February 1854. See also Geoffrey Serle, *The Golden Age: A History of the Colony of Victoria 1851–1861*, 108.

2: Marriage and Career in Troubled Times

1   Susan Priestley, 'In Defence of George Higinbotham: New Evidence on Family Relationships', 15.

2   Edward E. Morris, *A Memoir of George Higinbotham: An Australian Politician and Chief Justice of Victoria*, 35.

3   'Public Meeting: Mackay and Harrison', *Melbourne Morning Herald* (*MMH*), 4 December 1854.

4   *Ibid.*

5   'Evidence and Proof' (Editorial), *MMH*, 8 November 1854. Higinbotham's reflections on the role of Crown Prosecutor.

6   'A Young Victim', *MMH*, 5 February 1856.

7   'Legal News', *MMH*, 19 September 1854; 'Legal News', *MMH*, 31 October 1854.

8   See 10, 23 and 26 March 1855, *MMH*.

9   Weston Bate, 'Cole, George Ward (1793–1879)', *Australian Dictionary of Biography* (*ADB*), Vol. 1.

10 Morris, *A Memoir of George Higinbotham*, 36.

11 *Ibid*, 39.

12 Priestley, 'In Defence of George Higinbotham', 13.

13 Online: <http://emhs.org.au/history/buildings/east_melbourne_wellington_parade_124_park_house>.

14 S.L. Devlin, 'Captain Arthur Devlin, 1810–1893: His Life and Times', online: <http://www.netspeed.com.au/Kdevlin/Stanley/CAPTAIN%20ARTHUR%20DEVLIN.pdf>.

15 Bate, 'Cole, George Ward (1793–1879)'.

16 Stanley Leighton, 'Stanley Leighton', 1868, National Library of Australia, MS 360 289815: 5, 11, 15.

17 Priestley, 'In Defence of George Higinbotham', 14.

18 Weston Bate, *A History of Brighton*, 336–9.

19 'The Scrap-Book of G.W. Cole 1862–1899', MS 10973, State Library of Victoria.

20 *Argus*, 29 April 1879, 5; Rosalind Landells, 'The Ward Coles and St Ninians', *Hampton Bugle*, March 1984, 14.

21 Priestley, 'In Defence of George Higinbotham', 13.

22 *Ibid*, 15.

23 'Ballaarat: From Our Own Correspondent', *MMH*, 3 August 1854. The spelling of 'Ballarat' as 'Ballaarat' was common at the time.

24 Advertisement, *MMH*, 20 September 1854.

25 'The Bank Embezzlement at Ballaarat', *MMH*, 18 October 1854; Suzanne G. Mellor, 'Levey, George Collins (1835–1919)', *ADB*, Vol. 5.

26 'Law and Lynch Law at the Diggings' (Editorial), *MMH*, 20 October 1854.

27 *Argus*, 29 December 1854, 4, reprinted 5 January 1855, 5. Hasleham's report of his wounding at the hands of troopers following the affray at Eureka.

28 Ian MacFarlane, *Eureka from the Official Records*, 192.

29 *Ibid*, 44–7.

30 'Ballaarat Important Public Meeting – Report of the Diggers' Delegates', *MMH*,

31 December 1853.

31 'Bendigo: From Our Own Correspondent, 2 January 1854', *MMH*, 5 January 1854.

32 *An Act to Enable Her Majesty to Assent to a Bill as amended of the Legislature of Victoria to Establish a Constitution in and for the Colony of Victoria, Act 55 (Imp).*

33 Geoffrey Serle, *The Golden Age: A History of the Colony of Victoria 1851–1861*, 256.

34 'Taxes on Gold Mining' (Leading article), *MMH*, 20 September 1854. The annual licence was not transferable to another goldfield.

35 'Bendigo', *MMH*, 12 December 1853 (Report of mass meeting at Golden Square on 3 December 1853); 'Bendigo: From Our Own Correspondent', *MMH*, 2 March 1854; 'The Squatters on "Class Taxation"', *MMH*, 8 April 1854.

36 'Law and Lynch Law at the Diggings' (Editorial), *MMH*, 20 October 1854.

37 *Ibid.*

38 'The Legislative Council: 31 October', *MMH*, 1 November 1854.

39 'The Administration of the Goldfields', *MMH*, 1 November 1854.

40 'Legislative Council' (Leading article), *Argus*, 1 November 1854, 4.

41 'Management of the Goldfields', *Argus*, 1 November 1854.

42 'The Administration of the Goldfields', *MMH*, 1 November 1854.

43 Elizabeth Morrison, 'Government Regulation of the Newspaper Press in Nineteenth Century Victoria', 128.

3: Reporting the Battle at Eureka

1 'Domestic Intelligence', *Argus*, 23 October 1854, 6.

2 'The Principles and Objects of the Ballarat Reform League', in Ian MacFarlane, *Eureka from the Official Records*, 207. See also Andrew Messner, 'Land, Leadership, Culture and Emigration: Some Problems in Chartist Historiography'.

3 'Why Diggers Riot' (Leading article), *Melbourne Morning Herald (MMH)*, 22 November 1854.

4 'The Conditions of the Goldfields' (Leading article), *MMH*, 20 November 1854.

5 VPRS 1095/P0000, Unit 3, Bundle 1, No.16; Peter Fitzsimons, *Eureka: The Unfinished Revolution*, 334–5.

6 *Ibid.*

7 *Ibid*, 29, 30.

8 'Bendigo: From Our Own Correspondent', *MMH*, 16 January 1854.

9 'Report on the New Constitution', *MMH*, 4 January 1854.

10 'The Electoral Districts', *MMH*, 22 February 1854.

11 Leading article (untitled), *MMH*, 2 February 1854.

12 VPRS 1095/P0000, Unit 3, Bundle 1, No. 16, 24–5.

13 Fitzsimons, *Eureka*, 334–5.

14 'Ballaarat' (Leading article), *MMH*, 28 November 1854. The facetious, almost

jocular tone at the start of the article suggests Aspinall, although the conclusion of the article is in a very grave tone that is more typical of Higinbotham. This article may have been a collaboration.

15 'The Last From Ballaarat' (Editorial), *MMH*, 29 November 1854. This article also quotes from Hamlet's famous 'To be or not to be' soliloquy in Shakespeare's *Hamlet*, Act III, Scene 1, in which Hamlet speaks of those 'who would rather bear those ills they bear than to fly to others that they know not of'. Higinbotham warns the leaders that rash policies and actions would alienate the moderates among the digging population.

16 'The Gold Puzzle' (Editorial), *MMH*, 1 December 1854.

17 Desmond O'Grady, *Raffaello! Raffaello! A Biography of Raffaello Carboni*, 160–1.

18 'Correspondence of Captain Thomas to Deputy Adjutant-General Reporting Collision with the Ballaarat Rebels', 3 December 1854, 2. Victorian Parliamentary Library.

19 'Retrenchment' (Leading article), *MMH*, 3 January 1855.

20 'The Right to Meet' (Editorial), *MMH*, 29 December 1854.

21 'Country News: Goldfields Reform League', *MMH*, 1 January 1855.

22 'Mr Michie's Reply to Mr Sinnett', *MMH*, 25 August 1855.

23 'Printing and Newspapers' (Editorial), *MMH*, 26 December 1854.

24 *Kinnahan v The Proprietors of Melbourne Morning Herald*; 'Legal News', *MMH*, 16 December 1854.

25 Laurel Blake and Larysa Demoor, *Dictionary of Nineteenth Century Journalism in Great Britain and Ireland*, 514.

26 MacFarlane, *Eureka from the Official Records*, 152.

27 'The Reform League', *Ballarat Times*, 18 November 1854. The word 'destiny' in the final sentence was actually printed as 'dynasty', but as this is clearly a mistake, it has been corrected in the quotation.

28 Editorial, *Argus*, 1 December 1854, 4.

29 'Geelong: From Our Own Correspondent', *Argus*, 29 November 1854, 4.

30 'The Ethics of Journalism', *Age*, 9 and 12 April 1855.

31 VPRS 1095/P0000, 'Newspapers'.

32 'The State of Things at Ballarat', *Geelong Advertiser*, 30 November 1854, 4.

33 *Ibid.*

34 'Ballaarat News', *MMH*, 1 December 1854.

35 Raffaello Carboni, *The Eureka Stockade* (reprint), 56.

36 *Geelong Advertiser*, 14 November 1854.

37 *Ballarat Times*, 18 November 1854; Fitzsimons, *Eureka*, 312–13.

38 *MMH*, 2 December 1854.

39 *The Goldfields Commission of Enquiry Report*, para. 16, quoted in MacFarlane, *Eureka from the Official Records*, 79, 37, 74–84.

40 *Ibid.*

41 *Geelong Advertiser*, 2 December 1854, 4.

42 Obituary, *Mount Alexander Mail*, 4 July 1862, quoted in *The Eureka Encyclopedia*, edited by J. Corfield, D. Wickham and C. Gervasoni.

43 *Argus*, 29 December 1854, 4, reprinted 5 January 1855, 5.

44 VPRS 1189: Box 839: 56/T 4107 in file 61/S 1823.

45 'Ballaarat', *MMH*, 5 February 1855.

46 MacFarlane, *Eureka from the Official Records*, 152–4.

47 VPRS 1189: Box 839 56/T 4107 in file 61/S 1823. Letter to the Chief Secretary, 19 December 1856.

48 Edward E. Morris, *A Memoir of George Higinbotham: An Australian Politician and Chief Justice of Victoria*, 321.

49 MacFarlane, *Eureka from the Official Records*, 208.

50 See *MMH* editorials of 11, 12 and 13 January 1855, and the leading article of 15 January 1855.

51 'What Will They Say in England?' (Leading article), *MMH*, 5 March 1855. On the issue of the penalty for high treason, see Richard Ireland's address to the jury in the trial of Jan Vennik, 'Legal News', *MMH*, 23 March 1855.

52 *Geelong Advertiser*, 30 November 1854, 4.

53 'Our Politics' (Editorial), *MMH*, 20 December 1854.

54 MacFarlane, *Eureka from the Official Records*, 42–3.

55 'Bendigo', *MMH*, 27 December 1854. Attack on Hotham, *MMH*, 12 December; attack on John Foster, Colonial Secretary, *MMH*, 10 and 12 January; attacks on Hugh Childers, Collector of Customs.

56 'Our Gold and Our Lands' (Leading article), *MMH*, 1 January 1855.

57 'Bendigo: From Our Own Correspondent: 23 December', *MMH*, 27 December 1854.

58 'The Ballaarat Riots: General Amnesty', 'Local News', *MMH*, 15 January 1855.

4: A Philosophical Watershed

1 Edward E. Morris, *A Memoir of George Higinbotham: An Australian Politician and Chief Justice of Victoria*, 41.

2 'London News', *Melbourne Morning Herald* (*MMH*), 8 December 1854.

3 Desmond Fitzgerald, 'The Trillick Derailment 1854', 33.

4 'The Attempt to Destroy a Railway Train', *Standard*, 20 September 1854; 'Law and Crime', *Household Narrative*, September 1854, 197, online: <http://www.djo.org.uk/household-narrative-of-current-events/year-1854/page-197.html>.

5 'A New Year's Rhapsody' (Editorial), *MMH*, 1 January 1855.

6 'The Murderous Railway Outrage', *Standard*, 16 October 1854.

7 'Address to the Right Honourable the Earl of Enniskillen and the Protestant Brethren', *Morning Chronicle*, 17 October 1854, Issue 27398.

8 Transcript of Proceedings, *R v Joseph*, Supreme Court of Victoria, 22–3 February

1855, 9–10, quoted in The Hon. Marilyn Warren, 'The Eureka Trials: 160 Years On', *Victorian Historical Journal*, 87, No. 1, 2016, 81–2.

9 *Argus*, 6 September 1880, 7.

10 *Ibid.*

11 Morris, *A Memoir of George Higinbotham*, 271.

12 P.S. O'Hegarty, *John Mitchel: An Appreciation, With Some Account of Young Ireland*, 19.

13 'Filibusters and Volunteers' (Leading article), *Herald*, 15 November 1855.

14 *Ibid.*

15 'Law and Lynch Law at the Diggings' (Editorial), *MMH*, 20 October 1854.

16 'The Land Regulations' (Leading article), *MMH*, 8 August 1855.

17 'The *Herald* and Its Progress' (Leading article), *Herald*, 10 September 1855.

18 For references to 'lynch law', see editorial 'Law and Lynch Law at the Diggings', *MMH*, 20 October 1854; 'Summary for the Norma', *MMH*, 24 November 1854.

19 'The Resumption of the State Trials' (Leading article), *MMH*, 19 March 1855.

20 'Ourselves' (Editorial), *MMH*, 20 August 1855.

21 'The Governor and the Governed', *MMH*, 8 December 1854.

22 Morris, *A Memoir of George Higinbotham*, 240–1.

23 Editorial (untitled), *Argus*, 4 February 1858, 4.

24 *Geelong Advertiser*, 30 November 1854, 4.

25 'Important Announcements', *Age*, 5 April 1855; 'The Exploded Thunderclap', *Age*, 3 May 1855.

26 'Summary for the *James Baines*' (Leading article), *MMH*, 10 March 1855.

27 *Ibid.*

28 Morris, *A Memoir of George Higinbotham*, 26, 58.

29 'Principles of Representation' (Leading article), *Argus*, 18 May 1857; Morris, *A Memoir of George Higinbotham*, 59.

5: Awaiting the New Constitution

1 'Hints for the New Dynasty', *Melbourne Morning Herald* (*MMH*), 10 July 1854.

2 'Home News' (Leading article), *MMH*, 19 August 1854.

3 J.M. Ward, 'Grey, Henry George (1802–1894)', *Australian Dictionary of Biography* (*ADB*).

4 Peter Burroughs, 'Liberal, Paternalistic or Cassandra? Earl Grey as a Critic of Colonial Self-Government', 33.

5 *Ibid*, 38, 43.

6 Peter Spiller, 'The Legal Career of Henry Chapman in Victoria 1854–1864', 47.

7 H.S. Chapman, *Parliamentary Government or Responsible Ministries for the Australian Colonies*.

8 *Ibid*, 22–4; Terry Newman, 'Tasmania and the Secret Ballot', 97.

9 Chapman, *Parliamentary Government or Responsible Ministries for the Australian Colonies*, 12.

10 R.S. Neale, 'Chapman, Henry Samuel (1803–1881)', *ADB*; G.C. Boase, 'Chapman, Henry Samuel (1803–1881)', rev. Jane Tucker, *Oxford Dictionary of National Biography*.

11 'The New Constitution' (Editorial), *Age*, 16 April 1855; 'Political Condition' (Editorial), *Age*, 1 May 1855.

12 'Legislative Council: 11 June', *MMH*, 12 June 1855.

13 Edward Sweetman, *Constitutional Development of Victoria 1851–1856*, 52–3.

14 Shirley Roberts, *Charles Hotham: A Biography*, 174.

15 'The *Red Jacket* and the Americans' (Leading article), *MMH*, 1 May 1855.

16 'Political Condition', *Age*, 1 May 1855.

17 'Political Apathy' (Leading article), *MMH*, 11 August 1855.

18 'Legislative Independence', *MMH*, 31 August 1855.

19 'Australian Nationality' (Editorial), *Herald*, 15 September 1855.

20 'Profound Indifference' (Leading article), *Herald*, 2 November 1855.

21 'Our Defences' (Leading article), *Herald*, 9 October 1855.

22 'The Land Regulations' (Leading article), *MMH*, 8 August 1855.

23 'Legislative Independence' (Leading article), *MMH*, 31 August 1855.

24 'The Chinese and the Goldfields' (Leading article), *MMH*, 5 June 1855; 'The Chinese Puzzle' (Editorial), *MMH*, 6 June 1855.

25 'Bendigo: From Our Own Correspondent: 26 June 1854', *MMH*, 29 June 1854; Editorial, *MMH*, 11 April 1855.

26 'Country News: The Governor at Geelong', *MMH*, 18 August 1854; *Argus*, 18 August 1854, 4; *Geelong Advertiser*, 11 September 1854.

27 'English Criticisms of Sir C. Hotham's Despatch' (reprinted from the *Australian and New Zealand Gazette*, undated), *MMH*, 8 August 1855; Hotham to Secretary of State, Separate, 25 October 1854; Geoffrey Serle, *The Golden Age: A History of the Colony of Victoria 1851–1861*, 199.

28 Serle, *The Golden Age*, 202.

29 'The New Constitution and the Governor's Despatch', Letter to the Editor, *MMH*, 1 August 1855.

30 'The Debate on the Victorian New Constitution Bill' (reprinted from the *Liverpool Mail*), *Herald*, 28 September 1855; Edward Jenks, *The Government of Victoria*, 196.

31 'Summary of Affairs in Victoria: August 22nd to September 29th', *Herald*, 29 September 1855.

32 'The Attorney General's Prediction' (Leading article), *Herald*, 4 February 1856.

33 'Profound Indifference' (Leading article), *Herald*, 2 November 1855.

34 'A Holiday' (Leading article), *Herald*, 17 November 1855.

35 *Victorian Parliamentary Debates*, 1873, Vol. 17, 1442.

36 This view contrasts with that of John Bennett, *George Higinbotham: Third Chief Justice of Victoria*, 21.

37 'Report of Meeting', *Age*, 6 December 1854.

38 *An Act to Alter 'The Victorian Electoral Act of 1851' and to Increase the Number of Elected Representatives of Victoria 1853* (Vic.), 16 Vic. No. 29.

39 *An Act to Further Alter 'The Victorian Electoral Act of 1851' and to Increase the Number of Members of the Legislative Council of Victoria 1855* (Vic.), 18 Vic. No. 34. This allowed the franchise to those who met a range of requirements including holding a gold mining licence for a full year.

40 Letter from Lieutenant-Governor Charles La Trobe to the Duke of Newcastle, 23 March 1854; Letter No. 10 of Parliamentary Papers on the table of the House of Commons between 31 July and 10 August 1854; 'New Constitution for Victoria', *MMH*, 7 February 1855.

41 Weston Bate, *Lucky City: The First Generation at Ballarat: 1851–1901*, 91.

42 W. Westgarth et al., *Report of the Commission Appointed to Enquire into the Condition of the Gold Fields of Victoria, &c. &c / Laid Upon the Council Table by the Colonial Secretary, by Command of His Excellency the Lieutenant Governor, and Order by the Council to Be Printed, 29th March, 1855* (Melbourne: Legislative Council of Victoria, 1855), Recommendation 5.

43 *Victorian Government Gazette*, No. 46, 22 May 1855, 1217, 1218.

44 'Bendigo: From Our Own Correspondent', *MMH*, 16 January 1854.

45 'Legislative Council', *MMH*, 2 and 4 May 1855.

46 'A Parliament at Last', *Argus*, 21 November 1856, 4; 'Justice to the Diggers', *Age*, 4 May 1855.

47 J.B. Hirst, *The Strange Birth of a Colonial Democracy: New South Wales 1848–1884*, 98–103.

48 Serle, *The Golden Age*, 184–5.

49 'Summary for the *James Baines*', *Age*, 27 November 1855.

50 'Opening of the Legislative Council', *Herald*, 24 November 1855. Another report gives the name of the Avoca Member as Duncan Longden JP: 'Avoca Election', *Herald*, 15 November 1855.

51 *Re-member: A Database of All Victorian MPs since 1851*, Parliament of Victoria, online: <http://www.parliament.vic.gov.au/re-member/bioregfull.cfm?mid=815>; 'Where Are the "Ninety"?', *Argus*, 22 July 1856.

52 Serle, *The Golden Age*, 210.

53 *Ibid*, 132–3; Margaret Kiddle, *Men of Yesterday: A Social History of the Western District of Victoria 1834–1890*, 245.

54 'Bendigo: From Our Own Correspondent', *Herald*, 26 October 1855.

55 'Sandhurst: From Our Own Correspondent', *MMH*, 16 March 1855; E. Daniel Potts and Annette Potts, *Young America and Australian Gold: Americans and the Gold Rush of the 1850s*, 188.

56 'Ballarat: From Our Own Correspondent', *Age*, 17 April 1855.

57 Ian MacFarlane, *Eureka from the Official Records*, 195; Peter Fitzsimons, *Eureka:*

The Unfinished Revolution, 332.

58 'Report of Meeting', *Age*, 6 December 1854.

59 'Profound Indifference' (Leading article), *Herald*, 2 November 1855; Serle, *The Golden Age*, 185; 'City Election', *Herald*, 25 October 1855.

60 *Herald*, 1 November 1855.

61 'Election for the Counties of Villiers and Heytesbury', *Herald*, 19 November 1855, and 'Country News: Warrnambool', *Herald*, 20 November 1855.

6: The First Constitutional Crisis

1 'Our Colonial Czar' (Leading article), *Herald*, 3 December 1855.

2 Frederick Madden and David Fieldhouse, *Select Documents on the Constitutional History of the British Empire and Commonwealth*, Vol. 4: *Settler Self-Government and Responsible Government 1840–1900*, 406. The Minute was reproduced in full in 'Summary for Europe', *Herald*, 24 December 1855. See also Geoffrey Serle, *The Golden Age: A History of the Colony of Victoria 1851–1861*, 201; Charles Parkinson, *Sir William Stawell and the Victorian Constitution*, 50–1. Parkinson details eleven propositions contained in Hotham's Minute.

3 'The Ministerial Crisis' (Editorial), *Age*, 28 November 1855. The *Age* included Childers amongst those who resigned their portfolios and were immediately reappointed, but another account of the incident by Edward Sweetman does not include him in this group. See Edward Sweetman, *Constitutional Development of Victoria 1851–1856*, 52.

4 'The Legislative Council: 27 November', *Herald*, 28 November 1855. Dr Greeves identified this government member as the Chief Secretary, William Haines.

5 'The Legislative Council: 27 November', *Herald*, 28 November 1855.

6 *Ibid*.

7 'Organized Hypocrisies' (Leading article), *Herald*, 30 November 1855; 'The Conspiracy', *Age*, 29 November 1855. The new ministry appointed by Hotham consisted of the following: William Haines (Chief Secretary), William Stawell (Attorney-General), Charles Sladen (Treasurer), Hugh Childers (Commissioner of Trade and Customs), Andrew Clark (Surveyor-General) and Robert Molesworth (Solicitor-General). See also Zelman Cowen, 'A Historical Survey of the Victorian Constitution: 1856–1956', 10. Cowen mentions two other Ministers: Charles Pasley (Commissioner of Public Works), who was a long-standing friend of Hotham from school days, and William Mitchell, a former Chief Commissioner of Police, who was not a member of the Legislative Council but was appointed an Honorary Minister. See too Anon., 'Mitchell, Sir William Henry Fancourt (1811–1884)', *Australian Dictionary of Biography (ADB)*, Vol. 5.

8 'Organized Hypocrisies' (Leading article), *Herald*, 30 November 1855; 'The Legislative Council: 4 December', *Herald*, 5 December 1855.

9 'Our Colonial Czar' (Leading article), *Herald*, 3 December 1855.

10 A.C.V. Melbourne, 'The Establishment of Responsible Government', 276. Melbourne comments: 'Self-government, even in local matters, could never be obtained while the Governor had command of a revenue which was free from

legislative supervision and while he consulted none but permanent officials who were appointed by the Secretary of State'.

11   'Our Colonial Czar' (Leading article), *Herald*, 3 December 1855.

12   'The Whole Question' (Editorial), *Age*, 4 December 1855; James Grant, 'Sladen, Sir Charles (1816–1884)', *ADB*, Vol. 6. Charles Sladen was newly appointed to the position of Colonial Treasurer, having been previously the Acting Treasurer.

13   *Ibid.*

14   'The Governor's Functions as He Understands Them' (Editorial), *Age*, 30 November 1855; Edward E. Morris, *A Memoir of George Higinbotham: An Australian Politician and Chief Justice of Victoria*, 45. Morris records that Haines and the editor of the *Argus*, Edward Wilson, had attended the same private school in Hampstead and implies that they were friends.

15   'Summary for the *James Baines*', *Age*, 27 November 1855.

16   'Observations on His Excellency the Governor's Minute, 30 November 1855'; 'Responsible Government' (Editorial), *Herald*, 8 December 1855. It is noticeable that the term 'responsible government' was avoided by the Ministers in favour of the phrase 'broad principles of the constitution'.

17   Letter from Sir Charles Hotham to the Legislative Council, 3 December 1855, *Herald*, 8 December 1855; 'Legislative Council', *Argus*, 5 December 1855; 'Responsible Government' (Editorial), *Herald*, 8 December 1855; 'Observations on His Excellency's Minute and Reply', *Votes and Proceedings of the Legislative Council of Victoria*, 1855–56 in Parliamentary Papers, Legislative Council 1855–56, Vol. 1, 2. A 30, 763.

18   'The Majority of One' (Leading article), *Herald*, 6 December 1855.

19   'The Debate' (Editorial), *Age*, 5 December 1855.

20   'The Legislative Council: 5 December', *Herald*, 6 December 1855.

21   'The Legislative Council: 5 December', *Age*, 6 December 1855, 5.

22   'The Legislative Council: 4 December', *Herald*, 5 December 1855.

23   'The Legislative Council: 5 December', *Age*, 6 December 1855, 5.

24   *Argus*, 6 December 1855.

25   'The Legislative Council: 4 December', *Herald*, 5 December 1855.

26   'The Legislative Council: 4 December', *Age*, 5 December 1855; *Greg Taylor, The Constitution of Victoria*, 36. Taylor discusses two radically different nineteenth-century understandings of 'responsible government'.

27   'The Majority of One' (Leading article), *Herald*, 6 December 1855.

28   Parkinson, *Sir William Stawell and the Victorian Constitution*, 49.

29   John Waugh, 'The Brummagem Coup: The Start of Self-Government in Victoria', 150. Waugh writes that Stawell informed Hotham that there was a need to clarify the Ministers' tenure under the new Constitution, and he comments that 'the argument was sound'. However, in concentrating on the legalities, he ignores the political significance, which was that the wider question of the meaning of 'responsible government' was at stake.

30   'The Legislative Council: 5 December', *Herald*, 6 December 1855.

31 *Ibid.*

32 *Ibid.*

33 'The Legislative Council: 5 December', *Herald*, 6 December 1855.

34 *Ibid.*

35 J.M. Bennett, *Sir William Stawell: Second Chief Justice of Victoria: 1857–1886*, 77. Bennett argues that 'Stawell and Molesworth were concerned, not with constitutional niceties, but with devising a means of excluding Hotham from the substantive process of government'. This interpretation cannot easily be reconciled with their support for Hotham's Minute, for its object was to claim expanded powers for the Governor at the expense of the legislature.

36 'The Legislative Council: 5 December', *Herald*, 6 December 1855.

37 'The Legislative Council: 5 December', *Argus*, 6 December 1855, 5.

38 *Age*, 6 December 1855, 5.

39 'Legislative Council: 5 December', *Argus*, 6 December 1855, 5.

40 'The Legislative Council: 4 December', *Herald*, 6 December 1855.

41 'The Traitors', *Age*, 6 December 1855.

42 'The Debate' (Editorial), *Age*, 5 December 1855.

43 'The Traitors', *Age*, 6 December 1855; 'Where Are the Ninety?', *Argus*, 22 July 1856, 4. The writer of this editorial (who may have been Higinbotham) wrote, 'We believe that Mr Longden was at that time [i.e., December 1855] a candidate for the secretaryship of the Railway Board … but so far from his "traitorous" vote assisting him on that occasion … it was necessarily fatal to his claims. The appointment if then given would have had all the appearance of a distinct bribe.'

44 'Public Meeting: Mackay and Harrison', *Melbourne Morning Herald* (*MMH*), 4 December 1854.

45 'The Traitors', *Age*, 6 December 1855.

46 *Ibid*; 'The Government's "Next Friend"' (Editorial), *MMH*, 22 January 1855.

47 Melbourne, 'The Establishment of Responsible Government', 275, 277. Melbourne argues that the colonists were not interested in responsible government (in its modern sense), but merely wanted 'self-government in matters of local interest'. See also Trevor Richard Reese, 'Short Notices Review of A.C.V. Melbourne's *Early Constitutional Development in Australia*', 206–7. Reese points out that Melbourne's section on public opinion in New South Wales regarding this issue is 'largely a review of the activities of W.C. Wentworth'.

48 'Legislative Council: 5 December', *Age*, 6 December 1855, 5.

49 Lalor's contribution to the debate about Hotham's Minute indicates that he was more sophisticated than he has been portrayed by historians such a Patrick O'Farrell, Bruce Kent and Clive Turnbull. Though in 1856 he denied being 'a Chartist, a communist or a republican', at the close of his life he spoke of the sweetness of living to see 'the principles for which you have risked your life triumphant', and he added, 'we not only got all we fought for, but a little more'. Clive Turnbull, *Eureka: The Story of Peter Lalor*, 1, 40, 45–7.

50 'Observations on His Excellency the Governor's Minute, 30 November 1855';

'Responsible Government' (Editorial), *Herald*, 8 December 1855.

51 'The Majority of One' (Leading article), *Herald*, 6 December 1855.

52 'Does He Wag His Tail?' (Leading article), *Herald*, 11 December 1855.

53 'The Result of the Debate', *Argus*, 6 December 1855, 4.

54 'The Governor's Minute' (Leading article), *Herald*, 7 December 1855; 'Does He Wag His Tail?' (Leading article), *Herald*, 11 December 1855.

55 'English Criticisms of Sir C. Hotham's Despatch', reprinted from the *Australian and New Zealand Gazette* (undated), *Herald*, 8 August 1855; 'Despatches from the Governor of Victoria to the Secretary of State', 1854, Typed transcripts (London, Colonial Office volumes, Public Record Office, 1926), 832–4. Hotham had raised some of these same objections with the Colonial Office as early as 25 October 1854. See also Serle, *The Golden Age*, 202. Serle notes that Hotham particularly objected to the proposed power of an incoming government to dismiss civil servants, which he argued would make Victoria 'a republic in reality'.

56 *Argus*, 16 February 1854. Clause 44 as recommended by the Select Committee on the Constitution read: 'the appointment of all public officers under the Government of Victoria hereafter to become vacant, or to be created (other than corporate offices) whether such officers be salaried or not, shall be vested in the Governor, with the advice of the Executive Council'. However, in its final form it read, 'the appointment of all public officers under the Government of Victoria hereafter to become vacant, or to be created, whether such officers be salaried or not, shall be vested in the Governor, with the advice of the Executive Council with the exception of the officers liable to retire from office on political grounds, which appointments shall be vested in the Governor alone'.

57 Sir George Grey was the Colonial Secretary from 12 June 1854 to 8 February 1855. He was succeeded briefly by Sidney Herbert, and from 23 February by Lord John Russell. See also J.M. Ward, *Colonial Self-Government: The British Experience 1759–1856*, 291. Ward notes that Grey 'did not believe in the political fitness of … the Australian colonies to have responsible government', and that 'he distrusted colonial democracy'.

58 Separate no. 1 of 25 October 1854, *Despatches from the Governor of Victoria to the Secretary of State 1851–1860*, compiled by M.E. Deane, online <http:// search.slv.vic.gov.au/MAIN:SLV_VOYAGER1026904>; Ward, *Colonial Self-Government*, 309. Ward notes that Russell believed that responsible government was 'a necessary reform', but he still believed that 'it was necessary for the Crown to continue to play a beneficial role in the colonies to which that reform was granted'.

59 Serle, *The Golden Age*. 202; Bennett, *Sir William Stawell*, 54.

60 Shirley Roberts, *Charles Hotham: A Biography*. See also Chapters 3, 4, 5 and 6.

61 The writer of the letter provides a clue to his identity when he refers to the fact that he arrived in the Colony in July 1854. This was approximately the date of arrival of Henry Chapman, whose name is prominently associated with this constitutional controversy.

62 'The New Constitution and the Governor's Despatch' (Letter to the editor), *MMH*, 1 August 1855; Sir Zelman Cowen, 'A Historical Survey of the Victorian

Constitution: 1856–1956', 19, 20. Cowen observes that references to responsible government in the Victorian Constitution were 'scanty', and that the provision of it 'was not very clearly apparent on the fact of the instrument'. He explains: 'Section 37 drew a distinction between appointments to public offices under the government: in general, appointments were in the hands of the Governor with the advice of the Executive Council, but the appointment of "officers liable to retire from office on political grounds" was vested in the Governor alone. Section 50 provided for the payment of pensions to existing incumbents of offices "who on political grounds may retire or be released", while Section 51 (with a marginal note "pensions to responsible officers") provided for the payment of pensions for future holders of office.'

63 *MMH*, 23, 24 and 26 May 1855, also 5, 14, 15 and 16 June 1855.

64 'The Position of the Government', *Argus*, 7 June 1855, 4; 'A Retrospect and a Suggestion', *The Melbourne Monthly Magazine of Original Colonial Literature*, Vol. 1, No. II, 1855, 119–27.

65 Roberts, *Charles Hotham*, 90.

66 'Military Governors', *Age*, 8 April 1855; 'The Virtue of Resignation', *Age*, 10 April 1855; 'Political Condition: The Real Remedy', *Age*, 1 May 1855.

67 Edward Jenks, *The Government of Victoria*, 212. This study is an exception, as Jenks argues that Hotham's Minute was 'of the highest importance as expressing the views of a colonial official of great position with regard to the [constitutional] changes'.

68 'The Legislative Council 27 November', *Herald*, 28 November 1855.

69 Ronald McNicoll, 'Pasley, Charles (1824–1890)', *ADB*, Vol. 5; Roberts, *Charles Hotham*, 41.

70 'Leave of Absence' (Leading article), *Herald*, 7 February 1856. This article denounces La Trobe's appointment of Mitchell as Chief Commissioner of Police as being 'of great detriment to the Public Service'. It criticises the rumoured proposal for the present meritorious incumbent of the office, Captain MacMahon, to be demoted to allow Mitchell to resume his office.

71 Anon., 'Mitchell, Sir William Henry Fancourt (1811–1884)', *ADB*, Vol. 5.

72 'The Governor's Minute' (Leading article), *Herald*, 7 December 1855.

73 *Ibid.*

74 'Constitutional Reform' (Leading article), *Herald*, 4 December 1855.

75 Peter Burroughs, 'Molesworth, Sir William, Eighth Baronet (1810–1855)', *Oxford Dictionary of National Biography*.

7: Challenging the New Constitution

1 'Summary for Europe: Political Retrospect' (Leading article), *Herald*, 30 January 1856.

2 *Ibid.*

3 *Herald*, editorials of 7 January, and 9, 12, 13 and 16 February 1856.

4 'The New Constitution' (Leading article), *Age*, 16 April 1855. See also 'Political Condition' (Leading article), *Age*, 1 May 1855.

5   'The Constitution Act', *Argus*, 1 September 1855, 4. The substituted provisions objected to in the editorial do not appear in the (*Victoria Constitution Act 1855* Imp) *18 & 19 Vict., c. 55*, Schedule 1. However, Clause LX of Schedule 1 of this Act requires the reservation of any Bill to amend the Victorian Constitution for 'the signification of Her Majesty's pleasure' (i.e., approval of the British Cabinet).

6   'The Legislative Council: 11 December', *Herald*, 12 December 1855.

7   'The Legislative Council: 30 November', *Herald*, 1 December 1855.

8   'The Legislative Council: 30 November', *Age*, 1 December 1855.

9   'The Legislative Council: 11 December', *Herald*, 12 December 1855.

10   'The Legislative Council: 6 December', *Herald*, 7 December 1855, also 'Legislative Council: 7 December', *Herald*, 8 December 1855.

11   'The Legislative Council: 7 December', *Herald*, 8 December 1855.

12   'Election for the Counties of Villiers and Heytesbury', *Herald*, 19 November 1855, and 'Country News: Warrnambool', *Herald*, 20 November 1855.

13   'Constitutional Reform' (Leading article), *Herald*, 4 December 1855.

14   *Ibid*; 'Triumph of the Ballot' (Leading article), *Argus*, 20 December 1855, 4.

15   Charles Parkinson, *Sir William Stawell and the Victorian Constitution*, 42.

16   John Ashton Cannon, *A Dictionary of British History*, 502.

17   Hugh Edward Egerton, *Selected Speeches of the Right Honourable Sir William Molesworth, Bart, MP*.

18   'The Legislative Council: 14 February', *Argus*, 16 February 1854, 4.

19   'The Legislative Council: 18 January', *Melbourne Morning Herald* (*MMH*), 19 January 1854.

20   'Constitution in Committee' (Leading article), 31 January 1854; Geoffrey Serle, *The Golden Age: A History of the Colony of Victoria 1851–1861*, 146. Serle, by contrast, argued that 'the final form differed only in minor detail from the proposals of the committee'.

21   D.H. Rankin, 'Sir William Stawell', 79–80.

22   'Ballaarat', *MMH*, 31 December 1853.

23   'The Legislative Council: 17 March', *Argus*, 18 March 1854, 4; 'The Debate on the New Constitution', *MMH*, 19 January 1854.

24   John Waugh, 'Framing the First Victorian Constitution, 1853–5', 331–61.

25   'The Whole Question', *Age*, 4 December 1855.

26   Peter Burroughs, 'Molesworth, Sir William, Eighth Baronet (1810–1855)', *Oxford Dictionary of National Biography*.

27   'The Late Sir William Molesworth' (Editorial), *Argus*, 10 October 1856, 4.

28   Shirley Roberts, *Charles Hotham: A Biography*, 183.

29   Russell to Hotham, 2 June 1855, 'Confidential Despatches from the Secretary of State 1852–1860', Vol. 1, Part 1, Public Record Office of Victoria.

30   'The State Trials', *MMH*, 13 March 1855.

31   'Military Governors', *Age*, 8 April 1855; 'The Virtue of Resignation', *Age*, 10 April 1855.

32 'Political Condition: The Real Remedy', *Age*, 1 May 1855.

33 *Ibid*, 181.

34 Hotham Family Papers, quoted in Roberts, *Charles Hotham*, 174.

35 'Death of the Governor' (Leading article), *Herald*, 1 January 1856.

36 Editorial (untitled), *Herald*, 30 January 1856.

37 'The Legislative Council: 15 February', *Herald*, 16 February 1856.

38 Waugh, 'Framing the First Victorian Constitution 1853–1855', 359.

39 'The Legislative Council: 15 February', *Herald*, 16 February 1856; Edward Jenks, *The Government of Victoria*, 205.

40 *Votes and Proceedings of the Legislative Council During the Session 1855–6*, Vol. 2, No. C34, 783.

41 Jenks, *The Government of Victoria*, 205. Jenks comments, 'It is difficult to discover what this opinion means'. Greg Taylor, *The Constitution of Victoria*, 36. Taylor supports this opinion of Stawell and Molesworth, arguing, 'the ultimate source of validity of the *Constitution Act* in Kelsenian terms at the time of its enactment was clearly the authority of the Imperial Parliament'.

42 'Topics for the Week' (Editorial), *Herald*, 3 June 1856.

43 'The Viper Bag' (Leading article), *Herald*, 24 July 1856.

44 Price Warung, 'The Greatest of Australia's Dead'.

45 Edward E. Morris, *A Memoir of George Higinbotham: An Australian Politician and Chief Justice of Victoria*, 37.

46 'The Constitutional Question' (Editorial), *Herald*, 13 February 1856.

47 Charles Parkinson, 'George Higinbotham and Responsible Government in Colonial Victoria', Part 11, Background, online <http://www.austlii.edu.au/au/journals/MULR/2001/6.html>. Parkinson argues that 'it was the events of the 1860s that shaped Higinbotham's views on responsible government'.

8: Higinbotham, Duffy and the Irish Legacy

1 'The Legislative Council: 3 February', *Melbourne Morning Herald* (*MMH*), 4 January 1854. Colonial Secretary John Foster defended the property qualification in the proposed new Constitution, arguing that it would deter 'scamps who would trade on politics and seek a seat in that house to carry out their dishonest purposes'.

2 Charles Gavan Duffy, *My Life in Two Hemispheres*, Vol. 2, 133.

3 University of Minnesota Law Library website: <https://www.law.umn.edu/library/irishlaw/intro>.

4 Christine Kinealy, *This Great Calamity: The Irish Famine 1845–52*.

5 *Hansard Parliamentary Debates*, 3rd series, 4: 24–5, 9 May 1843.

6 Hereward Senior, 'Orangeism in Ireland and Britain', 274.

7 *Ibid*, 250.

8 *Ibid*, 76.

9   Jacqueline Hill, 'The 1847 General Election in Dublin City', 49.

10 House of Commons, Debate on The Corn Importation Bill, 8 May 1846, online <http://hansard.millbanksystems.com/commons/1846/may/08/corn-importation-bill>, line 243. See also Verner's comments re the Protection of Life (Ireland) Bill, 27 April 1846, 1103, online <http://hansard.millbanksystems.com/commons/1846/apr/27/protection-of-life-ireland-adjourned#S3V0085P0_18460427_HOC_28>.

11 John Kerr, 'Churchill: Home of the Verners'; H.W. Coffey, *The Anglican Church, South Melbourne, Emerald Hill Canvas Town 1852–1977*, 18. Coffey states that George Higinbotham's paternal grandmother was the sister of Sir William Verner, MP of Churchill, Vernersbridge, County Armagh. But Kerr's study of the generations of the family seems to be more detailed and therefore reliable, and by this evidence, she was the aunt of Sir William Verner. However, Coffey's account, even if wrong in this detail, is further evidence of a relationship between George Higinbotham and Sir William Verner.

12 Kerr, 'Churchill: Home of the Verners'.

13 *Ibid.*

14 House of Lords, 'Third Report of the Select Committee Appointed to Inquire into the Nature, Character, Extent and Tendency of Orange Lodges, Associations or Societies in Ireland, 3 July 1835', *Sessional Papers*, House of Lords, 3 July 1835, Vol. 24, 10 July 1835.

15 *Ibid.* For a wider discussion of this, see Sean Farrell, *Rituals and Riots: Sectarian Violence and Political Culture in Ulster, 1784–1886*, 26–8.

16 House of Lords, 'Third Report of the Select Committee … 3 July 1835', Vol. 24, Questions 9522, 9524, 8970, 8971, 8972 8979.

17 Farrell, *Rituals and Riots*, 81.

18 House of Lords, 'Third Report of the Select Committee … 3 July 1835'; Farrell, *Rituals and Riots*, 26–8.

19 House of Lords, 'Third Report of the Select Committee … 3 July 1835', 178.

20 Farrell, *Rituals and Riots*, 456. Judge William Fletcher, before a grand jury in County Wexford, denounced 'those societies called Orange societies' for having produced 'most mischievous effects, and particularly in the North of Ireland'.

21 *Ibid*, 45–6; House of Lords, 'Third Report of the Select Committee … 3 July 1835', 187. Sub-Inspector William Henry of the Armagh Constabulary deposed that those who broke the law known as 'An Act Restraining Party Processions in Ireland' were impossible to prosecute because the magistrates at Portadown would not hear charges for this offence.

22 Thomas Verner, 'What Is an Orangeman?', 484.

23 *Ibid*, 487.

24 Hereward Senior, 'Orangeism in Ireland and Britain', 236.

25 Kerr, 'Churchill: Home of the Verners'.

26 Edward E. Morris, *A Memoir of George Higinbotham: An Australian Politician and Chief Justice of Victoria*, 37. Morris noted that Higinbotham loved the challenge of handling a refractory horse.

27   Kerr, 'Churchill: Home of the Verners'.

28   *Ibid*, 15; Henry Brougham's letter to Edward Morris. Higinbotham was, in later years, a founding member of the Brighton Yacht Club in Victoria.

29   Morris, *A Memoir of George Higinbotham*, 7.

30   She was christened Jane Verner, but known as Jenny Verner.

31   Peter O'Shaughnessy (ed.), *The Gardens of Hell: John Mitchel in Van Diemen's Land: 1850–1853*, 12.

32   K. Molloy, 'An Irish Radical and His Nephew: The Papers of John Mitchel and Sir William Hill Irvine', 37–8, 42, 141.

33   John Mitchel, 'June in the Famine Year', in *The Nation*, quoted in Brian P. McGovern, *John Mitchel: Irish Nationalist, Southern Secessionist*, 34. The reference to doors off their hinges relates to the custom of the Irish poor of placing corpses on doors for transportation to a cemetery.

34   See Chapter 4 for the account of the derailment of a train at Trillick.

35   Duffy, *My Life in Two Hemispheres*, Vol. 2, 292.

36   John Fawkner, 'Open Column: Mr C.G. Duffy and the "Nation" of Dublin', *Herald*, 24 July 1856.

37   'Ireland and Catholicism' (Leading article), *Herald*, 25 July 1856. This was published after the date that Higinbotham declared himself to have been 'unconnected with the colonial press', but it may have been submitted for publication by Aspinall.

38   Cayetano Ripoll was hanged by the state authorities despite the Inquisition's sentence that he should be burned.

39   Paul de Serville, *Pounds and Pedigrees: The Upper Class in Victoria 1850-1880*, 92.

40   Duffy, *My Life in Two Hemispheres*, Vol. 2, 69.

41   Joy E. Parnaby, 'Duffy, Sir Charles Gavan (1816–1903)', *Australian Dictionary of Biography (ADB)*, Vol. 4.

42   Duffy, *My Life in Two Hemispheres*, Vol. 2, 292.

43   Morris, *A Memoir of George Higinbotham*, 5; Documents Relating to the Charles Willson Peale Portrait of George Washington, Vol. 1, CO242, Manuscripts Division, Department of Rare Books and Special Collections, Princeton University Library, online <https://rbsc.princeton.edu/collections/documents-relating-charles-willson-peale-portrait-george-washington>. These two sources provide evidence that this famous portrait was a gift from George Washington to Higinbotham's grandfather, Joseph Wilson.

44   Charles Allen Munn, *Three Types of Washington Portraits*, 36–7. Munn quotes from a copy of the will of Joseph Wilson of 13 February 1809.

45   Jonathon Smyth, 'John Richard Darley (1799–1884): Bishop, Scholar and Philanthropist', 687. See also Geraldine Moore, 'The Young George Higinbotham: 1826–1856', 29–33.

46   'Summary for Europe: Political Retrospect', *Herald*, 30 January 1856; 'The Late Sir William Molesworth', *Argus*, 10 October 1856, 4.

9: The *Argus*, Duffy and the 1856 Election

1 T.L. Work, 'The Early Printers of Melbourne'.

2 'The *Herald* and Its Future' (Leading article), *Herald*, 3 September 1855.

3 'The European News' (Leading article), *Herald*, 19 November 1855.

4 'The Abbe Le Gras', translated by Peter Perfume, *Herald*, 25 October 1855.

5 'The Demonstrative Herald', *Melbourne Punch*, Vol. 1, 1855, 194.

6 Janice Burns Woods, 'Evans, George Samuel: 1802–1868', *Australian Dictionary of Biography* (*ADB*), Vol. 4. Woods describes the speaking style of Evans as 'ponderous', a comment which also describes his writing style.

7 Advertisement, *Herald*, 17 October 1855.

8 'A New Epoch' (Leading article), *Herald*, 5 November 1855.

9 Woods, 'Evans, George Samuel (1802–1868)'. Dr George Evans, who became the editor of the *Herald* at some time in 1855, was also a candidate for the seat of Richmond in the new legislature, and may have written some of these articles.

10 'Our Pillars of the State' (Leading article), and 'The Italian Opera' (Editorial), *Herald*, 12 November 1855.

11 J.M. Bennett, *George Higinbotham: Third Chief Justice of Victoria*, 18.

12 Edward E. Morris, *A Memoir of George Higinbotham: An Australian Politician and Chief Justice of Victoria*, 51-52.

13 'Summary for Europe' (Leading article), *Herald*, 30 January 1856. See quotation from the article, Chapter 11.

14 'Ourselves at the Antipodes' (Editorial), *Herald*, 22 July 1856.

15 Ian MacFarlane, *Eureka from the Official Records*, 159–63.

16 Editorial, *Argus*, 1 December 1854, 4.

17 'The Election' (Leading article), *Argus*, 6 September 1855, 4.

18 Charles Patrick Smith, 'Men Who Made the *Argus* and the *Australasian*: 1846–1923'.

19 'The Report of the New Constitution' (Leading article), *Melbourne Morning Herald* (*MMH*), 12 December 1853; 'Squattocratic Impudence' (Leading articles), *MMH*, 23, 24 and 25 January 1854.

20 'The Duke of Newcastle to the Squatters: Greeting', *MMH*, 15 March 1854.

21 Jacqueline Templeton, 'Mackinnon, Lauchlan: 1817–1888', *ADB*, Vol. 5.

22 'The Crisis' (Editorial), *Argus*, 1 December 1854, 4.

23 'Financier Foster' (Editorial), *MMH*, 2 December 1854.

24 VPRS 1095/P0000, Public Record Office of Victoria.

25 'A Forgotten Democrat', William Astley Papers, MS Q51330, State Library of New South Wales, January 1893, 169. Astley's pen-name was Price Warung.

26 Stuart Macintyre, *A Colonial Liberalism: The Lost World of Three Victorian Visionaries*, 33.

27 'Mr Duffy's Election' (Leading article), *Argus*, 27 October 1856, 4.

28 Charles Gavan Duffy, *My Life in Two Hemispheres*, Vol. 2, 154.

29 *Argus*, 23 August, 3, 4 and 13 September, 8, 21, 22 and 23 October 1856.

30 Morris, *A Memoir of George Higinbotham*, 226–7; 'The North Bourke Election', *Argus*, 4 September 1855, 4.

31 'Benefits of the Ballot' (Leading article), *Argus*, 30 August 1856, 4.

32 Brian P. McGovern, *John Mitchel: Irish Nationalist, Southern Secessionist*, 90; *The Crime and Outrage Act*.

33 Jacqueline Hill, 'The 1847 General Election in Dublin City'.

34 Brian Walker, 'Politicians, Elections and Catastrophe: The General Election of 1847', 9. Walker refers to the report of Verner's speech in the *Northern Whig*, 12 August 1847.

35 'The Irish Party', *Dublin Evening Mail*, No. 4403, 11 January 1847.

36 Hill, 'The 1847 General Election in Dublin City', 58, 61.

37 *Ibid*, 58.

38 Mun/soc/hist/26. College Historical Society, Trinity College Dublin, *Journals*, 1843–49.

39 'Mr O'Shanassy's Speech' (Editorial), *Argus*, 30 August 1856, 4.

40 Morris, *A Memoir of George Higinbotham*, 316.

41 'A Parliament at Last', *Argus*, 21 November 1856, 4.

42 'Benefits of the Ballot' (Leading article), *Argus*, 30 August 1856, 4.

43 Leading article, *MMH*, 2 February 1855.

44 R.S. Neale, 'H.S. Chapman and the Victorian Ballot', 518.

45 Peter Cook, 'Nicholson, William (1816–1865), *ADB*, Vol. 5.

46 Charles Parkinson, *Sir William Stawell and the Victorian Constitution*, 52.

47 Shirley Roberts, *Charles Hotham: A Biography*, 182–3.

48 *Ibid*.

10: Metamorphosis

1 Geoffrey Serle, *The Golden Age: A History of the Colony of Victoria 1851–1861*, 252.

2 Jarlath Ronayne, *The Irish in Australia: Rogues and Reformers, First Fleet to Federation*, 137.

3 Charles Gavan Duffy, *My Life in Two Hemispheres*, Vol. 2, 160.

4 Serle, *The Golden Age*, 254.

5 *Ibid*.

6 Duffy, *My Life in Two Hemispheres*, Vol. 2, 136.

7 *Ibid*, 162.

8 *Ibid*, 164–5.

9 Charles Parkinson, *Sir William Stawell and the Victorian Constitution*, 9.

10 Serle, *The Golden Age*, 238–48, 261 footnote.

11 Betty Malone, 'Haines, William Clarke (1810–1866)', *Australian Dictionary of*

Biography (*ADB*), Vol. 4.

12 'The New Ministry' (Leading article) and 'Government by Party' (Editorial), *Argus*, 9 March 1857, 4.

13 Duffy, *My Life in Two Hemispheres*, Vol. 2, 165.

14 *Ibid*, 169.

15 H.L. Hall, 'Michie, Sir Archibald (1813–1899)', *ADB*, Vol. 5.

16 Duffy, *My Life in Two Hemispheres*, Vol. 2, 172.

17 *Ibid*, 205.

18 Susan Priestley, 'In Defence of George Higinbotham: New Evidence on Family Relationships', 23–4.

19 *Freeman's Journal*, 7 January 1826, reprinted in the *Newcastle Courant*, 7 January 1826; *Glasgow Herald*, 2 January 1826.

20 John Watson Stewart, *Watson's or the Gentleman's and Citizen's Almanack* (Dublin: Stewart and Hopes, 1829).

21 Geraldine Moore, 'The Young George Higinbotham: 1826–1856', 30–3. Henry Higinbotham's whereabouts can be traced from the voting registers for the City of Dublin, from the Deeds Registry, Dublin, where he registered the sale of property leases, and from the records of Trinity College and King's Inn Dublin when he registered his sons for tertiary studies. See also Priestley, 'In Defence of George Higinbotham', 24.

22 Moore, 'The Young George Higinbotham', 25–35.

23 Fergus Whelan, *Dissent into Treason: Unitarians, King-Killers and the Society of United Irishmen*, 100, 159, 160.

24 *Ibid*.

25 Priestley, 'In Defence of George Higinbotham', 17.

26 Ethel is buried with her Uncle Thomas in the graveyard of St Andrew's Church, Brighton.

27 Edward E. Morris, *A Memoir of George Higinbotham: An Australian Politician and Chief Justice of Victoria*, 40.

28 Paul de Serville, *Pounds and Pedigrees: The Upper Class in Victoria 1850–1880*, 344 (William Verner) and 305 (Thomas Higinbotham).

29 Stanley Leighton, 'Stanley Leighton Journal', National Library of Australia, 1868, MS 360 289815. 5, 11, 15.

30 Morris, *A Memoir of George Higinbotham*, 49.

31 *Ibid*, 273.

32 Serle, *The Golden Age*, 242.

33 *Ibid*, 241–8.

34 Stuart Macintyre, *A Colonial Liberalism: The Lost World of Three Victorian Visionaries*, 31-32.

35 'The Unemployed', *Argus*, 14 August 1857, 5; 'Working Men's Association', *Argus*, 15 September 1857, 5.

36 'The Unemployed', *Argus*, 1 August 1857, 4; 'The Unemployed', *Argus*, 22

September 1857, 4.

37 'The Land Convention' (Editorial), *Argus*, 18 July 1857, 4.

38 *Ibid*.

39 Serle, *The Golden Age*, 318.

40 Letter from Higinbotham to Chapman (undated), quoted in Serle, *The Golden Age*, 278. This series of letters, formerly in the State Library of Victoria, is now lost.

41 Serle, *The Golden Age*, 281.

42 *Ibid*, 282.

43 'Immigration and the Labour Market' (Leading article), 9 June 1857, 4.

44 *Argus*, 1 September 1858, 4.

45 Morris, *A Memoir of George Higinbotham*, 50.

46 Leading article (unnamed), *Argus*, 7 December 1858, 4.

47 'The Land Bill', *Argus*, 23 September 1857, 4.

48 *Argus*, 15 September 1858, 4; 'Labor', *Argus*, 24 June 1857, 5.

49 Ken S. Inglis, *The Australian Colonists: An Exploration of Social History 1788–1870*, 117–25.

50 Richard Kennedy, 'Embling, Thomas (1814–1893)', *ADB*, Vol. 4; Serle, *The Golden Age*, 213–14.

51 'Representative Reform' (Letter to the editor), *Argus*, 8 April 1858, 5.

52 'Principles of Representation' (Leading article), *Argus*, 18 May 1857.

53 *Argus*, 8 April 1858, 4.

54 Wilson to Henry Parkes, 12 April 1858, Mitchell Library of New South Wales, MS A930. See also Macintyre, *A Colonial Liberalism*, 35.

55 Morris, *A Memoir of George Higinbotham*, 48.

56 John Quick, *The History of Land Tenure in the Colony of Victoria*, 45.

57 Leading article, *Argus*, 29 August 1860, 4.

58 'Serious Riot at the Parliament Houses', Argus, 29 August 1860, 5; Serle, *The Golden Age*, 298–9.

59 Serle, *The Golden Age*, 299.

60 G. Serle, 'The Victorian Legislative Council 1856–1950', 186–203.

61 Morris, *A Memoir of George Higinbotham*, 62.

62 *Ibid*.

63 *Ibid*, 76.

64 *Ibid*, 73.

11: The Member for Brighton

1 John Quick, *The History of Land Tenure in the Colony of Victoria*, 59.

2 Janette Finch and Ruth Teale, 'Brodribb, William Adams' (1809–1886)', *Australian Dictionary of Biography (ADB)*, Vol. 3.

3 'Anecdotal Photograph: Mr J.G. Burtt', *Table Talk* (Melbourne: 1885–1939),

Friday 12 June 1896, 2.

4   'The Brighton Election', *Argus*, 4 April 1862, 5.

5   *An Act to Consolidate and Amend the Laws relating to the Sale and Occupation of Crown Lands*, CLXV, 18 June 1862.

6   'The Brighton Election', *Argus*, 4 April 1862, 5.

7   *Ibid.*

8   Sylvia Morrissey, 'Clarke, Sir William John (1831–1897)', *ADB*, Vol. 3.

9   J.M. Bennett, *George Higinbotham: Third Chief Justice of Victoria*, 56.

10 Edward E. Morris, *A Memoir of George Higinbotham: An Australian Politician and Chief Justice of Victoria*, 73.

11 'The Constitutional Question' (Editorial), *Herald*, 13 February 1856. In this editorial, Higinbotham repeated the accusation of 'lawless usurpation' against the British Parliament.

12 'Summary for Europe' (Leading article), *Herald*, 30 January 1856. See also see Chapter 9.

13 Leading article (unnamed), *Argus*, 4 April 1862, 4.

14 Leading article (unnamed), *Argus*, 6 May 1862, 4.

15 S. Merrifield, 'Don, Charles Jardine (1820–1866)', *ADB*, Vol. 4.

16 Leading article (unnamed), *Argus*, 25 April 1860, 4.

17 Guy Featherstone, 'Smith, Louis Lawrence (1830–1910)', *ADB*, Vol. 6.

18 Leading article (unnamed), *Argus*, 6 May 1862, 4.

19 'Summary for Europe', *Argus*, 25 April 1862, 5.

20 'Report of Debate in the Legislative Assembly: 2 April', *Argus*, 3 April 1862.

21 Leading Article (unnamed), *Argus*, 4 April 1862, 4.

22 'Mr William Frazer' (Obit.), *Argus*, 15 December 1870, 3.

23 'Death of Mr George Dill' (Obit.), *Argus*, 2 August 1901, 5.

24 Leading article (unnamed), *Argus*, 2 May 1862, 4.

25 *Ibid*; *Argus*, 5 May 1862, 4.

26 Leading article (unnamed), *Argus*, 2 May 1862, 4.

27 Leading article (unnamed), *Argus*, 24 April 1862, 4.

28 Charles Parkinson, *Sir William Stawell and the Victorian Constitution*, 70–2.

29 Weston Bate, *A History of Brighton*, 2nd edition, 348.

30 Leading article (unnamed), *Argus*, 24 April 1862, 4.

31 Letter from George Rusden to Charles Dickens, 4 December 1868, in Rusden Papers (Leeper Library, Trinity College, University of Melbourne). Quoted in Parkinson, *Sir William Stawell and the Victorian Constitution*, 68.

32 *An Act to Establish a Constitution in and for the Colony of Victoria*, Schedule D, Part 4.

33 'Feathering Official Nests' (Leading article), *Melbourne Morning Herald* (*MMH*), 16 February 1854.

34 'The Legislative Council: 15 February', *MMH*, 16 February 1854.

35 'Summary for Europe: Statistical and Commercial Summary of the Colony of Victoria from the 24th December 1855 to the 30 January 1856', *Herald*, 30 January 1856.

36 'The Crisis' (Editorial), *Argus*, 1 December 1854, 4.

37 See Chapter 9.

38 G.W. Rusden, *A History of Australia*, Vol. 3.

39 Quick, *The History of Land Tenure in the Colony of Victoria*, 70.

40 Charles Gavan Duffy, *My Life in Two Hemispheres*, Vol. 2, 240. See also Leading article (unnamed), *Argus*, 16 September 1864, 4.

41 Jarlath Ronayne, *The Irish in Australia: Rogues and Reformers, First Fleet to Federation*, 130–3.

42 Duffy, *My Life in Two Hemispheres*, Vol. 2, 240; *Appropriations Act (No. 2) 1862* (Vic.), 25 Vict., No. 139.

43 Duffy, *My Life in Two Hemispheres*, Vol. 2, 232.

44 Quick, *The History of Land Tenure in the Colony of Victoria*, 64.

45 Duffy, *My Life in Two Hemispheres*, Vol. 2, 233–4.

46 Janice Burns Wood, 'Ireland, Richard Davies (1815–1877), *ADB*, Vol. 4.

47 Duffy, *My Life in Two Hemispheres*, Vol. 2, 235–6.

48 *Ibid*, 288.

49 Geoffrey Serle, *The Golden Age: A History of the Colony of Victoria 1851–1861*, 315.

50 Robin Gollan, *Radical and Working Class Politics: A Study of Eastern Australia: 1850–1910*, 67.

51 Walter Bagehot, *The English Constitution*, 2nd edition, 129. See also Parkinson, *Sir William Stawell and the Victorian Constitution*, 68–9.

52 'The Constitution Debate' (Leading article), *MMH*, 4 February 1854.

53 'The Legislative Council: 18 January', *MMH*, 19 January 1854; *Argus*, 2 September 1853.

54 'The Legislative Council: 25 January', *MMH*, 26 January 1854.

55 *Victorian Hansard*, Vol. 8, p. 145. Quoted in Quick, *The History of Land Tenure in the Colony of Victoria*, 58.

56 Leading article (unnamed), *Argus*, 18 December 1858; Serle, *The Golden Age*, 286.

57 Quick, *The History of Land Tenure in the Colony of Victoria*, 58.

58 'The Constitutional Question' (Leading article), *Herald*, 13 February 1856.

59 *Ibid*; Morris, *A Memoir of George Higinbotham*, 37.

12: Attorney-General George Higinbotham

1 Leading article (unnamed), *Argus*, 26 September 1864, 4.

2 Leading article (unnamed), *Argus*, 21 September 1864, 4.

3 'Death of Mr Matthew Hervey' (Obit.), *Ovens and Murray Advertiser*, 5 December 1874, 5.

4   Gwyneth M. Dow, *George Higinbotham: Church and State*, 25–6. Dow explores the precariousness of McCulloch's hold on power.

5   Edward E. Morris, *A Memoir of George Higinbotham: An Australian Politician and Chief Justice of Victoria*, 80. Morris attributed this quote to an unnamed 'member of the Legislature' when Higinbotham was Attorney-General in the ministry of James McCulloch.

6   *Ibid.*

7   *Ibid*, 79.

8   John Quick, *The History of Land Tenure in the Colony of Victoria*, 76.

9   *Ibid*, 74.

10   *Age*, 24 October 1864. See also speech of William Hull quoting Higinbotham, 'The Legislative Council: 31 January', *Argus*, 1 February 1865, 5.

11   Quick, *The History of Land Tenure in the Colony of Victoria*, 77.

12   *Ibid*, 78.

13   *Ibid*, 70–1.

14   *Ibid*, 83.

15   *Ibid*, 77.

16   *Ibid*, 83.

17   *Ibid*, 87.

18   *Ibid*, 82.

19   Morris, *A Memoir of George Higinbotham*, 85.

20   Terry Smyth, *Australian Confederates: How 42 Australians Joined the Rebel Cause and Fired the Last Shot in the American Civil War*, 75.

21   *Ibid*, 76.

22   Morris, *A Memoir of George Higinbotham*, 90.

23   Barry J. Crompton, *Dixie Down Under: Report of the Shenandoah's Cruise by James I. Waddell*, 17.

24   *Argus*, 30 January 1865, 5.

25   Editorial (unnamed), *Argus*, 1 February 1865, 4.

26   Morris, *A Memoir of George Higinbotham*, 85.

27   *Age*, 27 January 1865, quoted in Barry J. Crompton, *The Visit of the CSS Shenandoah to Australia*, 6.

28   <http://www.burkeandwills.net.au/Explorers/Relief_Parties/HMCSS_Victoria.htm>.

29   'The Colonial Steamship *Victoria*', *Courier* (Hobart), 1 August 1856, 2; Geoffrey Serle, *The Golden Age: A History of the Colony of Victoria 1851–1861*, 313, online <https://en.wikipedia.org/wiki/HMVS_Victoria_(1855)>.

30   Crompton, *Dixie Down Under*, 73.

31   *Ibid*, 86.

32   J.M. Bennett, *George Higinbotham: Third Chief Justice of Victoria*, 68–70.

33   *Ibid*, 70.

34 Gary McKay, *The Sea King: The Life of James Iredell Waddell*, 153.

35 Morris, *A Memoir of George Higinbotham*, 89.

36 *Ibid*, 92.

37 (1873) XVI *Victorian Parliamentary Debates*, 236–7; Bennett, *George Higinbotham*, 69.

38 A.G.L. Shaw, 'Verdon, Sir George Frederic (1834–1896)', *Australian Dictionary of Biography*, Vol. 6.

39 George Higinbotham to Sir Charles Darling, Minute of 16 April 1864, quoted in Morris, *A Memoir of George Higinbotham*, 113.

40 Morris, *A Memoir of George Higinbotham*, 115.

41 'The Report on the New Constitution' (Leading article), *Melbourne Morning Herald* (*MMH*), 4 January 1854.

42 Morris, *A Memoir of George Higinbotham*, 112–16.

43 'The Legislative Council: 31 January', *Argus*, 1 February 1865, 5.

44 *Ibid*.

45 *Ibid*.

46 'The Loddon Election' (Leading article), *MMH*, 10 June 1854.

13: The Struggle for the Public Purse

1 *Australian News for Home Readers*, 25 September 1865, 15. This table gives the population of Victoria for March 1865 as 610,893 and notes that there had been an increase during the previous quarter of 5,770.

2 C.E. Sayers, 'Syme, David (1827–1908)', *Australian Dictionary of Biography* (*ADB*), Vol. 6.

3 N.G. Butlin, *Australian Domestic Product, Investment and Foreign Borrowing 1861–1938/39*, 160; H.G. Turner, *A History of the Colony of Victoria from Its Discovery to Its Absorption into the Commonwealth of Australia*, Vol. 2, 116. Turner presents a contrary view, stating that the Colony was 'basking in prosperity', and disapproving of the popular demand for protection of native industries.

4 Editorial (unnamed), *Argus*, 20 September 1864.

5 Leading article (unnamed), *Argus*, 22 September 1864, 4.

6 Leading article (unnamed), *Argus*, 21 September 1864, 4.

7 *Ibid*.

8 Edward E. Morris, *A Memoir of George Higinbotham: An Australian Politician and Chief Justice of Victoria*, 107.

9 *Ibid*, 95.

10 *Ibid*, 118.

11 Frank Crowley, 'Aspects of the Constitutional Conflicts between the Two Houses of the Victorian Legislature, 1864–1868', quoted in Charles Parkinson, *Sir William Stawell and the Victorian Constitution*, 80.

12 Gwyneth M. Dow, *George Higinbotham: Church and State*, 32.

13 *Ibid.*

14 *Ibid*, 33.

15 Morris, *A Memoir of George Higinbotham*, 99.

16 Robin Gollan, *Radical and Working Class Politics: A Study of Eastern Australia, 1850–1910*, 55.

17 Dorothy P. Clarke, 'The Colonial Office and the Constitutional Crises in Victoria: 1865–68', 163.

18 Paragraph 21 of the Petition quoted in full in 'The Political Situation', *Argus*, 25 September 1865, 5, 6.

19 *Ibid*, paragraph 24.

20 Enclosure in Despatch No. 152, Darling to Cardwell, 23 December 1865.

21 Morris, *A Memoir of George Higinbotham*, 120.

22 J.M. Bennett, *George Higinbotham: Third Chief Justice of Victoria*, 81.

23 Darling to Cardwell, No. 152, 23 December 1865.

24 *Stevenson v. The Queen* (1865) 2 W.W. & a'B. (L.) 148.

25 *Stevenson v. The Queen* (1865) 2 W.W. & a'B. (L.) 149.

26 Cardwell to Darling, 26 January 1866, quoted in Bennett, *George Higinbotham*, 82.

27 Paragraph 23 of the Petition quoted in full in 'The Political Situation', *Argus*, 25 September 1865, 5, 6.

28 Bennett, *George Higinbotham*, 82–3.

29 Morris, *A Memoir of George Higinbotham*, 103.

30 Gollan, *Radical and Working Class Politics*, 55.

31 Morris, *A Memoir of George Higinbotham*, 103.

32 *Ibid*, 107.

33 Bennett, *George Higinbotham*, 84.

34 Morris, *A Memoir of George Higinbotham*, 107.

35 'Mr Higinbotham at Brighton', *Argus*, 29 January 1867, 6.

36 See Chapter 11, section 'The incubus of the Council'.

37 Bennett, *George Higinbotham*, 84.

38 Minute by Cardwell, 17 November 1865, C.O. 309/74, quoted in Clarke, 'The Colonial Office and the Constitutional Crises in Victoria: 1865–68', 161.

39 *Ibid*, 86.

40 Bennett, *George Higinbotham*, 87; Morris, *A Memoir of George Higinbotham*, 133.

41 Speech on Darling's Treatment, Morris, *A Memoir of George Higinbotham*, 129–31.

42 Bennett, *George Higinbotham*, 88.

43 'Letter from Lord Carnarvon to the Spreaker of the Legislative Assembly', laid before the Assembly on 19 February 1867; Morris, *A Memoir of George Higinbotham*, 134.

44 *Ibid.*

45 Clarke, 'The Colonial Office and the Constitutional Crises in Victoria: 1865–68', 167.

46 Turner, *A History of the Colony of Victoria*, Vol. 2, 144.

47 Manners Sutton to Buckingham No. 148, 26 October 1867, C.O. 309/84, *Ibid*.

48 Turner, *A History of the Colony of Victoria*, Vol. 2, 144; Clarke, 'The Colonial Office and the Constitutional Crises in Victoria: 1865–68', 168–9.

49 Minutes by Rogers (undated), Adderley (26 May 1868) and Buckingham (25 and 27 May 1868), quoted in Clarke, 'The Colonial Office and the Constitutional Crises in Victoria 1865–68', 169.

50 Morris, *A Memoir of George Higinbotham*, 140.

51 *Ibid*, 141.

52 Dow, *George Higinbotham*, 36.

53 Turner, *A History of the Colony of Victoria*, Vol. 2, 137.

54 Bruce Knox, 'Imperial Consequences of Constitutional Problems in New South Wales and Victoria 1865–1870', (1985), 515–17.

55 Colonial Office 323/77/175, quoted in Geoffrey Serle, *The Golden Age: A History of the Colony of Victoria 1851–1861*, 197.

56 <http://search.slv.vic.gov.au/MAIN:Everything:SLV_VOYAGER1635430>. See online <http://eurekapedia.org/Bendigo_Goldfields_Petition>.

57 *Ibid*.

58 Graeme Tucker, 'Chronology', in Ian MacFarlane, *Eureka from the Official Records*, 188, 189.

59 'Bendigo: From Our Own Correspondent: 2 January 1854', *Melbourne Morning Herald* (*MMH*), 5 January 1854.

60 *Australian and New Zealand Gazette*, 1854, 487.

61 'Bendigo: From Our Own Correspondent', *MMH*, 16 January 1854.

62 'Bendigo: From Our Own Correspondent: 2 January 1854', *MMH*, 5 January 1854 – Report of Public Meeting held at View Point, Bendigo, 31 December 1853; 'Bendigo: From Our Own Correspondent', *MMH*, 2 September 1854.

63 *MMH*, 2, 7 and 23 February 1854. See also Serle, *The Golden Age*, 108.

64 'News from the Goldfields of Bendigo', *Australian and New Zealand Gazette*, 24 June 1854, 584.

65 MacFarlane, *Eureka from the Official Records*. Tucker's 'Chronology' of events on the goldfields, located at the back of MacFarlane's book, does not mention some of the public meetings that were reported in the *Melbourne Morning Herald*.

66 'Bendigo: From Our Own Correspondent', *MMH*, 1 September 1854.

67 'The Principles and Objects of the Ballarat Reform League', in *MacFarlane, Eureka from the Official Records*, 207. See also Andrew Messner, 'Land, Leadership, Culture and Emigration: Some Problems in Chartist Historiography'.

68 See Chapter 3.

69 'The New Constitution', *Australian and New Zealand Gazette*, 17 June 1854, 558; 'Defects of the New Constitution', *Australian and New Zealand Gazette*, 1 July 1854, 67.

70 Serle, *The Golden Age*, 198, 195.

71   <http://www.thecanadianencyclopedia.ca/en/article/province-of-canada-1841-67/>.

72   Speech on the Resolutions, Morris, *A Memoir of George Higinbotham*, 183.

73   'A Jesuitical Apology' (Leading article), *Herald*, 8 December 1855.

14: The Aftermath of the Struggle

1   A Royal Commission to Inquire Into and Report Upon the Operation of the System of Public Education in the Colony of Victoria.

2   Gwyneth M. Dow, *George Higinbotham: Church and State*, 65.

3   Henry Gyles Turner, *A History of the Colony of Victoria from Its Discovery to Its Absorption into the Commonwealth of Australia*, Vol. 2, 164.

4   A Bill to Amend the Law Relating to Public Instruction, 1867.

5   'Mr Aspinall at Buninyong', *Argus*, 18 December 1865, 7.

6   *Ibid.*

7   Editorial, *Argus*, 7 December 1865. 4.

8   Leading article (unnamed), *Argus*, 4 December 1865, 4, 5; *Argus*, 20 December 1865, 4.

9   Editorial (unnamed), *Argus*, 20 December 1865.

10   Stuart Macintyre, *A Colonial Liberalism: The Lost World of Three Victorian Visionaries*, 52.

11   Turner, *A History of the Colony of Victoria*, Vol. 2, 139.

12   'Sir Francis Murphy on Election', *Ballarat Star*, 29 December 1865, 3.

13   Editorial (unnamed), *Argus*, 6 October 1870, 4.

14   *Ibid*, 5.

15   *Ibid.*

16   Sean Farrell, *Rituals and Riot: Sectarian Violence and Political Culture in Ulster 1784–1886*, 45–6.

17   Geraldine Moore, 'The Young George Higinbotham: 1826–1856', 47–50.

18   Edward E. Morris, *A Memoir of George Higinbotham: An Australian Politician and Chief Justice of Victoria*, 273.

19   'Third Report of the Select Committee appointed to Inquire into the Nature, Character, Extent and Tendency of Orange Lodges, Associations or Societies in Ireland', *Sessional Papers*, House of Lords, 3 July 1835, Vol. 24. See also Chapter 8.

20   Moore, 'The Young George Higinbotham', 44–9.

21   Macintyre, *A Colonial Liberalism*, 60.

22   Margaret Kiddle, *Men of Yesterday: A Social History of the Western District of Victoria 1834–1890*, 249; J.E. Senyard, 'Glass, Hugh, 1817–1871', *Australian Dictionary of Biography* (*ADB*), Vol. 4.

23   J.M. Bennett, *Sir William Stawell: Second Chief Justice of Victoria: 1857–1886*, 123.

24   Kiddle, *Men of Yesterday*, 259–60.

25 *Ibid*, 124.

26 See Chapter 11.

27 Charles Parkinson, *Sir William Stawell and the Victorian Constitution*, 71–2.

28 Speeches on the Resolutions, Morris, *A Memoir of George Higinbotham*, 176.

29 Morris, *A Memoir of George Higinbotham*, 160.

30 *Ibid*, 161.

31 *Ibid*, 181–2.

32 *Ibid*, 177.

33 *Ibid*, 177–8; Bruce Knox, 'Imperial Consequences of Constitutional Problems in New South Wales and Victoria 1865–1870'.

34 Morris, *A Memoir of George Higinbotham*, 171.

35 Quoted by Higinbotham during his speech on the five resolutions. *Ibid*, 173.

36 'The Legislative Council: 25 January', *Melbourne Morning Herald* (*MMH*), 26 January 1854.

37 Morris, *A Memoir of George Higinbotham*, 174.

38 *Ibid*, 184.

39 *Ibid*, 188–9.

40 Parkinson, *Sir William Stawell and the Victorian Constitution*, 69.

41 'The General Election: Mr Higinbotham at Brighton', *Argus*, 10 March 1871, 5.

42 Morris, *A Memoir of George Higinbotham*, 191.

43 *An Act to Amend the Law relating to Education* (1872) Vic. 447.

44 Ann Shorten, 'Matters of Fact and Fiction: The Lauriston School Cases, 1871 and 1872', 8; Geraldine Moore, 'The Victorian Education Act of 1872: A New View', 42–52.

45 John Tregenza, *Professor of Democracy: The Life of Charles Henry Pearson, Oxford Don and Australian Radical: 1830–1894*, 123–4.

46 Susan Priestley, 'In Defence of George Higinbotham: New Evidence on Family Relationships', 17.

15: Last Years in Parliament

1 'Mr Higinbotham at Brunswick', *Leader*, 17 May 1873, 20.

2 *Ibid*, 21.

3 *Ibid*.

4 'Mr Higinbotham at Brunswick', *Argus*, 22 May 1873, 7.

5 'Mr Higinbotham at Brunswick', *Leader*, 17 May 1873, 21.

6 Edward E. Morris, *A Memoir of George Higinbotham: An Australian Politician and Chief Justice of Victoria*, 192.

7 Leading article (unnamed), *Argus*, 24 May 1873, 4.

8 *Victorian Parliamentary Debates*, Vol. 17, 1438–43; Geoffrey R. Quaife, 'The Nature of Political Conflict in Victoria, 1856-1857', 478–80.

9 *Victorian Parliamentary Debates*, Vol. 16, 596–9.

10 *Votes & Proceedings*, Legislative Council, 1872, Vol. 2, 1364.

11 *An Act to Make Better Provision for the Public Service of Victoria* (1883), Vic. 1273.

12 *An Act to Amend 'The Married Women's Property Act'* (1882), Vic. 1236.

13 Hansard, Vol. 11, 416, quoted in Stuart Macintyre, *A Colonial Liberalism: The Lost World of Three Victorian Visionaries*, 247, n. 47.

14 Leading article (unnamed), *Argus*, 18 December 1865, 4.

15 'Italic Virtue' (editorial), *Herald*, 7 June 1856. See also Geraldine Moore, 'The Young George Higinbotham: 1826–1856', 278.

16 'A Congratulatory Effusion', *Melbourne Punch*, 12 May 1870, 151.

17 Susan Priestley, *Henrietta Augusta Dugdale: An Activist: 1827–1918*, 104.

18 *An Act to Amend the Law relating to the Property of Married Women* (1870), Vict. 384; *Table Talk*, 20 October 1899, 6.

19 'An Appeal to Mr Higinbotham', *Argus*, 13 April 1869, 7.

20 *Argus*, 8 April 1869, 5.

21 Susan Priestley, 'In Defence of George Higinbotham: New Evidence on Family Relationships', 23; Moore, 'The Young George Higinbotham', 25–8.

22 Priestley, 'In Defence of George Higinbotham', 24; Moore, 'The Young George Higinbotham', 32–3.

23 Moore, 'The Young George Higinbotham', 31–2.

24 Copy of the Last Will & Testament with Three Codicils (1809) of Joseph Wilson, late of the City of Dublin, merchant and American Consul, deceased. Original perished. Exemplified copy of same, as recorded in Will Book 6, 105–20, of Register of Wills Office, Philadelphia, Pennsylvania, USA, copied by Henry Hollingsworth, 3250 W. 108th St, Inglewood, California, USA, from microfilms of said Will Books. Original grant registered in Prerogative Grants Index, 1815, folio 198. Copy supplied to the writer courtesy of Rory Delany of the Strand Street Unitarian Church, Dublin.

25 Macintyre, *A Colonial Liberalism*, 221.

26 Will of Margaret Higinbotham, VPRS 000028/P0003, Unit 000310.

27 Priestley, 'In Defence of George Higinbotham', 23.

28 Will of Sarah Higinbotham (certified copy), T6301, National Archives of Ireland, Dublin.

29 Morris, *A Memoir of George Higinbotham*, 25, 234, 318.

30 *Ibid*, 56.

31 K.D. Reynolds, 'Molesworth, Andalusia Grant, Lady Molesworth (c.1809–1888)', *Oxford Dictionary of National Biography*.

32 *Trinity College Dublin Journal, 1843–1849* (Journals of the College Historical Society), Mun/soc/hist/26.

33 Morris, *A Memoir of George Higinbotham*, 15.

34 *Ibid*, 13; Dean Hussey Burgh Macartney Files, MS 10924, Vol. 1, State Library of Victoria.

35 J.M. Bennett, *George Higinbotham: Third Chief Justice of Victoria*, 5.

36 Morris, *A Memoir of George Higinbotham*, 15.

37 R.B. McDowell and D.A. Webb, *Trinity College Dublin: 1592–1952*, 115–20.

38 Morris, *A Memoir of George Higinbotham*, 15.

39 *Ibid*, 14.

40 Priestley, *Henrietta Augusta Dugdale*, 133.

41 H.A. Dugdale, *A Few Hours in a Far-Off Age*, 22.

42 Priestley, *Henrietta Augusta Dugdale*, 158.

43 Morris, *A Memoir of George Higinbotham*, 281.

44 The Hon. Alfred Deakin, *The Crisis in Victorian Politics 1879 to 1881: A Personal Retrospect*, 65.

45 Denis Grundy, *Free, Secular and Compulsory: An Introduction to the Education Act of 1872*, 57; J.S. Gregory, *Church and State*, 137.

46 'O'Shanassy, Sir John (1818–1883)', *Australian Dictionary of Biography (ADB)*, Vol. 5.

47 Charles Parkinson, *Sir William Stawell and the Victorian Constitution*, 82–5.

48 *Ibid*, 87.

49 *Ibid*, 88–9.

50 *Ibid*, 86. See footnote 89.

51 *Ibid*, 90.

52 Robert Herbert, 25 December 1875, Minute attached to letter from Sir William Stawell, Acting Governor of Victoria, to Lord Carnarvon, Secretary of State for the Colonies, 4 November 1875, CO 309/113 (AJCP), quoted in Parkinson, *Sir William Stawell and the Victorian Constitution*, 90.

53 H.G. Turner, *A History of the Colony of Victoria from Its Discovery to Its Absorption into the Commonwealth of Australia*, Vol. 2, 185.

54 Morris, *A Memoir of George Higinbotham*, 195.

55 'Letter to the Electors of East Bourke Boroughs', *Ibid*, 196.

56 Geoffrey Serle, 'Service, James (1823–1899)', *ADB*, Vol. 6.

16: Supreme Court Judge

1 *Argus*, 29 May 1878. 5.

2 Geoffrey Bartlett, 'Berry, Sir Graham (1822–1904), *Australian Dictionary of Biography (ADB)*, Vol. 3.

3 Geoffrey Serle, *The Rush to Be Rich: A History of the Colony of Victoria: 1883–1889*, 8.

4 *An Act to Impose a Land Tax 1877* (Vic.), 1525.

5 John Tregenza, *Professor of Democracy: The Life of Charles Henry Pearson, Oxford Don and Australian Radical: 1830–1894*, 133.

6 Geraldine Moore, 'The Victorian Education Act of 1872: A New View', 161–70.

7   Joy Enid Parnaby, 'The Economic and Political Development of Victoria 1877–1881', 28.

8   R.L. Wettenhall, 'Higinbotham, Thomas 1819–1880', *ADB*, Vol. 4.

9   'The Town', *Leader*, 8 February 1879; Edward E. Morris, *A Memoir of George Higinbotham: An Australian Politician and Chief Justice of Victoria*, 258.

10 Henry Gyles Turner, *A History of the Colony of Victoria from Its Discovery to Its Absorption into the Commonwealth of Australia*, Vol. 2, 212.

11 Higinbotham to Service, 16 July 1880, La Trobe Library, Melbourne, Australian Manuscripts Collection, MS10035, p. 8. Quoted in J.M. Bennett, *George Higinbotham: Third Chief Justice of Victoria*, 123.

12 Letter to Richard Richardson, 29 July 1880, Morris, *A Memoir of George Higinbotham*, 259.

13 Serle, *The Rush to Be Rich*, 32.

14 Charles Parkinson, *Sir William Stawell and the Victorian Constitution*, 102.

15 *Ibid*, 103.

16 *Ibid*, 107.

17 Bennett, *George Higinbotham*, 124.

18 *Ibid*, 153.

19 *Ibid*, 155–6.

20 'The Prerogative of Mercy', *Argus*, 9 January 1886, 10.

21 Letter to the Right Honourable Sir Henry T. Holland, Bart., GCMG, 28 February 1887, Part 4, Morris, *A Memoir of George Higinbotham*, 216.

22 *Ibid*, Part 6, 219.

23 'A Working Man's College', *Herald*, 17 December 1881, 2.

24 'The Proposed Working Men's College', *Argus*, 20 June 1882, 6.

25 <http://www.kingscollections.org/catalogues/kclca/collection/m/10ma85-1>.

26 <https://www.britannica.com/biography/Frederick-Denison-Maurice>.

27 <http://diobeth.typepad.com/files/holy-women-holy-men.pdf>.

28 'The Working Man's College', *Age*, 27 June 1882.

29 'The Working Men's College', *Argus*, 27 June 1882, 6.

30 Stephen Murray-Smith and Anthony John Dare, *The Tech: A Centenary History of the Royal Melbourne Institute of Technology*, 123, 210.

17: Chief Justice Higinbotham

1   Higinbotham to Kerferd, 14 May 1866, quoted in J.M. Bennett, *George Higinbotham: Third Chief Justice of Victoria*, 157.

2   Jill Eastwood, 'Wrixon, Henry John (1839–1913)', *Australian Dictionary of Biography (ADB)*, Vol. 6.

3   Cambridge Alumni Database, University of Cambridge, online <http://venn.lib.cam.ac.uk/cgi-bin/search-2016.pl?sur=&suro=w&fir=&firo=c&cit=&cito=c&c=all&z=all&tex=HLNT843HT&sye=&eye=&col=all&maxcount=50>.

4   'Death of Chief Justice Higinbotham' (Obit.), *Argus*, 2 January 1893, 6.

5   Edward E. Morris, *A Memoir of George Higinbotham: An Australian Politician and Chief Justice of Victoria*, 201–2. The first of these two letters is printed as an Appendix to Chapter 20 of Morris's memoir.

6   Part 6, Letter to the Right Honourable Sir Henry T. Holland, Bart., GCMG, 28 February 1887, in Morris, *A Memoir of George Higinbotham*, 218.

7   Morris, *A Memoir of George Higinbotham*, 201.

8   *Ibid*. Morris does not include the subsequent letter with the reference to 'the sinister and clandestine policy' but extracts this quotation only.

9   Part 6, Letter to the Right Honourable Sir Henry T. Holland, Bart., GCMG, 28 February 1887, in Morris, *A Memoir of George Higinbotham*, 214–15.

10 'The Chief Justice and the Governorship', Letter to the editor from Sir Archibald Michie QC, *Argus*, 22 February 1889, 5.

11 K.H. Bailey, 'Self-Government in Australia, 1860–1900', 401; Bennett, *George Higinbotham*, 216, 217.

12 Geoffrey Serle, *The Rush to Be Rich: A History of the Colony of Victoria 1883–1889*, 304; Davis McCaughey, Naomi Perkins and Angus Trumble, *Victoria's Colonial Governors 1839–1900*, 260.

13 Morris, *A Memoir of George Higinbotham*, 294.

14 Geoffrey Serle, 'Mackinnon, Donald (1859–1932)', *ADB*, Vol. 10.

15 Bennett, *George Higinbotham*, 229.

16 Jarlath Ronayne, *The Irish in Australia: Rogues and Reformers, First Fleet to Federation*, 126–30.

17 'Distressed Lawyers' (Leading article), *Melbourne Morning Herald* (*MMH*), 10 May 1854.

18 Sue Reynolds, 'The Old Supreme Court of Victoria Buildings', 241.

19 'Mr Pohlman's Resignation' (Leading article), *MMH*, 26 October 1854.

20 Morris, *A Memoir of George Higinbotham*, 265.

21 Andrew Markus, *Fear and Hatred: Purifying Australia and California 1850–1901*, 249.

22 'Sir Henry Parkes and the Chinese', *Western Mail* (Perth), 19 May 1888, 22.

23 Markus, *Fear and Hatred*, 256.

24 'Sir Henry Parkes and the Chinese', *Western Mail* (Perth), 19 May 1888, 22.

25 Bennett, *George Higinbotham*, 192.

26 Charles Parkinson, *Sir William Stawell and the Victorian Constitution*, 116.

27 *Toy v Musgrove* (1888), 14 *VLR*, 349, 395 (Higinbotham CJ); David Wood, 'Responsible Government in the Australian Colonies: *Toy v. Musgrove* Reconsidered', 776–7.

28 Sir Ninian Stephen, 'George Higinbotham', Daniel Mannix Memorial Lecture, Melbourne University, 13 September 1983, Papers of Sir Ninian Stephen (Manuscript), 1982–1998, National Library of Australia, 28.

29 Serle, *The Rush to Be Rich*, 304.

30 Robin Gollan, *Radical and Working Class Politics: A Study of Eastern Australia, 1850–1910*, 58.

31 'The Legislative Council: 5 December', *Argus*, 6 December 1855, 5.

32 *The Great Maritime Strike of 1890: Report of Committee of Finance and Control* (Trades Hall Council) (Melbourne: H.W. Mills & Co.), 1891, 9, 10.

33 Stuart Svensen, *The Sinews of War: Hard Cash and the 1890 Maritime Strike*, xi.

34 *Ibid.*

35 *Ibid*, xvii.

36 *Ibid*, 244.

37 *Ibid*, 243.

38 'The Maritime Dispute of 1891', *Adelaide Register*, 17 November 1909, 8.

39 'Death of Colonel Tom Price' (Obit.), *Age*, 4 July 1911, 7.

40 *Victorian Parliamentary Debates*, Vol. 85, 1309, quoted in S.M. Ingham, 'Some Aspects of Victorian Liberalism: 1880–1900', 147.

41 *The Great Maritime Strike of 1890*, 26, 27. The final quote is from a speech by Lady Macbeth in William Shakespeare's play *Macbeth*, Act 1, Scene 5.

42 *The Great Maritime Strike of 1890*, 31.

43 *Ibid*, 35.

44 S. Merrifield, 'Douglass, Benjamin (1830–1904)', *ADB*, Vol. 4.

45 Morris, *A Memoir of George Higinbotham*, 285.

46 Reproduced in E.J. Holloway, 'From Labour Council to Privy Council', Typescript, Holloway Papers, National Library of Australia, MS 2098. Quoted in Stuart Macintyre, '"The Blessed Reign of Mobocracy": George Higinbotham and the Maritime Strike', 60.

47 Price Warung, *Bulletin*, 7 January 1893, 9.

48 Gwyneth M. Dow, 'Higinbotham, George (1826–1892)', *ADB*, Vol. 4.

Conclusion

1 Edward E. Morris, *A Memoir of George Higinbotham: An Australian Politician and Chief Justice of Victoria*, 309.

2 S. Merrifield, 'Douglass, Benjamin (1830–1904)', *Australian Dictionary of Biography (ADB)*, Vol. 4; J.M. Bennett, *George Higinbotham: Third Chief Justice of Victoria*, 249.

3 Morris, *A Memoir of George Higinbotham*, 311.

4 Bennett, *George Higinbotham*, 250–6.

5 Leading article (unnamed), *Argus*, 2 January 1893, 4.

6 Morris, *A Memoir of George Higinbotham*, ix.

7 *Ibid*, 36.

8 Stuart Macintyre, 'The Political Penance of George Higinbotham', Unpublished paper.

9   Geraldine Moore, 'The Young George Higinbotham: 1826–1856', Appendix A.

10   The motto means 'you will succeed by persevering'.

11   'Political Retrospect: Summary for Europe', *Herald*, 30 January 1856; 'The Constitutional Question' (Editorial), *Herald*, 13 February 1856. See also Chapters 6, 7.

12   For Captain and Mrs Devlin, see Chapter 2. For Colonel Sir William Verner, see Chapter 14. For William Higinbotham, see Chapter 15.

13   Geoffrey Serle, *The Rush to Be Rich: A History of the Colony of Victoria 1883–1889*, 7. See also Geoffrey Serle, 'The Gold Generation', 269.

14   Raymond Wright, *A Blended House: A History of the Legislative Council of Victoria 1851–1856*, 63; Sir Zelman Cowen, 'A Historical Survey of the Victorian Constitution, 1856–1956', 13.

15   Amongst those who view the 1855 Constitution positively are: Charles Parkinson, *Sir William Stawell and the Victorian Constitution*; J.M. Main, 'Making Constitutions in New South Wales and Victoria 1853–1854', 73; Wright, *A Blended House*, 63; and Cowen, 'A Historical Survey of the Victorian Constitution, 1856–1956', 13.

16   Parkinson, *Sir William Stawell*, 73.

17   See Chapter 3.

18   See

19   See Chapter 11 for Dill, Chapter 14 for Glass.

20   See Chapter 12.

21   See Chapter 15.

22   Jarlath Ronayne, *The Irish in Australia: Rogues and Reformers, First Fleet to Federation*, 30; Fergus Whelan, *Dissent Into Treason: Unitarians, King-Killers and the Society of United Irishmen*, 158.

23   Gordon Goodwin, 'Foster, John Leslie (1780/81?–1842)', rev. Sinéad Agnew, *Oxford Dictionary of National Biography*, online edition January 2008, <http://www.oxforddnb.com/view/article/9963>.

24   Ronayne, *The Irish in Australia*, 107.

25   Carole Woods, 'Griffith, Charles James (1808–1863)', *ADB*, Vol. 4.

26   A.F. Kimber, 'Chomley, Hussey Malone (1832–1906)', *ADB*, Vol. 3.

27   Ronayne, *The Irish in Australia*, 108.

28   *The Review of Reviews* (Australasian edition), 20 May 1895, 509.

29   Bennett, *George Higinbotham*, 116.

30   Charles Parkinson, 'George Higinbotham and Responsible Government in Colonial Victoria', 181.

31   A.C.V. Melbourne, 'The Establishment of Responsible Government', 277; Geoffrey Blainey, *The Story of Australia's People: The Rise and Rise of a New Australia*.

32   Sean Scalmer, 'Containing Contention: A Reinterpretation of Democratic Change and Electoral Reform in the Australian Colonies', 337.

33 Bennett, *George Higinbotham*, 116.

34 *Melbourne Morning Herald* (*MMH*), 7 February 1854; 'The Legislative Council: 3 February', *MMH*, 4 February 1854.

35 'Report on the New Constitution' (Leading article), *MMH*, 20 December 1853; 'The New Constitution', *Argus*, 12 December 1853, 5; 'Constitutions for Australia', *Argus*, 5 January 1854, 4.

36 Morris, *A Memoir of George Higinbotham*, 232.

37 *Ibid*, 231.

38 Geoffrey Bartlett. 'Political Organisation and Society in Victoria 1864–1883', 198, 199; Ronald Fogarty, *Catholic Education in Australia 1806-1950*, Vol. 1, 141; The Hon. Michael Kirby, 'Secularism and Constitutionalism: The Legacy of George Higinbotham'.

39 Morris, *A Memoir of George Higinbotham*, 322.

40 'The Representation of Brighton', *Argus*, 13 May 1861, 5.

41 Gwyneth M. Dow, *George Higinbotham: Church and State*, 103.

42 *The Higinbotham Report: Summary of Recommendations*; Dow, *George Higinbotham*, 194, Appendix A (Discussion) and 93.

43 Price Warung, 'The Greatest of Australia's Dead', *Bulletin*, 7 January 1893.

44 Geoffrey Serle, 'The Victorian Legislative Council: 1856–1950'.

45 Parkinson, *Sir William Stawell and the Victorian Constitution*, 117; David Dunstan, 'Exhibition Review: Naked Democracy: Governing Victoria 1856–2006', 230–1.

46 Parkinson, *Sir William Stawell and the Victorian Constitution*, 118.

Appendix

1 Edward E. Morris, *A Memoir of George Higinbotham: An Australian Politician and Chief Justice of Victoria*, 240.

2 *Ibid*, 56.

3 *Ibid*, 57.

4 'The Fourth of July' (Leading article), *Herald*, 4 July 1856; 'The Anniversary of American Independence' (Editorial), *Argus*, 4 July 1857. There are also striking similarities between a leading article in the *Melbourne Morning Herald*, 22 March 1854, entitled 'Public Education Bill' and Higinbotham's 'Speech to the Electors of Brighton', *Argus*, 13 May 1861.

ACKNOWLEDGEMENTS

My interest in Higinbotham started in about 1995, when my friend Frances Scholtz lent me her copy of Professor Stuart Macintyre's book, *A Colonial Liberalism: The Lost World of Three Victorian Visionaries*. It stimulated my interest to know more, particularly about one of the three: George Higinbotham. In 2016, I was surprised and delighted when I discovered that Professor Macintyre had examined my PhD thesis on Higinbotham's early life. Since then, he has encouraged me to expand the thesis into a book, and has provided much helpful advice.

In the century and a quarter since George Higinbotham died, a number of scholars have written about his life. They have done so under difficulty, because so many of the primary sources have been lost. In writing this account of his life, I acknowledge the pioneering works of a number of historians who have embarked upon this challenge. His contemporaries who knew him – such as Edward Morris, Henry Gyles Turner, Price Warung and George Rusden – have woven their own first-hand impressions of the man into their works. Their divergent views about Higinbotham are fascinating, and as much a part of the story as Higinbotham himself. In the twentieth century, historians such as Gwyneth Dow, Geoffrey Serle, Manning Clark and Stuart Macintyre examined Higinbotham's contributions to Victoria's history, particularly in the areas of public education, constitutional law and advocacy of liberal political ideals. In the twenty-first century, historians such as John Bennett and Charles Parkinson have more closely examined Higinbotham's role in the legal and constitutional history of Victoria. Susan Priestley has explored his work for women's rights, and in the process revealed new information about his early life and that of his wife, Margaret. This work builds upon the foundations that these and other historians have laid.

Special thanks are due to the supervisors of my PhD study into George Higinbotham's early life – Professor Christina Twomey, Dr David Dunstan and Professor John Rickard – and also to Dr Kate Cregan. I benefited considerably from the research skills that I gained under the collaborative learning model from the staff of the Matheson Library at Monash University, including Dr Jenny Casey and Dr Anne Holloway, and from their encouragement. I also gratefully acknowledge the help of Dr Georgina Heydon of RMIT University. I was extremely fortunate to receive guidance in using the Irish sources from Dr Breandán Ó Conaire of Dublin City University and Dr Jacqueline Hill of Maynooth University. The Reverend Bridget Spain and Mr Rory Delany of the Strand Street Unitarian Church in Dublin provided valuable assistance in researching Higinbotham's mother's family, the Wilsons. Mary and Jonathan Smyth of the Cavan Library and Archives in Ireland kindly assisted me with finding resources regarding Higinbotham's headmaster, the Reverend John Darley. I also acknowledge the help of the staff of Trinity College in Dublin, the National Library of Ireland and the Public Record Office of Northern Ireland. This book could not have been written without the rich resources of the State Library of Victoria, and of their helpful staff, particularly including Paul Dee. I also received assistance from Jon Breukel of the Parliamentary Library, Melbourne. I thank Lovell Chen Pty Ltd, Architects and Heritage Consultants, for permission to use the image on the front cover, and Liz Beattie, Trades Hall Literary Institute and Project Officer, for her enthusiastic support of this project. My husband Dr Garry Moore took a keen interest in the project, advised on some of the legal aspects and greatly encouraged my work. I thank him for his forbearance with what has become a lengthy project.

I have greatly appreciated working with the team of Australian Scholarly Publishing: the publisher, Nick Walker, the editor, Diane Carlyle, the manager, Anastasia Buryak, and the graphic designer, Wayne Saunders. I thank them for their work in bringing this project to fruition.

Geraldine Moore

BIBLIOGRAPHY

Books and journal articles

Articles from the *Australian Dictionary of Biography* and the *Oxford Dictionary of National Biography* are available online, respectively at <http://www.adb.anu.edu.au> and <http://www.oxforddnb.com>, and have not been included in this list.

Bagehot, Walter, *The English Constitution*, London: Nelson, 1865; 2nd edition, 1872.

Bailey, K.H., 'Self-Government in Australia, 1860–1900', in *The Cambridge History of the British Empire*, Vol. 7, 395–432, edited by J. Holland Rose, A.P. Newton and E.A. Benians, London: Cambridge University Press, 1929.

Bartlett, Geoffrey, 'Political Organisation and Society in Victoria: 1864–1883', PhD thesis, Australian National University, 1964.

Bate, Weston, *A History of Brighton*, Melbourne: Melbourne University Press, 1962; 1983, 2nd edition.

——— *Lucky City: The First Generation at Ballarat: 1851–1901*, Melbourne: Melbourne University Press, 1978.

Bennett, J.M., *Sir William Stawell: Second Chief Justice of Victoria: 1857–1886*, Sydney: Federation Press, 2004.

——— *George Higinbotham: Third Chief Justice of Victoria*, Sydney: Federation Press, 2006.

Blair, David, 'Three Melbourne Barristers: A Recollection', *Centennial Magazine*, Vol. 2, No. 9, April 1890: 692.

Blainey, Geoffrey, *The Story of Australia's People: The Rise and Rise of a New Australia*, Hawthorn, Vic.: Viking, 2016.

Blake, Laurel and Larysa Demoor, *Dictionary of Nineteenth Century Journalism in Great Britain and Ireland*, London: British Library, 2009.

Bland, William, *Letters to Charles Buller, Jnr, Esq., MP, from the Australian Patriotic Association*, Sydney: D.L. Welch (printer), Atlas Office, 1849.

Bonwick, James, *Early Struggles of the Australian Press*, Melbourne: Gordon & Gotch, 1890.

Buller, Charles, *Responsible Government for the Colonies*, London: James Ridgway, Piccadilly, 1840.

Burroughs, Peter, 'Liberal, Paternalistic or Cassandra? Earl Grey as a Critic of Colonial Self-Government', *Journal of Imperial and Commonwealth History*, 18, No. 1, 1990.

Butlin, N.G., *Australian Domestic Product, Investment and Foreign Borrowing 1861–1938/39*, Cambridge, England: Cambridge University Press, 1962.

Cannon, John Ashton, *A Dictionary of British History*, Oxford: Oxford University Press, 2009, 2nd edition.

Carboni, Raffaello, *The Eureka Stockade*, 1855, original edition; Windsor, Vic.: Currey O'Neil, 1980, reprint.

Chapman, Henry S., *Parliamentary Government or Responsible Ministries for the Australian Colonies*, Tasmania: Pratt & Sons, 1854.

Clark, Manning, *A History of Australia*, Vol. 4, Melbourne: Melbourne University Press, 1978.

Clarke, Dorothy P., 'The Colonial Office and the Constitutional Crises in Victoria 1865–68', *Historical Studies: Australia and New Zealand*, 5, No. 18, May 1952: 160–71.

Coffey, H.W., *The Anglican Church, South Melbourne, Emerald Hill Canvas Town 1852–1977*, Melbourne: Centenary Committee of the Church of England, 1947.

Corfield, J., D. Wickham and C. Gervasoni (eds), *The Eureka Encyclopedia*, Ballarat, Vic.: Ballarat Heritage Services, 2004.

Cowen, Sir Zelman, 'A Historical Survey of the Victorian Constitution: 1856–1956', *Melbourne University Law Review*, 1, No. 2, 1957: 9–63.

Crompton, Barry J., *The Visit of the CSS Shenandoah to Australia*, Melbourne: Archer Memorial Civil War Library, 2010.

——— *Dixie Down Under: Report of the Shenandoah's Cruise by James I. Waddell*, Melbourne: Archer Memorial Civil War Library, 2014.

Crowley, F.K., 'Aspects of the Constitutional Conflicts between the Two Houses of the Victorian Legislature 1864–1868', MA thesis, Melbourne University, 1947.

de Serville, Paul, *Pounds and Pedigrees: The Upper Class in Victoria, 1850–1880*, South Melbourne, Vic.: Oxford University Press, 1991.

Deakin, The Hon. Alfred, *The Crisis in Victorian Politics 1879 to 1881: A Personal Retrospect*, Carlton, Vic.: Melbourne University Press, 1957.

Dean, Arthur, *A Multitude of Counsellors: A History of the Bar of Victoria*, Melbourne, Canberra: Cheshire for the Bar Council of Victoria, 1968.

Dow, Gwyneth M., *George Higinbotham: Church and State*, Melbourne: Sir

Isaac Pitman and Sons Ltd, 1964.

Duffy, Charles Gavan, *My Life in Two Hemispheres*, Vols 1 & 2, London: Fisher Unwin, 1898.

Dugdale, H.A., *A Few Hours in a Far-Off Age*, Melbourne: McCarron, Bird & Co., 1883.

Dunstan, David, 'Exhibition Review: Naked Democracy: Governing Victoria 1856–2006', *The Victorian Historical Journal*, 27, No. 2, 2006: 229–35.

Egerton, Hugh Edward, *Selected Speeches of the Right Honourable Sir William Molesworth, Bart, MP*, London: J. Murray, 1903.

Farrell, Sean, *Rituals and Riots: Sectarian Violence and Political Culture in Ulster, 1784–1886*, Lexington, USA: University of Kentucky Press, 2000.

Fawcett, Dame Millicent Garrett, *Life of the Right Honourable Sir William Molesworth, Bart, MP, FRS*, London: McMillan & Co., 1901.

Finnane, Mark, 'Habeas Corpus Mongols – Chinese Litigants and the Politics of Immigration in 1888', *Australian Historical Studies*, 45, No. 2, 2014: 165–83.

Fitzgerald, Desmond, 'The Trillick Derailment 1854', *Clogher Record*, Vol. 15, No. 1, 1994: 31–47.

Fitzsimons, Peter, *Eureka: The Unfinished Revolution*, Sydney: William Heinemann, 2012.

Fogarty, Ronald, *Catholic Education in Australia 1806–1950*, Vol. 1, Melbourne: Melbourne University Press, 1959.

Forde, John L., *The Story of the Bar of Victoria*, Melbourne: Whitcombe & Tombs, 1913.

Forth, Gordon, 'The Anglo-Irish in Australia: Old World Origins and Colonial Experiences', in *Irish-Australian Studies: Papers Delivered at the 6th Irish-Australian Conference, July 1990*, edited by Philip Bull, Chris McConville and Noel McLachlan, Melbourne: La Trobe University, 1991.

Galbally, Ann, *Redmond Barry: An Anglo-Irish Australian*, Melbourne: Melbourne University Press, 1989.

Gollan, Robin, *Radical and Working Class Politics: A Study of Eastern Australia, 1850–1910*, Parkville, Vic.: Melbourne University Press in Association with the Australian National University, 1960.

Gregory, J.S., *Church and State*, Melbourne: Cassell, 1973.

Grote, Mrs Harriet, *The Philosophical Radicals of 1832, Comprising the Life of Sir William Molesworth and Some Incidents Connected with the Reform Movement from 1832 to 1842*, London: Savill & Edwards, 1866, online: <https://babel.hathitrust.org/cgi/pt?id=uc2.ark:/13960/t5m90913g;view=1up;seq=5>.

Grundy, Denis, *Free, Secular and Compulsory: An Introduction to the Education Act of 1872*, Carlton, Vic.: Melbourne University Press, 1972.

Hagan, Jim and Andrew Wells (eds), *The Maritime Strike: A Centennial Retrospective, Essays in Honour of E.C. Fry*, Wollongong, NSW: Five Islands Press, 1992.

Hereward Senior, 'Orangeism in Ireland and Britain', in *Studies in Irish History*, Second Series, Vol. IV, London: Routledge and Kegan Paul, 1966.

Hill, Jacqueline, 'The Protestant Response to Repeal: The Case of the Dublin Working Class', in *Ireland under the Union: Essays in Honour of T.W. Moody*, Oxford: Clarendon Press, 1980.

——— 'The Intelligentsia and Irish Nationalism in the 1840s', *Studia Hibernica*, XX, 1980: 73–109.

——— 'The 1847 General Election in Dublin City', in *Politics and Political Culture in Britain and Ireland 1750–1850*, edited by Allan Blackstock and Eoin Magennis, Essays in Tribute to Peter Jupp, Belfast: Ulster Historical Foundation, 2007.

Hirst, J.B., *The Strange Birth of a Colonial Democracy: New South Wales 1848–1884*, North Sydney: Allen and Unwin, 1988.

Ingham, S.M., 'Some Aspects of Victorian Liberalism: 1880–1900', MA thesis, Melbourne University, 1949.

Inglis, Ken S., *The Australian Colonists: An Exploration of Social History 1788–1870*, Melbourne: Melbourne University Press, 1974.

Irving, T.H., 'The Idea of Responsible Government in New South Wales before 1856', *Historical Studies: Australia and New Zealand*, 11, No. 42, 1964: 192–205.

——— '1850–1870', in *A New History of Australia*, edited by Frank Crowley, 125–65, Melbourne: Heinemann, 1974.

——— *The Southern Tree of Liberty*, Leichhardt, NSW: Federation Press, 2006.

Jenks, Edward, *The Government of Victoria*, London: Macmillan, 1891.

Kelly, Mary C., *The Shamrock and the Lily: The New York Irish and the Creation of a Transatlantic Identity, 1845–1921*, New York: Peter Lang, 2005.

Kent, Bruce, 'Agitations on the Victorian Goldfields 1851–1854: An Interpretation', *Historical Studies: Australia and New Zealand*, 6, No. 23, 1954: 261–81.

Kerr, John, 'Churchill: Home of the Verners', *Review* (Craigavon Historical Society), 3, No. 6, 1993, online: <http://www.craigavonhistoricalsociety. org.uk/rev/kerrchurchill.html>.

Kiddle, Margaret, *Men of Yesterday: A Social History of the Western District of Victoria 1834–1890*, Melbourne: Melbourne University Press, 1961.

Kinealy, Christine, *This Great Calamity: The Irish Famine 1845–52*, Dublin: Gill & Macmillan, 1994.

Kirby, The Hon. Michael, 'Secularism and Constitutionalism: The Legacy of George Higinbotham', Rationalist Society of Australia, Inaugural Higinbotham Lecture, Melbourne: RMIT University, 18 March 2013, online <http://www.rationalist.com.au/secularism-and-constitutionalism-the-legacy-of-george-higginbotham/>.

Knight, Ruth, *Illiberal Liberal: Robert Lowe in New South Wales 1848–1850*, Melbourne: Melbourne University Press, 1966.

Knox, Bruce, 'Imperial Consequences of Constitutional Problems in New South Wales and Victoria 1865–1870', *Historical Studies*, 21, No. 60, 1985.

MacFarlane, Ian, *Eureka from the Official Records*, Melbourne: Public Record Office of Victoria, 1995.

Macintyre, Stuart, *A Colonial Liberalism: The Lost World of Three Victorian Visionaries*, Oxford: Oxford University Press, 1991.

——— '"The Blessed Reign of Mobocracy": George Higinbotham and the Maritime Strike', in *The Maritime Strike: A Centennial Retrospective, Essays in Honour of E.C. Fry*, edited by Jim Hagan and Andrew Wells, Wollongong, NSW: Five Islands Press, 1992.

——— 'What Makes a Good Biography?', *Adelaide Law Review*, 32, 2011: 7–16.

——— 'The Political Penance of George Higinbotham', Unpublished essay.

Macintyre, Stuart and Anna Clark, *The History Wars*, Melbourne: Melbourne University Press, 2004.

McKay, Gary, *The Sea King: The Life of James Iredell Waddell*, Edinburgh: Birlinn Ltd, 2009.

Madden, Frederick and David Fieldhouse, *Select Documents on the Constitutional History of the British Empire and Commonwealth*, Vol. 4: *Settler Self-Government and Responsible Government 1840–1900*, Documents in Imperial History (series), London: Greenwood Press, 1990.

Main, J.M., 'Making Constitutions in New South Wales and Victoria 1853–1854', *Historical Studies: Selected Articles*, No. 2, 1967: 51–74.

McCaughey, Davis, Naomi Perkins and Angus Trumble, *Victoria's Colonial Governors 1839–1900*, Carlton, Vic.: Melbourne University Press, 1993.

McConville, Sean, *Irish Political Prisoners 1848–1922: Theatres of War*, Oxon and New York: Routledge, 2003.

McDowell, R.B. and D.A. Webb, *Trinity College Dublin: 1592–1952*, London: Cambridge University Press, 1982.

McGovern, Brian P., *John Mitchel: Irish Nationalist, Southern Secessionist*, Knoxville, USA: University of Tennessee Press, 2009.

Markus, Andrew, *Fear and Hatred: Purifying Australia and California 1850–1901*, Sydney: Hale and Iremonger, 1979.

Melbourne, A.C.V., 'The Establishment of Responsible Government', in *The Cambridge History of the British Empire*, 272–95 of Vol. VII, edited by J. Holland Rose, A.P. Newton and E.A. Benians, London: Cambridge University Press, 1929.

Messner, Andrew, 'Land, Leadership, Culture and Emigration: Some Problems in Chartist Historiography', *The Historical Journal*, 42, No. 4, December 1999: 1093–109.

Mills, J.E., 'The Composition of the Victorian Parliament: 1856–1861', *Historical Studies: Australia and New Zealand*, 5, No. 1, 1942: 25–39.

Molloy, K., 'An Irish Radical and His Nephew: The Papers of John Mitchel and Sir William Hill Irvine', *La Trobe Journal*, State Library of Victoria, No. 84, Spring 2009: 37–8, 42 and 141.

Molony, John N., *Eureka*, Melbourne: Melbourne University Press, 2001.

Moore, Geraldine, 'The Victorian Education Act of 1872: A New View', MEd thesis, Monash University, 1987.

———— 'The Young George Higinbotham: 1826–1856', PhD thesis, Monash University, 2016.

Morris, Edward E., *A Memoir of George Higinbotham: An Australian Politician and Chief Justice of Victoria*, London: MacMillan & Co., 1895.

Morrison, Elizabeth, 'Government Regulation of the Newspaper Press in Nineteenth Century Victoria', *Bulletin* (Bibliographical Society of Australia and New Zealand), Vol. 13, No. 4, December 1990: 121–36.

———— 'The Contribution of the Country Press to the Making of Victoria: 1840–1890', PhD thesis, Monash University, 1991.

Munn, Charles Allen, *Three Types of Washington Portraits*, Privately printed, New York: Gilliss Press, 1908. Digitised 9 October 2007.

Murray-Smith, Stephen and Anthony John Dare, *The Tech: A Centenary History of the Royal Melbourne Institute of Technology*, South Yarra, Vic.: Hyland House, 1987.

Neale, R.S., 'H.S. Chapman and the Victorian Ballot', *Historical Studies: Australia and New Zealand*, Vol. 12, No. 48, 1967: 506–21.

Newman, Terry, 'Tasmania and the Secret Ballot', *Australian Journal of Politics and History*, Vol. 49, No. 1, 2003: 93–101.

Nowlan, Kevin B., *The Politics of Repeal: A Study in the Relations between Great Britain and Ireland 1841–1850*, London: Routledge & Kegan Paul, 1965.

O'Farrell, Patrick, *The Irish in Australia*, Kensington, NSW: New South Wales University Press, 1986.

O'Grady, Desmond, *Raffaello! Raffaello! A Biography of Raffaello Carboni*, Melbourne: Hale & Iremonger, 1985.

O'Hegarty, P.S., *John Mitchel, an Appreciation: With Some Account of Young Ireland*, Dublin: Maunsel, 1917; London: Forgotten Books, 2013, reprint.

O'Shaughnessy, Peter (ed.), *The Gardens of Hell: John Mitchel in Van Diemen's Land: 1850–1853*, Kenthurst, Kangaroo Press, 1988.

Palmer, Vance, *National Portraits*, Melbourne: Melbourne University Press, 1954, 3rd edition.

Parkhill, T. and J. Bardon et al., *The Castle and the Crown*, Belfast: The Dungannon Royal School, 2004.

Parkinson, Charles, 'George Higinbotham and Responsible Government in Colonial Victoria', *Melbourne University Law Review*, 25, 2001: 1, online: <http://www.austlii.edu.au/au/journals/MULR/2001/6.html>.

———— *Sir William Stawell and the Victorian Constitution*, Melbourne: Australian Scholarly Publishing, 2004.

———— 'William Foster Stawell and the Making of Victoria's Constitution', *Victorian Historical Journal*, 77, No. 2, 2006: 106–42.

Parnaby, Joy Enid, 'The Economic and Political Development of Victoria: 1877–1881', PhD thesis, Melbourne University, 1951.

Pickering, Paul A., 'Ripe for a Republic: British Radical Responses to the Eureka Stockade', *Australian Historical Studies*, 34, No. 121, 2003: 60–90.

Potts, E. Daniel and Annette Potts, *Young America and Australian Gold: Americans and the Gold Rush of the 1850s*, St Lucia, Qld: University of Queensland Press, 1974.

Pratt, Ambrose, *The Centenary History of Victoria*, Melbourne: Robertson & Mullens, 1934.

Priestley, Susan, *Henrietta Augusta Dugdale: An Activist: 1827–1918*, Melbourne: Melbourne Books, 2011.

———— 'In Defence of George Higinbotham: New Evidence on Family Relationships', *Royal Historical Society of Victoria Journal*, Vol. 82, No. 1, June 2011.

Quaife, Geoffrey R., 'The Nature of Political Conflict in Victoria, 1856–1857', MA thesis, Melbourne University, 1964.

Quick, John, *The History of Land Tenure in the Colony of Victoria*, Sandhurst: J.G. Edwards, *Bendigo Independent*, 1883, online <http://www5.austlii.edu.au/au/journals/AUColLawMon/1883/2.pdf>.

Rankin, D.H., 'Sir William Stawell', *The Victorian Historical Magazine*, XXVII, No. 3, 1956: 73–86.

———— 'George Higinbotham', *The Victorian Historical Magazine*, 2, No. 27, 1956: 41–56.

Reese, Trevor Richard, 'Short Notices Review of A.C.V. Melbourne's *Early Constitutional Development in Australia*', *The English Historical Review*, 81, No. 318, 1966: 206–7.

Reynolds, Sue, 'The Old Supreme Court of Victoria Buildings', *Victorian Historical Journal*, 81, No. 2, November 2010.

Roberts, Shirley, *Charles Hotham: A Biography*, Melbourne: Melbourne University Press, 1985.

Ronayne, Jarlath, *The Irish in Australia: Rogues and Reformers, First Fleet to Federation*, Camberwell, Vic.: Penguin, Viking, 2002.

Rusden, G.W., *A History of Australia*, Vol. 3, Melbourne: Melville, Mullen & Slade, 1897.

Sawer, Marian, *Elections: Full, Free and Fair*, Annandale, NSW: Federation Press, 2001.

Scalmer, Sean, 'Containing Contention: A Reinterpretation of Democratic Change and Electoral Reform in the Australian Colonies', *Australian Historical Studies*, Vol. 42, No. 3, 2011: 337–56.

Senior, Hereward, *Orangeism in Ireland and Britain*, Studies in Irish History (series), Vol. 4, London: Routledge and Kegan Paul, 1966.

Serle, Geoffrey, 'The Causes of Eureka', *Historical Studies: Australia and New Zealand* – Eureka Centenary Supplement, 1954: 15–24.

———'The Victorian Legislative Council 1856–1950', *Historical Studies: Australia and New Zealand*, Vol. 6, No. 23, 1954: 186–203.

——— 'The Gold Generation', *Victorian Historical Journal*, Vol. 41, No. 1, 1970: 265–72.

——— *The Rush to Be Rich: A History of the Colony of Victoria 1883–1889*, Melbourne: Melbourne University Press, 1974, 2nd edition.

——— *The Golden Age: A History of the Colony of Victoria 1851–1861*, Melbourne: Melbourne University Press, 1977, 3rd edition.

Shorten, Ann, 'Matters of Fact and Fiction: The Lauriston School Cases, 1871 and 1872', Unpublished essay, Education Faculty, Monash University, 1983.

Smith, Charles Patrick, 'Men Who Made the *Argus* and the *Australasian*: 1846–1923', Typescript with photos, c. 1923, State Library of Victoria.

Smith, Simon, *Judging for the People: A Social History of the Supreme Court in Victoria 1841–2016*, Sydney: Allen & Unwin, 2016.

Smyth, Terry, *Australian Confederates: How 42 Australians Joined the Rebel Cause and Fired the Last Shot in the American Civil War*, North Sydney, NSW: Ebury Press, 2015.

Smyth, Jonathon, 'John Richard Darley (1799–1884): Bishop, Scholar and Philanthropist', *Breifne* (Journal of the Briefne Historical Society), Vol. XI, No. 44, 2008: 683–710.

Spiller, Peter, 'The Legal Career of Henry Chapman in Victoria 1854–1864', *Law and History in Australia: A Collection of Papers presented at the 1989 Law and History Conference, University of Adelaide*, 1989: 47–56.

Svensen, Stuart, *The Sinews of War: Hard Cash and the 1890 Maritime Strike*, Kensington, NSW: University of New South Wales Press, 1995.

Swanzy, Henry Biddall, *The Families of French of Belturbet and Nixon of Fermanagh and Their Descendants*, Dublin: Alex, Thom & Co. Ltd, 1908, online: <http://www.ebooksread.com/authors-eng/henry-biddall-swanzy/the-families-of-french-of-belturbet-and-nixon-of-fermanagh-and-their-descendant-naw/page-14-the-families>.

Sweetman, Edward, *Constitutional Development in Victoria: 1851–1856*, Melbourne: Whitcombe & Tombs, 1920.

Taylor, Greg, *The Constitution of Victoria*, Annandale, NSW: Federation Press, 2006.

Tregenza, John, *Professor of Democracy: The Life of Charles Henry Pearson, Oxford Don and Australian Radical: 1830–1894*, Melbourne: Melbourne University Press, 1968.

Turnbull, Clive, *Eureka: The Story of Peter Lalor*, Melbourne: Hawthorn Press, 1946.

Turner, Henry Gyles, *A History of the Colony of Victoria from Its Discovery to Its Absorption into the Commonwealth of Australia*, Vols 1 & 2, London: Longmans, Green, 1904.

——— *Our Own Little Rebellion: The Story of Eureka*, Melbourne: Whitcombe & Tombs, 1913.

Verner, Thomas, 'What Is an Orangeman?', *Dublin University Magazine: A Literary and Political Journal*, Vol. 5, No. 28, 1835.

Walker, Brian, 'Politicians, Elections and Catastrophe: The General Election of 1847', *Irish Political Studies*, 22, No. 1, March 2007: 1–34.

Walshe, R.D., 'The Significance of Eureka in Australian History', *Historical Studies: Australia and New Zealand* – Eureka Centenary Supplement, 1954: 62–81.

———'Bibliography of Eureka', *Historical Studies: Australia and New Zealand* – Eureka Centenary Supplement, 1954: 81–91.

Ward, J.M., *Colonial Self-Government: The British Experience 1759–1856*, Cambridge Commonwealth Series, London: Macmillan Press Ltd, 1976.

Warren, The Hon. Marilyn, 'The Eureka Trials: 160 Years On', *Victorian Historical Journal*, 87, No. 1, 2016.

Warung, Price, 'The Greatest of Australia's Dead', *Bulletin*, 7 January 1893.

Waugh, John, 'Framing the First Victorian Constitution, 1853–5', *Monash University Law Review*, Vol. 23, No. 2, 1997: 331–61.

——— 'The Brummagem Coup: The Start of Self-Government in Victoria', *Victorian Historical Journal*, Vol. 77, No. 2, November 2006: 143–61.

Whelan, Fergus, *Dissent into Treason: Unitarians, King-Killers and the Society of United Irishmen*, Ireland: Brandon, 2010.

Wickham, D., C. Gervasoni and W. Phillipson (eds), *The Eureka Encyclopaedia*, Ballarat: Ballarat Heritage Services, 1999.

Wood, David, 'Responsible Government in the Australian Colonies: *Toy v. Musgrove* Reconsidered', *Melbourne University Law Review*, 16, No. 4, 1987: 760–83.

Woollacott, Angela, 'Frontier Violence and Settler Manhood', *History Australia*, 6, No. 1, 2009, 11.1–11.15.

——— 'A Radical's Career: Responsible Government, Settler Colonialism and Indigenous Dispossession', *Journal of Colonialism and Colonial History*, 16, No. 2, 2015, online: <https://muse.jhu.edu.ezproxy.lib. monash.edu.au/journals/journal_of_colonialism_and_colonial_history/ v016/16.2.woollacott.html>.

——— *Settler Society in the Australian Colonies: Self-Government and Imperial Culture*, Oxford: Oxford University Press, 2015.

Work, T.L., 'The Early Printers of Melbourne', *Australasian Typographical Journal*, March 1898.

Wright, Clare, *The Forgotten Rebels of Eureka*, Melbourne: Text Publishing, 2013.

Wright, Raymond, *A People's Counsel: A History of the Parliament of Victoria 1856–1890*, South Melbourne, Vic.: Oxford University Press, 1992.

——— *A Blended House: A History of the Legislative Council of Victoria 1851–1856*, Melbourne: Parliament of Victoria, 2001.

Yule, Peter, *In the Public Interest: 150 Years of the Victorian Auditor-General's Office*, Melbourne: Victorian Auditor-General's Office, 2002.

INDEX